Adobe®
PageMaker® 7.0
Illustrated

Kevin Proot

THOMSON
™
COURSE TECHNOLOGY

Australia • Canada • Mexico • Singapore • Spain • United Kingdom • United States

THOMSON

COURSE TECHNOLOGY

Adobe PageMaker 7.0 - Illustrated

Kevin Proot

Managing Editor:
Nicole Jones Pinard

Contributing Authors:
Carol Cram, Marjorie Hunt

Associate Product Manager:
Christina Kling Garrett

Production Editor:
Catherine G. DiMassa

Product Manager:
Julia Healy

Editorial Assistant:
Elizabeth Harris

QA Manuscript Reviewers:
Shawn Day and Jeff Schwartz

Developmental Editor:
Mary Kemper

Composition House:
GEX Publishing Services

Text Designer:
Joseph Lee, Black Fish Design

Disclaimer
Course Technology reserves the right to revise this publication and make changes from time to time in its content without notice.

Trademarks
Some of the product names and company names used in this book have been used for identification purposes only and may be trademarks or registered trademarks of their respective manufacturers and sellers.

ISBN 0-619-10956-4

The Illustrated Series Vision

Teaching and writing about computer applications can be extremely rewarding and challenging. How do we engage students and keep their interest? How do we teach them skills that they can easily apply on the job? As we set out to write this book, our goals were to develop a textbook that:

▶ works for a beginning to advanced student

▶ provides varied, flexible, and meaningful exercises and projects to reinforce the skills

▶ serves as a reference tool

▶ makes your job as an educator easier, by providing resources above and beyond the textbook to help you teach your course

Our popular, streamlined format is based on advice from instructional designers and customers. This flexible design presents each lesson on a two-page spread, with step-by-step instructions on the left, and screen illustrations on the right. This signature style, coupled with high-caliber content, provides a comprehensive yet manageable introduction to Adobe PageMaker 7.0—it is a teaching package for the instructor and a learning experience for the student.

–The Illustrated Team

ACKNOWLEDGMENTS

Writing a book involves a great deal of coordination and effort by a team of individuals. I would like to thank Julia Healy, Product Manager, for keeping the project on track and ensuring that the many details involved in producing this book were addressed with professionalism and accuracy. I would like to thank my Development Editor for her constant support, encouragement, and her willingness to go the extra mile to make sure that this book exceeds her high standards of perfection.

No preface would be complete without acknowledging the support I receive from my parents. Thank you.

–Kevin Proot, Author

I'd like to thank Nicole Pinard for giving me the opportunity to join the authoring team for this revision. I'd also like to thank my editor for her careful and thoughtful developmental edits, and Julia Healy for keeping us all on schedule.

–Marjorie Hunt, Contributing Author

I wish to acknowledge the support of my Developmental Editor Mary Kemper and, as always, my wonderful family!

–Carol Cram, Contributing Author

Preface

Welcome to *Adobe PageMaker 7.0–Illustrated*. Each lesson in the book contains the elements pictured to the right in the sample two-page spread.

▶ How is the book organized?

This book is organized into 12 units on PageMaker 7.0, covering creating a publication; working with text and graphics; customizing a publication with advanced graphics; formatting multiple pages; adding color to publications; working with long publications; and publishing electronically.

▶ What kinds of assignments are included in the book? At what level of difficulty?

The lesson assignments are based on a fictional character, Sara Norton, and her freelance desktop publishing business. The assignments on the blue pages at the end of each unit increase in difficulty. Project Files and case studies provide a great variety of interesting and relevant business applications for skills. Assignments include:

- **Concepts Reviews** include multiple choice, matching, and screen identification questions.

- **Skills Reviews** provide additional hands-on, step-by-step reinforcement.

- **Independent Challenges** are case projects requiring critical thinking and application of the skills learned in the unit. The Independent Challenges increase in difficulty, with the first in each unit being the easiest (most step-by-step with the most detailed instructions). Independent Challenges become increasingly open-ended, requiring more independent thinking and problem solving.

- **E-Quest Independent Challenges** are case projects with a Web focus. E-Quests require the use of the World Wide Web to conduct research to complete the project.

- **Visual Workshops** show a completed file and require that the file be created without any step-by-step guidance, involving problem solving and an independent application of the unit skills.

Hints, design tips, and troubleshooting advice appear right where you need them — next to the step itself.

Concise text introduces the basic principles in the lesson and integrates the brief case study (indicated by the paintbrush icon).

Each 2-page spread focuses on a single skill.

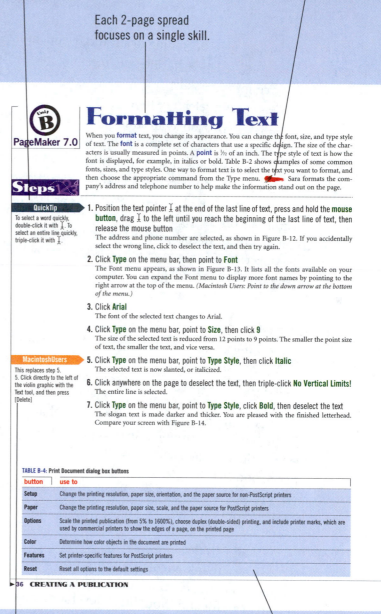

The steps and figures in this book feature PageMaker 7.0 for Windows. However the two software releases are very similar. Where there are differences, specific steps are given in tips for Macintosh Users.

Tables provide quickly accessible summaries of key terms, toolbar buttons, or keyboard alternatives connected with the lesson material. Students can refer easily to this information when working on their own projects.

Every lesson features large, full-color representations of what the screen should look like as students complete the numbered steps.

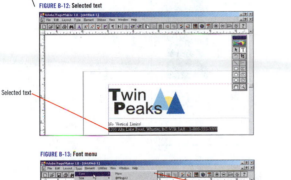

FIGURE B-12: Selected text

Selected text

FIGURE B-13: Font menu

Point to the arrow to display more font names

Your list of fonts might differ

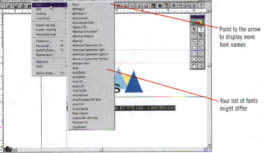

CLUES TO USE

Spacing around inline graphics

By simply pressing [Spacebar], you can add space between text and an inline graphic. Another way to control the horizontal space between text and inline graphics is to use indents and tabs. You can control the vertical space between paragraph text and an inline graphic by changing the leading. Whenever you place an inline graphic, PageMaker applies an autoleading format to it that is different from the paragraph's leading, creating odd line spacing in the paragraph. To make the line spacing consistent in a paragraph that includes an inline graphic, you can either reduce the size of the inline graphic or increase the leading of the paragraph.

CREATING A PUBLICATION 37 ◄

PageMaker 7.0

Clues to Use boxes provide concise information that either expands on the major lesson skill or describes an independent task that in some way relates to the major lesson skill.

► How are design concepts covered?

In addition to being covered in the lessons, each unit concludes with a two-page Design Workshop. Design Workshops focus on strong design skills, and offer a valuable review and check of key concepts.

► Is this book dual-platform?

Yes. All the lessons and exercises can be completed on either the Windows or Macintosh platform.

► Is this book ACE Certified?

Adobe PageMaker 7.0 – Illustrated covers the Adobe Certified Expert (ACE) product proficiency exam objectives for PageMaker 7.0. See the inside front cover for more information on other Course Technology titles meeting ACE certification. A grid in the back of the book lists the exam objectives and cross-references them with the units.

► What online learning options are available to accompany this book?

Options for this title include a testbank in MyCourse 2.0, WebCT, and Blackboard ready formats to make assessment using one of these platforms easy to manage. Visit www.course.com for more information on our online learning materials.

Instructor Resources

The Instructor's Resource Kit (IRK) CD is Course Technology's way of putting the resources and information needed to teach and learn effectively into your hands. All the components are available on the IRK (pictured below), and many of the resources can be downloaded from www.course.com. The Project Files, Solution Files, and Figure Files are provided in Macintosh and Windows formats. The testbank, as well, is dual-platform. Macintosh users can access the Instructor's Manual and Sample Syllabus provided they have Microsoft Office for the Macintosh. All the Instructor Resources are compatible with both the Windows and Macintosh platforms.

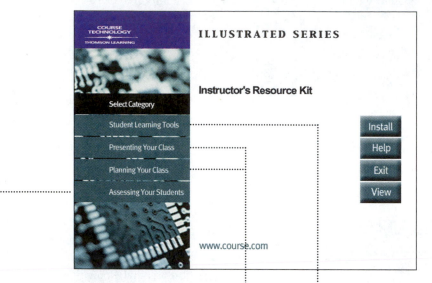

ASSESSING YOUR STUDENTS

Solution Files

Solution Files are Project Files completed with comprehensive answers. Use these files to evaluate your students' work. Or, distribute them electronically or in hard copy so students can verify their own work.

ExamView

ExamView is a powerful testing software package that allows you to create and administer printed, computer (LAN-based), and Internet exams. ExamView includes hundreds of questions that correspond to the topics covered in this text, enabling students to generate detailed study guides that include page references for further review. The computer-based and Internet testing components allow students to take exams at their computers, and also save you time by grading each exam automatically.

PRESENTING YOUR CLASS

Figure Files

Figure Files contain all the figures from the book in .jpg format. Use the figure files to create transparency masters or in a PowerPoint presentation.

STUDENT LEARNING TOOLS

Project Files and Project Files List

To complete most of the units in this book, your students will need **Project Files**. Put them on a file server for students to copy. The Project Files are available on the Instructor's Resource Kit CD-ROM, the Review Pack, and can also be downloaded from www.course.com.

Instruct students to use the **Project Files List** at the end of the book. This list gives instructions on copying and organizing files.

PLANNING YOUR CLASS

Instructor's Manual

Available as an electronic file, the Instructor's Manual is quality-assurance tested and includes unit overviews, detailed lecture topics for each unit with teaching tips, comprehensive sample solutions to all lessons and end-of-unit material, and extra Independent Challenges. The Instructor's Manual is available on the Instructor's Resource Kit CD-ROM, or you can download it from www.course.com.

Sample Syllabus

Prepare and customize your course easily using this sample course outline (available on the Instructor's Resource Kit CD-ROM).

Brief Contents

Contents

⌈ PageMaker 7.0 ⌉

Contents

Contents

Unit G: Formatting Text   177

Contents

Read This Before You Begin

Project Files

In this book, you will create desktop publications for print and electronic distribution. Before beginning your work, make sure that you have the Project Files provided by Course Technology. Check with your instructor or go to **www.course.com** to download the files. You can store your Project Files on a Zip disk, hard drive, network drive, or other file location. The Project Files are referenced in the book as "the drive and folder where your Project Files are stored," because actual file locations will vary.

Macintosh Users

Macintosh User tips are included in the margins and steps of this text. These tips were written and tested on Macintosh OS 9 and can be used for Macintosh OS X as well. Project Files are provided in Macintosh format. Please follow the above directions to store your Project Files.

Browsers

We recommend using Microsoft Internet Explorer 5.0 or higher or Netscape Navigator 4.7x or higher for browser output.

Getting
Started with Adobe PageMaker 7.0

Objectives

- ► **Define desktop publishing software**
- ► **Start PageMaker 7.0**
- ► **Open a publication**
- ► **View the PageMaker program window**
- ► **Set the zero point and use ruler guides**
- ► **Work with the toolbox**
- ► **View a publication**
- ► **Get Help**
- ► **Close a publication and exit PageMaker**

Adobe PageMaker 7.0 is a popular desktop publishing program that is used to create professional-quality business publications for print and electronic distribution. PageMaker includes sophisticated text, graphic, and layout tools that allow you to create a wide variety of publications such as advertisements, brochures, and newsletters. Sara Norton is a freelance graphic designer who runs a small desktop publishing business from her home. Sara uses PageMaker to design publications for her clients. One of her clients, the Lakeview Swan Theatre, has hired her to design a newsletter called the *Swan Report*, which Sara has almost finished.

Defining Desktop Publishing Software

PageMaker is a desktop publishing application. A **desktop publishing application** lets you integrate text, graphics, spreadsheets, charts, and other elements created in different applications into one document. With PageMaker, you can create many types of publications, including brochures, newsletters, and even books. A **publication** is any document produced in PageMaker. Some types of publications you can create with PageMaker are listed in Table A-1. Figure A-1 shows an example of a publication Sara created for one of her clients using PageMaker. PageMaker makes it easy for Sara to produce a variety of sophisticated publications from her home office.

Details

Some of the benefits of using PageMaker include:

► Professional-quality publications

With PageMaker, you can create publications from scratch or you can use a PageMaker template to quickly create a professionally designed publication. In addition, PageMaker includes a library of clip art and photographs that you can use to enhance your publications. Sara frequently uses the templates and graphics that come with PageMaker to create publications with effective designs.

► Extensive layout and design features

PageMaker includes tools for importing text and graphics produced in other applications as well as tools for creating and formatting text and graphics in PageMaker. PageMaker's professional typographic capabilities give you the power to create dynamic effects with text, and sophisticated layout features make it easy to position text and graphic objects on a page. Sara's publications often include text files from word processing programs, graphics captured by a digital camera or scanner, and charts created in a spreadsheet or presentation application. PageMaker's layout and design features make it easy for Sara to combine these elements into a cohesive publication.

► Control of the production process

PageMaker provides tools for controlling each step of the production process—from design to final layout, proofing, and printing. With PageMaker, you can output files to any printing device, including a desktop printer or a commercial press. You can also save a publication in a format acceptable for the Internet. Sara can accomplish each task involved in the production of a publication using PageMaker. For her clients, she routinely prepares publications for printing by a commercial printer.

► Color publications

PageMaker includes features for producing sophisticated color publications, including spot and full-color publications. A publication with **spot color** uses just one color in a particular area. Other publications, such as a color advertisement, use four basic colors—cyan, magenta, yellow, and black—printed over each other to create other colors. These are known as **process colors**, and the result is a **full-color** publication. Sara creates both spot and full-color publications for her clients. PageMaker allows her to output her color publications directly to a commercial press for printing on high capacity printers.

FIGURE A-1: A PageMaker publication

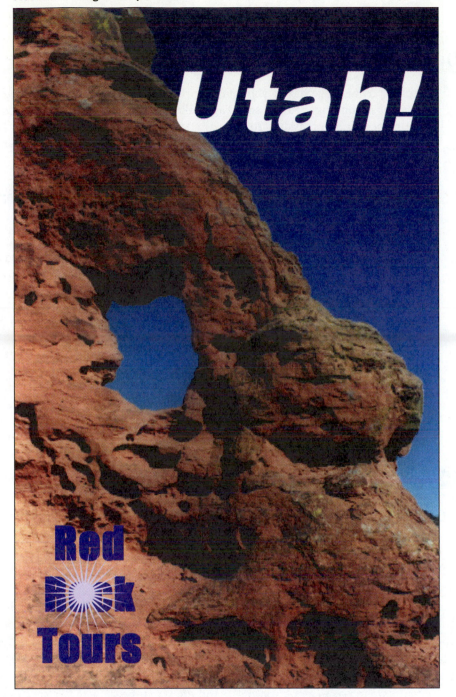

TABLE A-1: Examples of PageMaker publications

type of publication	examples
Periodical	Magazines, newsletters, newspapers
Promotional	Advertisements, flyers, press releases, prospectuses
Informational	Brochures, bulletins, catalogs, fact sheets, schedules, programs
Stationery	Business cards, envelopes, fax cover sheets, interoffice memos, letterheads
Instructional	Training manuals, employee handbooks, text books
Presentation	Overheads, posters, handouts

Starting PageMaker 7.0

Before starting PageMaker, you must start Windows by turning on your computer. Once Windows is running, you can start PageMaker or any other application by using the Start button on the Windows taskbar. You can also start PageMaker by clicking the PageMaker icon on the Windows desktop if that item is available on your computer. ✏️ Sara starts PageMaker so she can review the newsletter she created.

Steps

1. **Make sure the Windows desktop is open, then click the Start button on the taskbar**
   The Start menu opens on the desktop.

2. **Point to Programs or All Programs on the Start menu**
   The Programs menu opens, as shown in Figure A-2. The programs listed on your Programs menu might vary from those shown in the figure depending on the programs installed on your computer.

3. **Point to Adobe on the Programs menu, point to PageMaker 7.0, then click Adobe PageMaker 7.0**
   If Adobe is not listed on your Programs menu, then click Adobe PageMaker 7.0 to start PageMaker. The PageMaker program window opens, as shown in Figure A-3. By default, the Templates palette also opens when you start PageMaker. The Templates palette includes options for creating a publication that is based on a template. A template is a professionally-designed publication that contains placeholder text and graphics that you can replace with your own text and graphics. The Templates palette remains open until you select a template or you close it. Don't worry if the Templates palette does not open when you start PageMaker.

QuickTip

If other palettes are visible in your publication window, click their Close buttons to close them.

4. **If the Templates palette is open, click the Close button in the upper-right corner of the Templates palette**
   The Templates palette closes. The PageMaker program window remains open.

CLUES TO USE

Using a template to create a publication

PageMaker includes a wide variety of templates for creating advertisements, brochures, business cards, flyers, newsletters, posters, and many other types of publications. Using a template to create a publication can save you time by allowing you to concentrate on the content rather than the design of the publication. To open the Templates palette if it is not already open, click Window on the menu bar, point to Plug-in Palettes, and then click Show Template Palette. In the Templates palette, first click the Category list arrow, and then select the type of publication you want to create, such as business cards, flyers, newsletters, menus, programs, or another type of publication. Each category of publication includes templates that are designed for beginning, intermediate, and advanced users, and the templates are labeled with numbers to indicate their level of difficulty. Beginning templates begin with "0" or "1." Those that begin with "0" include design and production tips and those that begin with "1" are designed to be printed on a desktop or laser printer. Intermediate templates begin with "2" and are designed for desktop printers or to be reproduced at a quick-print shop. Finally, advanced templates, which begin with "3," are intended to be printed in full-color on a commercial press. To create a publication that is based on a template, double-click the template you want to use in the Templates palette to open it in the publication window, clicking OK in the PANOSE Font Matching Results dialog box if necessary, and then save the untitled publication with a new filename.

FIGURE A-2: Programs menu

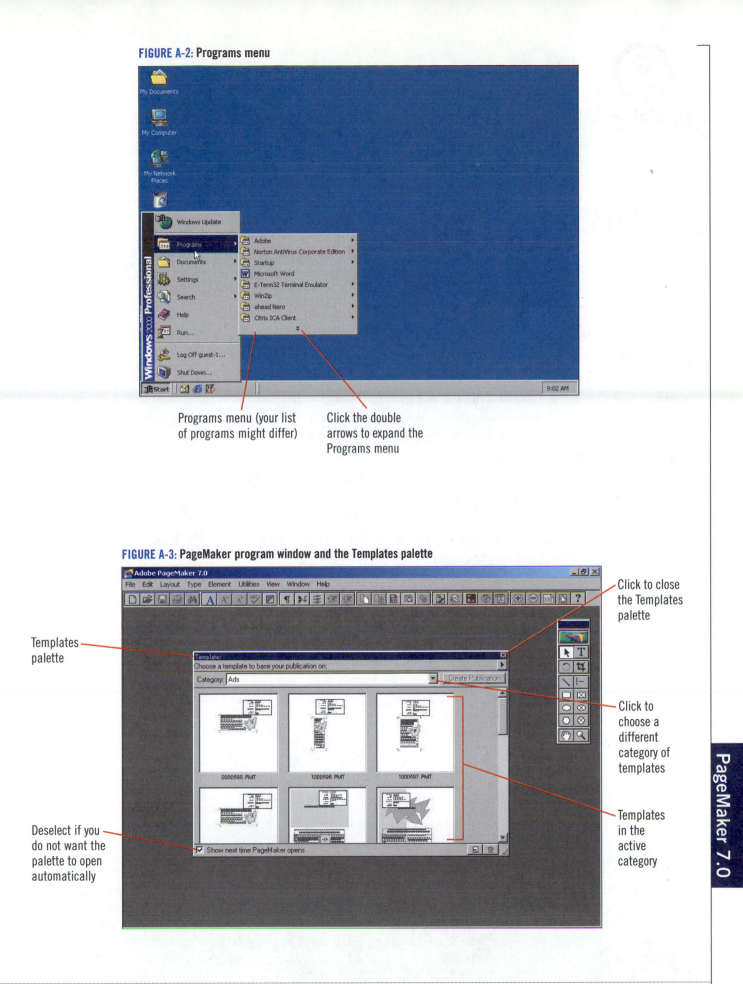

Programs menu (your list
of programs might differ)

Click the double
arrows to expand the
Programs menu

FIGURE A-3: PageMaker program window and the Templates palette

Templates
palette

Deselect if you
do not want the
palette to open
automatically

Click to close
the Templates
palette

Click to
choose a
different
category of
templates

Templates
in the
active
category

Opening a Publication

Once you start PageMaker, you have the option to open an existing publication, create a new publication that is based on a template, or create a new publication from scratch. When you start a new publication or open an existing publication, the publication appears in the PageMaker **publication window**. Sara opens the newsletter she is creating for the Lakeview Swan Theatre so that she can review it.

Steps

1. Click File on the menu bar, then click Open

The Open Publication dialog box opens, as shown in Figure A-4. You can also click the Open button 📁 on the toolbar to open the Open Publication dialog box. The Look in list box in the dialog box displays the name of the active drive or folder.

MacintoshUsers

This replaces Steps 2-4.
2. Click the drive or folder where your Project Files are located
3. Click PM A-1.pmd
4. Click OK

2. Click the Look in list arrow, then click the drive or folder where your Project Files are located

The list of files and folders in the active drive or folder appear in the dialog box.

3. Click the file PM A-1.pmd in the dialog box

Depending on your computer configuration, the file extension .pmd might or might not appear after the filename in the dialog box.

Trouble?

When you open a publication, if a warning box opens saying PageMaker cannot load your target printer, click Continue.

4. Click Open

The publication, the *Swan Report*, opens in the publication window with page 1 displayed, as shown in Figure A-5. The newsletter includes graphics and text. Notice that the filename PM A-1.pmd appears in the title bar at the top of the program window.

5. If the filename does not appear in the title bar, click the Maximize button in the upper-right corner of the publication window

The publication window is maximized and your screen should match Figure A-5.

Matching fonts when opening a publication

If you open a publication that uses a font that is not installed on your computer, PageMaker matches the missing font with an available font that is similar to the original. If the PANOSE Font Matching Results dialog box opens when you open a publication, it means one or more of the fonts used in the publication is not available on your computer, and you must select a substitute. To accept the font substitutions suggested by PageMaker, click OK in the PANOSE Font Matching Results dialog box.

FIGURE A-4: Open Publication dialog box

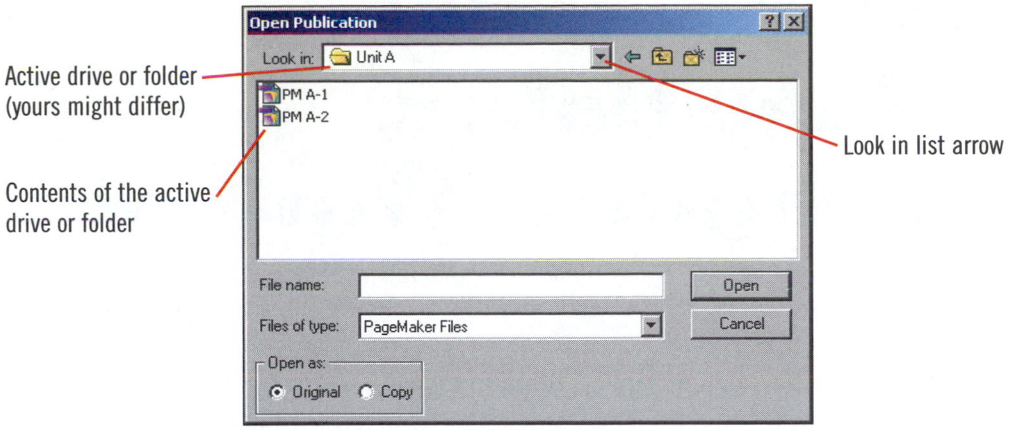

Active drive or folder
(yours might differ)

Contents of the active
drive or folder

Look in list arrow

Open Publication

Look in: Unit A

PM A-1
PM A-2

File name:

Open

Files of type: PageMaker Files

Cancel

Open as:
⦿ Original   ○ Copy

FIGURE A-5: Page 1 of PM A-1.pmd

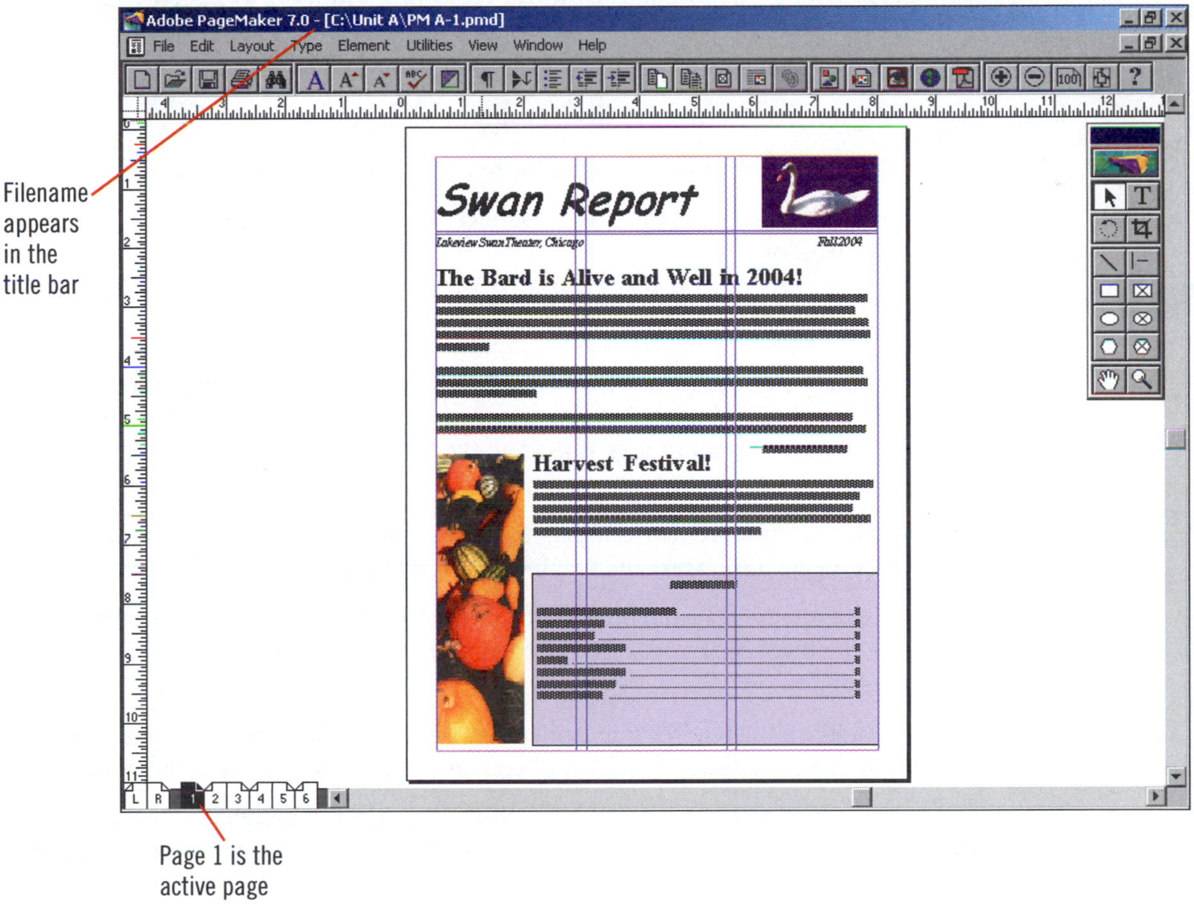

Filename
appears
in the
title bar

Adobe PageMaker 7.0 - [C:\Unit A\PM A-1.pmd]

File Edit Layout Type Element Utilities View Window Help

Swan Report

Lakeview Swan Theater, Chicago   Fall 2004

The Bard is Alive and Well in 2004!

Harvest Festival!

Page 1 is the
active page

L R 1 2 3 4 5 6

PageMaker 7.0

Viewing the PageMaker Program Window

When you open a new or existing publication in PageMaker, it appears in the publication window. Figure A-6 shows the *Swan Report* newsletter in the publication window.

Using Figure A-6 as a guide, find the following elements in your program window:

► The **title bar** displays the name of the program and the name of the publication. The title bar also contains resizing buttons and the program Close button, common to all Windows programs.

► The **menu bar** contains the names of the PageMaker menus. Clicking a menu name opens a list of commands from which you can choose.

MacintoshUsers

There is no toolbar for Macintosh users.

► The **toolbar** contains buttons for 30 of the most commonly used menu commands, including buttons for saving and printing a publication, formatting text, changing the publication view, and creating Web-based publications. When you point to a button, a **ScreenTip** showing the name of the button appears.

► The **horizontal and vertical rulers** are located on the top and left edges of the publication window, respectively. You use the rulers to size and align text and graphics.

QuickTip

To hide or show the rulers in the publication window, click View on the menu bar, then click Hide Rulers or Show Rulers.

► The **zero point marker** is the intersection of the horizontal and vertical rulers.

► The **publication window** displays the current publication. You lay out and design a publication in the publication window.

► The **toolbox** contains tools that you use to create and modify text and graphics. The toolbox is a **floating palette**, which is a movable window within the publication window.

QuickTip

To hide or show the toolbox, click Window on the menu bar, then click Hide Tools or Show Tools.

► The **publication page** is the solid-lined, boxed area in which you build a publication. The publication page can be displayed as a single page or with two facing pages. The bottom and the right or left side of the publication page is shadowed so that you can see if you are working on a right or a left page.

► The **pasteboard** is the white area surrounding the publication page. You use the pasteboard as a work area for creating or storing text and graphics that you intend to include in your publication.

► The **margin guides** are the magenta lines on the publication page that show the page margins. The margins are the blank space between the edge of the page and the part of the page where text and graphics appear.

► The **column guides** are the blue vertical guides that define the columns on a publication page. Column guides help you to control the flow of text on a page or to align text and graphics.

► The **scroll bars** are used to display portions of the publication and pasteboard that are not visible in the publication window. The scroll bars are located on the right and bottom edges of the publication window.

► The **master pages icon**, which appears in the lower-left corner of the publication window, provides access to the right and left master pages. **Master pages** are nonprinting pages used for placing text and graphics that appear on every page in a publication.

► The **page icons** are the numbered rectangles used to navigate between the pages in a publication. The page icons are located to the right of the master pages icon at the bottom of the publication window. You click a page icon to display that page in the publication window.

FIGURE A-6: PageMaker program window

Title bar

Menu bar

Toolbar

Zero point marker

Horizontal ruler

Pasteboard

Publication page

Vertical ruler

Master pages icon

Toolbox

Publication window

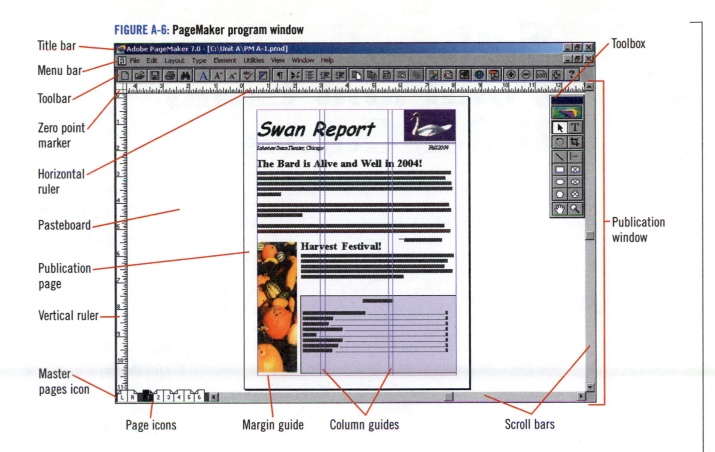

Page icons

Margin guide

Column guides

Scroll bars

PageMaker 7.0

Setting the Zero Point and Using Ruler Guides

Ruler guides are nonprinting lines that are used to help align text and graphics on a page. They usually appear in turquoise on the screen. You set a ruler guide by dragging it onto a page from the horizontal or vertical ruler. A publication page can accommodate up to 40 ruler guides. Another way to help align text and graphics on a page is to work with the zero point. The **zero point** is the point at which the zero marks on the horizontal and vertical rulers intersect. The default zero point is the upper-left corner of the page, but you can move the zero point to help you quickly measure and align objects on a page. Sara resets the zero point to the intersection of the top and left margin guides so that she can easily measure the size of a photo. She also sets ruler guides to help her verify the positioning of the text and graphics on the publication page.

Steps

1. Make sure your toolbox is in the upper-right corner of the publication window; if it is not, place the pointer over the **toolbox title bar**, press and hold the **mouse button**, drag the toolbox until its outline is in the upper-right corner of the publication window, then release the mouse button

2. Without pressing the mouse button, move the pointer slowly around the publication window

   As you move the pointer, dotted lines on the horizontal and vertical rulers indicate the location of the pointer on the page. These dotted lines are called **pointer guides**.

3. Position the pointer over the **zero point marker** ⊞, press and hold the **mouse button**, then drag the pointer down and to the right to the point where the top and left margin guides meet

   As you drag, two dotted lines that span the length and width of the publication window intersect at the pointer and represent the location of the zero point.

4. Release the mouse button

   The zero point is now located at the intersection of the top and left margin guides, as shown in Figure A-7.

5. Position the pointer over the **horizontal ruler**, then press and hold the **mouse button**

   The pointer changes to ↕.

6. Drag down until the pointer guide is at the **5" mark** on the vertical ruler, then release the mouse button

   A ruler guide moves with ↕ as you drag. When you release the mouse button, the ruler guide is located on the page, as shown in Figure A-8. The ruler guide confirms that the photo is aligned correctly with the top of the Harvest Festival headline.

7. Position the pointer over the vertical ruler, then drag a second **ruler guide** to the **1.5" mark** on the horizontal ruler

   A vertical ruler guide appears on the screen aligned with the 1.5" mark on the horizontal ruler. The ruler guide confirms that the photo is 1.5" wide.

8. Position the pointer over the vertical ruler guide, drag the **ruler guide** left off the publication page, then release the mouse button

   The ruler guide disappears. You remove a ruler guide by dragging it off the publication page and onto the pasteboard or to the ruler.

> **QuickTip**
>
> You can reposition a ruler guide at any time by dragging it to a new location.

> **QuickTip**
>
> To hide or show the ruler guides in the publication window, click View on the menu bar, then click Hide Guides or Show Guides.

FIGURE A-7: Repositioned zero point

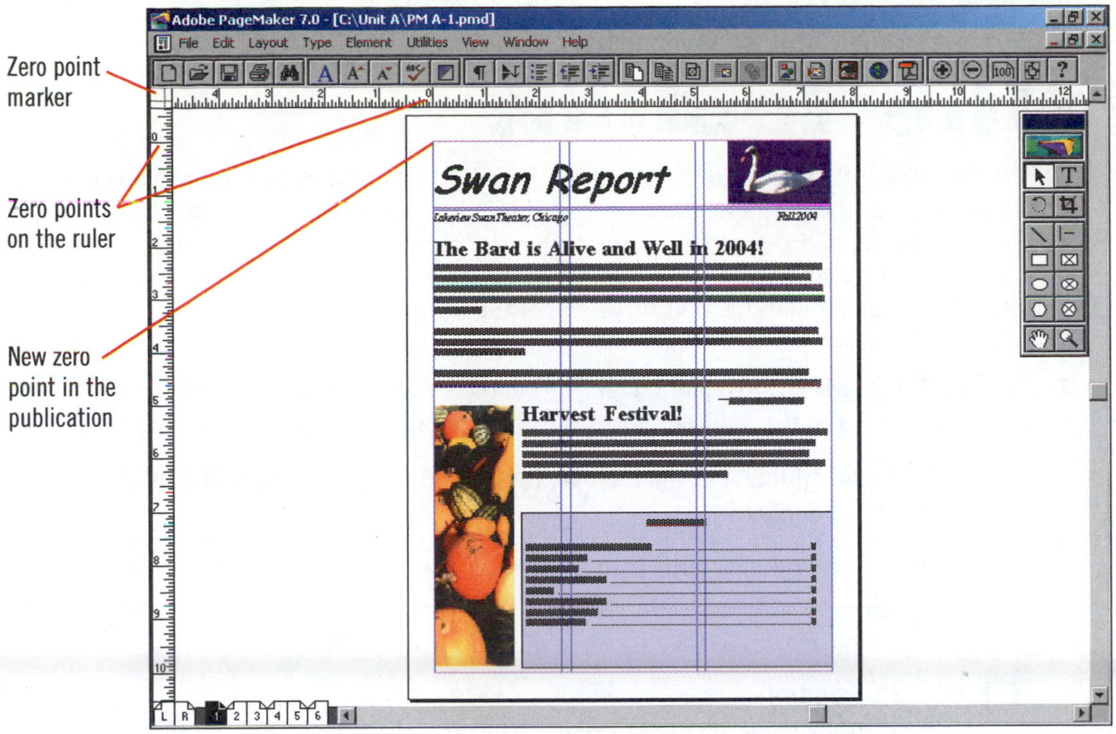

Zero point marker

Zero points on the ruler

New zero point in the publication

FIGURE A-8: Ruler guide on the publication page

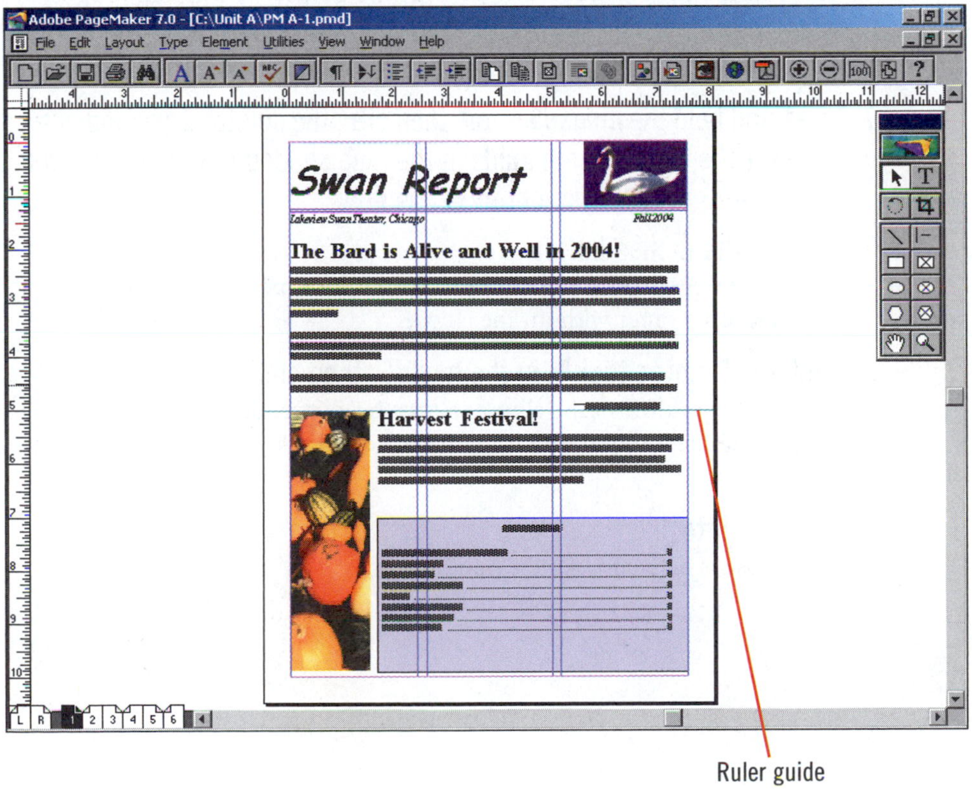

Ruler guide

Working with the Toolbox

The **toolbox** contains tools used to create and modify text and graphics. When you click an icon in the toolbox, the shape of the mouse pointer changes to reflect the active tool. Table A-2 describes the function of each tool and shows the corresponding pointer shape. Sara displays pages 2 and 3 and notices a spelling mistake, which she corrects. She also experiments with adding an ellipse to the bottom of one of the stories.

Steps

1. Click the **pages 2 and 3 page icon** 2 3 in the lower-left corner of the publication window
   Pages 2 and 3 of the publication appear in the publication window as facing pages.

2. Click the **Text tool** T in the toolbox, then move the pointer over the publication page
   The pointer changes to I.

3. Position I between **h** and **o** in the word "Anthony" in the headline on page 2, then click
   The blinking cursor is located between the letters "h" and "o."

MacintoshUsers

This replaces Step 4.
4. Press [Delete]

4. Press **[Backspace]**
   The "h" is deleted and the name is now correctly spelled "Antony," as shown in Figure A-9.

5. Click the **Ellipse tool** in the toolbox, then move the pointer over the publication page
   The pointer changes to +.

6. Position the pointer below the Antony and Cleopatra story and over the left column guide in the blue shaded box, so that the pointer is aligned roughly with the **8" mark** on the vertical ruler and with the **-3 3/8" mark** on the horizontal ruler
   Notice that the values to the left of the zero point on the horizontal ruler are negative values.

7. Press and hold the **mouse button**, then drag the pointer down and across to page 3 until it is over the right column guide in the blue shaded box, as shown in Figure A-10
   The outline of the ellipse appears as you drag.

8. Release the mouse button
   When you release the mouse button, the ellipse appears in the publication. Sara decides the spread looks cleaner without the ellipse.

Trouble?

If you accidentally select a different object, click the outline of the ellipse again to select the ellipse.

9. Click the **Pointer tool** in the toolbox, then click the outline of the ellipse
   Clicking the outline of the ellipse selects the ellipse. Black squares called sizing handles surround the object to indicate it is selected. You must select an object before modifying it or deleting it.

10. Press **[Delete]**
    The ellipse is deleted from the publication.

FIGURE A-9: Pages 2 and 3 of the publication

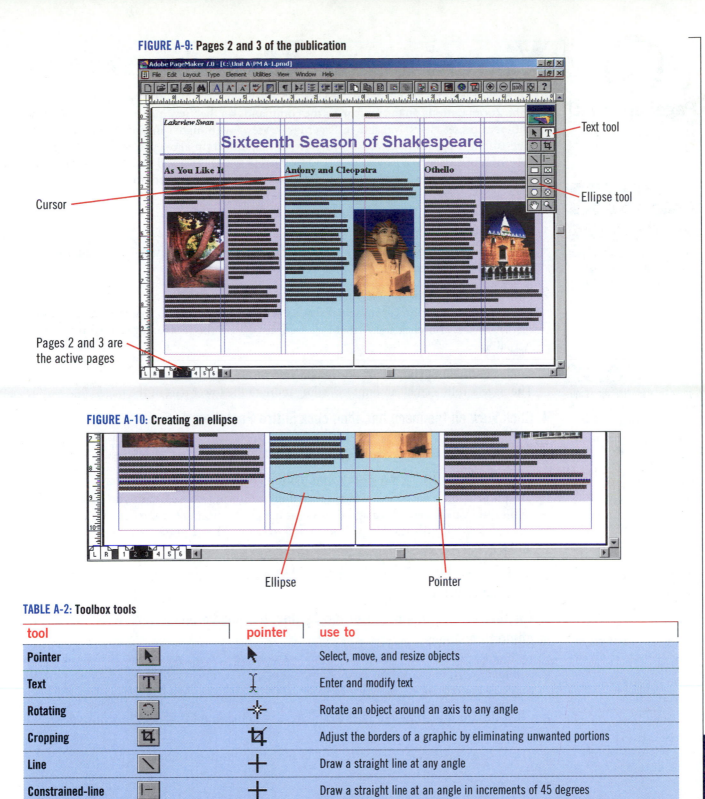

Cursor

Text tool

Ellipse tool

Pages 2 and 3 are the active pages

FIGURE A-10: Creating an ellipse

Ellipse

Pointer

TABLE A-2: Toolbox tools

tool		pointer	use to
Pointer			Select, move, and resize objects
Text	T		Enter and modify text
Rotating			Rotate an object around an axis to any angle
Cropping			Adjust the borders of a graphic by eliminating unwanted portions
Line			Draw a straight line at any angle
Constrained-line			Draw a straight line at an angle in increments of 45 degrees
Rectangle			Draw a rectangle or a square
Ellipse			Draw an ellipse or a circle
Polygon			Draw multisided figures
Hand			Move a different part of the page into view in the publication window
Zoom			Magnify the page view
Frame Tools	, ,		Draw shapes to use as placeholders for text and graphics

Viewing a Publication

In PageMaker, you can change the **page view**, or the magnification of the page, using the Zoom tool, the Zoom buttons on the toolbar, or the commands on the View menu. Table A-3 describes the different preset views available in PageMaker. Views with higher magnifications are useful for fine-tuning a publication. Views with a lower magnification allow you to check the overall composition of a page or a two-page spread. You can also use the scroll bars to display portions of a page that are not displayed in the publication window. Sara increases the magnification of pages 2 and 3 so she can read the text and look closely at the Sphinx photo.

Steps

Trouble?

Depending on the size of your monitor, your screen might not match the figures exactly.

1. Click View on the menu bar

The View menu opens. The check mark next to Fit in Window on the View menu indicates that this is the current view.

2. Point to Zoom To on the View menu, then click 100% Size

The publication appears at its actual size, as shown in Figure A-11, making the text easy to read. You can also click the Actual Size button 100 on the toolbar to change the view to Actual Size.

QuickTip

You can also click the scroll bar above or below the scroll box, or drag a scroll box in the scroll bar to scroll a publication.

3. Click the down scroll arrow on the vertical scroll bar

The page scrolls a small amount, revealing more of the lower part of the page.

4. Click View on the menu bar, then click Entire Pasteboard

A full view of the pasteboard appears with the pages centered in it, as shown in Figure A-12. This view is useful for finding objects that are stored on the pasteboard.

MacintoshUsers

This replaces Step 5.
5. Click View on the menu bar, then click Zoom In

5. Click the Zoom In button ⊕ on the toolbar

The publication is enlarged to 25% in the publication window. Each time you click the Zoom In button, you increase the magnification of the publication to the next greater preset view. You can also click the Zoom Out button ⊖ to reduce the magnification of the publication to the next lesser preset view.

QuickTip

Windows Users: To quickly change the view to Actual Size, double-click the Zoom tool 🔍 in the toolbox; to quickly change the view to Fit in Window, double-click the Hand tool 🖑 in the toolbox.

6. Click the Zoom tool 🔍 in the toolbox, then move the pointer over the pasteboard

The pointer changes to ⊕.

7. Position ⊕ over the photo of the Sphinx, the middle photo, then click the Sphinx photo three times

Each time you click, the publication is enlarged to the next greater preset view. You can also press and hold [Ctrl] to change the Zoom pointer to ⊖. Each time you click with ⊖, the publication is reduced to the next lower preset view. (*Macintosh Users: Press [Option] instead of [Ctrl].*)

MacintoshUsers

This replaces Step 8.
8. Click View on the menu bar, then click Fit in Window

8. Click the Pointer tool ▶ in the toolbox, then click the Fit in Window button 🔲 on the toolbar

The view changes so that pages 2 and 3 fit in the publication window.

Using the grabber hand

Instead of using the scroll bars to move around a publication, you can use the grabber hand. The **grabber hand** acts like a hand on a piece of paper and lets you move the page in any direction in the publication window. To use the grabber hand, click the Hand tool 🖑 in the toolbox. The pointer changes to 🖑, and the page moves in the direction you move the mouse.

FIGURE A-11: Publication in Actual Size view

FIGURE A-11: Publication in Actual Size view

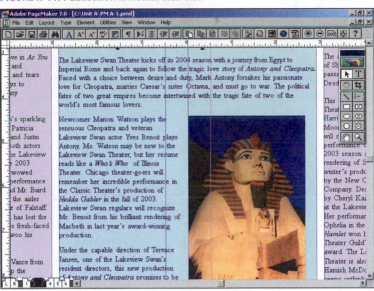

FIGURE A-12: Publication in Entire Pasteboard view

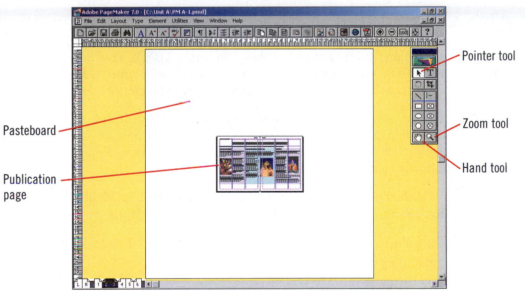

Pointer tool

Pasteboard

Zoom tool

Publication page

Hand tool

TABLE A-3: Publication page views

view	keyboard shortcut*	use to display
Fit in Window	[Ctrl][0]	The entire page(s) and some of the surrounding pasteboard
Entire Pasteboard	[Ctrl][Shift][0]	The entire pasteboard with the page(s) centered on it
25% Size		The page(s) at 25% of the actual size
50% Size	[Ctrl][5]	The page(s) at 50% of the actual size
75% Size	[Ctrl][7]	The page(s) at 75% of the actual size
Actual Size	[Ctrl][1]	The page(s) at 100% of the actual size
200% Size	[Ctrl][2]	A detail of the page(s) at twice the actual size
400% Size	[Ctrl][4]	A detail of the page(s) at four times the actual size

* *(Macintosh Users: Press [Option] instead of [Ctrl].)*

PageMaker 7.0

PageMaker 7.0

Getting Help

PageMaker provides an extensive Help system that gives you immediate access to definitions, explanations, and useful tips. The PageMaker Help system is HTML-based, and help information appears in your default browser window. Your browser must be Netscape Communicator 4.0 or Internet Explorer 4.0 or later to be able to use all the features of Help. Sara searches the Help system to learn more about using the toolbox and the magnification features.

1. **Click Help on the menu bar, then click Help Topics**
   The Adobe PageMaker Help system opens in the default browser window, as shown in Figure A-13. The contents, or the categories of Help topics, are displayed in the left frame of the Help window. You use the Contents, Index, and Search hyperlinks at the top of the Help window to locate help on a topic.

2. **Click Looking at the Work Area in the left frame**
   A list of Help topics related to the PageMaker work area appears in the right frame of the Help window.

3. **Click Using the Toolbox in the right frame**
   A picture of the toolbox and an explanation of each tool appear in the right frame.

4. **Click the Index hyperlink, then click the letter M in the left frame of the Help window**
   The left frame of the Help window displays an alphabetical index and the list of Help topics that begin with the letter M, as shown in Figure A-14. You use the index by clicking the first letter of the topic you want to learn more about. When you click a letter, the index of Help topics scrolls to display the topics that begin with that letter.

5. **Click 1 next to magnifying and reducing in the left frame**
   The Magnifying and reducing with the zoom tool Help topic is displayed in the right frame of the Help window. To display a Help topic using the Index feature, you must click the number next to the topic in the index list in the left frame.

6. **Read about using the zoom tool, clicking the down scroll arrow on the vertical scroll bar in the right frame of the Help window to scroll through the entire Help topic**

7. **Click File on the menu bar, click Print, then click Print or OK in the Print dialog box, depending on your Web browser**
   The Help topic prints.

8. **Click the Close button in the Help window**
   The browser closes and you return to the PageMaker program window.

FIGURE A-13: Help window with the Contents displayed

Click to access help on using the Help system

Contents hyperlink

Index hyperlink

Search hyperlink

Contents of the Help system appear in the left frame

Help system appears in the browser window (your browser might differ)

Right frame

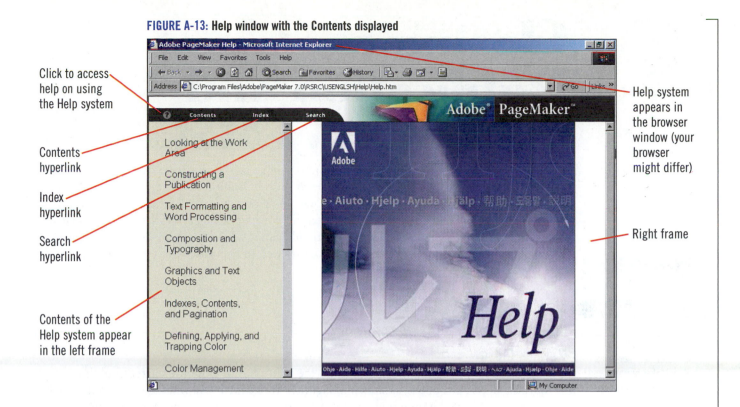

FIGURE A-14: Help window with the Index displayed

Click a letter to see the Help topics that begin with the letter

Index of Help topics beginning with "m"

Click the Back and Forward buttons to navigate between Help topics

Click a number next to a topic to display the topic

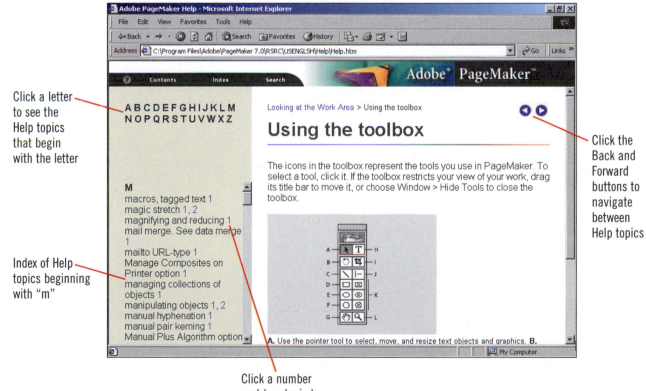

PageMaker 7.0

Unit A

PageMaker 7.0

Closing a Publication and Exiting PageMaker

When you are finished working on a publication, you generally save your work, and then close the file. You won't save the changes you made to this publication because you were only practicing. When you close a file, its publication window closes, but the PageMaker program window remains open. When you have completed all your work in PageMaker, you can exit the application. Exiting PageMaker closes all open publications, if any, and closes the program window. Sara is finished reviewing her newsletter, so she closes the publication and exits PageMaker.

Steps

QuickTip

To exit PageMaker and close several files at once, click File on the menu bar, then click Exit. PageMaker prompts you to save changes to each publication before exiting.

1. Click **File** on the menu bar

   The File menu opens, as shown in Figure A-15.

2. Click **Close**

   You could also click the Close button on the menu bar to close the current publication. A warning dialog box opens, as shown in Figure A-16, asking if you want to save changes to the file before closing. Because this was a practice session, you do not need to save the file.

3. Click **No**

   The publication closes, but the program window remains open.

4. Click **File** on the menu bar, then click **Exit**

   You could also click the Close button on the right end of the title bar to exit the application. PageMaker closes, and you are returned to the desktop.

MacintoshUsers

This replaces Step 4.

4. Click File on the menu bar, then click Quit

Close command closes the publication

Exit command closes PageMaker

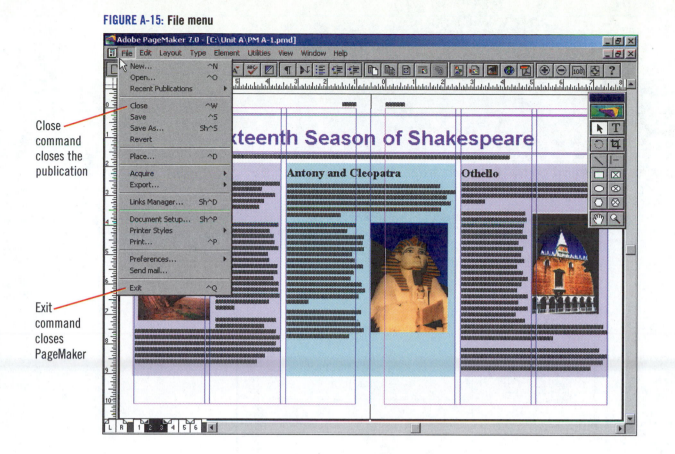

FIGURE A-16: Save changes warning dialog box

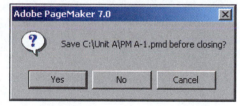

Practice

► Concepts Review

Label each element of the program window shown in Figure A-17.

FIGURE A-17

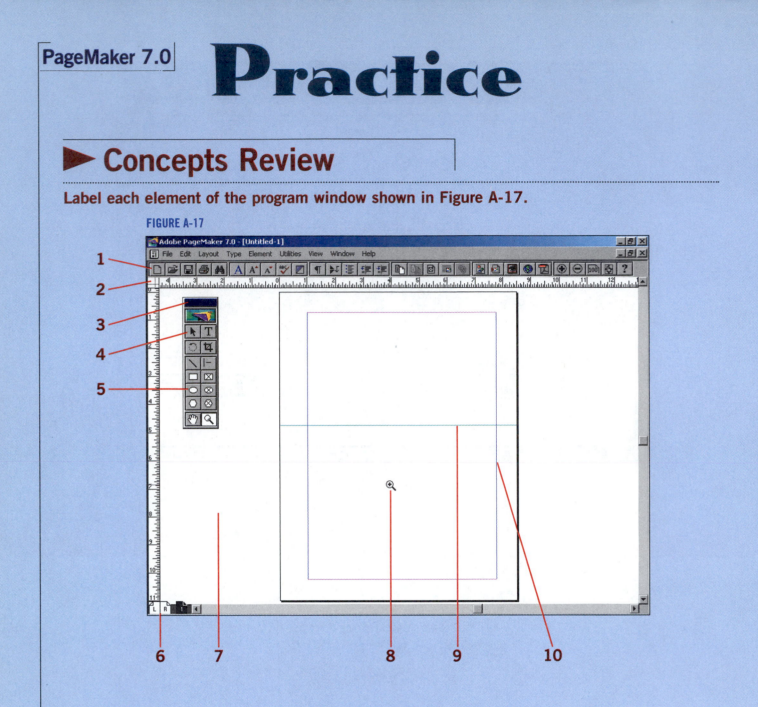

Match each term with the statement that best describes it.

11. **Master pages**
12. **Margin guides**
13. **Pasteboard**
14. **Publication page**
15. **Zero point marker**

a. Magenta box inside the page borders
b. Work area that is used as a temporary storage area for text and graphics
c. Boxed area of the publication window in which you build a publication
d. The intersection of the horizontal and vertical rulers
e. Nonprinting pages used for placing text and graphics that appear on all pages of the publication

Select the best answer from the list of choices.

16. **To precisely make small adjustments to a publication, which view would be the most useful?**
    a. 400% Size
    b. Actual Size
    c. 25% Size
    d. Entire Pasteboard

17. **Which tool is used to modify text?**
    a.
    b.
    c.
    d.

18. **Which element of the publication window helps you to align text and graphics on a page?**
    a. Master page
    b. Page icon
    c. Pasteboard
    d. Ruler guides

19. **Where do you place text that you want to appear on every page in a publication?**
    a. Master pages
    b. Pasteboard
    c. Normal pages
    d. Publication window

20. **Which of the following cannot be used to locate a Help topic in the PageMaker Help system?**
    a. Search hyperlink
    b. Index hyperlink
    c. Find hyperlink
    d. Contents hyperlink

▶ Skills Review

1. **Start PageMaker 7.0.**
   a. Click the Start button on the taskbar, point to Programs, then start PageMaker. *(Macintosh Users: Start PageMaker.)*
   b. Close the Templates palette if it is open in the PageMaker program window.

2. **Open a publication.**
   a. Click on the menu bar, then click Open.
   b. Open the file PM A-2.pmd from the drive and folder where your Project Files are located.
   c. Maximize the publication window if necessary.

3. **View the PageMaker program window.**
   a. Identify as many elements of the program window as you can without referring to the unit material.
   b. Click each menu name on the menu bar, then drag the pointer through the commands on each menu. Notice the additional menus that appear when you point to a command that has an arrow pointing to the right.
   c. Point to each button on the toolbar, and read the ScreenTip that appears in order to identify each button.

4. **Set the zero point and use ruler guides.**
   a. Move the pointer slowly around the publication window and notice how the pointer guides on the horizontal and vertical rulers move as the pointer moves.
   b. Reset the zero point to the upper-left corner of the publication page.
   c. Drag a horizontal ruler guide to the 1.5" mark on the vertical ruler.
   d. Drag another horizontal ruler guide to the 6.5" mark on the vertical ruler.
   e. Drag a vertical ruler guide to the .25" mark on the horizontal ruler. (*Hint:* The .25" mark to the left of 0 is actually -.25"; be sure to align the guide with the .25" mark to the right of 0.)
   f. Drag another vertical ruler guide to the 1.5" mark on the horizontal ruler.
   g. Remove the horizontal ruler guide at the 6.5" mark.

PageMaker 7.0

5. Work with the toolbox.

a. Click the Text tool in the toolbox, then move the pointer over the middle of the publication page. Notice the pointer has changed.

b. Click each additional tool in the toolbox, and notice how the pointer changes.

c. Click the Constrained-line tool in the toolbox, then position the pointer over the left vertical ruler guide, just under the word Tours.

d. Click and drag the pointer under the word Tours to the right vertical ruler guide, then release the mouse button.

e. Click the Text tool, then type the letter **t** between the "U" and the "a" to correct the misspelling of Utah.

f. Click the Pointer tool, then select the Red Rock Tours logo in the lower-left corner of the page by clicking it once.

6. View a publication.

a. Click the right scroll arrow on the horizontal scroll bar two times.

b. Click the down scroll arrow on the vertical scroll bar four times.

c. Using the View menu, change the view to 25% Size.

d. Make sure the Red Rocks Tour logo is selected, then change the view to 200% Size, as shown in Figure A-18.

e. Using the View menu, change the view to Entire Pasteboard.

f. Using the Zoom tool in the toolbox, increase the view so the logo is prominent.

g. Change the view to Fit in Window.

FIGURE A-18

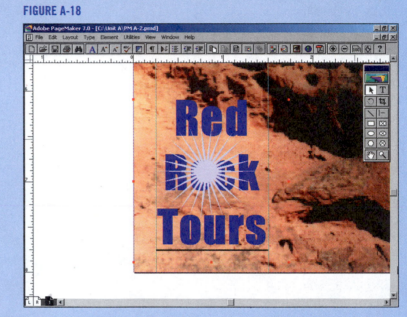

7. Get Help.

a. Open the Adobe PageMaker Help window.

b. Click Looking at the Work Area in the left frame.

c. Click the Viewing pages topic in the right frame, click the subtopic Scrolling within a window in the right frame, then read the information in the Help topic.

d. Click the Index hyperlink, click Z in the left frame, click the 1 to the right of the topic zero point, then read the information in the Help topic.

e. Click the Choosing a measurement system and setting up rulers hyperlink at the bottom of the Help topic, then read the information.

f. Click the Contents hyperlink, select a topic you want to know more about, read the information that appears, then print the topic.

g. Close the PageMaker Help window.

8. Close a publication and exit PageMaker.

a. Close the publication without saving your work.

b. Exit PageMaker.

► Independent Challenge 1

The Adobe PageMaker Help system provides detailed information on PageMaker commands and features. In this exercise, you explore the Help system to find information on several features.

a. Start PageMaker, then open the PageMaker Help window.

b. Click the Looking at the Work Area topic in the left frame of the Help window, then use the Forward and Back buttons in the right frame to scroll through the Help topics in this category. Print two Help topics that interest you.

c. Use the Search feature to find information on templates. Write a short essay describing how to create a publication using a template.

d. Use the Index feature to find information about guides. Write a short essay describing the three types of nonprinting PageMaker guides.

e. Close the PageMaker Help window, then exit PageMaker.

► Independent Challenge 2

Some examples of PageMaker publications are described at the beginning of this unit. To familiarize yourself with design features, search for examples of publications that could be produced using PageMaker and compile them into a sample design packet.

a. Gather at least five different types of publications. Make sure at least one sample is a full-color publication, as shown in Figure A-19, and at least one sample includes only spot color, as shown in Figure A-20.

b. Keep this design packet and refer to it as you learn about designing publications with PageMaker.

FIGURE A-19

FIGURE A-20

PageMaker 7.0

▶ Independent Challenge 3

You work in the marketing department of a landscaping company. Your organization has just installed PageMaker so that publications can now be produced in-house, and your boss has asked you to begin thinking about the kinds of publications you can create for your company.

a. Using pencil and paper, sketch a plan for a publication that advertises a wide variety of lawn maintenance services, including mowing, tree care, fertilization, weed control, and site analysis.

b. Include text, graphics, and a company logo in your sketch.

(e) Independent Challenge 4

The Adobe Web site includes additional resources for learning about PageMaker. In addition, you can read about the latest product features and troubleshooting techniques. In this exercise, search the Adobe Web site for information about the new features of PageMaker 7.0.

a. Open your browser, then go to the Adobe Web site at www.adobe.com.

b. Search the Web site for information on the new features of PageMaker 7.0. Print the information you find.

c. Search the Web site for information on system requirements, then print the information you find.

d. Search the Web site for information on design tips, then print the information you find.

Creating

a Publication

► **Plan a publication**
► **Create a new publication**
► **Place a graphic**
► **Resize and move a graphic**
► **Add text and lines to a publication**
► **Format text**
► **Save a publication**
► **Print a publication**
► **Design Workshop: Letterhead**

PageMaker makes it easy to create publications that include text and graphics. You can use PageMaker tools to create and modify text and graphics directly in a publication, or you can insert text and graphics created in other applications into a PageMaker publication. In this unit, you learn to create a simple publication that includes text and graphics. You also learn how to save and print a publication. Sara Norton has been hired to create a new company letterhead for the Twin Peaks Resort. The letterhead will include the Twin Peaks logo, address, and slogan.

Planning a Publication

Before you create a publication in PageMaker, it is important to plan its content and design. Planning and designing a publication involves determining the information to include and sketching a layout. At the beginning of each unit, you learn design tips for creating different types of publications. This unit focuses on letterhead. Letterhead should be eye-catching and memorable. It usually contains the company logo and the company name, as well as the company's mailing address, telephone and fax numbers, e-mail address, and Web site address, if applicable. ✒ Sara keeps the following guidelines in mind as she plans and designs the letterhead for the Twin Peaks Resort.

Details

Keep the following guidelines in mind when designing letterhead:

► **Place the company logo in a logical position on the page**

A company's logo is used in almost all forms of visual communication to reinforce the connection between the graphic logo and the company name. Logos on letterhead are often at the top of the page, but they can also run down a side or be at the bottom of the page. The logo should be large enough to catch the reader's attention, but not so large that it is overwhelming. Sara decides to place the Twin Peaks Resort logo at the top of the page in the center.

► **Include the company address and any other contact information**

The placement of the address, telephone and fax numbers, and e-mail and Web site addresses is usually based on the placement of the logo. Sara decides to put the company's address and toll free telephone number below the logo.

► **Consider adding the company motto or slogan**

Adding the motto or slogan is not required, but it can help reinforce the company's image. Sara decides to put the Twin Peaks Resort slogan "No Vertical Limits!" above the address line.

► **Evaluate the final design, and add lines, boxes, or shading, if necessary**

Sara wants the logo and the address line to be visually distinct from the rest of the page, so she adds a thin horizontal line below the logo. Figure B-1 shows Sara's sketch of the letterhead.

FIGURE B-1: Sara's sketch of the new letterhead

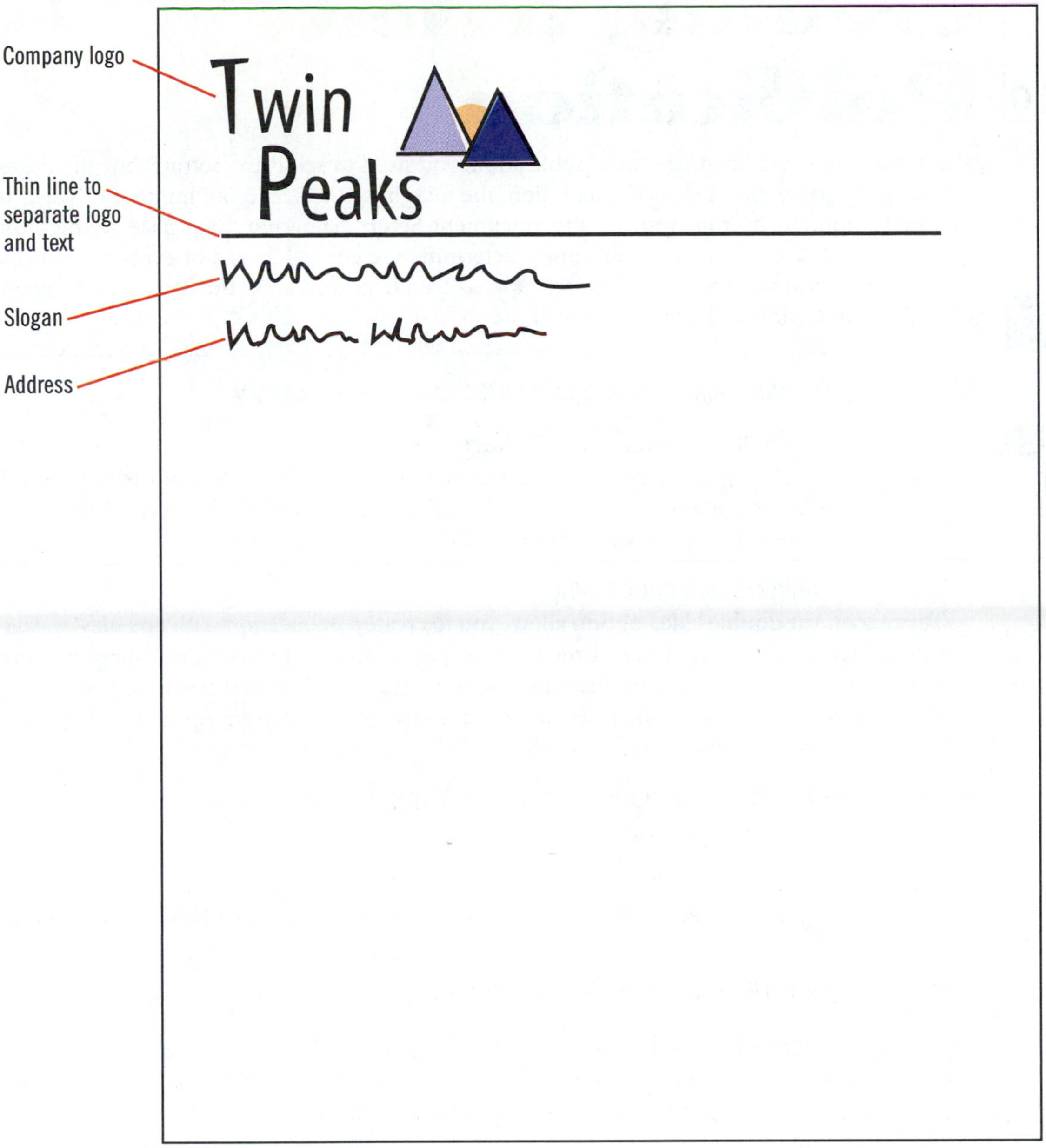
Company logo
Twin
Peaks
Thin line to separate logo and text
Slogan
Address

Creating a New Publication

Before you can begin creating a new publication, you need to select the settings for the pages, including the paper size, the page orientation, the margin settings, and the number of pages in the publication. To do this, you use the Document Setup dialog box. The page settings you choose when you set up a new publication determine the general layout of every page in the publication, unless you specify otherwise. ◆ Sara begins creating the letterhead by opening a new publication and setting up the pages.

Steps 1234

1. Start PageMaker, then close the Templates palette if necessary

2. Click **File** on the menu bar, then click **New**

The Document Setup dialog box opens, as shown in Figure B-2. The company letterhead will be a one-page publication on standard 8 ½" × 11" paper, so the default PageMaker settings for the page size, dimensions, orientation, and number of pages are fine.

3. Click the **Double-sided check box**

Turning off the double-sided option allows you to create a publication with one master page, rather than with different left and right master pages. Because this is a single-page publication, you do not need the letterhead to be double-sided. Notice that when you turned off double-sided pages, the Facing pages option dimmed and the margin options in the dialog box changed from "Inside" and "Outside" to "Left" and "Right".

4. Double-click **0.75** in the Top text box in the Margins section

The value 0.75 is selected.

5. Type **.5**

The top margin is now set at .5", which will allow Sara to put the logo close to the top edge of the page.

6. Double-click **0.75** in the Right text box, then type 1

7. Press **[Tab]** twice to select the value in the Bottom text box, then type **1**

You can move the insertion point in a dialog box by clicking in a text box or by pressing [Tab] to move from option to option. The right and bottom margins will be 1", the same as the left margin.

8. Click **OK**

The Document Setup dialog box closes, and a new blank publication with the filename Untitled-1 opens in the publication window.

9. Click the **Maximize button** in the publication window, if necessary

The Untitled publication window fills the screen, as shown in Figure B-3. The blank publication page is a letter-size page with a .5" top margin and 1" left, right, and bottom margins. The pink margin guides show the top and bottom margins. The blue column guides show the left and right margins. Notice that there is only one master page icon because this is a single-sided publication. The number of pages in the publication is one.

FIGURE B-2: Document Setup dialog box

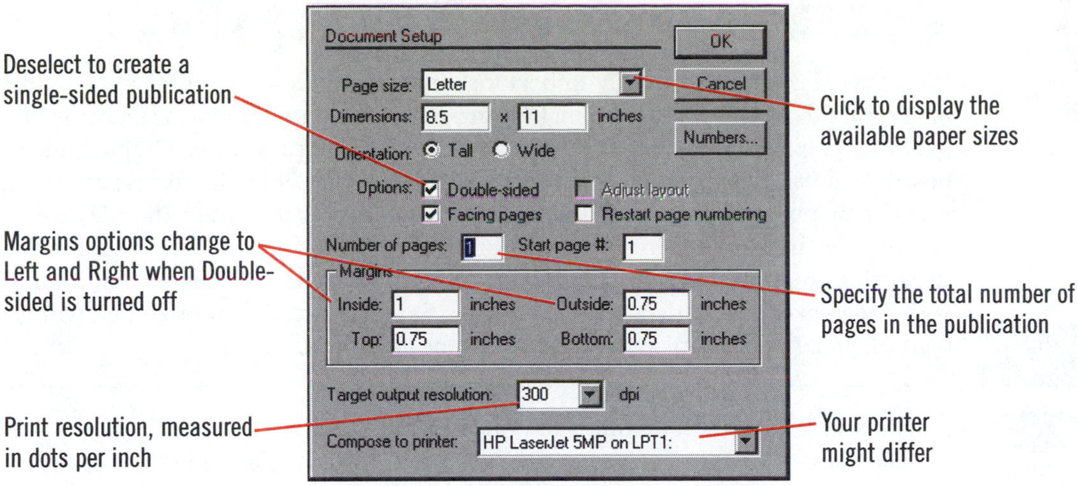

Deselect to create a single-sided publication
Margins options change to Left and Right when Double-sided is turned off
Print resolution, measured in dots per inch
Click to display the available paper sizes
Specify the total number of pages in the publication
Your printer might differ
Document Setup
OK
Cancel
Numbers...
Page size: Letter
Dimensions: 8.5 x 11 inches
Orientation: Tall Wide
Options: Double-sided Adjust layout
Facing pages Restart page numbering
Number of pages: 1 Start page #: 1
Margins
Inside: 1 inches Outside: 0.75 inches
Top: 0.75 inches Bottom: 0.75 inches
Target output resolution: 300 dpi
Compose to printer: HP LaserJet 5MP on LPT1:

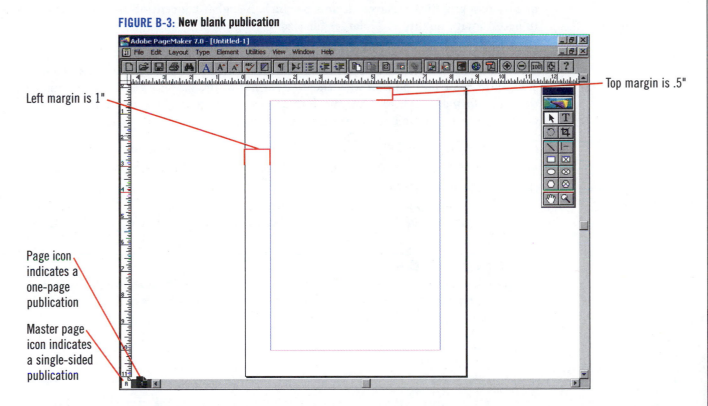

FIGURE B-3: New blank publication

Left margin is 1"
Top margin is .5"
Page icon indicates a one-page publication
Master page icon indicates a single-sided publication
Adobe PageMaker 7.0 - [Untitled-1]
File Edit Layout Type Element Utilities View Window Help

PageMaker 7.0

Placing a Graphic

With PageMaker, you can easily import, or insert, graphics into a publication. Some examples of graphics that can be imported include images created in a drawing or painting program, digital photographs, and art scanned into the computer using a scanner. Graphic images are composed of dots, called **pixels**, and can be saved as many different file types. The greater the number of pixels in a graphic, the richer the colors and the larger the file size. You import graphic files using the Place command on the File menu or the Place button on the toolbar. Importing graphics allows you to enhance your publications with images that cannot be created with PageMaker's basic design tools. Sara has already scanned the Twin Peaks Resort logo. She now wants to place it at the top of the letterhead.

Steps

QuickTip

Windows users can also click the Place button on the toolbar to open the Place dialog box.

1. Click **File** on the menu bar, then click **Place**

   The Place dialog box opens. Because Importable Files is selected in the Files of type list box, only files that can be imported into a PageMaker publication are listed in the dialog box. *(Macintosh Users: The Place document dialog box opens and does not include a Files of type list box.)*

2. Click the **Look in list arrow**, click the **drive** or **folder** where your Project Files are located, then click **Logo.tif**

   The dialog box displays information about the Logo.tif file, including the file type (TIFF image) and size (52K), as shown in Figure B-4. Different types of graphic files have a different resolution and take up a different amount of disk space. **Resolution** is the print quality of a graphic measured in dots per inch. A higher concentration of dots results in better image quality and a larger file size.

3. Click **Open** *(Macintosh Users: Click OK)*

   The dialog box closes, and the pointer changes to ⊠. *(Macintosh Users: The pointer changes to* ✛*.)* This pointer identifies the format of the graphic file as tagged image file (.tif) format. Each graphic file format has a different place pointer. Table B-1 describes several graphic file types and shows the associated place pointer.

4. Position the .tif place pointer ⊠ so that the top border of the pointer is over the top margin guide and the pointer guide is aligned with the **3.25"** mark on the horizontal ruler, as shown in Figure B-5

   Try to position the upper-left corner of the place pointer where you want the upper-left corner of the graphic to be. This saves time moving the graphic to the correct position after it is placed.

5. Click the **mouse button**

   The graphic appears on the page, and the pointer changes back to ↖, as shown in Figure B-6. The **selection handles**, the small black squares at the corners and sides of the graphic, indicate that the graphic is selected.

TABLE B-1: Graphic file types

place pointer	Macintosh place pointer	file extension	file type
		.bmp	Bitmap file
PS		.eps	Encapsulated PostScript file
⊠		.jpg	Joint Photographic Experts Group file
		.pic	Picture/Draw file
⊠		.tif	Tagged image file (TIFF)

Files that can be placed into PageMaker

Drive or folder where Project Files are stored (yours might differ)

Place

Look in: Unit B

CD Logo.jpg
Corner Bookstore.jpg
Hilltop Ski Shop Logo.jpg
Island Paradise Logo.jpg
Logo.tif
School.tif

File name: Logo.tif

Files of type: Importable Files

Open

Cancel

Kind: TIFF Image

Size: 52K   Last modified: 11/11/2001 9:14 PM

CMS source...

Place URL...

Information about the selected file

Logo.tif file is selected

Place
- ○ As independent graphic
- ○ Replacing entire story
- ○ Inserting text

Options
- ☐ Show filter preferences   ☑ Convert quotes
- ☑ Retain format   ☐ Read tags
- ☑ Retain cropping Data

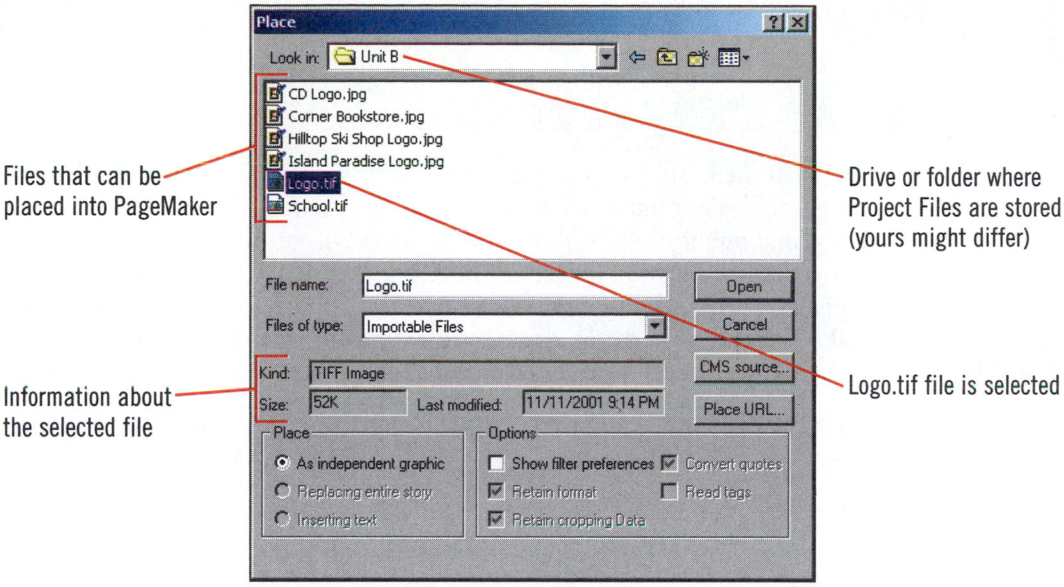

FIGURE B-5: TIF pointer on the publication page

Pointer guide at 3.25" mark

.tif place pointer

Adobe PageMaker 7.0 - [Untitled-1]
File Edit Layout Type Element Utilities View Window Help

FIGURE B-6: Placed graphic

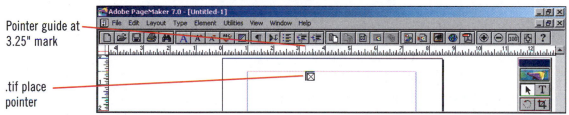

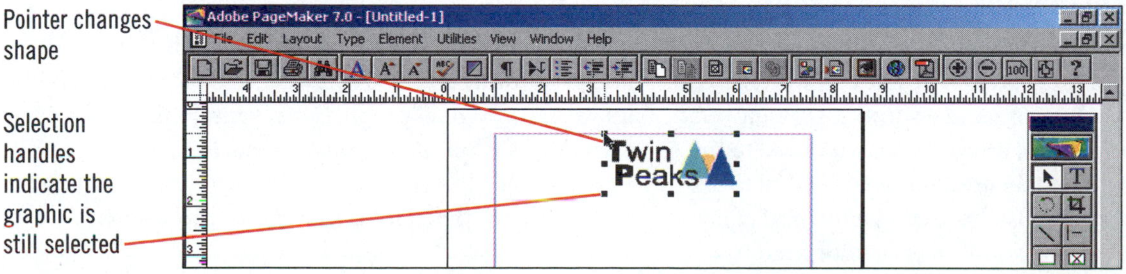

Pointer changes shape

Selection handles indicate the graphic is still selected

Adobe PageMaker 7.0 - [Untitled-1]
File Edit Layout Type Element Utilities View Window Help

Twin
Peaks

PageMaker 7.0

Resizing and Moving a Graphic

An **object** is an item, such as a graphic or a line, that you can select and then resize or move. Usually a graphic is not imported at the correct size, so often you need to resize a graphic after you place it in a publication. You can make a graphic larger or smaller by dragging a selection handle. You can also move an object to a different location on the same page, between pages, or onto the pasteboard for temporary storage outside the page. Sara needs to resize the Twin Peaks Resort logo so that it is more prominent at the top of the page.

Steps

1. If the graphic is not selected, position the ➤ pointer over the middle of the logo, then click

   The graphic is selected.

   Trouble?

   If you make a mistake, click Edit on the menu bar, click Undo Stretch, then try again.
   ---

2. Move the pointer over the lower-right selection handle of the logo, press and hold **[Shift]**, then press and hold the **mouse button**

   The pointer changes to the resize pointer ↘, and a box appears around the graphic to show its dimensions, as shown in Figure B-7. Pressing [Shift] while you resize a graphic maintains the proportions of the graphic as you resize it. By dragging a corner selection handle, you change the length and width of the image simultaneously.

3. Drag the **selection handle** until it is aligned with the **6.25"** mark on the horizontal ruler

   Use the pointer guides to help you size the logo correctly.

   DesignTip

   Move the zero point to the upper-left corner of a graphic to help you determine the measurements of the graphic as you resize it.
   ---

4. Release the **mouse button** and **[Shift]**

   The logo is enlarged, as shown in Figure B-8. The selection handles indicate the logo is still selected.

5. Position the pointer over the middle of the logo, but not over a selection handle, then press and hold the **mouse button**

   The pointer changes to the move pointer ➤.

6. Drag the **logo** to the upper-left corner of the page so that the top and left borders of the logo outline overlap the top and left margin guides, then release the **mouse button**

   If the logo outline disappears as you drag, then use the pointer guides to help position the logo. The left pointer guide should align with the 1" mark on the horizontal ruler. The upper pointer guide should align with the .5" mark on the vertical ruler. When you release the mouse button, the logo appears in its new location, as shown in Figure B-9.

7. Click outside the logo to deselect the graphic

CLUES TO USE

Distorting the image design

Sometimes you want to resize a graphic without maintaining its proportion between height and width. To do this, you drag a selection handle without pressing [Shift]. This distorts the image. When you need to fit an image within a certain area, it can be helpful to distort it. Distortion can also be used as a method of creative design in your publication. It is important to make sure that the distortion does not affect the integrity of the image. If you want to restore a distorted image to its original proportions, press [Shift], and then drag a selection handle to create the desired size. Pressing [Shift] as you drag a selection handle restores and maintains the graphic's original proportions.

FIGURE B-7: Preparing to resize the logo

Pointer guide in the horizontal ruler

Pointer guide in the vertical ruler

Outline shows the dimensions of the graphic

Resize pointer

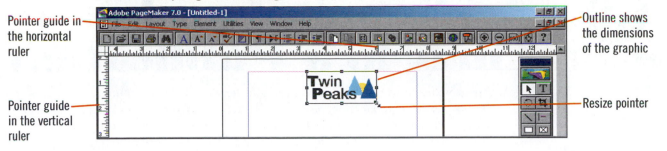

FIGURE B-8: Resized logo

Selection handles indicate the graphic is still selected

Right side of logo aligns with the 6.25" mark

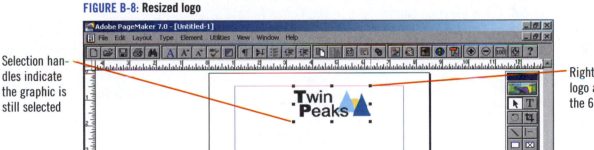

FIGURE B-9: Repositioned logo

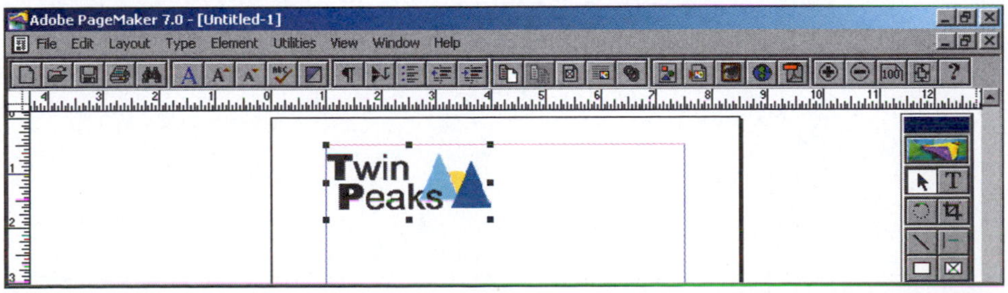

Adding Text and Lines to a Publication

PageMaker provides tools with which you can add text and lines to a publication easily and quickly. To add text to a publication, you select the Text tool from the toolbox, click the page, and then type. To add a straight line to a publication, you use the Constrained-line tool. Sara needs to add the company's address and telephone number to the letterhead. She also wants to draw a line to separate the logo from the rest of the page.

Steps

1. Click the **Constrained-line tool** ⊢ in the toolbox
   The pointer changes to +.

2. Position the + pointer over the left margin guide just below the graphic, drag to the right until the + pointer is directly over the right margin guide, then release the mouse button
   A horizontal line appears just below the logo, as shown in Figure B-10.

3. Click the **Pointer tool** in the toolbox, then click the **logo** to select it

4. Click **View** on the menu bar, then click **Actual Size**
   The screen appears at 100% with the logo in the center of the screen. Selecting an object before changing the view ensures that the object is centered on the screen when the view is magnified or reduced.

5. Click the **Text tool** T in the toolbox, then position the pointer over the page
   The pointer changes to Ⅰ.

6. Click below the line and just to the right of the left margin guide
   A blinking cursor appears at the left margin guide just below the line you drew. The **cursor**, also called the insertion point, shows where the next character you type will appear. If you clicked in the wrong place, reposition the cursor by clicking again in the correct place.

7. Type **No Vertical Limits!**, then press **[Enter]** *(Macintosh Users: Press [Return])*
   Characters appear at the location of the cursor as you type, and the cursor moves down one line when you press [Enter]. See Figure B-11.

8. Type **1200 Alta Lake Road, Whistler, BC V7R 1A8**, press **[Spacebar]** three times, then type **1-800-555-1200**

Line is selected

Constrained-line
tool

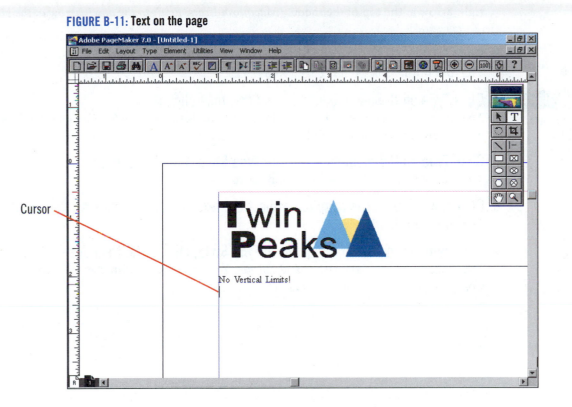

Cursor

Formatting Text

When you **format** text, you change its appearance. You can change the font, size, and type style of text. The **font** is a complete set of characters that use a specific design. The size of the characters is usually measured in points. A **point** is ½ of an inch. The type style of text is how the font is displayed, for example, in italics or bold. Table B-2 shows examples of some common fonts, sizes, and type styles. One way to format text is to select the text you want to format, and then choose the appropriate command from the Type menu. Sara formats the company's address and telephone number to help make the information stand out on the page.

Steps

1. Position the text pointer ⏋ at the end of the last line of text, press and hold the **mouse button**, drag ⏋ to the left until you reach the beginning of the last line of text, then release the mouse button

The address and phone number are selected, as shown in Figure B-12. If you accidentally select the wrong line, click to deselect the text, and then try again.

2. Click **Type** on the menu bar, then point to **Font**

The Font menu appears, as shown in Figure B-13. It lists all the fonts available on your computer. You can expand the Font menu to display more font names by pointing to the right arrow at the top of the menu. *(Macintosh Users: Point to the down arrow at the bottom of the menu.)*

3. Click **Arial**

The font of the selected text changes to Arial.

4. Click **Type** on the menu bar, point to **Size**, then click **9**

The size of the selected text is reduced from 12 points to 9 points. The smaller the point size of text, the smaller the text, and vice versa.

5. Click **Type** on the menu bar, point to **Type Style**, then click **Italic**

The selected text is now slanted, or italicized.

6. Click anywhere on the page to deselect the text, then triple-click **No Vertical Limits!**

The entire line is selected.

7. Click **Type** on the menu bar, point to **Type Style**, click **Bold**, then deselect the text

The slogan text is made darker and thicker. You are pleased with the finished letterhead. Compare your screen with Figure B-14.

TABLE B-2: Types of fonts and formatting

font	12 point	24 point	12 pt bold	12 pt italic
Arial	PageMaker	PageMaker	**PageMaker**	*PageMaker*
Century Schoolbook	PageMaker	PageMaker	**PageMaker**	*PageMaker*
Times New Roman	PageMaker	PageMaker	**PageMaker**	*PageMaker*

FIGURE B-12: Selected text

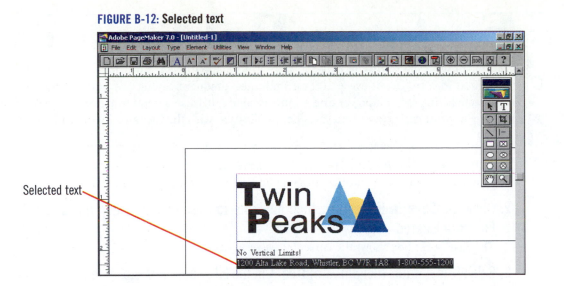

Selected text

FIGURE B-13: Font menu

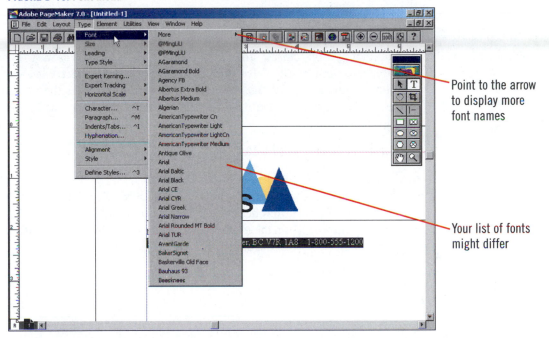

Point to the arrow to display more font names

Your list of fonts might differ

FIGURE B-14: Sara's completed letterhead

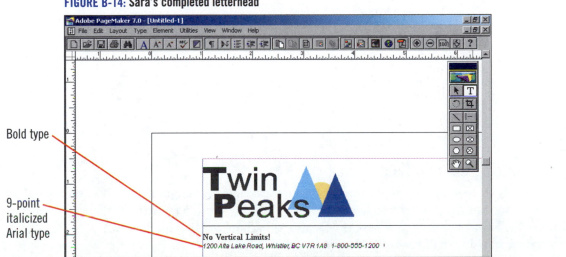

Bold type

9-point italicized Arial type

Saving a Publication

You must save a file to disk in order to store it permanently. As you work on your publication, it's a good idea to save it every 10 or 15 minutes. Frequent saving prevents losing your work unexpectedly in case of a power or equipment failure. It's also a good practice to save your work before you print it.   Sara saves her publication with the filename Twin Peaks Letterhead.

Steps

1. Click **File** on the menu bar, then click **Save As**

   The Save Publication: Untitled 1 dialog box opens, as shown in Figure B-15.

2. Click the **Save in list arrow**, then navigate to the drive or folder where your Project Files are located

   The Save in list box shows the current drive or folder.

3. Select the default filename **Untitled-1** in the File name text box if necessary, then type **Twin Peaks Letterhead**

   Filenames can contain up to 250 characters. These characters can be lowercase or uppercase letters, numbers, punctuation, or symbols.

QuickTip

You can also use the shortcut key combination [Shift] [Ctrl] [S] to save a file with a new filename. *(Macintosh Users: Use the shortcut key combination [Shift] [Command] [S] to save a file with a new filename.)*

4. Click **Save**

   The dialog box closes, and the publication is saved as a file named Twin Peaks Letterhead.pmd to the drive and folder where your Project Files are located. PageMaker automatically adds the PageMaker file extension .pmd after the filename when you save a file. A **file extension** identifies the program in which a file was created. The new filename appears in the title bar.

5. Double-click the word **Road**, then type **Rd.**

6. Click **File** on the menu bar, then click **Save**

   The change you made to the publication is saved. The Save command saves the changes made to a file after it has been saved with a unique filename. Windows users can also click the Save button 🖫 on the toolbar to save your changes to a publication. Table B-3 describes the difference between the Save and Save As commands.

Creating backup files

It's good practice to back up your files in case something happens to your disk. To create a backup copy of a file, use the Save As command to save the file to a different location with a slightly modified name. For example, you might name a backup copy of a file named "Brochure" with the filename "Brochure-backup" or "Brochure-copy."

Default filename is selected

Indicates file will be saved as a PageMaker publication

Current drive or folder (yours might differ)

PageMaker 7.0

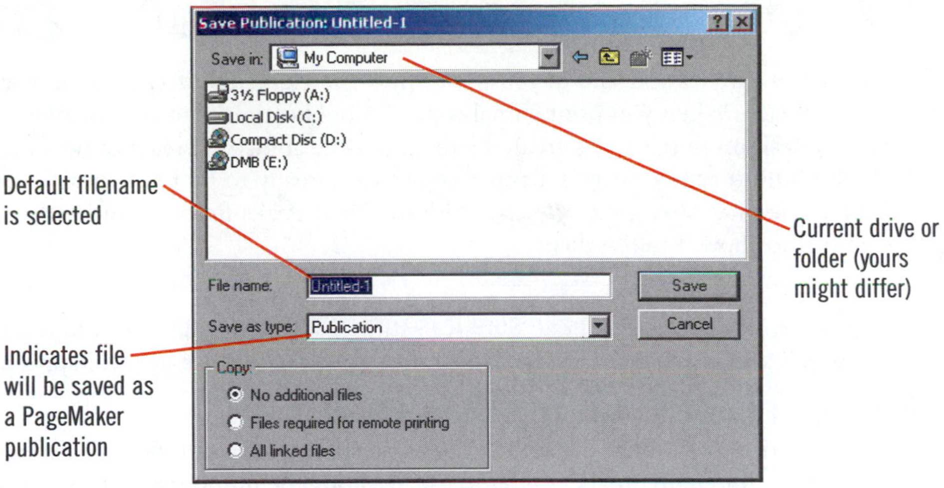

TABLE B-3: The Save and Save As commands

command	use to
Save As	Save a file for the first time, save a file with a different filename or in a different location, or save a file in a different file format (such as a template)
Save	Save the changes made to a file; overwrites the original copy of the file with the changes

B

PageMaker 7.0

Printing a Publication

Printing a publication allows you to see how the elements of each page work together on a printed page. When you print a final copy of a publication on a laser printer, you capitalize on one of desktop publishing's greatest strengths—the ability to create camera-ready copy at your desk. **Camera-ready copy** is a paper copy that is ready to be photographed for reproduction without further alteration. With the Twin Peaks Resort letterhead saved to disk, Sara prints it to show it to the client.

Steps

1. **Check the printer to make sure it is turned on, has paper, and is ready to print**
   If you send a file to a printer that is not ready, an error message will appear.

QuickTip

Always save a publication before printing it.

2. **Click File on the menu bar, then click Print**
   The Print Document dialog box opens, as shown in Figure B-16. The dialog box contains options for changing the printer to use, selecting the number of copies to print, selecting the pages to print, and selecting the page orientation of the publication, among other options. For the Twin Peaks letterhead, the default print settings are correct. Table B-4 describes the function of some of the command buttons in the Print Document dialog box. Windows users can also click the Print button 🖨 on the toolbar to open the Print Document dialog box.

3. **If you are using a non-PostScript printer, click Setup in the Print Document dialog box; if you are using a PostScript printer, click Paper in the Print Document dialog box**
   The Document Properties or Print Paper dialog box opens. The Document Properties dialog box is shown in Figure B-17. Depending on your non-PostScript printer, the options available in your Document Properties dialog box might be different. The Print Paper dialog box is shown in Figure B-18. You can use these dialog boxes to select the paper size on which to print, to add printer marks to the printed pages, and to change the scale of the printed publication, among other options.

QuickTip

Depending on your hardware and the size of the publication, a status window might appear while the printer receives the publication information. Click the Cancel button in the status window to cancel the print job if necessary.

4. **If you are using a non-PostScript printer, click OK to close the Document Properties dialog box, then click Print in the Print Document dialog box; if you are using a PostScript printer, click Print in the Print Paper dialog box**
   The publication prints. If you don't have a color printer, the printer converts the colors in the logo to black, white, and shades of gray.

5. **Click File on the menu bar, click Save, click File on the menu bar, then click Exit**
   The publication and PageMaker close.

TABLE B-4: Print Document dialog box buttons

button	use to
Setup	Change the printing resolution, paper size, orientation, and the paper source for non-PostScript printers
Paper	Change the printing resolution, paper size, scale, and the paper source for PostScript printers
Options	Scale the printed publication (from 5% to 1600%), choose duplex (double-sided) printing, and include printer marks, which are used by commercial printers to show the edges of a page, on the printed page
Color	Determine how color objects in the document are printed
Features	Set printer-specific features for PostScript printers
Reset	Reset all options to the default settings

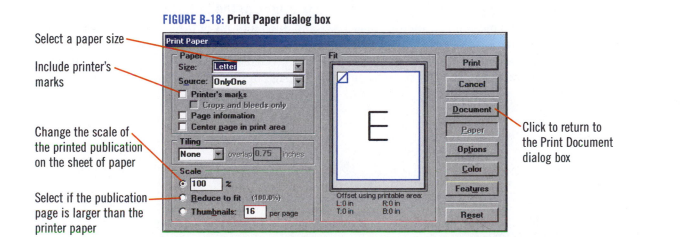

FIGURE B-16: Print Document dialog box

Print Document
Enter the number of copies to print
Select the pages to be printed
Tall orientation is selected
Current printer (yours might differ)
This button appears as "Paper" for PostScript printers

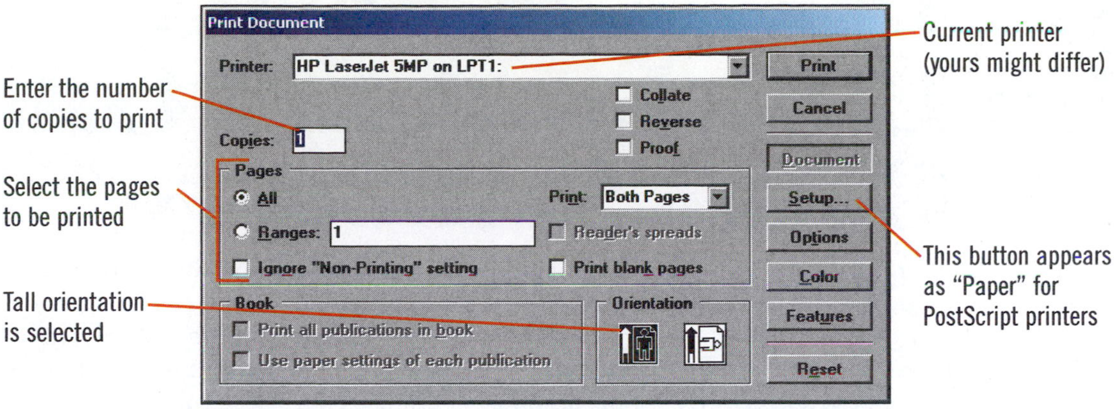

FIGURE B-17: Document Properties dialog box

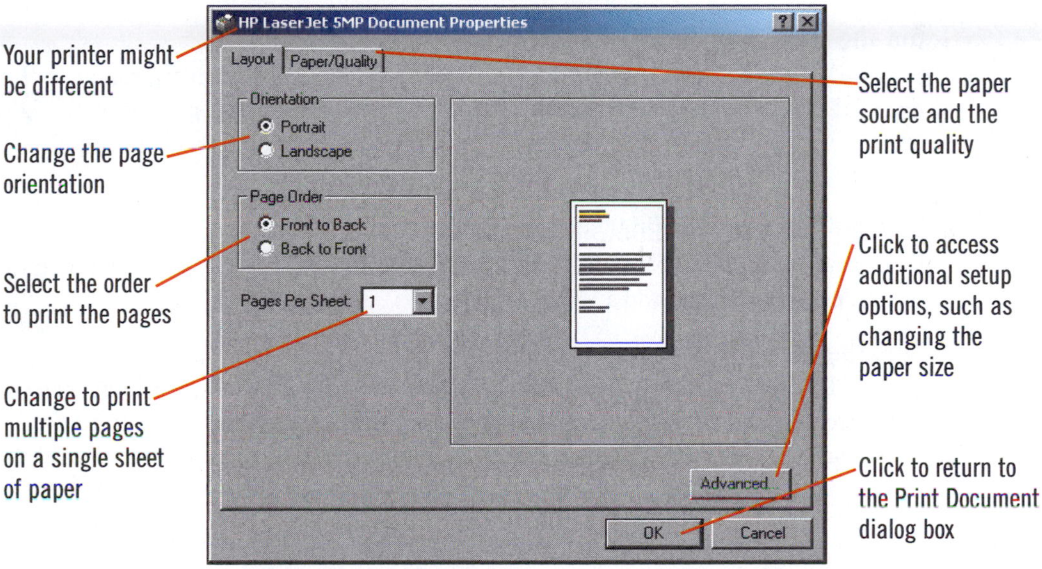

HP LaserJet 5MP Document Properties
Your printer might be different
Change the page orientation
Select the order to print the pages
Change to print multiple pages on a single sheet of paper
Select the paper source and the print quality
Click to access additional setup options, such as changing the paper size
Click to return to the Print Document dialog box

FIGURE B-18: Print Paper dialog box

Print Paper
Select a paper size
Include printer's marks
Change the scale of the printed publication on the sheet of paper
Select if the publication page is larger than the printer paper
Click to return to the Print Document dialog box

Design Workshop: Letterhead and Other Office Stationery

After you create a publication, it is important to critique your final output to see if it meets your original goals. Designing letterhead can seem simple, but there are certain techniques that can make a company's letterhead and stationery stand out. When creating office stationery such as letterhead, memos, business cards, fax cover sheets, and envelopes, it is important to use a consistent design in each type of publication. For example, the placement of the logo and the fonts, sizes, and text styles used in each type of publication should be similar. Sara critiques her design of the Twin Peaks Resort letterhead, shown in Figure B-19, before she gives it to the client for approval.

Details

Sara asks the following questions when she critiques the letterhead design:

▶ **Did the logo placement add to the overall design?**
Sara added the company logo to the letterhead and moved it from the center to the top left corner of the page. She could also have attractively positioned the logo at the top right, in the center, or on the bottom of the page. The logo seems to be an appropriate size and does not overwhelm the information on the page, which is important.

▶ **Was all the relevant information included?**
Sara included all the information the client requested. Letterhead also often includes a fax number, an e-mail address, and a Web site address.

▶ **Was the use of the slogan appropriate?**
Sara added the Twin Peaks Resort slogan to reinforce the company's message. Depending on the audience, slogans or mottoes might not be appropriate or necessary on a letterhead. She also could have placed the slogan and company information across the bottom of the page to serve as an anchor, or border, for the overall design of the letterhead.

▶ **Did the placement of the decorative line enhance the layout?**
Sara separated the logo from the rest of the layout by adding a line across the page below the logo. She could also have oriented the address vertically under the logo and then added a vertical line down the left side of the page to separate this information from the blank space reserved for the body of the letter.

▶ **Are you pleased with the overall appearance of the letterhead?**
Sara is pleased because the smaller size and different font of the address distinguish this information from the slogan and from the text of the letters that will be printed on the letterhead. However, she recognizes that she could have created a more balanced layout by placing the text above the line in the top-right corner of the page, or by placing it across the bottom of the page.

No Vertical Limits!
1200 Alta Lake Rd., Whistler, BC V7R 1A8   1-800-555-1200

Practice

► Concepts Review

Label each element of the publication window shown in Figure B-20.

FIGURE B-20

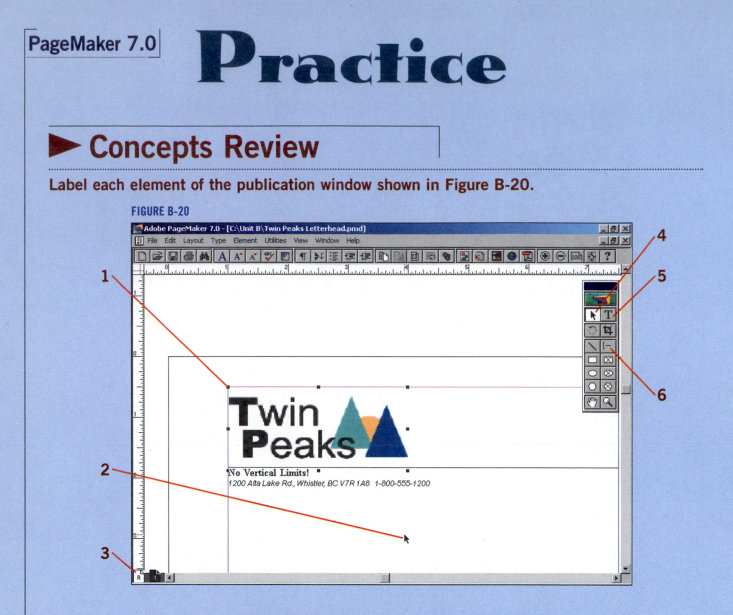

Match each term with the statement that best describes it.

7. **Graphic**
8. **Font**
9. **Resolution**
10. **Point**
11. **Place**

a. Measured in dots per inch
b. Image created in a drawing or painting program
c. ½ of an inch
d. The command used to import a graphic
e. A complete set of characters with a specific design

Select the best answer from the list of choices.

12. **The term used to describe the image quality and clarity of a publication's output is:**
   a. Resolution.
   b. Laser print.
   c. Image view.
   d. None of the above.

13. **In the Document Setup dialog box, you can set all of the following, except:**
   a. Number of pages.
   b. Size of the page.
   c. Number of columns.
   d. Size of the margins.

14. **All of the following are true statements concerning filenames, except:**
   a. Filenames must be less than eight characters.
   b. Punctuation marks can be used in a filename.
   c. Numbers can be used in a filename.
   d. All of the above are true statements.

15. **PageMaker allows you to place all of the following, except:**
   a. Graphic images.
   b. Images created with a paint program.
   c. Digital photographs.
   d. All of the above can be placed.

16. **While resizing a graphic by dragging a corner selection handle, which key do you press to resize the image proportionally?**
   a. [Alt]
   b. [Ctrl]
   c. [Shift]
   d. The image is automatically resized proportionally.

▶ Skills Review

1. **Create a new publication.**
   a. Plan a design for memo stationery for the Twin Peaks Resort. The memo should include the company logo and a memo header that includes a To, From, Date, and Re line.
   b. Start PageMaker, then close the Templates palette.
   c. Click File on the menu bar, then click New.
   d. In the Document Setup dialog box, make sure the page size is set to Letter and the orientation is set to Tall.
   e. Set the publication to be single-sided and set all margins to 1".
   f. Click OK.
   g. Reposition the zero point at the intersection of the top and left margin guides.

2. **Place a graphic.**
   a. Click File on the menu bar, then click Place.
   b. Use the Look in list arrow to navigate to the drive and folder where your Project Files are located, if necessary.
   c. Select the Logo.tif file, then click Open. *(Macintosh Users: Click OK.)*
   d. Position the .tif place pointer at the zero point in the upper-left corner of the publication, then click.

3. **Resize and move a graphic.**
   a. Select the graphic if necessary.
   b. Move the pointer over the lower-right corner selection handle of the logo.
   c. Press and hold [Shift], then drag the selection handle to resize the graphic so the bottom edge aligns with the 1" mark on the vertical ruler.
   d. Move the pointer over the logo, then drag the logo until it is centered between the left and right margins, with its top aligned with the top margin guide.

4. **Add text and lines to a publication.**
   a. Click the Text tool in the toolbox.
   b. Position the text pointer below the logo and at the left margin, then click.
   c. Change the view to Actual Size.

PageMaker 7.0

d. Type **MEMO**, then press [Enter] twice.

e. Type the following memo header, pressing [Enter] twice after each line:
   TO:
   FROM:
   DATE:
   RE:

f. Change the view to Fit in Window.

g. Click the Constrained-line tool in the toolbox.

h. Position the constrained-line pointer over the left margin guide just below the word MEMO (the first line of text, which might appear shaded).

i. Draw a line from the left margin to the right margin, then release the mouse button.

j. Position the pointer over the left margin guide below RE:, (the last line of text), then draw a line to the right margin.

k. Draw another line just below the line you just drew.

l. Deselect the line by clicking the Pointer tool in the toolbox.

m. Click the third line to select it, then press [Delete].

5. Format text.

a. Click the Text tool in the toolbox, click near the first line of text (MEMO), then change the view to Actual Size.

b. Select the word MEMO.

c. Change the size to 14 points.

d. Change the type style to Bold.

e. Change the type style to Italic.

f. Click anywhere on the page to deselect the text.

6. Save a publication.

a. Click File on the menu bar, then click Save As.

b. Use the Save in list arrow to navigate to the drive or folder where your Project Files are located.

c. Save the file as **Memo**.

7. Print a publication.

a. Click File on the menu bar, then click Print.

b. Click the Paper button or the Setup button, depending on your printer.

c. Check to see that all your printer settings are accurate.

d. If you are in the Print Paper dialog box, click Document to return to the Print Document dialog box. If you are in the Print Setup dialog box, click OK.

e. Make any other adjustments necessary.

f. Click Print to print the file.

g. Save and close the document, then exit PageMaker.

► Independent Challenge 1

You are the graphic designer for the Hilltop Ski Shop. Your manager has asked you to design a letterhead, a memo letterhead, and a business card for the company. The company logo is shown in Figure B-21.

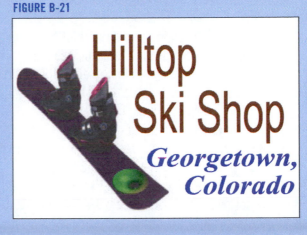

a. Plan a design for the letterhead, the memo letterhead, and the business card by sketching them on paper.

b. Start PageMaker, then create a new single-sided, one-page publication with 1" margins on all sides.

c. Save the new publication as **Hilltop Letterhead** to the drive and folder where your Project Files are located.

d. Place the image file Hilltop Ski Shop Logo.jpg, found in the drive and folder where your Project Files are located, on the page.

e. Resize the logo to a more appropriate size, then move the logo to an appropriate position on the letterhead.

f. Draw a line on the page, if appropriate.

g. Use the Text tool to add text for the address, phone number, and other contact information. (Make up this information.)

h. Save your changes, print the publication, then close the file.

i. Create a new single-sided, one-page publication with 1" margins on all sides, then save it as **Hilltop Memo** to the drive and folder where your Project Files are located.

j. Place the logo Hilltop Ski Shop Logo.jpg on the page. Resize the logo to an appropriate size, then move the logo to an appropriate position in the memo.

k. Use the Text tool to create a memo header that includes the words **MEMO:**, **TO:**, **FROM:**, **DATE:**, and **RE:**.

l. Add lines to enhance the design of the memo.

m. Save your changes, print the publication, then close the file.

n. Create a new single-sided, one-page publication with .25" margins on all sides and Wide orientation. In the Document Setup dialog box, select Custom in the Page size list box, then change the page dimensions to 2" x 3.5".

o. Save the publication as **Hilltop Business Card** to the drive and folder where your Project Files are located.

p. Place the logo Hilltop Ski Shop Logo.jpg on the page. Reduce the size of the logo so it fits within the page margins, then move the logo to an appropriate position on the business card.

q. Type your name, your title, and the company address, telephone number, and other relevant contact information on the business card.

r. Select your name, change the type style to bold, then change the type size to an appropriate size. Format your title and the company address, telephone number, and other contact information with fonts, sizes, and type styles as appropriate.

s. Save your changes, print the publication, close the file, then exit PageMaker.

▶ Independent Challenge 2

You are a freelance graphic artist hired by your school to redesign their stationery. Obtain a sample of the letterhead or memo letterhead currently in use. Compare this example to what you learned in this unit, and think about the following:

- Is a logo used in the publication? Is the logo large enough to be seen, but not overwhelming?
- Is all the relevant information included? Should you include a fax number or the e-mail or Web site address?
- Is the school's slogan included in the letterhead? Is it appropriate to include it?
- Do you need a graphic to separate the logo and other information from the body text of the letterhead?

a. Sketch a new design for the letterhead.

b. What information did you include? Why?

c. Start PageMaker, then create a new one-page, single-sided publication.

d. Create the letterhead you sketched.

e. Place the graphic file School.tif, found on the drive and folder where your Project Files are located, as a place-holder for the school logo. Resize the graphic if necessary.

f. Add the text to the letterhead, then enhance it with lines if necessary.

g. Save the publication as **New Letterhead** to the drive and folder where your Project Files are located.

h. Print the publication, close the file, then exit PageMaker.

▶ Independent Challenge 3

You have been hired by the Corner Bookstore to create two business cards, one for the store managers and one for the buyers.

a. Sketch a design for the two business cards. Each should include a logo, the name, address, and phone number of the bookstore, and the name and title of the manager or buyer. Make the layout of each business card different.

b. Start PageMaker, then create a new single-sided, one-page publication with .25" margins on all sides and Wide orientation. In the Document Setup dialog box, select Custom in the Page size list box, then change the page dimensions to 2" x 3.5".

c. Save the publication as **Manager Business Card** to the drive and folder where your Project Files are located.

d. Place the logo graphic file Corner Bookstore.jpg, found on the drive and folder where your Project Files are located, in the publication.

e. Add text to the business card. Use your name and the employee title **Manager**. Format the text so that the most important elements stand out.

f. Add lines as necessary to make the layout of the business card compelling.

g. Save the publication, then print it.

h. Use the Save As command to save the publication with the new filename **Buyer Business Card** to the drive and folder where your Project Files are located.

i. Change the employee title to **Buyer**, then reorganize the elements of the business card to create a different layout. Adjust the formatting of the text and add and remove lines as necessary.

j. Save your changes to the publication, print it, close the file, then exit PageMaker.

Independent Challenge 4

You have been asked to create a new company letterhead for an online retailer of music CDs, tapes, and records.

a. Open your browser, then use your favorite search engine to search the World Wide Web for the Web site of a music retailer. For example, you might go to the Yahoo! search engine at www.yahoo.com and enter keywords such as **CD music store** to perform your search. You can also use AltaVista, Excite, Infoseek, or another search engine. If your search does not result in appropriate links, try looking at the following Web sites: www.musicland.com or www.cduniverse.com.

b. Select one of the online music retailers that you find, then sketch a design for a letterhead, including a logo and an appropriate slogan. Make sure to keep the guidelines that you learned in this unit in mind as you plan and design the letterhead.

c. Start PageMaker, then create the letterhead you designed.

d. Place the graphic file CD Logo.jpg, found on the drive and folder where your Project Files are located, as a place-holder for the company logo.

e. Save the publication as **Music Letterhead** to the drive and folder where your Project Files are located.

f. Print the publication, close the file, then exit PageMaker.

g. Critique your final letterhead.

▶ Visual Workshop

Create the letterhead shown in Figure B-22, using .75" margins on all sides. For the logo, place the graphic file Island Paradise Logo.jpg, found on the drive and folder where your Project Files are located, in the publication, adjusting it as necessary. Save the file as **Island Paradise Letterhead** to the drive and folder where your Project Files are located, then print a copy.

FIGURE B-22

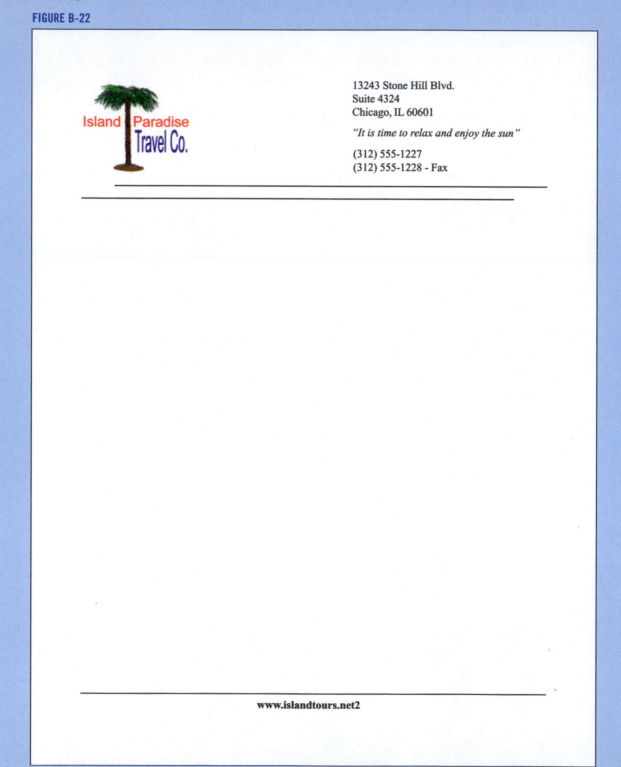

13243 Stone Hill Blvd.
Suite 4324
Chicago, IL 60601

"It is time to relax and enjoy the sun"

(312) 555-1227
(312) 555-1228 - Fax

www.islandtours.net2

Working
with Text

Objectives

► **Plan a fact sheet**
► **Create columns**
► **Import and place text**
► **Control the flow of text**
► **Manipulate text blocks**
► **Move and resize text blocks**
► **Drag-place text**
► **Use reverse text**
► **Design Workshop: Fact Sheets**

PageMaker includes tools that make it easy to lay out a publication that includes a lot of text. In this unit, you learn how to create columns, how to import, place, and control the flow of text, and how to format headlines. Mousing Around supplies souvenir stores and corporate customers with custom-designed mouse pads. Sara Norton has been hired by Mousing Around to create a series of fact sheets for prospective customers with information about their products. The first fact sheet will contain information about three categories of custom mouse pads.

Details

Planning a Fact Sheet

A **fact sheet** is an informational publication that describes a company's products or services in detail. Fact sheets can be one page or several pages, and usually contain large amounts of text. When designing a fact sheet, it is important to plan the layout carefully and to use graphical elements to support the text. Sara's first fact sheet must include information about Mousing Around's three categories of custom mouse pads: landscapes, landmarks, and logos. Figure C-1 shows Sara's sketch of the fact sheet.

Keep the following guidelines in mind when designing a fact sheet:

► Keep the layout simple

While it is important to catch the reader's attention, fact sheets should provide detailed information about a product or service in a succinct and organized way. If your fact sheet relies too heavily on creative design, some of your message might get lost. Sara has decided to use a three-column format for the fact sheet. Each column will provide information about a category of mouse pad.

► Keep the format consistent among fact sheets in a series

Fact sheets in a series should present similar types of information consistently. Sara's fact sheets will provide the same information about each Mousing Around product: the name of the product, a description, the cost, and the point of response. The **point of response** is the phone number, Web site, or address the reader can use to respond to information in the fact sheet. Formatting this text in the same manner creates a consistent look among fact sheets in a series.

► Use graphical elements strategically to enhance the overall layout

Graphical element is an umbrella term that describes anything on a page other than text. Graphical elements, such as lines or photos, can make your fact sheets more interesting. Because fact sheets provide information, graphical elements should support the text without overshadowing the message you are trying to convey. Sara decides to include a photograph or an illustration of each type of mouse pad in her fact sheet.

► Include a headline that instantly conveys the purpose of the fact sheet

Publications that are dense with text can be so overwhelming that readers ignore them. A fact sheet should include a headline that conveys the purpose of the publication immediately and clearly. Sara wants to include a headline that identifies the purpose of her fact sheet across the top of the page. She decides to set the headline for her fact sheet in **reverse text**, white text on a black background, so the reader knows at first glance what information the fact sheet contains.

► Use high-quality paper stock

People keep fact sheets as reference material, so it's important to print a fact sheet on paper that is able to withstand repeated handling.

FIGURE C-1: Sara's sketch of the fact sheet

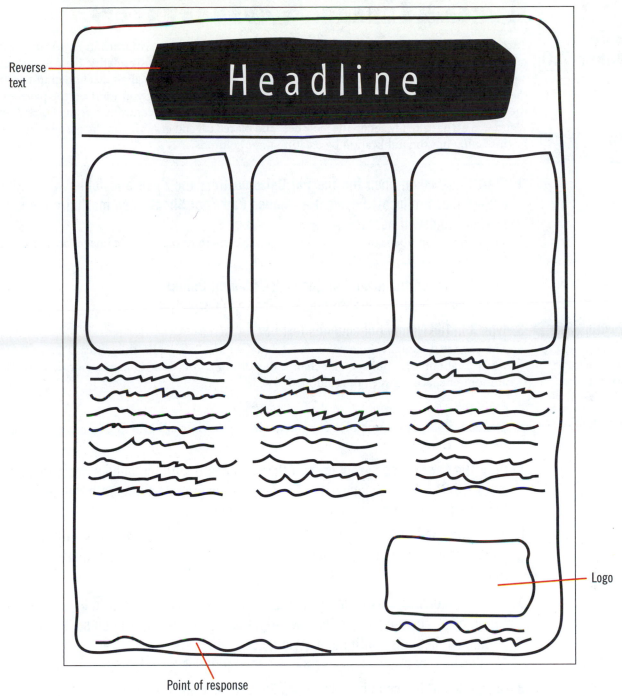

Reverse text

Headline

Logo

Point of response

Creating Columns

Text can be easier to read when it is formatted in columns. To create columns in PageMaker, you use the Column Guides command on the Layout menu. **Column guides** define the columns on a publication page, and are used to control the flow of text or to help align text and graphics. In the Column Guides dialog box, you specify the number of columns you want on the page and the amount of space between the columns. The space between columns is called a **gutter**. Sara has already set up the fact sheet and placed several graphics on the pasteboard. She begins laying out the publication by creating three columns.

Steps

1. Start PageMaker, open the file **PM C-1.pmd** from the drive and folder where your Project files are located, save it as **Mouse Pad Fact Sheet**, then maximize the publication window if necessary
   The publication opens in Fit in Window view. Notice that four graphic images are stored on the pasteboard.

2. Click **Layout** on the menu bar, then click **Column Guides**
   The Column Guides dialog box opens, as shown in Figure C-2.

3. Type **3** in the Number of columns text box
   The page will contain three columns of equal width. By default, the gutter is set at .167", which is about 1/6", but you can change the setting if you want to increase or decrease the amount of space between the columns.

4. Click **OK**
   The dialog box closes, and blue column guides divide the page into three equal columns, as shown in Figure C-3.

5. Drag the **Landscapes graphic** from the pasteboard onto the publication page, then place it in the first column so the top border of the graphic aligns with the ruler guide
   The Landscapes graphic is placed in the first column.

6. Place the **Landmarks graphic** in the second column so its top aligns with the ruler guide, then place the **Logos graphic** in the third column so its top aligns with the ruler guide

7. Drag the **Mousing Around logo** from the right side of the pasteboard onto the publication page, then place it in the lower-right corner of the publication so its right and bottom borders align with the margin guides
   The graphics are placed in the publication as shown in Figure C-4.

8. Click **File** on the menu bar, then click **Save** to save your changes to the publication

Changing column widths

PageMaker automatically creates columns of equal width, but you can change the width of columns by simply dragging the column guides. After you create the number of columns you want on a page, position the pointer over one of the column guides that divide two columns, and then press and hold the left mouse button. The pointer changes to ◄┃►. Drag the column guides left or right to widen and narrow the columns on either side. As you drag, both column guides move, making one column wider and the other narrower. The width of the gutter does not change.

FIGURE C-2: Column Guides dialog box

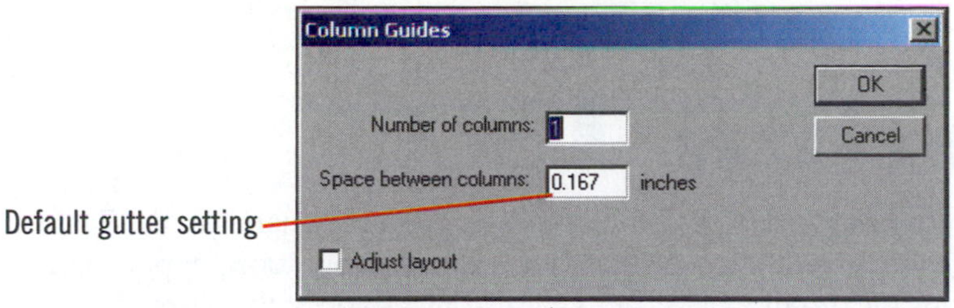

Default gutter setting

FIGURE C-3: Page with three columns

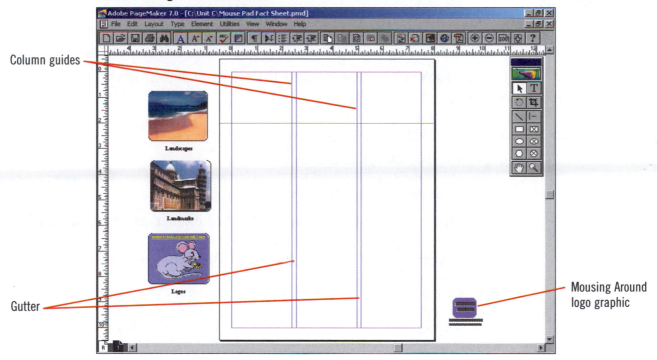

Column guides

Gutter

Mousing Around
logo graphic

FIGURE C-4: Graphics placed in the fact sheet

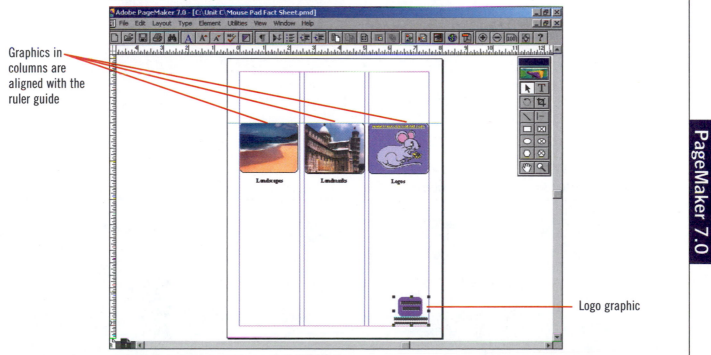

Graphics in
columns are
aligned with the
ruler guide

Logo graphic

Importing and Placing Text

In addition to placing graphics, you can use the Place command on the File menu to import a text file created in a word-processing program into a publication. Importing text files saves you having to retype the text in PageMaker. Table C-1 lists some of the types of text files you can place in a PageMaker publication. ◆━━ Sara uses the Place command to place a point of response in her fact sheet. The point of response was created using a word-processing application.

1. Click **File** on the menu bar, then click **Place**

The Place dialog box opens. (*Macintosh Users: The Place document dialog box opens.*)

2. Click the **Look in list arrow**, navigate to the drive and folder where your Project Files are located, then click **PM C-2.doc**

The Place dialog box shows the file type and size of the selected file, and offers options for how the text should be placed, as shown in Figure C-5.

3. Click **Open** (*Macintosh Users: Click OK*)

The pointer changes to the manual text flow pointer 📝. When a text flow pointer appears, it is said to contain, or be **loaded**, with text.

4. Position 📝 in the upper-left corner of the third column, as shown in Figure C-6, then click

The text appears on the page in a text block in the third column, as shown in Figure C-7. A **text block** is an object that contains text. The width of the text block is determined by the width of the page or column into which it was placed. The **windowshade handles** at the top and bottom of the text block define its top and bottom borders. The windowshade handle at the bottom of the text block is empty, indicating that all the text appears in the text block. The selection handles around the text block indicate it is selected.

5. Save your changes to the publication

TABLE C-1: Types of text files that PageMaker accepts

file extension	application
.wks	Microsoft Works
.doc	Microsoft Word
.wpd	Corel WordPerfect
.rtf	Rich Text Format
.txt	Text or ASCII file

FIGURE C-5: Place dialog box

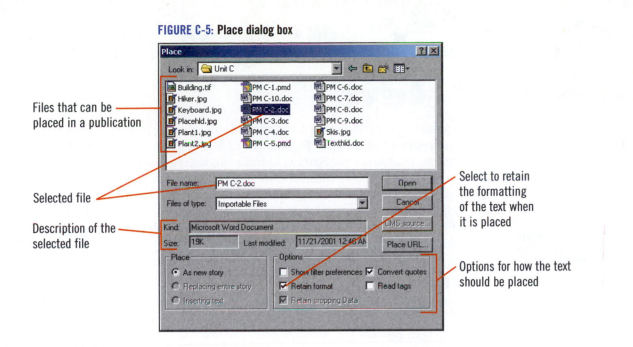

Files that can be placed in a publication

Selected file

Description of the selected file

Select to retain the formatting of the text when it is placed

Options for how the text should be placed

FIGURE C-6: Manual text flow pointer

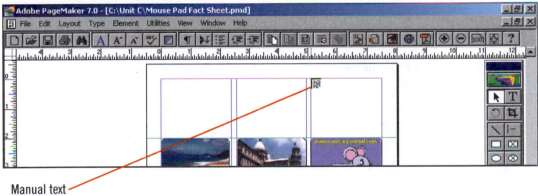

Manual text flow pointer

FIGURE C-7: Text block placed in the third column

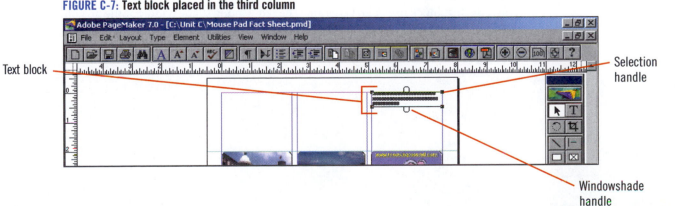

Text block

Selection handle

Windowshade handle

Controlling the Flow of Text

PageMaker includes three options for controlling the flow of text in a publication: Autoflow, semi-Autoflow, and manual flow. These are described in Table C-2. By default, you control the flow of text manually in a publication, but you can also turn on the **Autoflow** feature so that when you place text it flows automatically from one column to the next, filling up as many columns and pages as necessary. Mousing Around provided Sara with a file that contains text describing the mouse pads. Before Sara places the text in her fact sheet, she makes sure the Autoflow option is turned off so that she can manually control the flow of the text between the columns. She then places the text in the fact sheet.

Steps 123 4

1. Click **Layout** on the menu bar
   The Layout menu opens. By default, the Autoflow feature is turned off in PageMaker. If a check mark appears next to the Autoflow command on the Layout menu, Autoflow is activated on your computer.

2. If a check mark appears next to the Autoflow command on the Layout menu, click **Autoflow** to turn the feature off

3. Click **File** on the menu bar, then click **Place**
   The Place dialog box opens. (*Macintosh Users: The Place document dialog box opens.*)

4. Click the **Look in list arrow**, navigate to the drive and folder where your Project Files are located, click the file **PM C-3.doc**, then click **Open** (*Macintosh Users: Click OK*)
   The pointer changes to 📰.

QuickTip

When the text placement pointer is loaded, you can switch between manual flow and semi-Autoflow by pressing and holding [Shift]. You can switch between manual flow and Autoflow by pressing and holding [Ctrl].

5. Position 📰 below the graphic in the first column so that the pointer guide aligns with the 4.75" mark on the vertical ruler, then click
   The text is placed at the location of the pointer, and flows to the bottom of the first column. A red triangle appears in the windowshade handle at the bottom of the column, indicating that the text file contains more text than could fit in the column, as shown in Figure C-8.

6. Click the **windowshade handle** 🔻 at the bottom of the first column
   The pointer changes to 📰.

7. Position 📰 in the second column so the pointer guide aligns with the 4.75" mark on the vertical ruler, then click
   Once again, text flows within the column to the bottom of the page, as shown in Figure C-9. Notice that the windowshade handle at the top of the second column contains a plus sign ⊞ . This indicates that the text is **threaded** from (connected to) another text block, in this case, the text block in the first column. The red windowshape handle at the bottom of the column indicates there is more text to be placed.

8. Save your changes to the publication

FIGURE C-8: Text flowing to the bottom of the first column

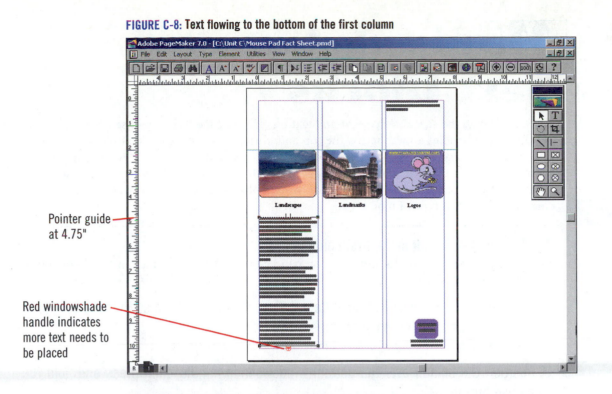

Pointer guide at 4.75"

Red windowshade handle indicates more text needs to be placed

FIGURE C-9: Threaded text block

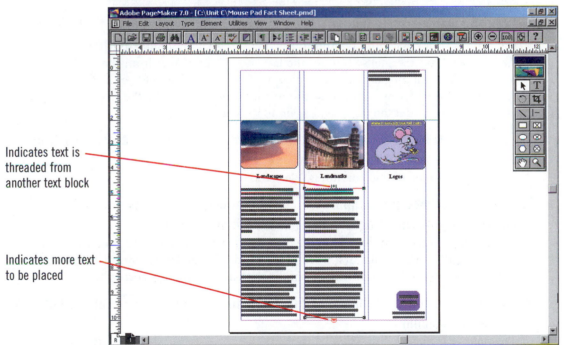

Indicates text is threaded from another text block

Indicates more text to be placed

TABLE C-2: Text flow methods

method	pointer	description
Manual		Text flows from the insertion point to the bottom of the column or page; you must reactivate the text flow pointer, and then specify where to place additional text, if necessary
Autoflow		Text flows from one column to the next, filling up as many columns and pages necessary to place the text; new pages are automatically inserted if necessary
Semi-Autoflow		Text flows to the bottom of the page or column; then the semi-Autoflow text pointer automatically appears ready to place more text

Manipulating Text Blocks

You can change the size and shape of any text block on a page. When you select a text block, windowshade handles appear across the top and bottom borders of the text block, and selection handles appear on the corners. You change the length of a text block by dragging a windowshade handle up or down. You change the width of a text block by dragging a selection handle. ✐ Sara changes the length of the text blocks so that the text under each graphic corresponds to that type of mouse pad.

Steps

QuickTip
Use ruler guides to make sure text blocks are aligned across all columns.

1. **Click the text block in the first column**
   The windowshade handles and selection handles around the text block in the first column indicate it is selected.

2. **Click View on the menu bar, click Actual Size, then scroll down so that the bottom of the text block is visible on your screen**
   The text in the first column describes the Landscape mouse pads.

3. **Position the pointer over the bottom windowshade handle, then press and hold the mouse button**
   The pointer changes to ↕, as shown in Figure C-10.

4. **Drag the windowshade handle ⊞ up approximately three lines to the bottom of the line that begins with "Landmarks", then release the mouse button**
   After you release the mouse button, the last three lines of text from the first column are forced to the beginning of the second column. "Landmarks" should be the first word in the second column. If you didn't drag the windowshade handle in the first column up far enough, or dragged it too far, drag it again to the correct position.

5. **Click the text block in the second column, then scroll down if necessary so that the bottom of the text block is visible on your screen**
   The text box in the second column is selected.

6. **Drag the windowshade handle ▽ up approximately five lines to the bottom of the line that begins with "Logos", then release the mouse button**
   The last five lines of text describing the logo mouse pads are removed from the second column. "Logos" should be the first word in the third column. Don't worry if it takes a couple of tries to position the windowshade handle so that the text flows correctly.

7. **Click View on the menu bar, click Fit In Window, then click ▽ at the bottom of the second column**
   The pointer changes to ▦.

8. **Position ▦ in the third column so the pointer guide aligns with the 4.75" mark on the vertical ruler, then click**
   The text describing the logo mouse pads fills the third column, as shown in Figure C-11. The empty windowshade handle ▽ at the bottom of the third column indicates that all the text has been placed in the publication.

9. **Save your changes to the publication**

FIGURE C-10: Changing the length of the text block

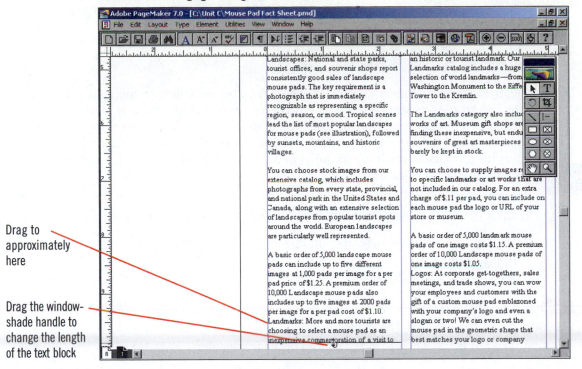

Drag to approximately here

Drag the window-shade handle to change the length of the text block

FIGURE C-11: Text in the third column

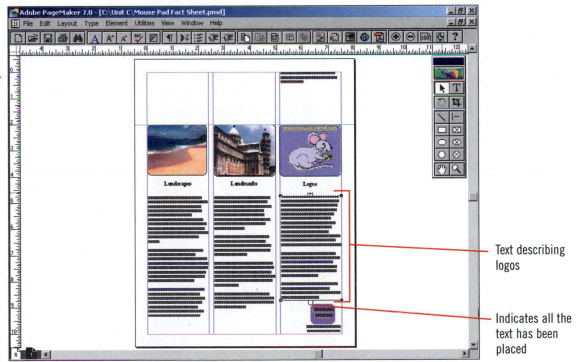

Text describing logos

Indicates all the text has been placed

Unit C

PageMaker 7.0

Moving and Resizing Text Blocks

One of PageMaker's most powerful options is its extensive ability to manipulate the dimensions and location of text blocks. The process for sizing and moving text blocks is similar to that used for resizing and moving graphics: drag a selection handle to change the size and shape of a text block, and drag the text block itself to move it to a new location. Sara moves the text block containing the point of response to the bottom of the page. She resizes it so that it stretches across the three columns.

Steps

1. **Click the point of response text block in the upper-right corner of the page to select it**
2. **Position the pointer over the middle of the text block, then press and hold the mouse button**
   The pointer changes to ▶.
3. **Drag the text block to the bottom of the first column in the lower-left corner of the page, then release the mouse button**
   The text block is moved to the bottom of the first column.
4. **Position the pointer over the lower-right selection handle of the text block, then drag the handle to the right margin guide in the third column, but do not release the mouse button**
   The pointer changes to ↘ as you drag the handle, and a box appears around the text block to show its dimensions, as shown in Figure C-12.
5. **When you are satisfied with the new dimensions, release the mouse button**
   The text block now spans the three columns.
6. **Position the pointer in the middle of the text block, drag the text block down until it is just above the bottom margin guide, then release the mouse button**
   The bottom of the text block aligns with the bottom margin, as shown in Figure C-13. Although the text block overlaps the logo object in the lower-right corner of the page, the text in the text block does not flow over the logo.
7. **Save your changes to the publication**

Trouble?

If you make a mistake, select the text block and try again.

FIGURE C-12: Resizing a text block

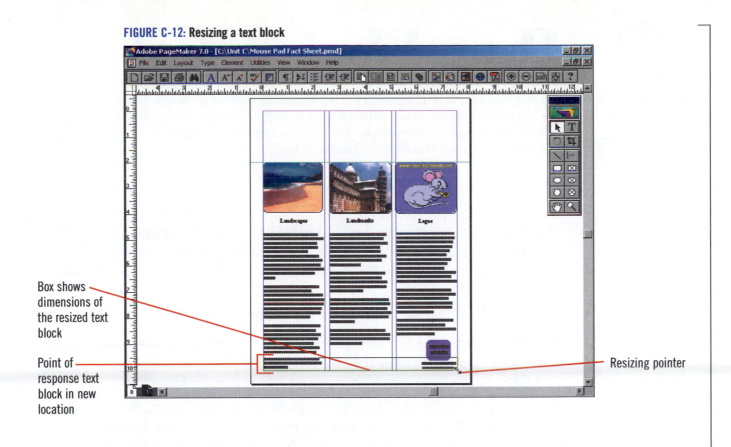

Box shows dimensions of the resized text block

Point of response text block in new location

Resizing pointer

FIGURE C-13: Text block moved to a new location

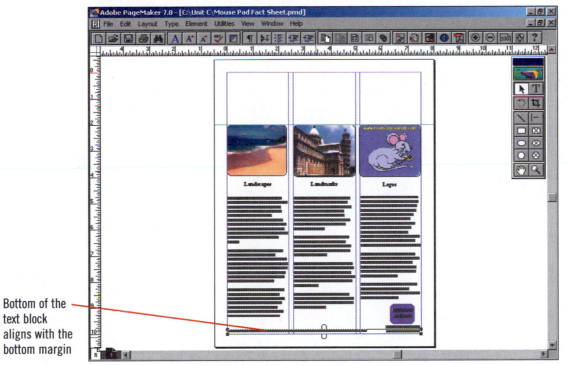

Bottom of the text block aligns with the bottom margin

Drag-Placing Text

In addition to resizing and moving a text block, you can automatically position text across columns or a page using the drag-place method. The **drag-place method** allows you to define the size of a text block at the same time you import text from another location. You can use this method with both manual and automatic text flows. You can also drag-place graphics. Sara drag-places a headline across the top of all three columns in her fact sheet.

Steps

1. Click **File** on the menu bar, then click **Place**

   The Place dialog box opens. (*Macintosh Users: The Place Document dialog box opens.*)

2. Click the **Look in list arrow**, navigate to the drive and folder where your Project Files are located, click the file **PM C-4.doc**, then click **Open** (*Macintosh Users: Click OK*)

   The pointer changes to the manual text flow pointer ▤. The file PM C-4.doc contains the headline text.

3. Position ▤ at the intersection of the top and left margin guides

4. Drag ▤ down to the 1.5" mark on the vertical ruler and across the page to the right margin guide, but do not release the mouse button

   A box shows the dimensions of the new text block, as shown in Figure C-14.

5. When you are satisfied with the text block dimensions, release the mouse button

   The headline appears in a text block that stretches from margin to margin, as shown in Figure C-15. The text, which was formatted in the word-processing program, retains its format when it is placed in a PageMaker publication.

6. Save your changes to the publication

FIGURE C-14: Drag-placing a text block

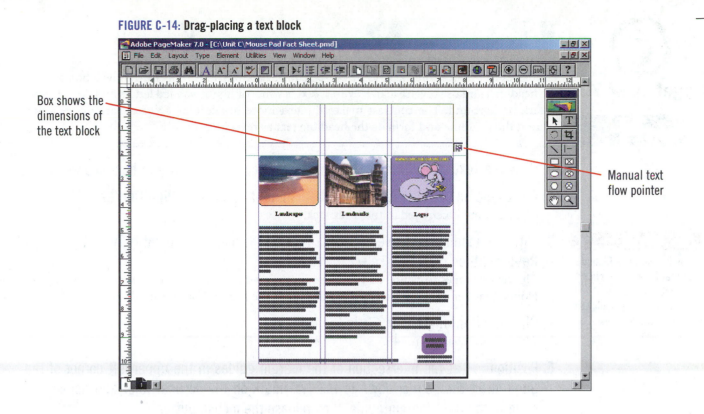

Box shows the dimensions of the text block

Manual text flow pointer

FIGURE C-15: Headline placed across three columns

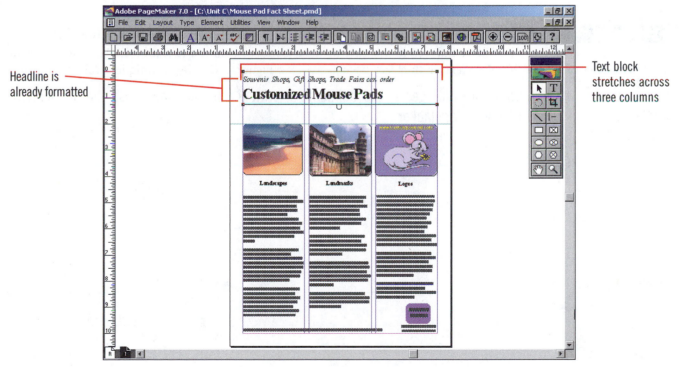

Headline is already formatted

Text block stretches across three columns

PageMaker 7.0

PageMaker 7.0

Steps 1 2 3 4

Using Reverse Text

Headlines in publications need to be eye-catching. One way to do this is to draw a box around the headline, and use reverse text. **Reverse text** is white or lightly shaded letters and lines against a dark background. The contrast makes the text more noticeable. ✎ Sara draws a box around the headline and formats the headline text as reverse text.

1. Click the **Text tool** T in the toolbox, then select the two lines of headline text

2. Click **Type** on the menu bar, point to **Alignment**, then click **Align Center**
   The headline is centered in the text block.

Trouble?

If you have trouble finding text that is reversed, click Edit on the menu bar, then click Select All to display the windowshade handles of all the text blocks.

3. With the headline text selected, click **Type** on the menu bar, point to **Type Style**, click **Reverse**, then click to deselect the text
   The text changes to white, and because it's on a white background, it seems to disappear. Notice that before you deselected the text, both the text and background color were black.

4. Click the **Rectangle tool** ▭ in the toolbox
   The pointer changes to ✛.

5. Position ✛ at the intersection of the margin guides in the upper-left corner of the page, drag the pointer down to the 1.5" mark on the vertical ruler and across the page to the right margin guide, then release the mouse button
   A box appears, as shown in Figure C-16.

6. With the box still selected, click **Element** on the menu bar, point to **Fill**, then click **Solid**
   The box fills with black. You cannot see the white text because the box is an object that is on top of the text block. To see the text in the text block, you need to move the box behind, or in back of, the text block.

DesignTip

Reverse text is an effective method to draw the reader's attention to headlines or subheadlines if the type is large enough.

7. Click **Element** on the menu bar, point to **Arrange**, then click **Send to Back**
   The selected object, in this case the box, is moved behind the text block. You can now read the white text on the black background. See Figure C-17. This technique is called **layering**.

8. Save your changes to the publication, print the publication, close the publication, then exit PageMaker

FIGURE C-16: A box drawn across three columns

New rectangle

Headline is currently white text on a white background

Rectangle tool

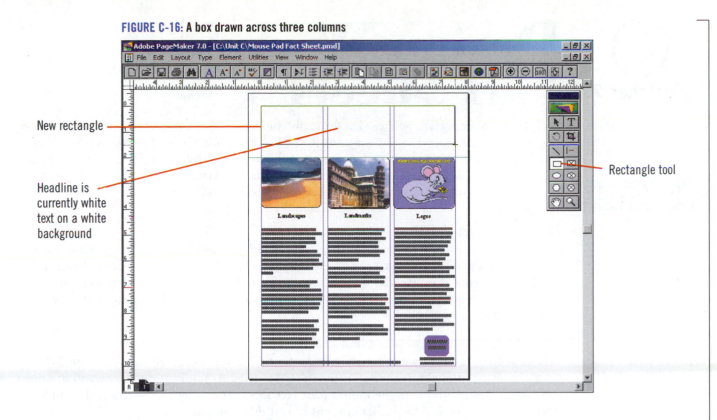

FIGURE C-17: White text on a black background

Text block with white text is layered on top of the black box

Box filled with black is layered behind the text block

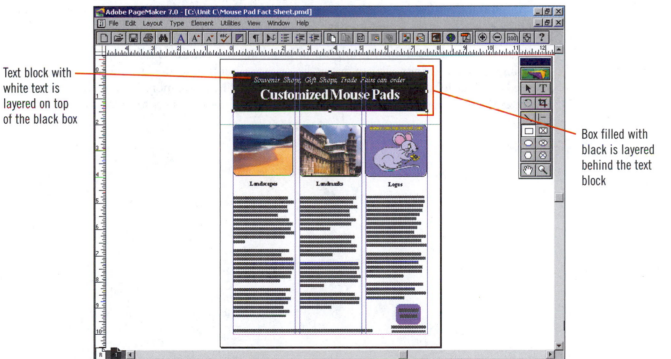

Unit C

Design Workshop: Fact Sheets

Fact sheets are important publications for many companies. These documents describe a company's products and services, and are often the first contact with potential customers. It is therefore important that fact sheets convey the information in an organized fashion. Consistency is essential in fact sheets that describe multiple products or services. Sara critiques her design for the Mousing Around fact sheet shown in Figure C-18.

Details

► Is the layout simple?

Graphical elements help to break up large amounts of text and add visual interest to a page. When you add graphical elements, be careful not to add too many, or the publication looks cluttered. Sara's layout is simple and well-balanced. Each of the three columns contains a graphic and an equal amount of text. The headline at the top and the point of response at the bottom pull the fact sheet together.

► Is the format consistent with other fact sheets?

It is important to portray a company's products and services in an organized fashion. When Sara creates additional fact sheets for the other Mousing Around products, she will use the same layout as she did with the mouse pads fact sheet. The other fact sheets will include a headline, small graphics, a similar amount of text describing the specific products, and the point of response.

► Do the graphical elements on the page enhance the overall layout?

Graphical elements can help the reader gain an immediate understanding of the purpose of the publication. Sara has included graphics to help stimulate the reader's desire for mouse pads. She also used the Mousing Around logo to help identify the company. Both of these graphical elements enhance the fact sheet message.

► Does the headline achieve its goal of catching the reader's attention?

Using reverse text immediately draws the reader's attention to the fact sheet. Sara could have used a bolder font and a larger point size to make her headline more striking. Before she completes the other fact sheets in the series, she will make these changes to the headline.

FIGURE C-18: Completed Mousing Around fact sheet

Souvenir Shops, Gift Shops, Trade Fairs can order

Customized Mouse Pads

Landscapes

Landmarks

Logos

Landscapes: National and state parks, tourist offices, and souvenir shops report consistently good sales of landscape mouse pads. The key requirement is a photograph that is immediately recognizable as representing a specific region, season, or mood. Tropical scenes lead the list of most popular landscapes for mouse pads (see illustration), followed by sunsets, mountains, and historic villages.

You can choose stock images from our extensive catalog, which includes photographs from every state, provincial, and national park in the United States and Canada, along with an extensive selection of landscapes from popular tourist spots around the world. European landscapes are particularly well represented.

A basic order of 5,000 landscape mouse pads can include up to five different images at 1,000 pads per image for a per pad price of $1.25. A premium order of 10,000 Landscape mouse pads also includes up to five images at 2000 pads per image for a per pad cost of $1.10.

Landmarks: More and more tourists are choosing to select a mouse pad as an inexpensive commemoration of a visit to an historic or tourist landmark. Our Landmarks catalog includes a huge selection of world landmarks from the Washington Monument to the Eiffel Tower to the Kremlin.

The Landmarks category also includes works of art. Museum gift shops are finding these inexpensive, but enduring souvenirs of great art masterpieces can barely be kept in stock.

You can choose to supply images related to specific landmarks or art works that are not included in our catalog. For an extra charge of $.11 per pad, you can include on each mouse pad the logo or URL of your store or museum.

A basic order of 5,000 landmark mouse pads of one image costs $1.15. A premium order of 10,000 Landscape mouse pads of one image costs $1.05.

Logos: At corporate get-togethers, sales meetings, and trade shows, you can wow your employees and customers with the gift of a custom mouse pad emblazoned with your company's logo and even a slogan or two! We can even cut the mouse pad in the geometric shape that best matches your logo or company image. Selling flowers? Have your corporate mouse pad cut in the shape of a daisy. Sports equipment? How about a baseball or basketball-shaped mouse pad?

You can supply a reproduction of your company's logo to us and we will transfer it directly to a mouse pad or you can supply a digital version of the logo and save the preprinting charge of $100 per order of 5,000 mouse pads.

A basic order of 5,000 Logo mouse pads costs $1.55 per mouse pad, while a premium order of 10,000 Logo mouse pads costs $1.30 per mouse pad.

Custom Mouse Pads
www.mousingaround.com

To order your completed set of custom mouse pads, call Mousing Around at 1-800-GOMOUSE.

PageMaker 7.0

Practice

► Concepts Review

Label each element of the publication shown in Figure C-19.

FIGURE C-19

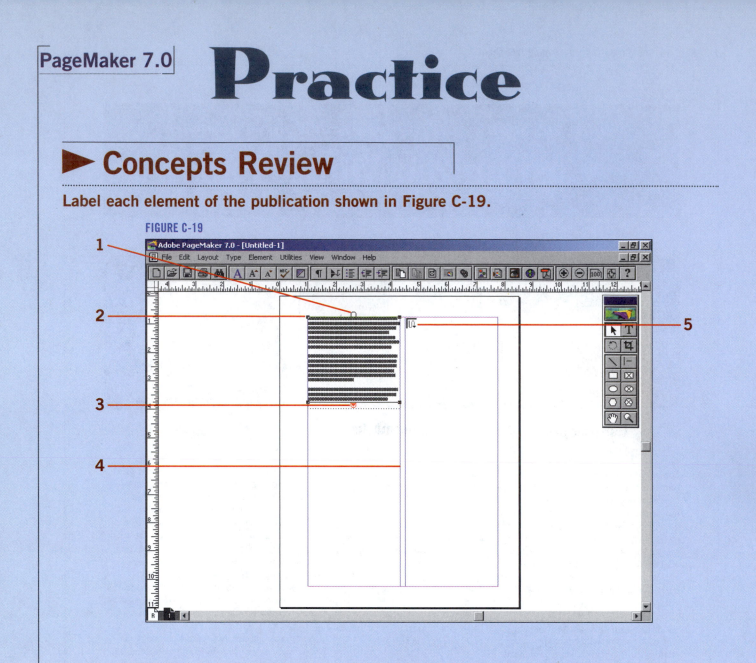

Match each term with the statement that best describes it.

6. Gutter

7. Autoflow

8. Column guide

9. Windowshade handle

10. Drag-placing

a. Element of the publication page that helps you to place text and graphics

b. Feature that threads text from one column to the next until all the text is placed

c. Technique that allows you to define the size of a text block as you place text

d. The space between columns

e. Element of a text block that allows you to define the length of the text block

Select the best answer from the list of choices.

11. **A fact sheet should include which of the following?**
    a. Detailed information about a product or service
    b. Graphic elements that instantly convey a message
    c. Headlines that instantly convey the purpose
    d. All of the above

12. **Which of the following is not true?**
    a. All publications must have at least two columns
    b. Column widths can be changed by dragging a column guide to a new location
    c. PageMaker automatically creates columns of equal width
    d. The space between columns is called the gutter

13. **A gutter is:**
    a. The margins within a column.
    b. The space between columns.
    c. The space between the margins and the edge of the page.
    d. None of the above.

14. **You can thread text from one column to the next, filling up as many pages as necessary, using:**
    a. Drag-placing.
    b. Autoflow.
    c. Reverse text.
    d. Balance columns.

▶ Skills Review

1. **Create columns.**
   a. Start PageMaker, open the file PM C-5.pmd from the drive and folder where your Project Files are located, then save it as **My Fact Sheet**.
   b. Change the number of columns in the publication to 3.
   c. Change the view to Entire Pasteboard.
   d. Drag the logo from the pasteboard onto the publication page, and place it so it is centered in the top part of the third column.
   e. Drag the photograph from the pasteboard onto the publication page, and place it below the logo, centered in the third column.
   f. Change the view to Fit in Window, then save your changes to the publication.

2. **Import and place text and control the flow of text.**
   a. Make sure the Autoflow feature is turned on.
   b. Click the Place command on the File menu to open the Place dialog box. (*Macintosh Users: Open the Place document dialog box.*)
   c. Use the Look in list arrow to navigate to the drive and folder where your Project Files are located, click the file PM C-6.doc, then click Open. (*Macintosh Users: Click OK.*)
   d. Place the text at the top of the first column. The text should fill the first column and flow into the second.
   e. Save your changes to the publication.

PageMaker 7.0

3. Manipulate text blocks.

   a. Change the view to Actual Size.

   b. Scroll so that the bottom of the first column is visible on your screen.

   c. Select the text block in the first column if necessary.

   d. Drag the bottom windowshade handle up until the pointer guide aligns with the 5.5" mark on the vertical ruler.

   e. Save your changes to the publication.

4. Move and resize text blocks.

   a. Change the view to Fit in Window.

   b. Select the text block in the first column, then drag it down so that its bottom aligns with the bottom margin guide.

   c. Drag the text block in the second column down so that the top of the text block is aligned with the top of the text block in the first column. Use a ruler guide to assist you in aligning the text blocks.

   d. Change the left and right margins to .5" using the Document Setup dialog box.

   e. Resize and reposition the text blocks so that they fit in the wider columns. Make sure the tops of the text boxes are still aligned.

   f. Adjust the flow of text so that "Rome, Italy" appears at the top of the second column.

   g. Save your changes to the publication.

5. Drag-place text.

   a. Turn off the Autoflow feature.

   b. Open the Place dialog box (*Macintosh Users: Open the Place Document dialog box*), select the text file PM C-7.doc, located in the drive and folder where your Project Files are located, then click Open. (*Macintosh Users: Click OK.*)

   c. Position the manual text flow pointer in the upper-left corner of the page, inside the margins.

   d. Drag-place the text so that it flows across the first two columns.

   e. Drag the text block down so it is located just above the body text, then save your changes to the publication.

6. Use reverse text.

   a. Change the view to Actual Size, then scroll so that the tops of the first two columns are visible on your screen.

   b. Type the following two lines at the top of the first column:
   Paris, London, and Rome
   Escorted Tour from $3,500

   c. Select the text you just typed, then change the font to Arial.

   d. Change the size of the first line to 30 points, then change the size of the second line to 24 points.

   e. Resize the text box so that it spans the first two columns.

   f. Select the two lines of text, then change the alignment to Align Center.

   g. Change the type style to Reverse.

   h. Use the Rectangle tool to draw a box around the text: drag from the intersection of the top and left margin guides to the right side of the second column at the 2" mark on the vertical ruler.

   i. Change the fill of the box to Solid, then send the box in back of the text.

   j. Change the view to Fit in Window, then compare your publication with Figure C-20.

   k. Save your changes, print the publication, close the file, then exit PageMaker.

FIGURE C-20

► Independent Challenge 1

You work in the Admissions Office at Jefferson College. One of your tasks is to standardize the descriptions for all degree programs in the various schools. You decide to keep a consistent format, and give each major its own fact sheet. You create a fact sheet for the Bachelor of Science degree in Computer Science.

a. Start PageMaker, then create a new one-page publication with a tall orientation and .5" margins on all sides.

b. Create three columns on the page.

c. Drag-place the text from the file PM C-8.doc, found in the drive and folder where your Project Files are located, across the top of the page from margin to margin.

d. Change the font, size, and text style of the headline "Jefferson College, Computer Science" so it is eye-catching and appealing.

e. Draw a box around the headline, then format the text as reverse text.

f. Place the graphic file Building.tif, found in the drive and folder where your Project Files are located, on the publication page. This file contains a drawing of the building that houses the Computer Science offices. Resize the graphic proportionally to fit the width of one column.

g. Make sure the Autoflow feature is turned on, then place the file PM C-9.doc, found in the drive and folder where your Project Files are located, on the publication page. The text in this file should flow automatically from one column to the next.

h. Arrange the text blocks and the graphic to create an appealing layout.

i. Use your own judgment to add lines or boxes to enhance the layout of the fact sheet.

j. Save the publication as **Computer Science Factsheet** to the drive and folder where your Project Files are located, print the fact sheet, close the publication, then exit PageMaker.

► Independent Challenge 2

Visit a hardware store, department store, or some other retailer and pick up copies of the informational fact sheets used to describe the products offered. In this exercise, redesign one of the fact sheets you found to improve its appearance and impact.

a. Critique one of the fact sheets you found by answering the following questions:
  • Is the layout simple, or are there too many graphics?
  • If the fact sheet contains too much text, is there a way to cut some of the text and add graphical elements without sacrificing the overall message of the publication?
  • Does the headline stand out and immediately catch your attention?
  • Can the overall design be consistently applied to other fact sheets?

b. Sketch a new design for the fact sheet.

c. Start PageMaker, open a new single-sided, one-page publication, then save it as **New Fact Sheet** to the drive and folder where your Project Files are located.

d. Create columns in your publication if necessary.

e. Create a headline for the fact sheet, then format the headline to be eye-catching.

f. Place the graphics in the fact sheet. Instead of placing actual graphics, place the graphic file Placehld.jpg, found in the drive and folder where your Project Files are located, as a placeholder graphic. Use this file for each graphic you want to include. Use the drag-place method to place the graphics, and then resize and move them as necessary.

g. Place the text in the fact sheet. Instead of placing actual text, place the text file Texthld.doc, found in the drive and folder where your Project Files are located, as placeholder text.

h. Adjust the text flow in the fact sheet so that the fact sheet looks visually balanced. (*Hint:* If there is too much text for your fact sheet, select some of the placeholder text, then press [Delete] to delete it.)

i. Add a point of response to the fact sheet by typing it directly on the page.

j. Enhance the publication with lines if necessary.

k. Save your changes, print the fact sheet, close the publication, then exit PageMaker.

▶ Independent Challenge 3

You received a freelance design project from Tom Grades, owner of Grades Used Computer Parts. He wants a simple fact sheet about the PCs, printers, and modems in stock at his store. Before Grades gives you the information needed for the fact sheet, he wants to see a dummy of the sheet. You design a fact sheet and place fake text and graphics to simulate where each element will be situated.

a. Start PageMaker, then create a new single-sided publication with a Wide orientation. Make the margins .75" on all sides.

b. Create three columns with a .5" gutter between the columns.

c. Type the headline, **Grades Used Computer Parts Store** to fit across the top of the page.

d. Format the headline in reverse type with a black background.

e. Add a point of response to the fact sheet.

f. Place the placeholder graphic file Keyboard.jpg, found in the drive and folder where your Project Files are located, into the publication three times. Resize the graphic placeholder to fit the width of the columns, and then move a graphic to each column. Use your judgment on how best to balance the page using the graphics.

g. Type a separate heading for each of the three columns: **PCs...**, **Printers...**, and **Modems...**. Arrange the headings in each column so they complement the graphics.

h. Place the placeholder text file Texthld.doc, found in the drive and folder where your Project Files are located, into the publication. This dummy text simulates the real text you'll create from the information Tom Grades gives you later. Delete any unnecessary text, and adjust the flow of text in the three columns so that the layout appears balanced.

i. Save the file as **Grades Factsheet** to the drive and folder where your Project Files are located, print the fact sheet, close the publication, then exit PageMaker.

e Independent Challenge 4

You work in the marketing department for a sporting goods company. You create a fact sheet that describes the products your company sells to retail stores.

a. Search the World Wide Web to find information on a company that sells sporting equipment. Use the keywords **sporting goods** or **sports equipment stores** to conduct your search. If your search does not result in appropriate links, try looking at the following Web sites: www.wilsonsports.com or www.thesportsauthority.com.

b. Using the information that you find, sketch a fact sheet for the sporting goods company keeping in mind the guidelines you learned in this unit. Don't forget to include a point of response, graphical elements, and a headline.

c. Start PageMaker, then create a fact sheet using your sketch as a guide.

d. Create a headline for the publication.

e. Create a point of response. Be sure to include the company's URL (Web address) in the point of response.

f. Place the files Skis.jpg and Hiker.jpg, found in the drive and folder where your Project Files are located, as placeholders for any graphics in the publication.

g. Place the file Texthld.doc as a placeholder for any text in the publication. Delete any unnecessary text, then adjust the flow of the text so that the publication is attractive and readable.

h. Save the publication as **Sporting Factsheet** to the drive and folder where your Project Files are located, print a copy, close the publication, then exit PageMaker.

i. Critique your final fact sheet.

► Visual Workshop

Create the inside of the brochure shown in Figure C-21. To begin, create a new publication with .75" margins on all sides. Create four columns and customize the width of the columns by moving the far-left column guide to the 2.5" mark on the horizontal ruler, and the far-right column guide to the 8.5" mark on the horizontal ruler. Place the graphic files Plant1.jpg, Plant2.jpg, and Placehld.jpg, all found on the drive and folder where your Project Files are located, then rearrange the graphics as shown in Figure C-21. Place the text file PM C-10.doc, found on the drive and folder where your Project Files are located, and arrange the body text as shown in the figure. Add the vertical lines, the headlines, the point of response, and the other text to the page, and format it as shown. Save the publication as **Independence Landscape Brochure** to the drive and folder where your Project Files are located, then print a copy.

FIGURE C-21

PageMaker 7.0

Unit D

Modifying

Text

Objectives

- ▶ **Plan a business report**
- ▶ **Open story editor**
- ▶ **Create and place text with story editor**
- ▶ **Edit text in story editor**
- ▶ **Check spelling**
- ▶ **Find and change text**
- ▶ **Apply multiple character formats to text**
- ▶ **Apply multiple paragraph formats to text**
- ▶ **Insert and remove pages**
- ▶ **Create a table**
- ▶ **Edit a table**
- ▶ **Enhance a table**
- ▶ **Design Workshop: Business reports**

PageMaker includes a built-in word processor called story editor that allows you to type, edit, format, and check the spelling of text easily. PageMaker also comes with the Adobe Table 3.0 program, which you can use to create and format tables for your publications. Sara Norton uses story editor to help her complete a business proposal for one of her clients. The client, Seaside Cycles, has hired Sara to design a proposal to expand its company Web site.

Unit D

Planning a Business Report

When developing a business report or proposal, consider that most business people have limited time to read your document. Your goal should be to create a high-impact report that takes advantage of innovative design and concise writing. It's important that the report be organized in a logical, consistent, and sequential fashion. A report that quickly and clearly conveys a message using a creative design captures the attention of busy people. ✐ The finished proposal for the expansion of the Seaside Cycles Web site will be presented to the president and vice presidents of the company. Sara plans to make the report concise and eye-catching. Sara's sketch of the proposal is shown in Figure D-1.

Details

Keep the following guidelines in mind when planning a business report:

▶ **Use a coherent writing style**

Keep report language simple, clear, and concise. Use headings and subheadings to organize the report in a logical and consistent fashion. Sara's proposal headings will serve as an outline for the report. The body text of the report will be written in a clear, to-the-point writing style.

▶ **Include an abstract**

An **abstract** is a summary at the beginning of a report that highlights the main points of the report. Sara's proposal will include a short, one-paragraph abstract that she will place on the proposal's cover.

▶ **Add a businesslike cover**

The cover of a report sets the tone for the report. The cover of a business report should emphasize the importance of the content and introduce the visual style used in the report. The cover for Sara's proposal will include a title, the Seaside Cycles logo, and the names of the people who prepared the proposal.

▶ **Include graphics to enhance the text**

Graphics can help to illustrate the important points in a report and offset heavy amounts of text. Graphics used in a business report can include charts, tables, photographs, or illustrations. The graphics used in a report should reinforce the report content, rather then detract from it. Sara plans to include charts to show how Seaside Cycles' revenue will increase by expanding the Web site.

▶ **Organize the text in columns**

A columnar layout allows you to include more text on a page. Often a layout that uses three or more columns offers more flexibility in sizing and placing graphics than layouts with only one or two columns. Since letter-sized pages look cramped with more than three columns, limit the number of columns on a letter-sized page to three. Sara decides to lay out the text for the body of the proposal in three columns so that she can use graphics that are one, two, or three columns wide.

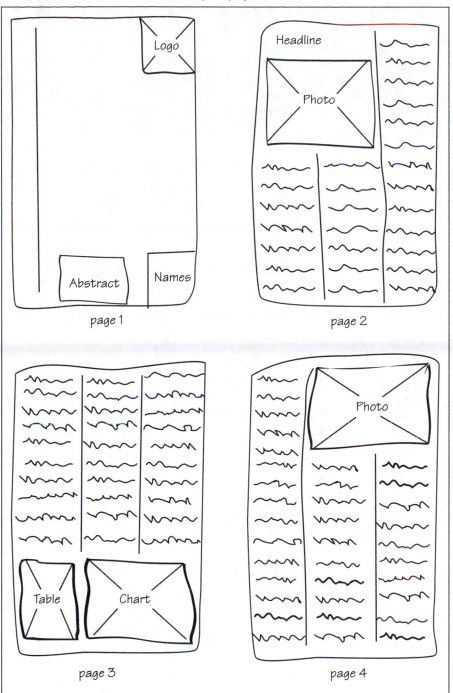

Steps 123 4

Opening Story Editor

Although you can type and edit text in layout view in PageMaker, if you are working with a large amount of text, layout view can be tedious and slow. **Story editor** is a word processing program within PageMaker that makes it easy to work with large amounts of text. Using story editor, you can enter, edit, find and replace, and check the spelling of text. ✎ Sara already placed the body text for the proposal in her publication. She plans to use story editor to type and place the abstract text on the cover. She begins by opening story editor.

1. Start PageMaker, open the file **PM D-1.pmd** from the drive and folder where your Project Files are stored, save it as **Seaside Cycle Web Proposal**, then maximize the publication window if necessary
   The cover page of the proposal, page 1 of the publication, appears in the publication window in Fit in Window view.

2. Drag a **vertical ruler guide** to the **6"** mark on the horizontal ruler

3. Drag a second **vertical ruler guide** to the **2.5"** mark on the horizontal ruler
   The cover page appears as shown in Figure D-2.

4. Click **Edit** on the menu bar, then click **Edit Story**
   The view changes to story editor, as shown in Figure D-3. The title bar in the story editor window shows the filename of the publication and the story name, in this case Untitled:1. Notice that the Layout and Element menus are not available on the menu bar in story editor view; instead the menu bar includes the Story menu.

5. Move the pointer over the right side of the story editor window
   The pointer changes to ⌶. You enter and edit text on the right side of the story editor window.

6. Move the pointer over the left side of the story editor window
   The pointer changes to ▷. The left side of the story editor window is the style bar. The **style bar** displays the name of the style applied to each paragraph of text. In this case, the default style for text is Body Text.

CLUES TO USE

Exporting text to other word processing programs

You can export text created in PageMaker to another word processing program, such as Corel WordPerfect or Microsoft Word. To export a story while in story editor view, click File on the menu bar, point to Export, and then click Text. In the Export Document dialog box, select the location to which you want to save the text file, type a filename, and then use the Save as type list arrow to select the file type you want to use for the exported file. You can save the file in a specific word processing program format, or you can save it in **text-only format**, which saves the text without the formatting applied in PageMaker. You can open a text-only file in most word processing programs. You can also export text in layout view by first selecting the text you want to export and then following the same set of steps.

FIGURE D-2: Page 1 of the proposal

Ruler guides

Abstract will be placed here

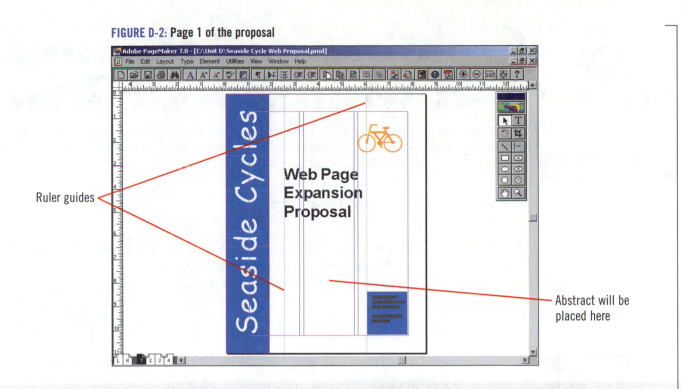

FIGURE D-3: Story editor window

Story menu

Style bar

Insertion point

Mark indicates the end of the story

Story name

Filename

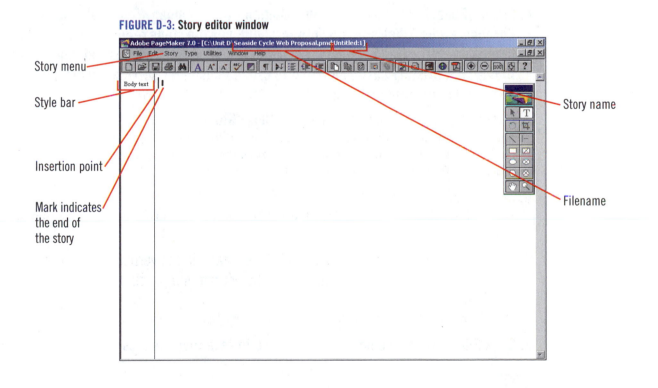

Creating and Placing Text with Story Editor

Once you finish typing text in story editor, you can close story editor and place the text in your publication using layout view. With story editor open, Sara is ready to type the text of the abstract and place it in the publication.

Steps

1. Type **ABSTRACT** then press **[Enter]** twice
   The text you type appears on the right side of the story editor window.

2. Click **Story** on the menu bar, then click **Display ¶**; if a check mark already appears next to the Display ¶ command on the menu, skip this step
   A check mark next to the Display ¶ command on the Story menu indicates the option is turned on. The Display ¶ command displays nonprinting characters such as paragraph markers, spaces, and tab markers. ¶ is the symbol for a new paragraph. Displaying non-printing characters makes it easier to edit text with precision.

Trouble?

If the toolbox is covering your view, move it by clicking the toolbox title bar, and dragging it to a new position.

3. Type **Seaside Cycles runs a very successful retail sales and bicycle repair operation with a loyal customer base.**, but do not press [Enter]
   Depending on the size of your screen, a word or words may move down to the next line as you type. This feature is called **word wrap**. When typing in story editor, you only need to press [Enter] when you want to start a new paragraph. Notice that spaces are represented by dots between words.

4. Press **[Spacebar]**, then type **In addition, the company maintains a simple "brochureware" Web site. This proposal outlines the steps required to expand the company's Web site to handle on-line sales, to distribute cycling-related content to new and existing customers, and to expand customer service opportunities.**
   The text appears as shown in Figure D-4.

5. Click **Story** on the menu bar, then click **Close Story**
   You could also click the Close button in the story editor window to close story editor. A dialog box opens offering three options for handling the text you created in story editor: Place, Discard, or Cancel. Table D-1 describes the three options.

6. Click **Place**
   Story editor closes, and page 1 of the publication appears in layout view. The pointer changes to ▤.

7. Position ▤ over the left ruler guide at the **6"** mark on the vertical ruler, drag to the intersection of the right ruler guide and the bottom margin guide, then release the mouse button
   The abstract is placed on page 1, as shown in Figure D-5.

8. Click **File** on the menu bar, then click **Save** to save your changes

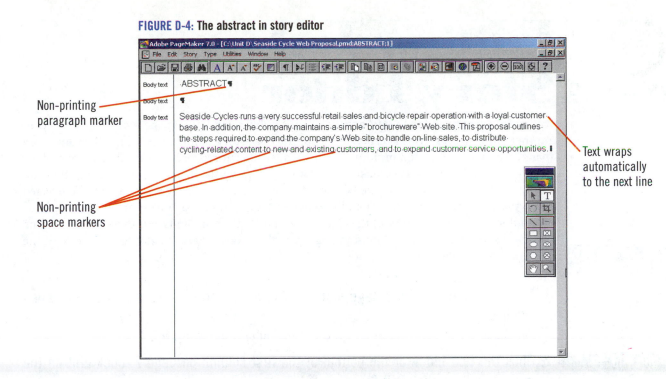

Non-printing paragraph marker

Non-printing space markers

Text wraps automatically to the next line

FIGURE D-5: Abstract on page 1

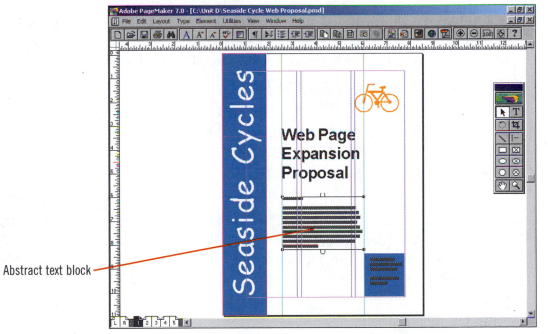

Abstract text block

TABLE D-1: Options for closing story editor

command	use to
Place	Close story editor and open layout view
Discard	Delete the text you just typed and return to layout view
Cancel	Stop the action and keep story editor open

Editing Text in Story Editor

You can use story editor to edit any story in a publication, even if the story was created in another word processor. It is especially helpful to use story editor for editing when the story spans several text blocks on multiple pages, because the entire story displays in the story editor window. You edit text in PageMaker by deleting and retyping characters or by using the Cut, Copy, and Paste commands on the Edit menu. When you cut or copy selected text, the selected text is placed on the Clipboard. The **Clipboard** is a temporary storage area for cut or copied text or graphics. Table D-2 describes the Cut, Copy, and Paste commands and their corresponding keyboard shortcuts. ✎ After looking over the proposal, Sara decides to move one of the paragraphs in the body text.

Steps 1234

1. Click the **pages 2 and 3 page icon** 〔2│3〕 in the lower-left corner of the publication window
   Pages 2 and 3 of the publication appear in the publication window.

2. Click the **text block** at the bottom of the first column on page 2, click **Edit** on the menu bar, then click **Edit Story**
   The selected story opens in story editor. "Body text" appears in the style bar next to each paragraph, indicating that the body text style is applied to the text. Notice that the default filename for the story is the first few words of the story.

3. Click **Story** on the menu bar, click **Display ¶**, then triple-click the **second body paragraph** under the Introduction heading
   The entire paragraph including the ¶ symbol is selected, as shown in Figure D-6.

4. Click **Edit** on the menu bar, then click **Cut**
   The selected paragraph is removed from the story and placed on the Clipboard.

5. Click before the word "In" at the beginning of the first body paragraph
   The insertion point is located at the beginning of the first paragraph.

6. Click **Edit** on the menu bar, then click **Paste**
   The cut paragraph is pasted at the location of the insertion point, as shown in Figure D-7.

7. Click immediately after the word "too" in the second line of the new first body paragraph, then press **[Backspace]**
   The "o" is removed and the word is correctly spelled "to". When you use the [Backspace] or [Delete] key to remove text, the text is not placed on the Clipboard and is permanently removed from the publication.

8. Save your changes to the publication

QuickTip
To quickly open a story in story editor, triple-click a text block with the ▶ pointer.

Default filename

Paragraph and ¶ symbol are selected

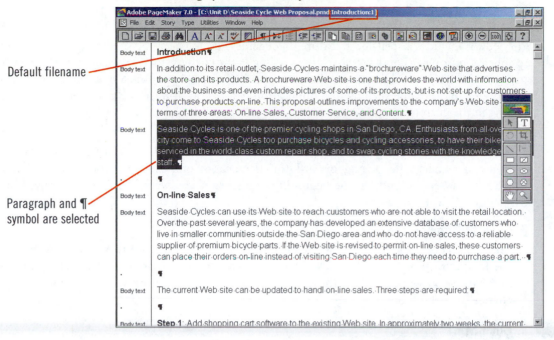

Paragraph is pasted in a new location

TABLE D-2: Editing commands

command	keyboard shortcut	description
Cut	[Ctrl][X]	Removes the selection from the publication and places it on the Clipboard
Copy	[Ctrl][C]	Places a copy of the selection on the Clipboard, leaving the selection in place in the publication
Paste	[Ctrl][V]	Places the contents of the Clipboard at the location of the insertion point

PageMaker 7.0

Checking Spelling

Story editor includes a spell check feature that enables you to check the spelling of the words in a publication. You can choose to check the spelling in the current story, in selected text, in all the stories in the current publication, or in all the stories in each open PageMaker publication. It's a good idea to check the spelling in a publication before you print it. ✎ Sara checks the spelling in the current story.

Steps

1. **Scroll up if necessary, then click before "Introduction" at the top of the story**
   PageMaker checks the spelling forward from the location of the insertion point, so you must place the insertion point at the beginning of a story if you want PageMaker to check the spelling of the entire story.

2. **Click Utilities on the menu bar, then click Spelling**
   The Spelling dialog box opens. Before beginning, you should select the options you want to use for performing the spell check. Table D-3 describes the options in the Spelling dialog box. Since you want to check the spelling in the current story only, you do not need to change the default options.

3. **Click Start**
   The first word flagged by PageMaker as a possible spelling error is "brochureware," as shown in Figure D-8. The word is not misspelled, but PageMaker flagged it as an error because "brochureware" is not in its dictionary.

4. **Click Ignore**
   PageMaker ignores the word "brochureware" and flags "cuustomers" as misspelled.

5. **Click customers in the Change to list box, then click Replace**
   PageMaker replaces the misspelled word with the alternative spelling you selected in the Change to list box. The next word flagged as misspelled is "purrchase."

6. **Click purchase in the Change to list box, click Replace, click handle in the Change to list box, then click Replace**
   Next, the word "for" is flagged because it appears twice.

7. **Click Replace to delete the duplicate word, then continue replacing or ignoring words, choosing the appropriate action for each flagged word**
   When PageMaker is finished checking the story, the message "Spelling check complete" appears at the top of the Spelling dialog box.

8. **When you finish, click the Close button in the Spelling dialog box to close it, then save your changes**

FIGURE D-8: Spelling dialog box

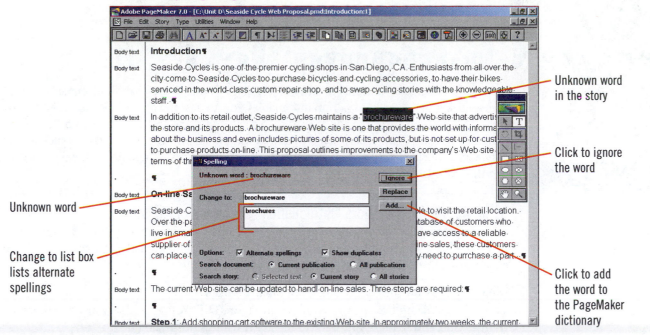

Unknown word in the story

Unknown word

Change to list box lists alternate spellings

Click to ignore the word

Click to add the word to the PageMaker dictionary

TABLE D-3: Spelling dialog box options

option	description
Alternate spellings	When turned on, lists alternate spellings for each word the PageMaker dictionary does not recognize
Show duplicates	When turned on, flags duplicate words such as "the the"
Current publication	Checks spelling in the current publication only
All publications	Checks spelling in all open publications
Selected text	Checks spelling in the selected text only
Current story	Checks spelling in the current story only
All stories	Checks spelling in all stories in the current publication

Finding and Changing Text

The Find and Change commands in story editor allow you to search for all instances of a word or phrase in a story. The Find command enables you to search for specific text. The Change command allows you to search for a word or phrase in a story and change it to different text. You can also use the Change command to search for and change format attributes such as font, type style, or font size. ✐ Sara wants to locate all instances of "agents" in the proposal and change the word to "representatives."

Steps 1234

1. **Scroll up, then click before "Introduction" at the top of the story**
   Since PageMaker searches forward from the location of the insertion point, it's important to place the insertion point at the beginning of a story if you want PageMaker to search the entire story.

2. **Click Utilities on the menu bar, then click Change**
   The Change dialog box opens, as shown in Figure D-9. You enter the word or phrase you want to find and the text you want to replace it with in this dialog box.

3. **Type agents in the Find what text box, type representatives in the Change to text box, then click Find**
   The first instance of the word "agents" is selected in the story, and the Change dialog box offers several choices for changing the word, as shown in Figure D-10. Table D-4 describes the options available in the Change dialog box.

4. **Click Change**
   "Agents" is replaced with "representatives."

5. **Click Find next**
   The Search complete dialog box opens, indicating that PageMaker did not find any more occurrences of the word "agents" in the story.

6. **Click OK to close the dialog box**

7. **Click the Close button to close the Change dialog box**
   The Change dialog box closes.

8. **Click Story on the menu bar, click Close Story, then save your changes to the publication**
   Story editor closes and pages 2 and 3 appear in layout view.

TABLE D-4: Change dialog box options

option	use to
Find next	Skip the selected occurrence of the text and find the next occurrence
Change	Replace the selected text with the text in the Change to text box
Change & find	Replace the selected text with the text in the Change to text box, and find the next occurrence of the text
Change all	Find and replace all occurrences of the text with the text in the Change to text box

FIGURE D-9: Change dialog box

Type the text you want to find

Type the text you want to replace it with

Select the publication and story to search

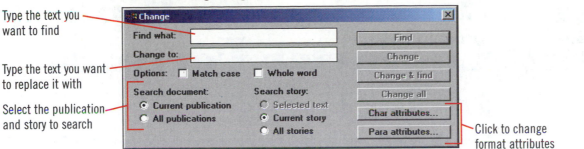

Click to change format attributes

FIGURE D-10: Found text

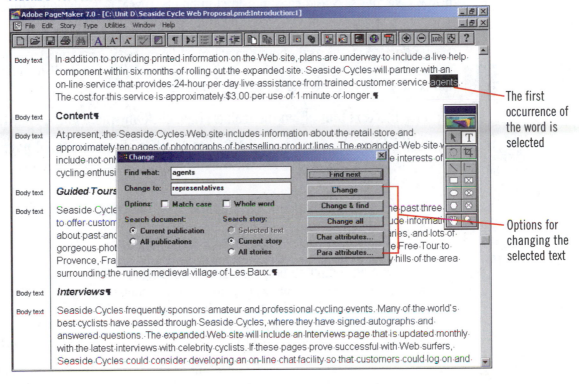

The first occurrence of the word is selected

Options for changing the selected text

Changing format attributes

You might need to find and change text that is formatted in a particular way. The Change dialog box includes a Para attributes button and a Char attributes button that enable you to change paragraph and character format settings. Clicking the Para attributes button opens the Change Paragraph Attributes dialog box, shown in Figure D-11. You can use this dialog box to find and change paragraph style, alignment, and leading settings. Similarly, you can click the Char attributes button to open the Change Character Attributes dialog box, and use this dialog box to change such character format settings as font, size, horizontal scale, type style, and tracking.

FIGURE D-11: Change Paragraph Attributes dialog box

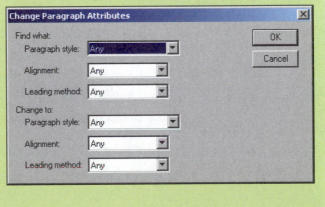

PageMaker 7.0

MODIFYING TEXT 89 ◀

Applying Multiple Character Formats to Text

A fast way to apply multiple character formats to text at once is to use the Character Specifications dialog box, which you can use to change the font, size, leading, and other settings applied to text. **Leading** is the vertical space between lines of text, specifically, the total height of a line from the top of the tallest character in the line to the top of the tallest character in the line below. Like font size, leading is measured in points. PageMaker's default setting for leading is 120% of the font size. For example, if the text is 10 points, the leading would be 12 points. You can format text using the Character Specifications dialog box in either story editor or layout view. Sara thinks the body text will be easier to read if it is formatted in a serif font with more white space on the page. She uses the Character Specifications dialog box to change the font, change the text size, and adjust the leading.

Steps

1. Click the **Text tool** T in the toolbox, then click anywhere in the body text on page 2

2. Click **Edit** on the menu bar, click **Select All**, then click the **page 4 page icon** 4
   All the text in the story is selected, including the text on page 4. The story is threaded across pages 2, 3, and 4.

3. Click **View** on the menu bar, click **Actual Size**, then scroll down until you can see the bottom margin guide
   The bottom half of page 4 appears in the publication window, with the text selected.

4. Click **Type** on the menu bar, then click **Character**
   The Character Specifications dialog box opens, as shown in Figure D-12. You can use the Character Specifications dialog box to change the font, size, leading, horizontal scale, color, type style, and case of text, among other options. Windows users can also click the Character Specs button A on the toolbar to open the Character Specifications dialog box.

MacintoshUsers

This replaces Step 5.
5. Click the Font list box, scroll down the Font list, click Times New Roman, click the Size list arrow, click 12, click the Leading text box, type 22.5, click OK, then click outside the text to deselect it

5. Click the **Font list arrow**, scroll down the Font list, click **Times New Roman**, click the **Size list arrow**, click **12**, click the **Leading text box**, type **24**, click **OK**, then click outside the text to deselect it
   The text is formatted in 12-point Times New Roman, and the space between the lines of text is increased, as shown in Figure D-13. Increasing the size and leading of the text changed the flow of text in the story.

6. Click the **Pointer tool** ▸ in the toolbox, click the text block in the second column, then drag the **windowshade handle** ⊞ up to align with the bottom margin guide
   The text now fits within the second column.

7. Click the **windowshade handle** ⊞ at the bottom of the second column, scroll up, align the pointer ▤ with the **4"** mark on the vertical ruler and the left column guide in the third column, then click
   The text flows into the third column. Notice that the windowshade handle ⊞ appears at the bottom of the third column, indicating that there is still text to be placed.

8. Save your changes to the publication

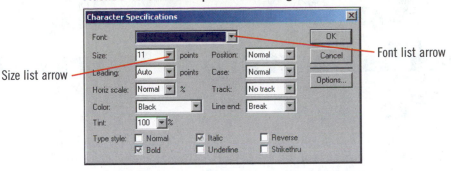

Size list arrow

Font list arrow

FIGURE D-13: Character changes applied

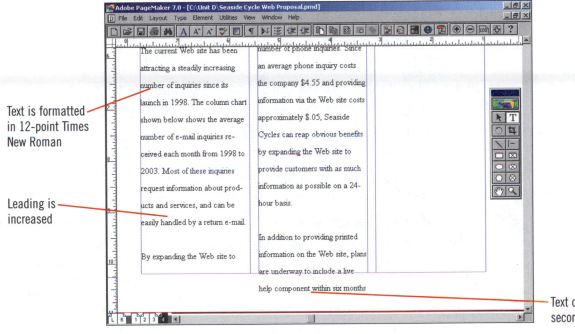

Text is formatted in 12-point Times New Roman

Leading is increased

Text overflows the second column

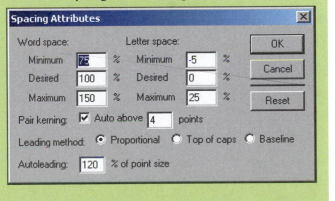

Positioning text within its leading

You can use the Spacing Attributes dialog box to adjust the position of text within its leading. To open the Spacing Attributes dialog box, shown in Figure D-14, click Type on the menu bar, click Paragraph, then click Spacing in the Paragraph Specifications dialog box. In the Leading method section of the dialog box, select one of the three options. **Proportional leading** is the default setting that allows for proportional amounts of space above the tallest character and the lowest character in a line. **Top of caps** leading measures the leading from the highest point on any character in a line. **Baseline leading** measures the leading from the baseline of the line of text.

FIGURE D-14: Spacing Attributes dialog box

Unit D

Applying Multiple Paragraph Formats to Text

You can also use the Paragraph Specifications dialog box to apply multiple paragraph formats at once. For example, you can set paragraph indents, adjust the space between paragraphs, change the alignment, or turn on widow and orphan control. In PageMaker, a **widow** is a line that begins a paragraph at the bottom of a column or page. An **orphan** is a line that ends a paragraph but falls at the top of the next column or page. ✎ Sara wants to alter the first line indent for the body text paragraphs and eliminate widows and orphans from the story. She makes these changes using the Paragraph Specifications dialog box.

Steps 1 2 3 4

1. Click the **Text tool** T in the toolbox, click anywhere in the body text, click **Edit** on the menu bar, then click **Select All**
   The entire story is selected.

2. Scroll down if necessary until you can see the bottom margin guide
   The paragraph at the bottom of the first column includes a widow, as shown in Figure D-15.

3. Click **Type** on the menu bar, then click **Paragraph**
   The Paragraph Specifications dialog box opens.

4. Double-click the **First text box** in the Indents section, then type **.15**
   The first line of every paragraph will be indented .15".

5. Click the **Widow control check box** in the Options section to turn on Widow control, then click the **Orphan control check box** to turn on Orphan control
   Turning on Widow and Orphan control instructs PageMaker to treat any one line that begins or ends a paragraph at the bottom of a column as a widow or orphan. Notice that you can change the number of lines to be treated as a widow or orphan by typing a different number in the Widow or Orphan text box in the dialog box. The Paragraph Specifications dialog box appears as shown in Figure D-16.

6. Click **OK**
   PageMaker indents the first line of every paragraph .15", and moves lines of text up to the next column or page or down to the previous column or page to eliminate widows and orphans, as shown in Figure D-17.

7. Save your changes to the publication

FIGURE D-15: Widowed text at the bottom of column one

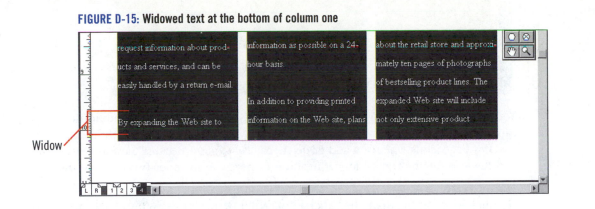

Widow

FIGURE D-16: Paragraph Specifications dialog box

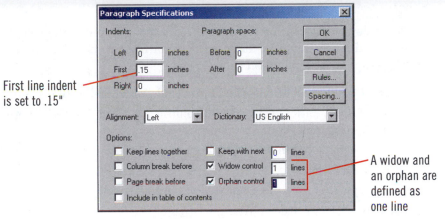

First line indent is set to .15"

A widow and an orphan are defined as one line

FIGURE D-17: Text after paragraph settings have been applied

First line of each paragraph is indented

Text flow of the story has changed

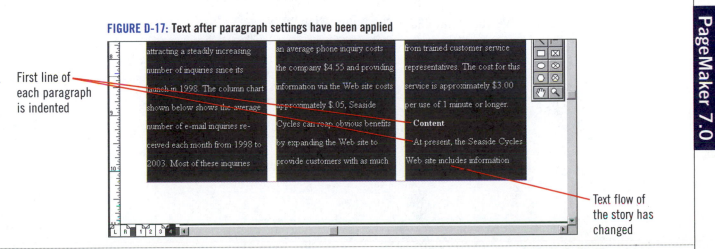

PageMaker 7.0

MODIFYING TEXT 93 ◄

Inserting and Removing Pages

You can insert pages before, after, or between the current pages in the publication window. You can also remove pages from a publication. PageMaker automatically rethreads text blocks and updates page icons when you add or delete pages. ✎ Because Sara increased the font size and the leading, the text no longer fits on four pages, so she adds two pages to the publication.

Steps

1. Click **View** on the menu bar, click **Fit in Window**, click the **Pointer tool** ⬉ in the toolbox, click the **text block** in the third column to select it, then click the **windowshade handle** ⊞ at the bottom of the third column
   The pointer changes to 🖹 and is loaded with the text that doesn't fit on page 4.

2. Click **Layout** on the menu bar, then click **Insert Pages**
   The Insert Pages dialog box opens, as shown in Figure D-18. You use this dialog box to specify how many pages you want to insert and where you want to insert them.

3. Make sure **2** appears in the Insert text box, make sure **after** appears in the page(s) text box, then click **Insert**
   The dialog box closes, and a new page 5 appears in the publication window as part of a page spread with page 4. Notice that page icons for pages 5 and 6 have been added to the lower-left corner of the publication window.

4. Press and hold **[Shift]**, click the upper-left corner of the first column on page 5, click the upper-left corner of the second column, click the upper-left corner of the third column, then release [Shift]
   All the text is placed in the publication, as shown in Figure D-19. Page 6 is an empty page that can be removed.

5. Click **Layout** on the menu bar, then click **Remove Pages**
   The Remove Pages dialog box opens.

6. Type **6** in the Remove page(s) text box, press **[Tab]**, type **6** in the through text box, then click **OK**
   An alert message appears, asking if you want to delete the specified pages.

7. Click **OK**
   PageMaker removes page 6 from the publication. Notice that the page 6 page icon no longer appears in the lower-left corner of the publication window.

8. Save your changes to the publication

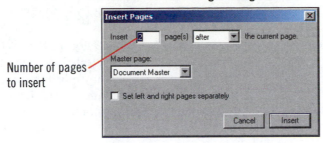

Number of pages
to insert

FIGURE D-19: Text placed on the new page

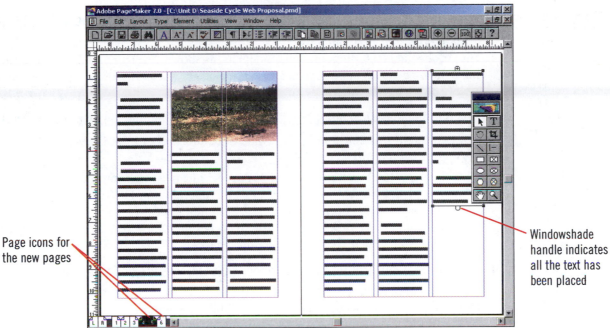

Page icons for
the new pages

Windowshade
handle indicates
all the text has
been placed

PageMaker 7.0

CLUES TO USE

Using the Go to Page command

In addition to clicking the page icons to move to a specific page in a publication, you can use the Go to Page command to display a certain page. This command is helpful if you are working on a large multiple-page document (usually more than 20 pages) and all the page icons do not appear at the bottom of the publication window. To display a specific page, click Layout on the menu bar, then click Go to Page to open the Go to Page dialog box, shown in Figure D-20. In the dialog box, click the Page number option button, type the page number you want to display in the Page number text box, then click OK.

FIGURE D-20: Go to Page dialog box

Creating a Table

PageMaker includes a stand-alone program called Adobe Table 3.0 that you can use to create and edit tables for your publications. One way to add a table created in Adobe Table 3.0 to a publication is to use the Insert Object command in PageMaker to embed the object in the publication. When an object is embedded, it can be edited in the program in which it was created. Sara wants to add a table to page 3 that shows the number of monthly e-mail inquiries each year since 1998. She uses the Insert Object command to create a new Adobe Table 3.0 object and embed it in her publication.

Steps

1. Click the **pages 2 and 3 page icon** ⌐2│3⌐, click **Edit** on the menu bar, then click **Insert Object**

    The Insert Object dialog box opens as shown in Figure D-21. You use this dialog box to insert an object created in a different program into your publication.

2. Make sure the **Create New option button** is selected, click **Adobe Table 3.0** in the **Object Type** list, then click **OK**

    The Adobe Table 3.0 program window opens, as shown in Figure D-22. You use the New Table dialog box that appears to determine the height and width of the table and the number of columns and rows you want your table to include.

3. Type **6** in the Rows text box, press **[Tab]**, type **2** in the Columns text box, press **[Tab]**, type **3** in the Height text box, press **[Tab]** twice (*Macintosh Users: Press [Tab] once*), type **2** in the Width text box, then click **OK**

    A blank table with 6 rows and 2 columns appears in a new window. The title bar of the new window reads Adobe Table 3.0 in Seaside Web Proposal.pmd. The Text Attributes and Table Attributes palettes also open. If these palettes do not appear on your screen, click Window on the menu bar, then click Show Text Attributes and Show Table Attributes (*Macintosh Users: Click Show Text Palette and Show Table Palette*).

4. Click the **Maximize button** of the Adobe Table 3.0 in Seaside Cycle Web Proposal.pmd window to maximize it

    The entire table is now visible in the Adobe Table 3.0 window.

5. Type **Year** in the first cell in the first row, press **[Tab]**, then type **Inquiries**

    Pressing [Tab] moves the insertion point from cell to cell. You can also click in a cell to move the insertion point to that cell.

6. Click **File** on the Adobe Table 3.0 menu bar, then click **Exit & Return to Seaside Cycle Web Proposal.pmd** (*Macintosh Users: Click Quit & return*)

    Adobe Table 3.0 closes. The table you created is located in the center of pages 2 and 3 in the publication.

7. Click the table to select it if necessary, drag the table to the bottom of column 1 on page 3, then place it in column 1 next to the Monthly E-mail Inquiries chart

    The table is now at the bottom of page 3, as shown in Figure D-23.

8. Save your changes to the publication

Trouble?

Windows Users: If Adobe Table 3.0 is not on your Object Type list, click Cancel, click the Start button on the taskbar, point to Programs, point to Adobe, point to PageMaker 7.0, click Adobe Table 3.0, click OK in the New Table dialog box, click File on the Adobe Table 3.0 menu bar, click Exit, click Don't Save, then repeat Steps 1 and 2.

Macintosh Users: If Adobe Table 3.0 is not on your Object Type list, click Cancel, double-click the hard drive icon on the desktop, double-click the Adobe PageMaker 7.0 folder, double-click the Adobe Table folder, click Adobe Table, click OK in the New Table dialog box, click File on the Adobe Table menu bar, click Exit, click Don't Save, then repeat Steps 1 and 2.

FIGURE D-21: Insert Object dialog box

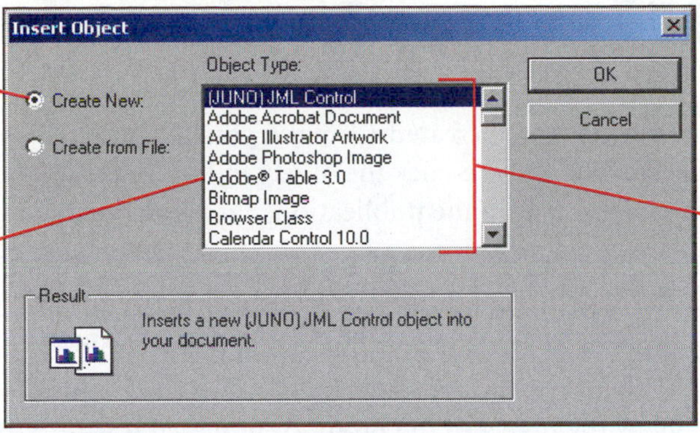

Create New option button

Adobe Table 3.0 object

The object types on your list might differ

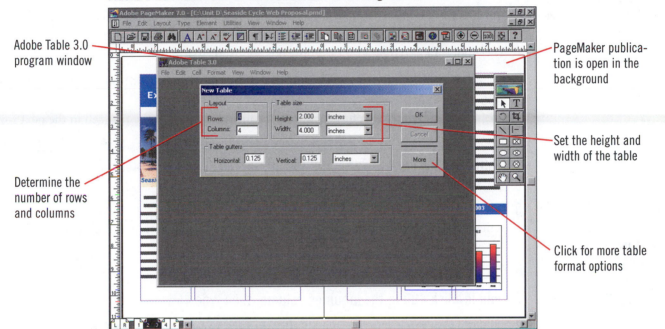

FIGURE D-22: Adobe Table 3.0 window and New Table dialog box

Adobe Table 3.0 program window

PageMaker publication is open in the background

Set the height and width of the table

Determine the number of rows and columns

Click for more table format options

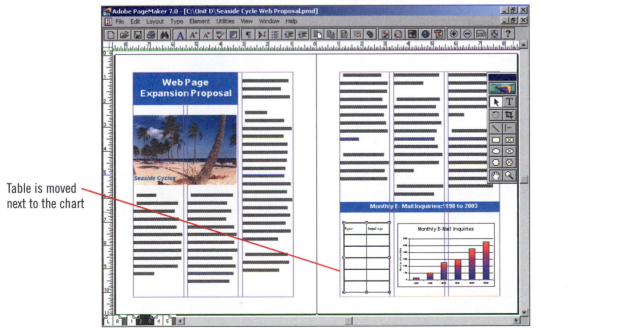

FIGURE D-23: Table moved to page 3

Table is moved next to the chart

Editing a Table

When you edit an object that is embedded in a PageMaker publication, you use the tools of the program in which it was created to make your changes. To open an embedded object in its source program, you double-click the object in PageMaker.  Now that she has placed the table where she wants it in the publication, Sara adds the data to the table.

1. Click **View** on the menu bar, click **Actual Size**, scroll so that the table and chart are visible on your screen, then double-click the table

   The table opens in the Adobe Table 3.0 program window. Double-clicking an embedded object opens the object in the program in which it was created.

Trouble?

If another window is in your way, drag it by its title bar to a new location.

2. Click the **Maximize button** in the Adobe Table 3.0 in Seaside Cycle Web Proposal.pmd window to maximize it, then click the **Maximize button** in the Adobe Table 3.0 program window to maximize it

   The Adobe Table 3.0 program window fills your screen.

3. Click the first blank cell in the Year column to move the insertion point to that cell, type **1998**, press **[Tab]**, type **30**, then press **[Tab]**

   Pressing [Tab] at the end of a row moves the insertion point to the first cell in the next row.

4. Type **1999**, press **[Tab]**, type **100**, press **[Tab]**, type **2000**, press **[Tab]**, type **250**, press **[Tab]**, type **2001**, press **[Tab]**, type **300**, press **[Tab]**, type **2002**, press **[Tab]**, then type **400**

   The text appears in the table as shown in Figure D-24.

MacintoshUsers

This replaces Step 5.
5. Click the grey bar to the left of the 2002 row, click Cell on the menu bar, then click Insert Row Below

5. Click **Cell** on the menu bar, then click **Insert Row Below**

   A new blank row is added below the row containing the insertion point, in this case, the last row of the table.

6. Click the first cell in the new row, type **2003**, press **[Tab]**, then type **550**

7. Double-click **400** in the Inquiries column, then type **450**

8. Click **File** on the menu bar, click **Exit & Return to Seaside Cycle Web Proposal.pmd** (*Macintosh Users: Click Quit & return*)

   The edited table appears in the publication as shown in Figure D-25.

9. Save your changes to the publication

FIGURE D-24: Table in the Adobe Table 3.0 program window

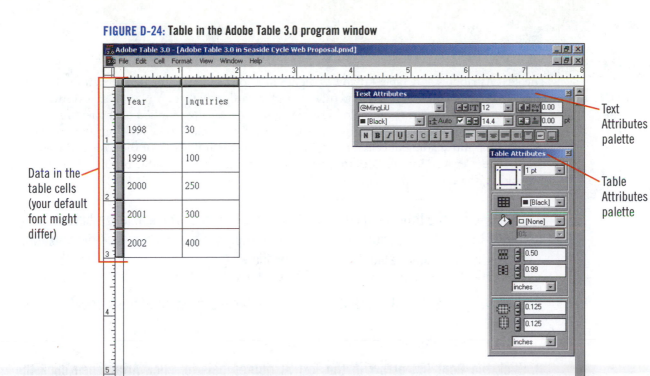

Data in the table cells (your default font might differ)

Text Attributes palette

Table Attributes palette

FIGURE D-25: Table in the PageMaker publication

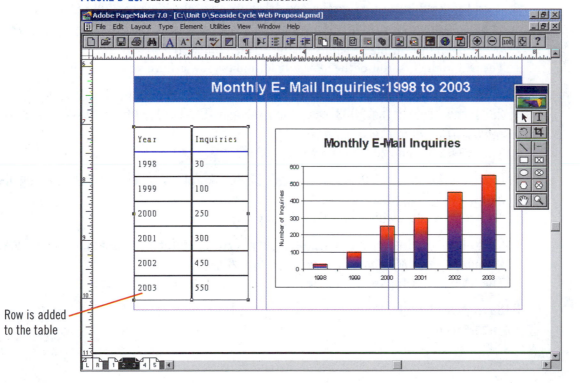

Row is added to the table

Enhancing a Table

The Text Attributes and Table Attribute palettes in Adobe Table 3.0 include tools for enhancing tables with fonts, colors, borders, and other table formatting features. You use the Text Attributes palette to change the font, size, color, leading, and other settings applied to the text in a table. You use the Table Attributes palette to change the width and color of the table borders, to change the fill color and shading of cells, and to change the height and width of the rows and columns in the table. ✎ Sara decides to spice up the appearance of the table by changing the font and adding shading to every other row.

1. Double-click the table to open it in Adobe Table 3.0, click the **Maximize button** in the Adobe Table 3.0 in Seaside Cycle Web Proposal.pmd window, then click the **Maximize button** in the Adobe Table 3.0 program window
   The Adobe Table 3.0 program window fills your screen.

2. Click the grey **Select All button** 🔲 located at the intersection of the vertical and horizontal rulers
   Clicking this button selects the entire table.

3. Click the **Font list arrow** in the Text Attributes palette, click **Arial**, then click the **Center alignment button** ▤ in the Text Attributes palette
   The font changes to Arial and the text is centered in each cell in the table, as shown in Figure D-26.

4. Click outside the table to deselect it, then click the grey bar to the left of the first row
   Clicking the grey bar to the left of a row selects the row. Clicking the grey bar above a column selects the column.

5. Click the **Bold button** ▣ on the Text Attributes palette, click the **Fill color list arrow** ◇ □[None] ▾ on the Table Attributes palette, click **Blue**, click the **Fill shading list arrow** 100% ▾ on the Table Attributes palette, then click **20%**
   The text in the first row of the table is bold, and the row is filled with light blue shading.

6. Click the grey bar next to the **1999 row** to select it, press and hold **[Ctrl]**, select the **2001 row**, select the **2003 row**, then release **[Ctrl]** (*Macintosh Users: Press and release [Command] instead of [Ctrl]*)
   The 1999, 2001, and 2003 rows are selected.

7. Click the **Fill color list arrow** ◇ □[None] ▾, click **Yellow**, click the **Fill shading list arrow** 100% ▾, then click **20%**
   The rows are filled with light yellow shading.

8. Click **File** on the menu bar, then click **Exit & Return to Seaside Cycle Web Proposal.pmd** (*Macintosh Users: Click Quit & return*)
   The completed table appears in the publication as shown in Figure D-27.

9. Save your changes to the publication, print the publication, close the file, then exit PageMaker

FIGURE D-26: Formatting the table

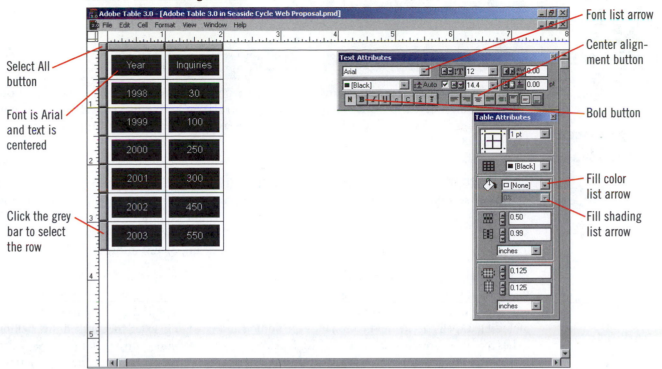

Select All button

Font is Arial and text is centered

Click the grey bar to select the row

Font list arrow

Center alignment button

Bold button

Fill color list arrow

Fill shading list arrow

FIGURE D-27: Completed table in PageMaker

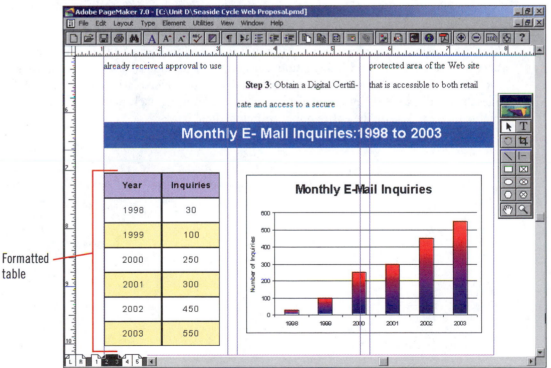

Formatted table

PageMaker 7.0

Design Workshop: Business Reports

Innovative design and concise writing in a business report help to capture the reader's attention. It's important that the information in a business report be organized in a logical and consistent fashion. ✐ Sara critiques her design of the Seaside Cycles business proposal shown in Figure D-28.

Details

► Does the cover invite the reader to read the report?

The cover sets the tone for the report. It should emphasize the importance of the content and introduce the visual style used in the report. The large headline and the abstract on the cover of Sara's proposal immediately let the reader know what the report contains. The Seaside Cycles logo on the cover adds a nice touch without crowding any important information.

► Is the text organized in a logical fashion?

It is critical that the text in a business report be coherent. PageMaker's story editor provides you with some of the tools commonly available in word processing applications to edit your stories, including a spell checker and commands for finding and changing text. Sara checked the spelling in her report before she printed it. She also replaced an awkward word with a better word. Sara also included headlines and subheads within the body of the report to help organize the information.

► Are the pages too heavy with text?

If possible, you should balance the excessive text used in reports with graphics. As with most business publications, the graphics in a business report should reinforce the content, not just decorate the pages. Sara included a table and chart on page 3 to reinforce the information contained in the text, and photos on pages 2 and 4 to add interest to the pages. Sara also adjusted the leading to add more white space to the proposal, giving the text a more manageable feel.

► Does each page of the report have a consistent design?

Using a consistent design provides continuity through all sections of the report and makes it easier for the reader to find information. Sara set up the proposal with three columns, which gave her more flexibility in placing the text and graphics. Her placement of the graphics on pages 2, 3, and 4 gives the proposal a consistent look. Looking back, Sara could have included a graphic on page 5 to tie the entire publication together.

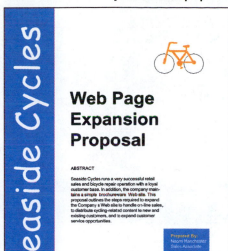

Seaside Cycles

Web Page
Expansion
Proposal

ABSTRACT

Seaside Cycles runs a very successful retail sales and bicycle repair operation with a loyal customer base. In addition, the company maintains a simple brochureware Web site. This proposal outlines the steps required to expand the Company's Web site to handle on-line sales, to distribute cycling-related content to new and existing customers, and to expand customer service opportunities.

Prepared By:
Naomi Manchester
Sales Associate

Kevin Williamson
Consultant

Web Page Expansion Proposal

Seaside Cycles

Introduction

Seaside Cycles is one of the premier cycling shops in San Diego, CA. Enthusiasts from all over the city come to Seaside Cycles too purchase bicycles and cycling accessories, to have their bikes serviced in the world-class custom repair shop, and to swap cycling stories with the knowledgeable staff.

In addition to its retail outlet, Seaside Cycles maintains a "brochureware" Web site that advertises the store and its products. A brochureware Web site is one that provides the world with information about the business and even includes pictures of some of its products, but is not set up for customers to purchase products on-line. This proposal outlines improvements to the company's Web site in terms of three areas: On-line Sales, Customer Service, and Content.

On-line Sales

Seaside Cycles can use its Web site to reach customers who are not able to visit the retail location. Over the past several years, the company has developed an extensive database of customers who live in smaller communities outside the San Diego area and who do not have access to a reliable supplier of premium bicycle parts. If the Web site is revised to permit on-line sales, those customers can place their orders on-line instead of visiting San Diego eachtime they need to purchase a part.

The current Web site can be updated to handle on-line sales. Three steps are required:

Step 1: Add shopping cart software to the existing Web site. In approximately two weeks, the current Web site designer can modify the Web site so that 25% of the inventory is available for purchase on-line. The full inventory can be made available within three months.

Step 2: Acquire access to a payment and transaction processing service. Seaside Cycles has already received approval to use its existing merchant account to handle on-line sales.

Inquiries are being made with the bank handling the current merchant account to determine the services offered with relation to handling on-line sales. Approximate monthly costs for processing an anticipated 100 transactions is $50.00 in addition to a $40.00 per month maintenance charge.

Step 3: Obtain a Digital Certificate and access to a secure server. The Seaside Cycles Web site must be hosted on a secure server to handle credit card transactions and to safeguard the contact information provided by customers.

The company is in the process of obtaining a Digital Certificate from a recognized Certificate Authority. In addition, the Web designer is developing procedures for setting up a password-protected area of the Web site that is accessible to both retail

Monthly E- Mail Inquiries:1998 to 2003

Year	Inquiries
1998	30
1999	100
2000	250
2001	300
2002	450
2003	550

Monthly E-Mail Inquiries

---

and Business-to-Business customers.

In fact, the next phase of the Web site expansion will be to make portions of the company's Intranet accessible to selected suppliers. Many of these suppliers are now in a position to sell on-line to their business customers.

Customer Service

Seaside Cycles is in a good position to provide on-line customer service, particularly to customers who purchase frequently from Seaside Cycles, are "web savvy," and are interested in receiving customer support outside of regular store hours. The current Web site has been attracting a steadily increasing number of inquiries since its launch in 1998. The column chart shown below shows the average number of e-mail inquiries received each month from 1998 to 2003. Most of these inquiries

request information about products and services, and can be easily handled by a return e-mail.

By expanding the Web site to include answers to questions asked most frequently, Seaside Cycles can reduce the number of individual e-mails that must be replied to and decrease the number of phone inquiries. Since an average phone inquiry costs the company $4.55 and providing information via the Web site costs approximately $.05, Seaside Cycles can reap obvious benefits by expanding the Web site to provide customers with as much

information as possible on a 24-hour basis.

In addition to providing printed information on the Web site, plans are underway to include a live help component within six months of rolling out the expanded site. Seaside Cycles will partner with an on-line service that provides 24-hour per day live assistance from trained customer service representatives. The cost for this service is approximately $3.00 per use of 1 minute or longer.

Content

At present, the Seaside Cycles Web site includes information

---

about the retail store and approximately ten pages of photographs of bestselling product lines. The expanded Web site will include not only extensive product information, but a wealth of content related to the interests of cycling enthusiasts. This content falls into the following categories:

Guided Tours

Seaside Cycles has been associated with *Cycle Free Tours* in Los Angeles for the past three years to offer customers 10% discounts on selected cycling tours. The Web site will include information about past and upcoming tours, interviews with tour participants, maps and itineraries, and lots of gorgeous photographs! Shown at the right is a photograph taken on a recent Cycle Free Tour to Provence, France. Cyclists on the tour wound through the lush vineyards and rocky hills of the area surrounding the ruined medieval village of Les Baux.

Interviews

Seaside Cycles frequently sponsors amateur and professional cycling events. Many of the world's best cyclists have passed through Seaside Cycles, where they have signed autographs and answered questions. The expanded Web site will include an Interviews page that is updated monthly with the latest interviews with celebrity cyclists. If these pages prove successful with Web surfers, Seaside Cycles could consider developing an on-line chat facility so that customers could log on and chat to celebrity cyclists at set times.

Testimonials

Customers of Seaside Cycles are an enthusiastic bunch who welcome the opportunity to swap stories and make product recommendations. The new Testimonials page will provide an ongoing forum that customers can contribute to and provide honest appraisals of products, services, and even personnel.

Summary

Seaside Cycles is in an excellent position to take advantage of the World Wide Web to reach more customers, better serve existing customers, and even develop new Business-to-Business connections and opportunities.

The proposed changes to the Web site will take effect within the next month, pending approval of the Board of Directors.

Practice

► Concepts Review

Label each element of the story editor window shown in Figure D-29.

FIGURE D-29

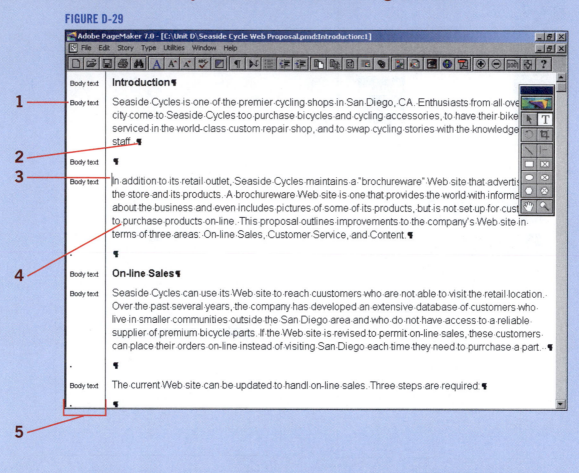

Match each term with the statement that best describes it.

6. Clipboard

7. Leading

8. Story editor

9. Word wrap

a. Temporary storage area for cut or copied text or graphics

b. PageMaker's word processor

c. The automatic movement of the insertion point and text to the next line

d. The space between lines of text

Select the best answer from the list of choices.

10. **All of the following are advantages of using story editor, except:**
    a. You can make multiple changes to a story that spans several text blocks.
    b. You can insert large amounts of text easily.
    c. You can use powerful utilities such as the spell checker and the Find and Change commands.
    d. You can see how the story fits on the page.

11. **When you use the spell checker, you can check only:**
    a. The current story.
    b. All stories in the current publication.
    c. All stories in open PageMaker publications.
    d. All of the above.

12. **An advantage of using the Character Specifications dialog box is that you can:**
    a. Set multiple formats at one time.
    b. Check the spelling of your entire publication.
    c. Set paragraph alignment.
    d. Both a and c.

13. **All of the following are true statements about leading, except:**
    a. Leading is automatically set when you choose a different font size.
    b. PageMaker's default for leading is 20% greater than font size.
    c. Leading is measured in points, the same as text.
    d. You change the height of the characters when you set leading.

14. **PageMaker's spell checker allows you to:**
    a. Add new words to the dictionary.
    b. Check for spelling in all stories in the publication.
    c. Find a word accidentally typed consecutively.
    d. All of the above.

15. **Setting the number of lines for a widow to 2 in the Paragraph Specifications dialog box means PageMaker will:**
    a. Not allow two lines that end a paragraph at the top of a page or column.
    b. Not allow three lines that end a paragraph at the bottom of a page or column.
    c. Not allow two lines that begin a paragraph at the end of a page or column.
    d. Not allow three lines that begin a paragraph at the end of a page or column.

PageMaker 7.0

▶ Skills Review

1. **Open story editor and create and place text with story editor.**
   a. Start PageMaker, open the file PM D-2.pmd from the drive and folder where your Project Files are located, then save it as **Sunrise Proposal**.
   b. Open story editor.
   c. Turn on the Display ¶ option.
   d. Type the following text:
   Story by Pete Kenwood
   Pete is a business editor for the Tampa Times. He has closely monitored the large food warehouse chains nationwide because many of these companies are headquartered in Tampa and the surrounding areas in Florida. He can be reached at his office at (602) 555-1234, or through e-mail at Kenwood@times.com.
   e. Close and place the story.
   f. Drag-place the story below the headline and across all three columns, then drag the windowshade handle down to fit all the text if necessary.
   g. Save your changes.

2. **Edit text in story editor.**
   a. Open the main story on page 1 in story editor.
   b. Turn on the Display ¶ option.
   c. Select the entire second paragraph, including the paragraph symbol, then cut the text.
   d. Position the insertion point at the beginning of the ninth paragraph, which begins "Sunrise cited…", then paste the text.
   e. Delete the last sentence of the seventh paragraph, which begins "We've been talking about surviving…".
   f. Save your changes.

3. **Check spelling.**
   a. Position the insertion point at the beginning of the story.
   b. Start the spelling check.
   c. Click food in the list of alternative spellings for "fod", then click Replace.
   d. Ignore the spelling of "Isis".
   e. Continue checking the spelling of the text, replacing or ignoring words as necessary.
   f. When you are finished, close the Spelling dialog box, then save your changes.

4. **Find and change text.**
   a. Position the insertion point at the beginning of the story.
   b. Using the Change command, replace the text "Sunrise Foods" with the text "Sunrise Distributors Inc."
   c. Click Find to select the first occurrence of the text.
   d. Click Change to change the text to the replacement text.
   e. Find all occurrences of the text you are searching for and change them to the new text.
   f. When you are finished, close the Change dialog box.
   g. Close the story, then save your changes.

5. **Apply multiple character formats to text.**
   a. Change the view to Actual Size, then scroll so the top half of the page is visible in the publication window.
   b. Select the Text tool, then click anywhere in the main story on page 1.
   c. Select all the text in the story.
   d. Open the Character Specifications dialog box.
   e. Change the Font to Arial.
   f. Change the Size to 10.
   g. Change the Leading to 20.
   h. Click OK, then save your changes.

6. **Apply multiple paragraph formats to text.**
   a. Make sure all the text in the main story is still selected.
   b. Open the Paragraph Specifications dialog box.
   c. Change the first line indent to .15".
   d. Turn on Widow control and define a widow as one line.
   e. Turn on Orphan control and define an orphan as one line.
   f. Click OK, then save your changes.

7. **Insert and remove pages.**
   a. Change the view to Fit in Window.
   b. Insert four new pages at the end of the publication.
   c. Display page 1.
   d. Using the Pointer tool, select the text block in the third column, then click the bottom windowshade handle once to load the pointer with the overflow text.
   e. Display pages 2 and 3.
   f. Turn on the Autoflow feature.
   g. Place the text at the top of the first column on page 2.
   h. Remove pages 4 and 5, then save your changes.

PageMaker 7.0

8. Create a table.

a. Click Edit on the menu bar, then click Insert Object to open the Insert Object dialog box.

b. Click Adobe Table 3.0 in the Object Type list, then click OK.

c. Create a table that has 5 rows, 2 columns, and is 2.5" high and 4" wide.

d. Type **Company** in the first cell in row 1, press [Tab], then type **Market Share** in the second cell in row 1.

e. Exit Adobe Table 3.0 and return to PageMaker.

f. Move the table to the lower-right corner of page 3.

g. Save your changes.

9. Edit a table.

a. Double-click the table to open it in Adobe Table 3.0.

b. Type the following data in the table:

Company	Market Share
Sunrise Distributors Inc.	35%
Kemper	30%
Stones Ltd.	23%
A & R Foods Inc.	12%

c. Click after Kemper in the table, press [Spacebar], then type **Industries**.

d. Exit Adobe Table 3.0 and return to PageMaker.

10. Enhance a table.

a. Double-click the table to open it in Adobe Table 3.0.

b. Select the entire table, then change the font to Arial.

c. Select the top row, bold the text, then change the fill color to red.

d. Change the fill color of the third and fifth rows to yellow.

e. Exit Adobe Table 3.0 and return to PageMaker.

f. Change the view to Actual Size, then compare your table with Figure D-30.

g. Save your changes, print the publication, close the file, then exit PageMaker.

FIGURE D-30

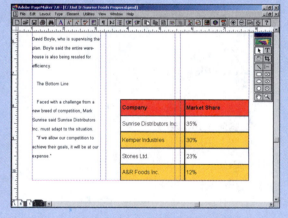

▶ Independent Challenge 1

As the desktop publisher for Peterson Consultants, you need to petition your manager for an upgrade of your computer equipment. You must justify the expense in a report that proves the upgrade will ensure an increase in productivity. The increase in productivity will translate into more time to do more projects, which equals more revenue. You know the report will be most effective if you make it simple and straightforward.

a. Create a new four-page, single-sided publication using the default margins. Format the master page with three columns, then save the publication as **Peterson Consultants Proposal** to the drive and folder where your Project Files are located.

b. Place the logo file Peterson Consultants.jpg, found on the drive and folder where your Project Files are located, on page 1, which is the cover page.

c. Type a headline, your name, and the date on the cover page. Format the text using the Character Specifications dialog box, then arrange the logo and text on the cover page to create an appealing design. Feel free to add other design elements to the cover page to make it more eye-catching.

d. Create a table that contains three columns and four rows. Type information in the table about the items you propose to purchase, including the computer parts, quantity, and price. Format the table to be attractive, then place the table on page 3.

e. Type a headline on page 2 that communicates the main point of your request for new equipment. Format the headline so that it spans all three columns.

f. Place the placeholder text file Proptxt.doc, found on the drive and folder where your Project Files are located, on pages 2 through 4.

g. Open the story in story editor and use the spell check to correct the misspelled words.

h. Close story editor, then format the body text and increase the leading to make the proposal more readable. Adjust the flow of text if necessary.

i. Evaluate the final design. Is the proposal too text heavy? Do you need to increase the leading? Would a different font be easier to read? Do you need to add more graphics? Make any changes necessary.

j. Save your proposal, print a copy, close the publication, then exit PageMaker.

▶ Independent Challenge 2

Find a copy of business reports from at least two different companies. They can be annual reports, proposals, or some other type of report.

    a. Analyze the writing style of the reports. Can you tell who is the intended audience for each report?

    b. Critique the reports using the guidelines discussed in this unit along with other criteria that you establish. For each, answer the following: Is the design of the cover effective? Is the text organized logically? How effective is the design in enhancing the readability of the publication? Do elements of design detract from or improve the complete report?

    c. How would you improve the design or readability of each report?

▶ Independent Challenge 3

You have been asked to create a report about the improved computer science program at Springfield University. The intended audience for the report is potential students. The report must include a table highlighting the average starting salaries for computer science graduates.

    a. Start PageMaker, then create a new single-sided publication with three pages and default margins. Format the master page with two columns, then save the publication as **Computer Science Proposal** to the drive and folder where your Project Files are located.

    b. Type a headline at the top of page 1, then place the text file Springfield Text.doc, found on the drive and folder where your Project Files are located, as the body text in the proposal.

    c. Check the spelling of the story, making corrections as necessary.

    d. Format the text of the proposal so that it is attractive and readable. Add or remove pages from the publication as necessary.

    e. Set Widow and Orphan control at two lines, and indent the first line of every paragraph .15".

    f. Format the headings and subheading to enhance the overall appearance of your report.

    g. Place the graphic file SU Logo.jpg, found on the drive and folder where your Project Files are located, as a placeholder graphic on one of the pages in the publication.

    h. Add a table that lists starting salaries for computer science graduates to your report using Adobe Table 3.0. Make up the data for the table.

    i. Insert a new page before page 1. This page will be the cover page.

    j. Open story editor, then type a short abstract describing the contents of your report.

    k. Place the abstract on the cover page, then add a headline and any other necessary text to the cover page.

    l. Place the graphic file Springfield University.jpg, found on the drive and folder where your Project Files are located, on the cover page.

    m. Add any design elements you think necessary, then arrange the elements of the cover page to make the page eye-catching and attractive.

    n. Evaluate the final design and make any necessary changes.

    o. Save your changes, print the publication, close the file, then exit PageMaker.

Independent Challenge 4

You have been chosen to put together a proposal for your Volunteer Corp's annual summer volunteer trip. The proposal will be presented to the organization's Board of Trustees. Your peers in the group want you to design an attractive, high-impact proposal that will justify the trip expense to the board and convince them that your trip will be beneficial to those you will be helping.

a. Search the World Wide Web for information on volunteer organizations and their areas of need. If your search does not result in appropriate links, try looking at the following Web sites: **www.habitat.org** or **www.unv.org**.

b. Create a thumbnail sketch of a four-page proposal, keeping in mind the guidelines you learned in this unit. Your proposal should include a cover sheet that includes the Volunteer Corp logo, a headline, and an abstract. The remaining three pages should include the body text, organized under headings and subheadings, a table, and graphics.

c. Start PageMaker, then create a four-page, single-sided publication, using your sketch as a guide.

d. Using the information that you find on the Web, write an abstract for your proposal using story editor. Check the spelling in the abstract, then place the abstract on the cover page of your proposal.

e. Place the graphic file Volunteer Corp.jpg, found on the drive and folder where your Project Files are located, on the cover page. Add a headline and any other necessary information to the cover page, then arrange the elements so the design of the cover page is compelling.

f. Create the body text for the proposal in story editor, making sure to organize the text under headings and subheadings. Check the spelling of the story, then place it in the publication.

g. Add a table detailing some aspect of the trip to the proposal.

h. Place the graphics in the proposal using the file Volunteer Corp.jpg as a placeholder graphic.

i. Format the text of the proposal.

j. When you are done formatting the proposal and enhancing its appearance, critique the final design and make any necessary adjustments.

k. Save your proposal as **Volunteer Trip Proposal** to the drive and folder where your Project Files are located, print the publication, close the file, then exit PageMaker.

PageMaker 7.0

► Visual Workshop

Using the file PM D-3.pmd, found on the drive and folder where your Project Files are located, create the report shown in Figure D-31. Use story editor to type the following abstract:

INTRODUCTION
This report is a supplement to the information found in the annual Hawthorne Investors Group Plan Summary booklet and is provided to help you understand the characteristics of your investment options. Please note that the historical data in this report is provided for information purposes only and should not be used to predict the future performance of group funds.

Place the abstract text as shown in Figure D-31, then format the text to make it attractive. Open the story that begins on page 2 in story editor, move point #3 above point #2, then renumber the points. Replace "Windlow Stock Fund" with "Altoffz Growth Stock Fund", check the spelling in the story, then close story editor. Format the body text of the report in 12-point Times New Roman or a similar font, and change the leading to 24 points. Turn on the Widow and Orphan control and set both to 2 lines. Finally, format the section headings in Arial or a similar font. Save the publication as **Hawthorne Report** to the drive and folder where your Project Files are located, then print a copy.

FIGURE D-31

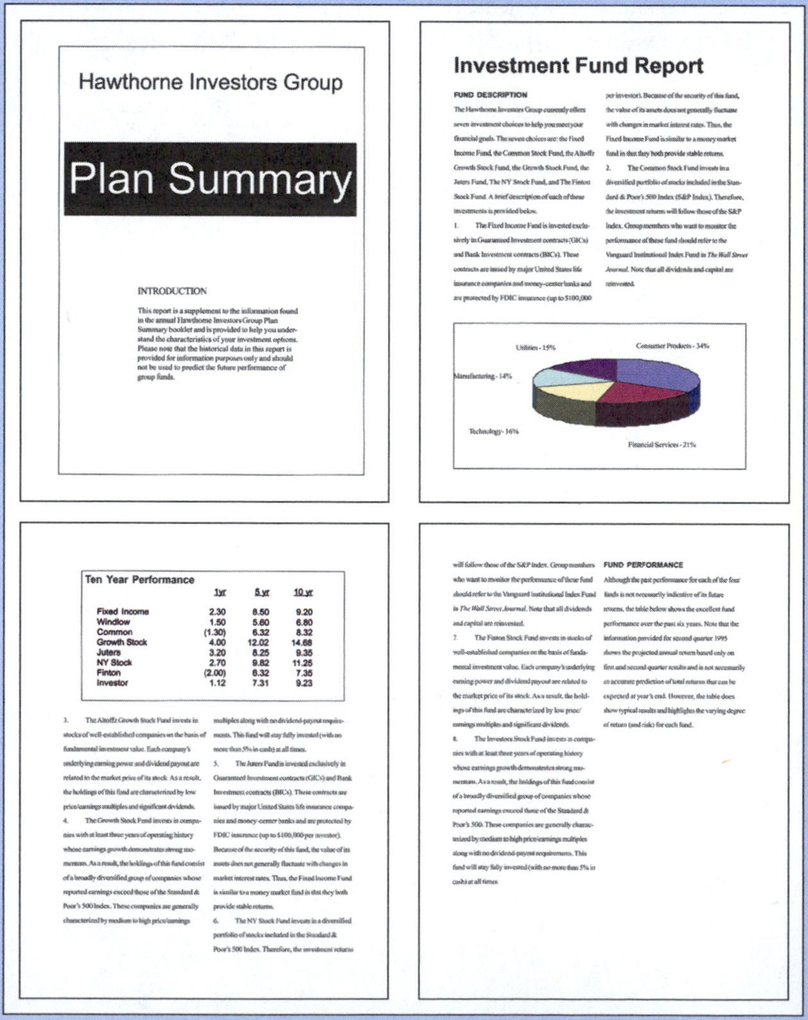

Working

with Multiple Pages

Objectives

- ► **Plan a newsletter**
- ► **Use master pages**
- ► **Create a new master page**
- ► **Modify a master page**
- ► **Apply master pages**
- ► **Use and define styles**
- ► **Apply styles**
- ► **Edit styles**
- ► **Add jump lines and balance columns**
- ► **Rearrange pages**
- ► **Mask objects**
- ► **Design Workshop: Newsletters**

PageMaker includes tools you can use to ensure a consistent look throughout your publication. In this unit, you learn how to use master pages to place text and objects that you want to appear on every page. You also learn to use styles to format paragraphs consistently and quickly. Finally, you learn to use some of PageMaker's plug-in features. ✐ Sara Norton has been hired to design the *Swan Report*, a newsletter produced by the Lakeview Swan Theater. Sara takes advantage of PageMaker's page formatting tools to enhance the final appearance of the *Swan Report*.

PageMaker 7.0

Details

Planning a Newsletter

Newsletters are one of the most common types of publications produced using PageMaker. The challenge is to create a newsletter that captures the reader's attention. Before creating your newsletter in PageMaker, it's important to take time to identify the audience for your newsletter, determine the information to include, establish such printing specifications as paper size and length, and then sketch the overall layout of each page in your newsletter. ✎▬ The *Swan Report* is produced twice a year and contains information for season ticket holders about upcoming productions. Sara's sketch for the *Swan Report* is shown in Figure E-1. The newsletter will be printed on letter-size paper and will be eight pages long.

Keep the following guidelines in mind when planning the layout of a newsletter:

► Include a masthead at the top of the newsletter
The **masthead**, also called a **nameplate** or **flag**, is the area on the first page of a newsletter or other periodical that contains the title of the publication, the date of issue, and other identifying information such as the volume number or company name. The masthead also can contain a graphical element such as a logo or other identifying symbol. Be careful not to crowd a masthead with too much information. Sara plans to include the title of the newsletter, an image of a swan, the name and location of the theater, and the date of issue of the *Swan Report* in its masthead.

► Focus the attention of the reader on the main article on each page
The reader should be able to glance at a page and immediately identify the most important article on the page. Creating a focus gives readers a place to begin reading each page of the newsletter. For example, the headline for the main article can be larger than other headlines on the page. Generally, it's best to place articles on a page in order of importance from the top left to the bottom right, because of the way we naturally read. In the *Swan Report*, the article that provides an overview of the season is the most important one, so Sara will place it at the top of page 1.

► Use graphics to show the importance of information
Graphics grab attention and often motivate readers to read an article. Generally, graphics associated with the main article are the largest on the page, and smaller articles might not even contain graphics. Sara plans to place three graphics on pages 2 and 3 to convey the themes related to the three upcoming productions. Since each production carries the same importance, she decides to make each graphic roughly the same size and to lay out pages 2 and 3 as a **spread**, or two facing pages that are designed to work together as a unit.

► Use shading, lines, or white space to break up text
It's important that the articles in a newsletter appear as separate blocks of text. A newsletter like the one Sara is creating should contain only one or two articles per page. However, for those occasions when you need to place several short articles on a page, you can use shading or lines to separate the articles. Sara will use colored boxes on pages 2 and 3 to separate the three articles on upcoming productions. She will also use shading for one of the articles on page 8 to help it stand out from the other two articles on the page.

► Select appropriate fonts for headlines and body text
Like photos and graphics, the headline for an article should invite the audience to read the article. Headlines compete with other design elements for attention on the page, so it's best to format headlines so that they stand out. Body text is usually formatted in a 10- or 12-point serif font, such as Times New Roman or Palatino, so that it is easy to read. In general, you should format headlines to be no smaller than 18 points, and in a complementary font. Sara plans to use a mix of fonts and sizes for headlines and to format the body text in 12-point Times New Roman.

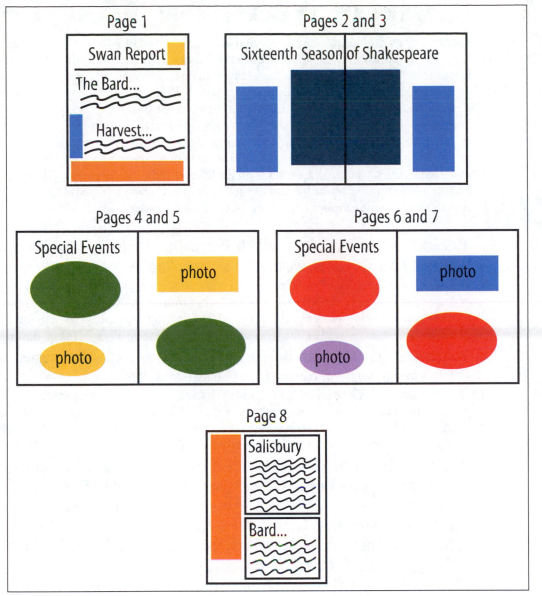

Using Master Pages

Master pages are nonprinting pages that serve as a foundation for the entire publication. All PageMaker publications include a **Document Master page** or, for double-sided publications, a **Document Master page spread**. Any element that you place on a master page appears on every page of your publication. Typically, **headers** (text that appears at the top of every page, such as a publication title) and **footers** (text that appears at the bottom of every page, such as a page number) are placed on a master page. Master pages also contain nonprinting layout guides, such as margin guides, column guides, and ruler guides. To include information on a master page, you must open the master page and then place the item on the master page itself. In a publication with facing pages, you can place objects on the left and right master pages. ✒️ Sara wants to include a page number at the bottom of each page in her newsletter. To do this, she adds a footer containing the page number to both the left and right master pages.

Steps

Trouble?

If the Templates palette opens, close it.

1. Start PageMaker, open the file **PM E-1.pmd** from the drive and folder where your Project Files are stored, then save it as **Swan Report**

   Pages 2 and 3 of the newsletter open in the publication window. The left and right master pages icon in the lower-left corner of the publication window indicates that this is a double-sided publication. Items placed on the left master page appear on all left (odd-numbered) pages, and items placed on the right master page appear on all right (even-numbered) pages.

2. Maximize the publication window, if necessary, then click the **master pages icon** in the lower-left corner of the publication window

   The master pages icon is highlighted and the left and right master pages appear in Fit in Window view. You can see that column guides have been added to the master pages. "Lakeview Swan" is also placed at the top of the left master page and is followed by a decorative, blue double line, and "Fall, 2004" is placed in the upper-left corner of the right master page, above the margin guide.

3. Click the **Text tool** in the toolbox, click just below the third column on the right master page, click **View** on the menu bar, then click **Actual Size**

   The area below the third column of the right master page appears magnified on your screen.

4. Drag-place a text block below the third column that is as wide as the column and ¼" high, type **Page**, press **[Spacebar]**, then press **[Ctrl][Shift][3]** *(Macintosh Users: Press [Command][Option][P])*

   Typing the key combination [Ctrl][Shift][3] inserts the symbol "RM". "RM" is the page number symbol for the right master page. The actual page number appears automatically on each page in the publication in place of the RM symbol.

5. Click **Type** on the menu bar, point to **Alignment**, then click **Align Right**

   The text is right-aligned in the text block, as shown in Figure E-2.

6. Scroll so that the lower-left corner of the left master page is visible on your screen, drag-place a text block below the first column that is as wide as the column and ¼" high, type **Page**, press **[Spacebar]**, then press **[Ctrl][Shift][3]** *(Macintosh Users: Press [Command][Option][P])*

   "Page LM" appears in the text block and is left-aligned. "LM" is the page number symbol for the left master page.

7. Click the **pages 2 and 3 page icon**, position the pointer near the lower-right corner of page 3, click **View** on the menu bar, then click **Actual Size**

   "Page 3" appears below the third column of page 3 in Actual Size view, as shown in Figure E-3. PageMaker automatically replaces the RM symbol with "3", the number of the page.

8. Click **View** on the menu bar, click **Fit in Window**, click **File** on the menu bar, then click **Save** to save your changes to the publication

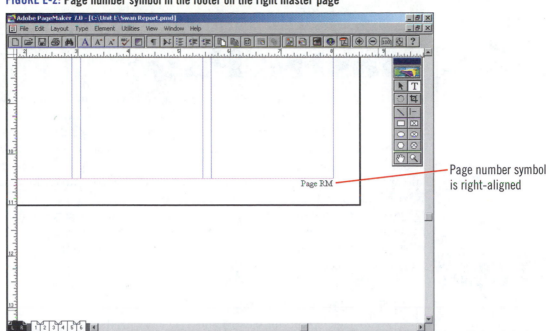

Page number symbol
is right-aligned

FIGURE E-3: Footer on page 3

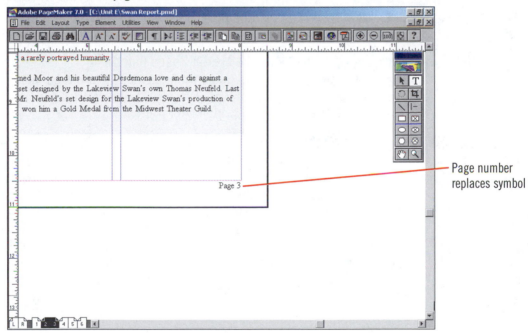

Page number
replaces symbol

Hiding master page items

The Display Master Items command on the View menu lets you choose whether to show or hide all the elements contained on the master pages on the active page or page spread. When Display Master Items is checked (the default), all items on the master page appear on the current pages. When Display Master Items is unchecked, the master page items do not appear on the current page. Sometimes you might want to hide only certain master page elements. For example, you might want to display a graphic, but not a page number. To hide a single unwanted element, click the Rectangle tool in the toolbox, drag a rectangle around the element, click Element on the menu bar, click Fill, and then click Paper. To remove the border of the rectangle, select the rectangle, click Element on the menu bar, click Stroke, and then click None.

PageMaker 7.0

Creating a New Master Page

By placing objects on the master pages, you can add page numbers, repetitive graphic elements, and headers and footers to all the spreads in your publication at once. However, sometimes master page objects can limit your ability to create a unique page layout for a spread. To remove some or all of the master page elements from a page can be very time consuming, especially in a multiple-page publication. Fortunately, you can create multiple master pages in PageMaker and apply them to different spreads in your publication. You can create a new master page that is based on an existing publication page, or you can create a new master page from scratch.   Sara is unhappy with the way some of the master page elements appear in the spread highlighting special events on pages 4 and 5. She decides to create a new master page spread that is based on the document master page spread, but which eliminates some of the elements. She names this master page spread "Special Events."

Steps 1 2 3 4

1. Click the **pages 4 and 5 page icon** ⁅4⁆5⁆

   The two-page spread for pages 4 and 5 opens, with the headline "Special Events" at the top of page 4. You can see that the Lakeview Swan header and the double line bump into the Special Events headline, making the top of page 4 look cluttered.

2. Click **Window** on the menu bar, then click **Show Master Pages**

   The Master Pages palette appears on the publication window, as shown in Figure E-4.

3. Click the **right arrow** on the Master Pages palette

   The Master Pages menu opens, as shown in Figure E-5. You can use this menu to create new master pages from existing publication pages or from scratch. This menu also contains other commands related to working with master pages.

Trouble?

If the Master Pages palette covers a screen element you're working with, click its title bar and drag it out of the way. If you can't see the full names of the master pages listed on the palette, click and drag the borders of the palette to resize it.

4. Click **Save Page as** on the Master Pages menu, type **Special Events** in the Save Page as Master dialog box, then click **Save**

   The highlight in the lower-left corner of the publication window moves from ⁅4⁆5⁆ to ⁅L⁆R⁆, indicating that the pages shown on screen are a master page spread. Notice that all the document master page elements and the page layout from pages 4 and 5 are automatically copied to the new master page spread, and that the name Special Events is highlighted in the Master Pages palette. Once you save a new master page spread, you can modify it, and apply it to any spread in your publication.

5. Save your changes to the publication

FIGURE E-4: Master Pages palette

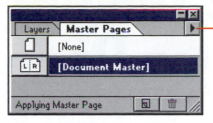

Click to open the
Master Pages menu

FIGURE E-5: Master Pages menu

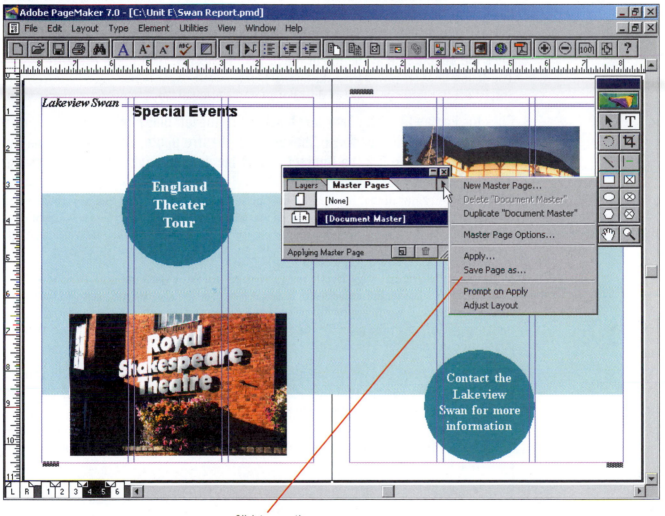

Click to save the
current page as a
master page

PageMaker 7.0

Modifying a Master Page

You can make modifications to a master page just as you would to any page of your publication. You can add text, place graphics, or remove an existing object. Any changes you make to a master page are instantly reflected in all pages to which the master is applied. ✒ Sara wants to remove the Lakeview Swan header and the decorative, blue double lines from the Special Events master page spread. She also wants to remove the information and photos relating to the England theater tour featured in this issue of the newsletter so that she can use the Special Events master page spread for future issues of the newsletter.

1. Click the **Pointer tool** in the toolbox, click the **Lakeview Swan** text block to select it, then press **[Delete]**
   The text Lakeview Swan is removed from the Special Events master pages.

2. Click the **double line** at the top of the pages to select it, then press **[Delete]**
   The double line is removed from the Special Events master pages. Removing objects from the Special Events master page spread does not affect the original Document Master page spread.

3. Click the **England Theater Tour text block** inside the left blue circle to select it, press and hold **[Shift]**, click the **Royal Shakespeare Theatre photo**, click the **photo** on the right master page, click the **Contact… text block** in the right blue circle, release **[Shift]**, then press **[Delete]**
   See Figure E-6. Now all that remains on the Special Events master page spread is the colored box across both pages, the blue circles which will contain future special events text, the Special Events headline, the header containing the date, and the footers containing the page numbers.

4. Click the **pages 4 and 5 page icon** 4 5
   Notice that the original page layout for these pages remains the same; the Lakeview Swan header text and double line still appear across the top. This is because the original Document Master page spread is still applied to pages 4 and 5. Before you apply the new Special Events master page spread to the pages, you need to delete the elements on pages 4 and 5 that are already included on the Special Events master page spread.

5. Click the **pale blue box** in the background of pages 4 and 5, press and hold **[Shift]**, click the **Special Events text block**, click the **blue circle** on page 4, click the **blue circle** on page 5, release **[Shift]**, then press **[Delete]**
   Now the spread includes only the custom objects for the layout on the England Theater tour, as shown in Figure E-7. The text that used to be inside the blue circles is still there, but you can't see it because it is white.

6. Save your changes to the publication

FIGURE E-6: Special Events master pages with issue-specific text and objects removed

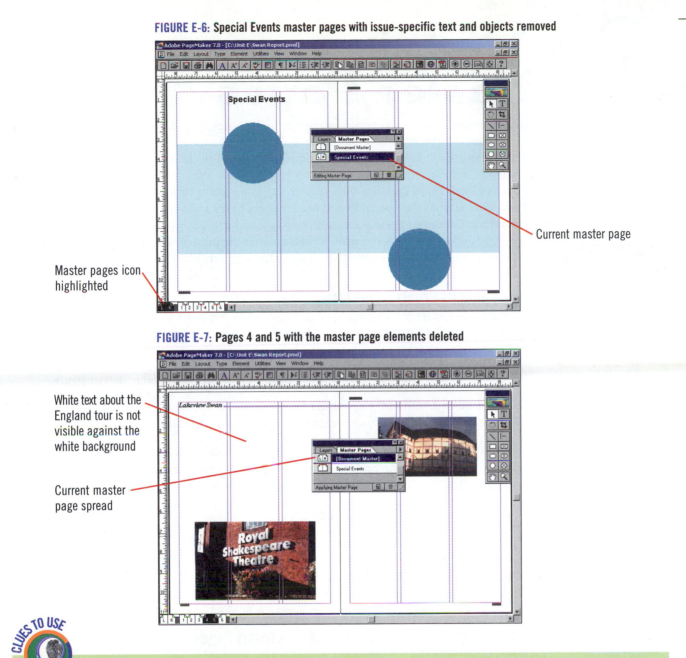

Master pages icon highlighted

Current master page

FIGURE E-7: Pages 4 and 5 with the master page elements deleted

White text about the England tour is not visible against the white background

Current master page spread

Creating a new master page from scratch

Sometimes you might need to create a master page that is not based on existing pages. To create a new master page from scratch, click New Master Page on the Master Pages menu. The New Master Page dialog box opens, as shown in Figure E-8. Type the name of the new master page in the Name text box, choose a one-page master page or a two-page master page spread, then select the margin and column settings. If you are creating a master page spread, the margin and column settings you choose are applied to both the left and right master pages. When you are finished, click OK, and the new blank master page(s) appear in the publication window. *(Macintosh Users: Click Create instead of OK.)* You can then customize the new master pages with text, graphics, and other elements.

FIGURE E-8: New Master Page dialog box

PageMaker 7.0

Applying Master Pages

After you create and save a new master page or master page spread, you can then apply it to any page or page spread in your publication. To apply a master page or master page spread to selected pages, first open the page or page spread you want to change, and then choose the master page you want to apply from the Master Pages palette. When you insert new pages in your publication, you must specify which master page or page spread to apply to the new pages. Sara applies the Special Events master pages to the page spread describing the England Theater Tour. After she applies the master, she decides the layout would be stronger if the Special Events heading were more prominent, so she modifies the master page spread. She also adds two additional pages that use the Special Events master page spread to the publication.

Steps

1. Click Special Events on the Master Pages palette

The Special Events master page spread is applied to pages 4 and 5, as shown in Figure E-9. Notice that the white text is now visible against the blue circles.

2. Right-click the master pages icon `L` `R`

The Master Pages shortcut menu opens, displaying the list of available master pages.

3. Click Special Events on the Master Pages shortcut menu

The Special Events master pages open in the publication window.

4. Click the Text tool `T` in the toolbox, select the headline Special Events on the left master page, click Type on the menu bar, point to Size, then click 60

The Special Events headline is enlarged.

5. Click the pages 4 and 5 page icon `4` `5`

The Special Events headline is larger, reflecting the changes you made to the master page, as shown in Figure E-10.

6. Click the page 1 page icon `1`

Page 1 opens. Notice that Document Master is now highlighted on the Master Pages palette, indicating that the default master page spread is applied to these pages.

7. Click Layout on the menu bar, then click Insert Pages

The Insert Pages dialog box opens.

8. Verify that 2 is entered in the Insert text box, verify that after is selected in the current page list box, click the Master page list arrow, click Special Events, then click Insert

Two new pages based on the Special Events master page spread are added to the publication following page 1. Sara will add information about additional special events to these pages later. New page icons for pages 7 and 8 appear.

9. Click Window on the menu bar, click Hide Master Pages, then save your changes to the publication

The Master Pages palette closes.

FIGURE E-9: Special Events master page spread applied to pages 4 and 5

Special Events master page elements

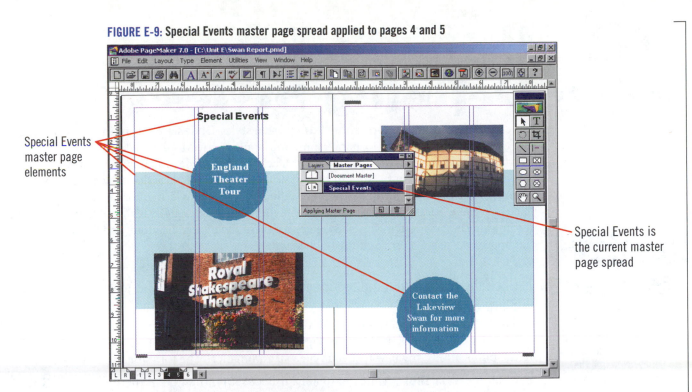

Special Events is the current master page spread

FIGURE E-10: Pages 4 and 5 reflecting change made to the Special Events master pages

Heading is larger, reflecting the change made to the master

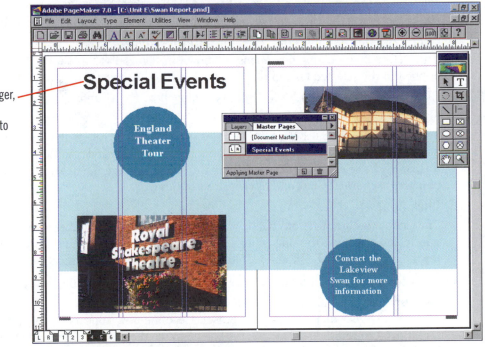

CLUES TO USE

Applying master pages to multiple pages

To apply the same master page to multiple pages in a publication, click the right arrow on the Master Pages palette to open the Master Pages menu, then click Apply. The Apply Master dialog box opens. You use the dialog box to select the master page you want to apply, and then to specify the pages you want to change. If you want to apply the master page to a select number of pages, click the Page Range option button and then type the page numbers in the Page range text box. Separate nonconsecutive page numbers with a comma (3, 5, 7), or enter the page numbers of the first and last page in a series separated by a hyphen (3-7). You can also select the Set left and right pages separately check box to apply different master pages to the left and right pages. When you have completed your selections, click Apply.

Using and Defining Styles

You can save a lot of time formatting text by using styles. **Styles** are sets of format settings that you name, save, and apply to paragraphs. You apply a style to a paragraph using the Styles palette. All new publications include PageMaker's default styles for body text, headings, sub-heads, captions and indents. You can also create or define your own styles using the Define Styles command on the Type menu. After you define styles, the style names appear on the Styles palette. Sara has already created styles for the headlines, body text, and table of contents headings in the newsletter. Now she creates styles for the special headline and for the play titles that appear on pages 4 and 5 of the publication.

Steps

QuickTip

The Styles palette is a floating palette. You can move it by dragging its title bar or resize it by dragging one of its borders. Enlarge the Styles palette to see the complete list of styles in the publication.

1. Click the **page 4 and 5 page icon**, click **Window** on the menu bar, then click **Show Styles**
   The Styles palette opens. It lists both the PageMaker default styles and the styles Sara created in alphabetical order, as shown in Figure E-11. The highlighted style is the default style for the publication. Any new text you type will automatically be formatted in this style.

2. Click the **Text tool** in the toolbox if necessary, then click the headline **Sixteenth Season of Shakespeare**
   [No Style] is selected in the Styles palette, indicating that this headline does not have a style applied to it. You can click any paragraph with the Text tool to determine the style applied to it.

3. Click **Type** on the menu bar, then click **Define Styles**
   The Define Styles dialog box opens, as shown in Figure E-12. It shows the format settings applied to the selected text, in this case the headline "Sixteenth Season of Shakespeare."

QuickTip

You use the Next style list box in the Style Options dialog box to select the style to apply to the next paragraph in the story when the style you are creating is applied.

4. Click **New** to open the Style Options dialog box, then type **Season Headline** in the Name text box
   See Figure E-13. You use the Style Options dialog box to create a new style that is based on an existing style. "Season Headline" is the name of the new style, and it will be based on the format of the selected text, the headline. You can customize the new style by modifying the paragraph, character, tab, and hyphenation settings.

5. Click **Char**
   The Character Specifications dialog box opens. It shows the character format settings for the selected text. You use this dialog box to specify the character format settings you want to use for the new style, such as the font, font size, color, and other specifications.

6. Click the **Bold check box**, click **OK** to close the Character Specifications dialog box, click **OK** to close the Style Options dialog box, then click **OK**
   The Define Styles dialog box closes. Season Headline now appears in the Styles palette. You might need to scroll down your Styles palette to see the new style added to the list. You will later apply the new style to the headline.

7. Select the headline **As You Like It**, click **Type** on the menu bar, click **Define Styles**, click **New**, then type **Play Title** in the Name text box in the Style Options dialog box
   Creating a style for the play titles will make it easy to format this spread in future issues of the newsletter. You decide to increase the font size of the play titles so they stand out more.

8. Click **Char**, click the **Size list arrow** in the Character Specifications dialog box, click **30**, click **OK** three times to close all the dialog boxes, then save your changes
   The new style Play Title is now listed in the Styles palette.

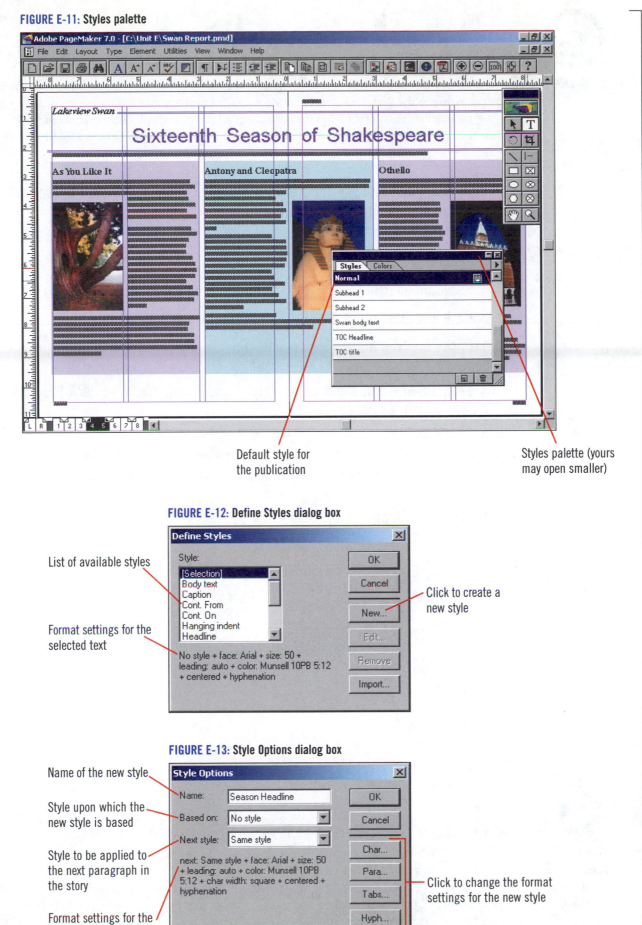

Default style for
the publication

Styles palette (yours
may open smaller)

FIGURE E-12: Define Styles dialog box

List of available styles

Format settings for the
selected text

No style + face: Arial + size: 50 +
leading: auto + color: Munsell 10PB 5:12
+ centered + hyphenation

Click to create a
new style

FIGURE E-13: Style Options dialog box

Name of the new style

Style upon which the
new style is based

Style to be applied to
the next paragraph in
the story

Format settings for the
new style

next: Same style + face: Arial + size: 50
+ leading: auto + color: Munsell 10PB
5:12 + char width: square + centered +
hyphenation

Click to change the format
settings for the new style

PageMaker 7.0

Applying Styles

After you define a style, you need to apply it to text in order for the style to take effect. You apply a style by placing the insertion point in the paragraph you want to format, and then clicking the style name in the Styles palette. The style is applied to the entire paragraph. If you want to apply a style to more than one paragraph, you select all the paragraphs before clicking the style name in the Styles palette. Sara applies the new Play Title and Season Headline styles to the headlines on pages 4 and 5.

Steps 123 4

1. Click the **Text tool** T in the toolbox, if necessary, then click anywhere in the headline **Sixteenth Season of Shakespeare**
   Notice that [No style] is selected on the Styles palette.

2. Click **Season Headline** on the Styles palette, scrolling down if necessary
   The headline text changes to bold to match the specifications you set in the Character Specifications dialog box when you defined this style. See Figure E-14.

3. Click anywhere in the heading **As You Like It**

4. Click **Play Title** in the Styles palette
   The font increases to 30 points to match the Play Title style you defined.

5. Click anywhere in the heading **Antony and Cleopatra**, then click **Play Title** in the Styles palette
   The font size increases to match the Play Title style you defined.

6. Click anywhere in the heading **Othello**, then click **Play Title** in the Styles palette
   All the headings on pages 2 and 3 now have styles applied to them. Compare your screen to Figure E-15.

7. Save your changes to the publication

Formatting text after applying a style

Once you have applied a style to text, you can make formatting changes to the text using the commands on the Type menu. Any changes you make to text to which a style has been applied affect only the selected text and not the style itself. When you make formatting changes to text that has a style applied to it, a plus sign (+) appears next to the name of the style on the Styles palette, indicating that additional formatting changes were made to the text after the style was applied.

Heading is now bold, reflecting the change made to the style

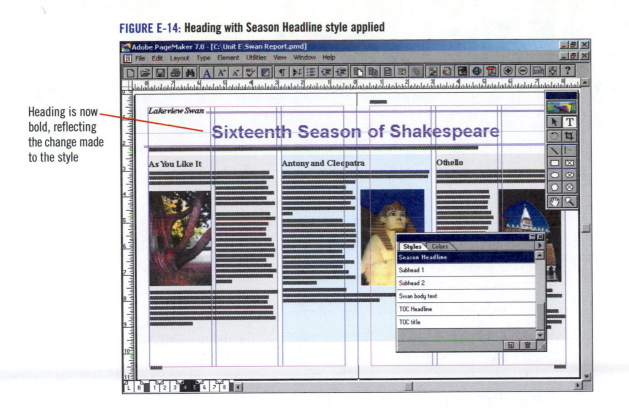

Font size is increased when the Play Title style is applied

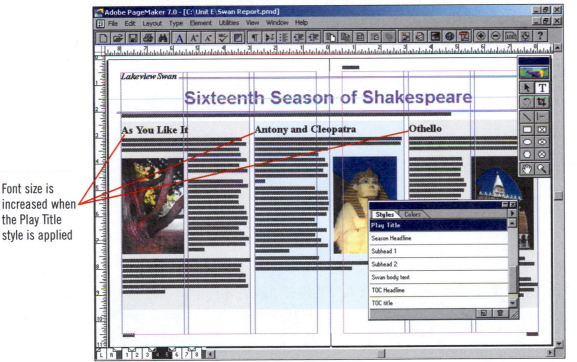

PageMaker 7.0

Editing Styles

After you define a style, you can modify it at any time using the Define Styles and Style Options dialog boxes. Any changes you make to a style are immediately reflected in all text to which the style has been applied throughout the publication. This is one reason why using styles is an efficient way to format text. ➜ Sara decides to modify the Play Title style she created to make the titles look more attractive on the page. She redefines the style to change the font color to cyan and the alignment to center.

Steps

1. Click **Type** on the menu bar, then click **Define Styles**
   The Define Styles dialog box opens.

2. Scroll down the Style list in the Define Styles dialog box, click **Play Title**, then click **Edit**
   The Style Options dialog box opens.

3. Click **Char** in the Style Options dialog box
   The Character Specifications dialog box opens.

4. Click the **Color list arrow** in the Character Specifications dialog box, click **Cyan**, then click **OK**
   The Character Specifications dialog box closes, and you return to the Style Options dialog box.

5. Click **Para** in the Style Options dialog box
   The Paragraph Specifications dialog box opens, as shown in Figure E-16. You use this dialog box to specify paragraph format settings, such as indents, alignment, and line spacing.

6. Click the **Alignment list arrow** in the Paragraph Specifications dialog box, click **Center**, then click **OK** to close each of the three dialog boxes
   The three play title headings now appear centered and in a shade of blue (cyan), reflecting the modifications you made to the style. Compare your screen with Figure E-17.

7. Close the Styles palette, then save your changes to the publication

Importing styles from another PageMaker publication

Sometimes you might want to use the styles you created in one publication in a different publication. To copy styles from another publication to the current publication, click Type on the menu bar, click Define Styles, and then click Import. The Import styles dialog box opens. Select the filename of the publication with the styles you want to use, then click Open. *(Macintosh Users: Click OK.)* Note that if the styles you are importing have names identical to the styles in the current publication, a dialog box opens asking if you want to overwrite the styles in the current publication with the new styles. Click OK to overwrite the styles; click Cancel if you don't want to overwrite them. Imported styles appear in the Styles palette of the current publication.

FIGURE E-16: Paragraph Specifications dialog box

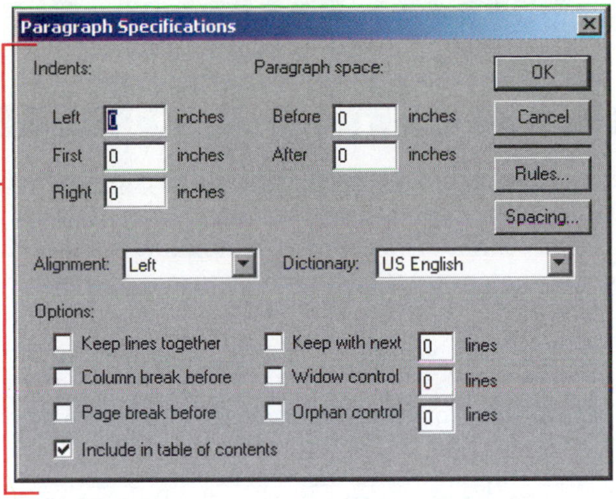

Paragraph format settings for the Play Title style

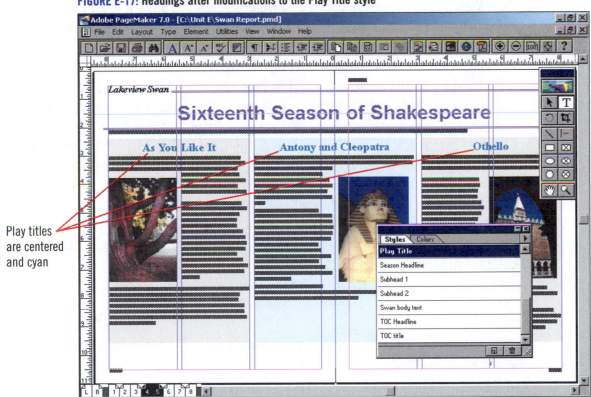

FIGURE E-17: Headings after modifications to the Play Title style

Play titles are centered and cyan

Adding Jump Lines and Balancing Columns

PageMaker includes many automated tools, called **plug-ins**, to help you improve the readability and appearance of your publications. For instance, you can add a jump line to a story that starts on one page and continues on another. A **jump line** is a short line of text that tells the reader a story is continued on or continued from a different page. You can also **balance** the columns in a story to make the text blocks in each column of the story the same length across a page or facing pages. The balance columns and add jump lines features are two of the 18 different PageMaker plug-ins. Sara adds jump lines to the article that begins on page 1 and continues on page 8. She also balances the text blocks in the Bard article on page 8.

Steps

QuickTip

PageMaker cut the last line from the article text block to make room for the jump line. The cut text is moved to the text block on page 8 where the article continues.

1. Click the **page 1 page icon** , click the **Pointer tool** in the toolbox, then click the **The Bard is Alive... text block** to select it

2. Click **View** on the menu bar, click **Actual Size**, click **Utilities** on the menu bar, point to **Plug-ins**, click **Add cont'd line**, click the **Bottom of textblock option button** in the Continuation notice dialog box, then click **OK**
   The text "Continued on page 8" appears in a new text block below the article text block, as shown in Figure E-18.

3. Click **View** on the menu bar, click **Fit in Window**, click the **page 8 page icon** , click , click the **text block** in the first column under the Bard headline, click **View** on the menu bar, then click **Actual Size**
   The Bard article on page 8 is magnified on your screen.

4. Click **Utilities** on the menu bar, point to **Plug-ins**, click **Add cont'd line**, verify that the **Top of textblock option button** is selected in the dialog box, then click **OK**
   The jump line "Continued from page 1" appears at the top of the first column.

5. Click the **text block** in the first column of the Bard article, press and hold **[Shift]**, click the **text block** in the second column of the Bard article, then release **[Shift]**
   The text blocks in both columns of the article are selected.

6. Click **Utilities** on the menu bar, point to **Plug-ins**, then click **Balance Columns**
   The Balance columns dialog box opens, as shown in Figure E-19.

7. Verify that the **Balance column top icon** is selected, then verify that the **Balance column left icon** is selected
   The settings indicate that the text blocks will align along their top edges, and any leftover text that cannot be divided equally between the two blocks will be placed in the left column.

8. Click **OK**
   The columns are now balanced to be roughly the same length. The text blocks are aligned at the top, with the one extra line of text appearing in the first column.

9. Click the first line of text in the left column to select the "Continued from page 1" text block, then drag the text block up approximately ¼" so that it no longer overlaps the article text
   See Figure E-20.

10. Click **View** on the menu bar, click **Fit in Window**, then save your changes

FIGURE E-18: Jump line added to page 1 story

One line of text was moved to page 8 to make room for the jump line

Jump line

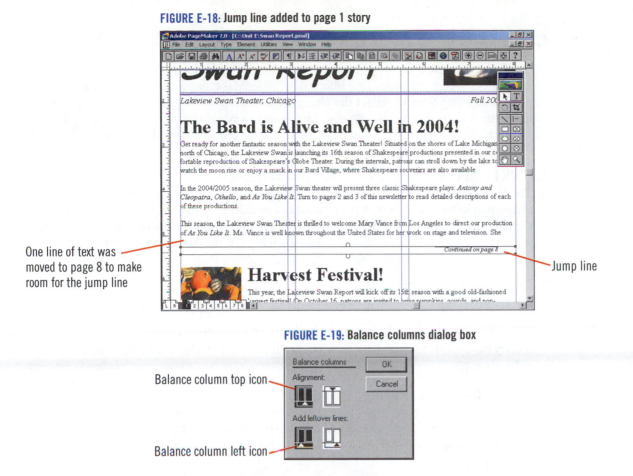

FIGURE E-19: Balance columns dialog box

Balance column top icon

Balance column left icon

FIGURE E-20: Balanced columns with jump line

Repositioned jump line

Columns balanced

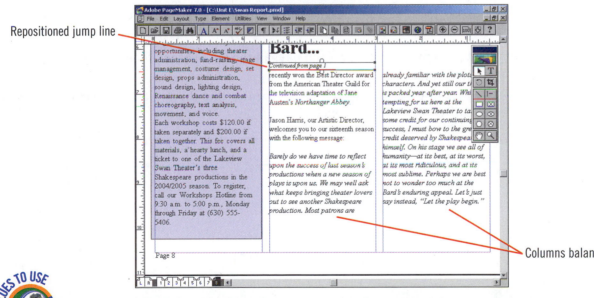

Using PageMaker plug-ins

PageMaker includes a variety of plug-ins that automate repetitive or complex tasks. To see the list of plug-ins installed on your computer, click Utilities on the menu bar, then point to Plug-ins. Plug-ins are of three types: text plug-ins, page layout plug-ins, and color and printing plug-ins. The text plug-ins automate such tasks as creating drop caps and adding bullets and numbers to lists. The plug-ins for page layout make balancing columns, creating running headers and footers, and other design tasks easier. The plug-ins for color and printing simplify such tasks such as defining printer styles, building booklets, and creating keylines.

Rearranging Pages

You can rearrange the order of pages in a publication easily by using the Sort Pages command. When you rearrange the pages in a publication, PageMaker automatically modifies the page numbers and jump lines to reflect the change, and rethreads the text. Reordering pages does not alter the text in the stories. Sara wants to reposition the new pages she inserted (pages 2 and 3) so that they fall after the England Tour Special Events page spread.

Steps

1. **Click Layout on the menu bar, then click Sort Pages**
   The Sort Pages dialog box opens, as shown in Figure E-21. Each page is represented by a small thumbnail in the dialog box. A **thumbnail** is a miniature rendering of the page. You reorder the pages by dragging the thumbnails to a new location. You might have to wait a few seconds while PageMaker creates the thumbnail for each page. If necessary, click and drag the bottom right corner of the dialog box to enlarge it so that all the thumbnails are visible.

2. **Click the page 2 thumbnail**
   Clicking the page 2 thumbnail selects the pages 2 and 3 spread.

3. **Drag the page 2 and 3 thumbnails to the right of page 7**
   A black bar appears to the right of page 7 indicating where the selection will be inserted, as shown in Figure E-22.

4. **Release the mouse button**
   The thumbnails are rearranged in the Sort Pages dialog box. Notice that two page number icons appear beneath each thumbnail affected by the move. The page number on the left is the new page number. The page number on the right is the original page number and is dimmed.

5. **Click OK**
   PageMaker sorts the pages in the publication and the dialog box closes. This process may take several minutes, depending on the speed of your computer.

6. **Click the page icons to view each page in the publication, then save your changes to the publication**
   The pages in the newsletter are reorganized so that the two Special Events spreads fall consecutively on pages 4 through 7.

FIGURE E-21: Sort Pages dialog box

Thumbnails

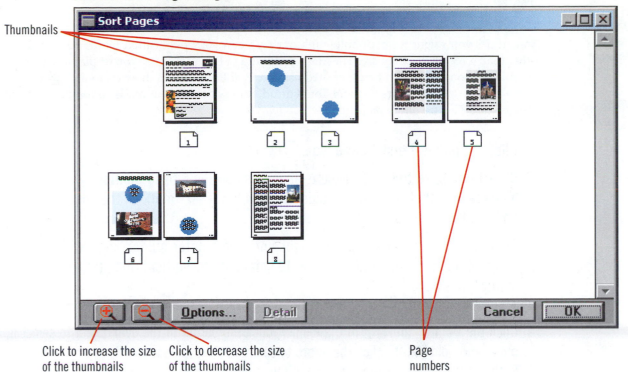

Click to increase the size
of the thumbnails

Click to decrease the size
of the thumbnails

Page
numbers

FIGURE E-22: Pages being moved

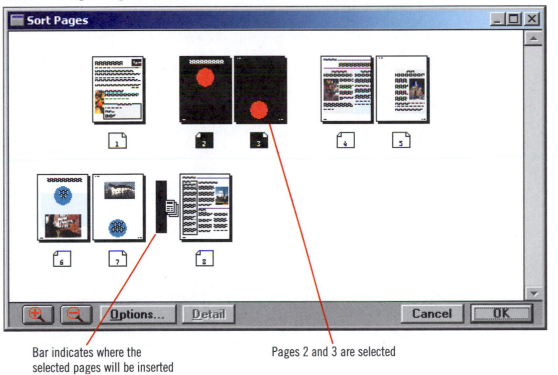

Bar indicates where the
selected pages will be inserted

Pages 2 and 3 are selected

Masking Objects

Sometimes you might want a photograph or graphic in your publication to appear as a shape other than a rectangle or square. The Mask command in PageMaker lets you display a portion of an object through a drawn figure created using one of PageMaker's drawing tools. To complete the Special Events England Tour spread, Sara places an oval mask on top of the Royal Shakespeare Theatre photo on page 4.

1. Click the **pages 4 and 5 page icon** [4|5]

2. Click the **Ellipse tool** [⬭] in the toolbox, position the **Ellipse pointer** over the photo on page 4 so that the pointer guides align with the **−7"** mark on the horizontal ruler and the **6.5"** mark on the vertical ruler

3. Click and drag down and to the right until the pointer guides align with the **−2"** mark on the horizontal ruler and the **10"** mark on the vertical ruler, then release the mouse button
   An oval appears on top of the Royal Shakespeare Theatre photo, as shown in Figure E-23.

4. Click the **Pointer tool** [▸] in the toolbox, click the border of the oval object to select it, press and hold **[Shift]**, click the **photo** to select it, then release **[Shift]**
   Both the oval and the photo are selected. You must select both the mask shape and the object you want to mask before creating the mask.

5. Click **Element** on the menu bar, then click **Mask**
   The photo is masked by the oval object, as shown in Figure E-24. Notice that both the oval object and the photo are still selected.

6. Click **Element** on the menu bar, then click **Group**
   A single set of selection handles appears around both objects, indicating they are a group. You can now move or resize the masked object as a single object.

7. Move the pointer over the middle of the masked object, then drag the masked object down ¼"
   The masked photograph moves as a single unit.

8. Save your changes, then print the publication
   The eight-page newsletter prints.

9. Close the publication, then exit PageMaker

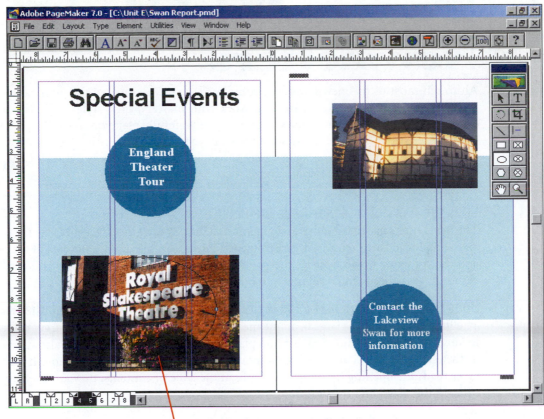

Oval drawn on top of photo

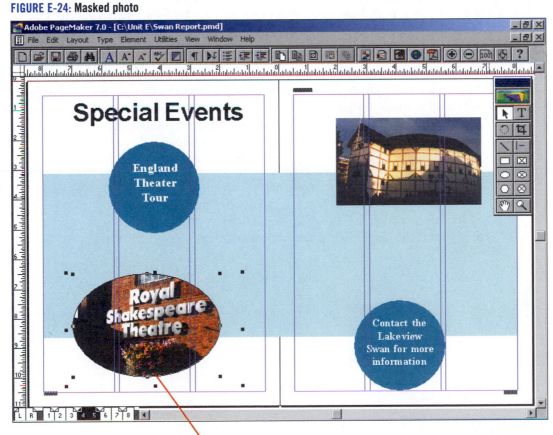

Photo is masked by the drawn oval object

PageMaker 7.0

PageMaker 7.0

Design Workshop: Newsletters

Although most of this newsletter was completed when you opened the publication, this unit provided the information you need to work with master pages, styles, and a multiple-page publication. Before creating a newsletter, you must carefully plan your overall layout to capture your reader's attention and to draw the reader's eye to the main article. Pages 1, 2, 3, 4, 5, and 8 of the *Swan Report* newsletter are shown in Figure E-25. Before showing the newsletter to the client, Sara critiques her design.

Details

► Does the newsletter's masthead stand out?

The newsletter's masthead serves as a graphic that quickly identifies the newsletter for readers. The swan graphic in Sara's masthead is easily identifiable. Sara also included the date of the publication and the company name. Because the newsletter is published only quarterly, Sara decided not to clutter the masthead with a volume number.

► Does the newsletter's first page invite the reader to continue to read the newsletter?

The first page contains a large headline meant to catch the attention of the target reader, namely, theater patrons who enjoy Shakespeare plays. The photo of the pumpkins also draws attention to the Harvest Festival article which announces the season kickoff celebration. If a Shakespeare lover reads the opening headlines and looks at the table of contents, they are likely to be moved to open the newsletter to read more.

► Are the pages too congested or too crowded?

Sara wanted page 1 to be visually appealing and focused on the two primary stories. To accomplish this, she kept the design simple and did not clutter the page with other stories or photos. The result is a strong first page. Page 8 acts as a "catch-all" page for Sara, where she placed the continuation of the page 1 article, and other smaller, less important stories. She separated the articles on page 8 with lines and a shaded box.

► Is the reader's attention drawn to the main article on each page?

Only pages 1 and 8 contain more than one article, so the features on the other pages compete only with graphics for attention. On page 1, the top article is clearly the focus of the page. On page 8, the article about student workshops is understood to be the most important because it is at the top left of the page, and is shaded for emphasis.

► Was each spread designed effectively?

Sara placed a large headline across pages 2 and 3 to unify this spread. The large headline also creates a feeling of excitement, meant to draw in the reader. Sara used colored boxes to separate each of the play descriptions and placed photos appropriate for each play within each of the colored boxes. The photos help create a mood to interest readers in attending the plays.

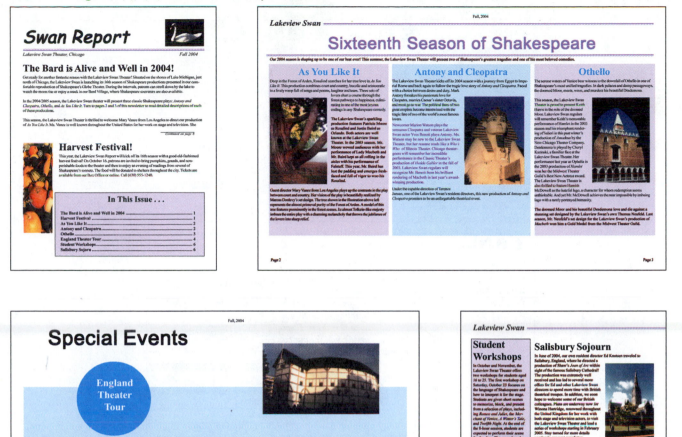

PageMaker 7.0

Practice

► Concepts Review

Label each element of the program window shown in Figure E-26.

FIGURE E-26

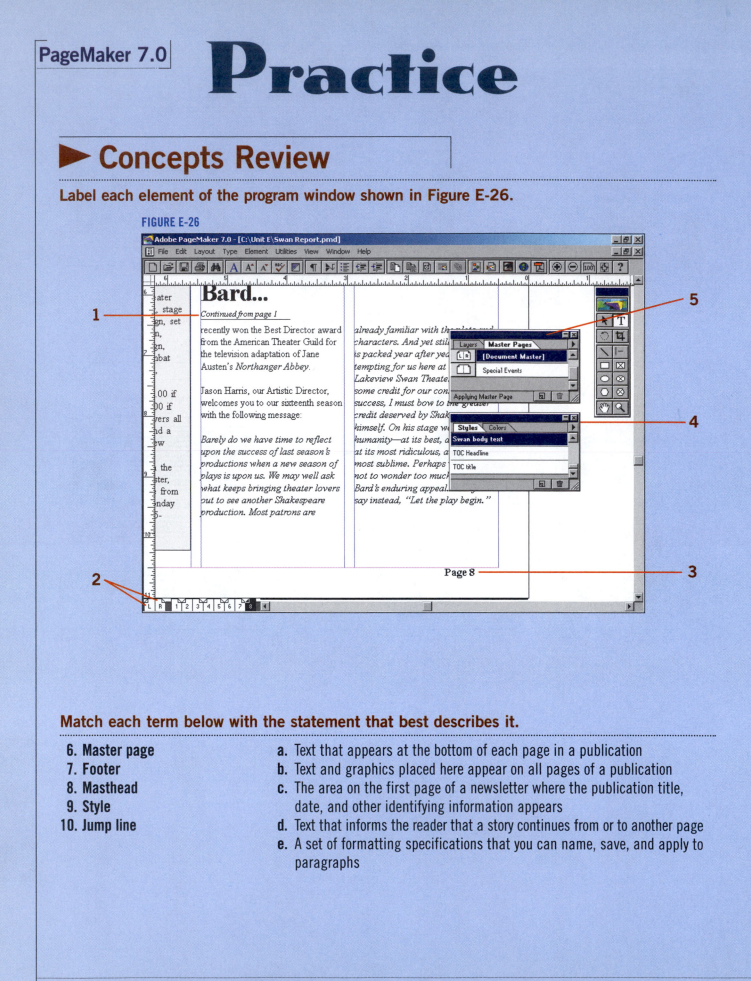

Match each term below with the statement that best describes it.

6. Master page
7. Footer
8. Masthead
9. Style
10. Jump line

a. Text that appears at the bottom of each page in a publication
b. Text and graphics placed here appear on all pages of a publication
c. The area on the first page of a newsletter where the publication title, date, and other identifying information appears
d. Text that informs the reader that a story continues from or to another page
e. A set of formatting specifications that you can name, save, and apply to paragraphs

11. **When you place stories on a page, how should you place them in order of importance?**
    a. Top left to bottom right
    b. Top left to bottom left
    c. Top right to bottom left
    d. Top right to bottom right

12. **Which of the following is NOT true about master pages?**
    a. You can use them to place page numbers.
    b. You can only have one master page or page spread in a publication.
    c. You can hide master page elements on certain pages if you wish.
    d. You can add layout guides to them.

13. **Which of the following is NOT true about styles?**
    a. You can create and name your own styles.
    b. Once you create a style, you must apply it to take effect.
    c. PageMaker comes with built-in styles for every new publication you create.
    d. When you modify a style, you must reapply it to every item formatted with that style in the publication.

14. **You can use the mask command to:**
    a. Inform a reader that an article continues on another page of the publication.
    b. Make a photograph appear in the shape of a circle.
    c. Group two objects together so that they can be moved or resized as a single object.
    d. Hide an object so that it cannot be seen.

15. **Which of the following key combinations do you use to add page numbers to a master page?**
    a. [Ctrl][Shift][1]
    b. [Ctrl][Shift][2]
    c. [Ctrl][Shift][3]
    d. [Ctrl][Shift][4]

► Skills Review

1. **Use master pages.**
    a. Start PageMaker, open the file PM E-2.pmd from the drive and folder where your Project Files are stored, then save it as **Health Notes**.
    b. Open the master page spread, then zoom in on the upper-right corner of the left master page.
    c. Above the third column of the left master page, drag-place a text block that is approximately ¼ inch tall and spans the width of the column.
    d. Type **Volume 7, Issue 3**, then right-align the text in the text block.
    e. Scroll to display the upper-left corner of the right master page, if necessary, then drag-place a text block above the first column that is approximately ¼ inch tall and spans the width of the column.
    f. Type **Spring 2004**, then left-align the text if necessary.
    g. Scroll to display the lower-left corner of the left master page, then drag-place a text block below the first column that is approximately ¼ inch high and spans the width of the column.
    h. Type **Page**, press [Spacebar] then insert a page number symbol using the key combination [Ctrl][Shift][3]. *(Macintosh Users: Use the key combination [Command] [Option] [P].)*
    i. Click the Pointer tool, select the Page LM text block, click Edit on the menu bar, then click Copy.
    j. Click Edit on the menu bar, then click Paste.
    k. Drag the copy of the Page LM text block to the right master page, then place it below the third column on the right master page. Notice that the LM symbol changes to an RM symbol. (*Hint*: Change the zoom level if necessary.)

    l. Click the Text tool, click anywhere in the Page RM text, then right-align the text in the text block.

    m. Click the Page 2 and 3 page icon. Notice that the Volume 7, Issue 3, and Spring 2004 headers appear at the top of the pages, and the page numbers appear at the bottom.

    n. Save your changes.

2. Create a new master page.

    a. Open pages 4 and 5.

    b. Open the Master Pages palette. (*Hint*: Use the Show Master Pages command on the Windows menu.)

    c. Click the right arrow in the Master Pages palette, click Save Page as, then save the page 4 and 5 spread as a new master page spread called **Exercise**.

    d. Save your changes.

3. Modify a master page.

    a. Delete the Running text block in the Exercise master page spread.

    b. Delete the three header text blocks containing the text Holistic Health Notes, Volume 7, Issue 3, and Spring 2004.

    c. Delete the image of the runner, then delete the text block in the largest blue rectangle on the right master page.

    d. Open pages 4 and 5.

    e. Delete the following from the left page: the Exercise text block, the blue rectangle at the top of the page, and the blue circle.

    f. Delete the following from the right page: The Key to Good Health text block, and the two blue rectangles.

    g. Save your changes.

4. Apply master pages.

    a. Apply the Exercise master page spread to pages 4 and 5.

    b. Right-click the Master pages icon, then click Exercise. *(Macintosh Users: Press [Command] and click the Master pages icon.)*

    c. Change the font size of the Exercise headline to 48 points.

    d. Open pages 4 and 5 and view the change to the Exercise headline.

    e. Insert a new page spread after pages 2 and 3 that is based on the Exercise master page spread.

    f. Close the Master Pages palette, then save your changes.

5. Use and define styles.

    a. Open pages 2 and 3.

    b. Click the Text tool, if necessary, click anywhere in the Plants Process Nuclear Contamination headline, click Type on the menu bar, then click Define Styles.

    c. In the Define Styles dialog box, click New, then type **Headline 2** in the Name text box.

    d. Make sure the new style is based on No style and the next style is Same style.

    e. Click Char, then change the size to 24 and the type style to bold.

    f. Click OK three times to close the dialog boxes, then save your changes.

6. Apply styles.

    a. Open the Styles palette.

    b. Click anywhere in the Plants Process... headline at the top of page 2, if necessary.

    c. Click Headline 2 in the Styles palette, scrolling down if necessary.

    d. Apply the Headline 2 style to the Organically Grown… headline at the bottom of page 2.

    e. Apply the Headline 2 style to the Non-traditional Health headline at the bottom of page 3.

    f. Save your changes.

7. Edit a style.

    a. Click Type on the menu bar, then click Define Styles.

    b. In the Define Styles dialog box, click Body text in the Style list, click Edit, then click Para.

    c. In the Paragraph Specifications dialog box, change the alignment to Justify.

    d. Click OK twice to return to the Define Styles dialog box.

e. Click Headline 2 in the Style list, click Edit, then click Char.

f. Click the Size list box to select 24, type **26**, then click OK three times to close the dialog boxes. Notice the style changes in the body text and headlines on pages 2 and 3.

g. Close the Styles palette, then save your changes.

8. **Add jump lines and balance columns.**

a. Open page 1, click the Pointer tool, then click anywhere in the third column of paragraph text to select the text block.

b. Click Utilities on the menu bar, point to Plug-ins, then add a continued line to the bottom of the text block. Zoom in to view the jump line.

c. Open page 8, click the Pointer tool, then add a continued line to the top of the paragraph text block in the first column on page 8.

d. Select the paragraph text block, then drag the bottom windowshade handle down so that all the text appears in the text block.

e. Open pages 2 and 3, press and hold [Shift], then select the three text blocks under the Organically Grown Controversy headline.

f. Click Utilities on the menu bar, point to Plug-ins, then balance the selected columns so that the columns are aligned at the top and any leftover lines appear in the left columns.

g. Balance the three text blocks under the Non-traditional Health Research headline.

h. Save your changes.

9. **Rearrange pages.**

a. Click Layout on the menu bar, then click Sort Pages to open the Sort Pages dialog box.

b. Move the thumbnails for pages 4 and 5 so they are positioned after pages 6 and 7.

c. Click OK, open pages 4 and 5 to confirm the change, then save your changes.

10. **Mask objects.**

a. Make sure pages 4 and 5 are open.

b. Click the Ellipse tool in the toolbox.

c. Referring to Figure E-27 for guidance, drag an oval shape over the jogger graphic that is roughly the same size as the jogger.

d. Use the Pointer tool to select both the oval and the jogger image, then use the Mask command to create an oval mask in front of the jogger. Compare your graphic to Figure E-27.

e. Save your changes, print your publication, close the file, then exit PageMaker.

FIGURE E-27

► Independent Challenge 1

As the marketing manager for the health research company BioBuilder, Inc, you decide to create a company newsletter covering health research issues. To meet your budgetary constraints, you decide the newsletter will be printed on the front and back of a letter-size page. For the first issue, the newsletter includes four short articles.

a. Start PageMaker, then create a new single-sided publication with two letter-size pages with .75 inch margins on all four sides.

b. Save the publication with the name **BioBuilder** to the drive and folder where your Project Files are stored.

c. Add column guides to the master page to divide each page into three columns.

d. Add page numbers to the master page that are center-aligned in the footer.

e. Using the Text tool and the line and shape tools, create a masthead at the top of page 1 that contains the name of the newsletter, **BioBuilder**, and the text **Cambridge, MA** and **Winter 2004**.

f. Use element and text formatting to make the masthead interesting and effective.

g. Place the following four stories in the newsletter: PM E-3.doc, PM E-4.doc, PM E-5.doc, and PM E-6.doc, all found in the drive and folder where your Project Files are stored.

h. Add appropriate headlines for each story based on each story's content.

i. Arrange the text boxes so that the layout is compelling and attractive. Add lines, boxes, and shading as necessary to separate the stories in the page layout.

j. Create new styles for the headlines, body text, and secondary headlines, and then apply the styles to the text.

k. Make sure the columns are evenly balanced to give the newsletter a professional appearance. Add jump lines to at least one of the stories.

l. Save and print the publication, close the publication, then exit PageMaker.

► Independent Challenge 2

You have been hired by the manager of a local bookstore to create a newsletter called *BookBuzz* to be sent to all members of the Frequent BookBuyers Club.

a. Sketch a plan for a four-page newsletter that includes at least six articles. Plan to use columns and graphics in your newsletter.

b. Start PageMaker, create a double-sided publication with four letter-size pages, then save it as **BookBuzz** to the drive and folder where your Project Files are stored.

c. Create a master page spread that includes page numbers, a header, and columns.

d. Create an interesting masthead on page 1. Include a fictional bookstore name and address for the masthead. Place the file Book.jpg, found on the drive and folder where your Project Files are stored, somewhere in the masthead and resize it so that it looks good.

e. Hide all the master page items on page 1.

f. Write and place headlines for at least six articles related to buying books in the newsletter. For instance, you could include a review of your favorite book or CD, a story about an author, or a story that highlights upcoming events at the store.

g. Place graphics in the newsletter. Use the file Apple.tif found on the drive and folder where your Project Files are stored, as a graphic placeholder.

h. Place the body text for the stories in the newsletter. Use the text placeholder file Texthold.doc, found on the drive and folder where your Project Files are stored, instead of real text. Delete any unnecessary placeholder text from each story.

i. Separate the stories using lines and/or shading so that the newsletter looks professional and is easy to read.

j. Create styles for headlines and body text.

k. Balance the columns in the newsletter, then add jump lines, if necessary.

l. Save and print your publication, then close the publication and exit PageMaker.

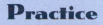# Independent Challenge 3

There are many causes and organizations that help people in the world. In this exercise, you create a two-page newsletter about a cause that is important to you and has some significance in the global community. To create the content for your newsletter, search for information about your cause on the World Wide Web.

a. Open your browser, then use your favorite search engine to search the World Wide Web for information about your cause. For example, you might go to the AltaVista search engine at www.altavista.com, and enter a keyword such as **homelessness**, **pollution**, or **literacy** to perform your search. You can also use Yahoo!, Excite, Infoseek, or another search engine.

b. Sketch your newsletter using the guidelines you learned in this unit. Include a masthead, headlines, and graphics in your sketch.

c. Start PageMaker, then create your newsletter using your sketch as a guide.

d. Create a master page that includes columns and a page number.

e. Create a masthead and the headlines for your stories.

f. Place graphics in your newsletter to illustrate your cause. You can download graphics from the Web, or use your own graphics. Apply a mask to at least one of the graphics, if appropriate.

g. Place the body text for your stories. Type the text in PageMaker or a word processor.

h. Define and apply styles to the different elements in your newsletter. Edit the styles as you wish.

i. Balance all of the columns, and add jump lines, if necessary.

j. Save your newsletter as **My Cause** to the drive and folder where your Project Files are stored, print a copy, close the file, then exit PageMaker.

▶ Visual Workshop

Use PageMaker to create the newsletter shown in Figure E-28. Start with the file PM E-7.pmd, found on the drive and folder where your Project Files are stored, and then place the stories and graphics as shown. The four stories in the newsletter are in the files PM E-8.doc, PM E-9.doc, PM E-10.doc, and PM E-11.doc, and the graphic in the masthead and in the header on the master page (shown on page 2) is the file Apple.tif. Define and apply the following styles in your newsletter: Headline 1 (for primary headlines), Headline 2 (for secondary headlines), and Health Body Text (for the body text). Hide all master page elements on the first page. Save the publication as **Health Connection**, and then print a copy.

FIGURE E-28

Health Connection

Sedona, Arizona   Summer 2004

Good Health Starts at Home

You may eat well, exercise regularly, and meditate twice a day. Perhaps you have a regular exercise regime that includes aerobics, lifting weights, and swimming. You might even subsist entirely on a gluten-free diet and drink carrot juice three times a day. All of these are great habits that you might think ensure your long-term health. However, a recent study shows that *where* you live may be just as important to your overall health as how you live.

The National Center for Health Statistics devised health indicators for 33 metropolitan areas. California, not unexpectedly, had several first-place rankings for unhealthy living standards. Sacramento was deemed the sickest city of any in the survey, although San Diego residents tallied

Continued on page 2

Alternative Health Victory

CompleteLife National Insurance Company recently launched its newest health insurance product, an alternative healthcare policy called CompleteCare. The plan—the most generous non-traditional policy offered by any private U.S. company—will pay for procedures by company-approved practitioners ranging from acupuncture to massage therapy.

Such non-traditional medicines as homeopathy and Chinese herbal remedies are among the four alternative medicines covered. Hypnotherapy is also covered under the plan for treating such illnesses as Cancer and Parkinson's Disease and for managing pain.

CompleteLife National consulted with many U.S. alternative-health experts in formulating its plan, which is being hailed by the alternative press as "a major breakthrough for consumers. It is expected that this new health insurance product will inspire other health insurance companies to offer similar plans.

In This Issue . . .

 Health Connection   Summer 2004

The Power of Fresh Juice

Studies show that our modern diet is destructive to our immune system. A meat diet is high in toxins. This is because cows and chickens eat food that has toxins in it. When we eat meat, our bodies have to work hard to break down the toxins, taxing our immune and metabolic systems.

Enzymes are crucial in breaking down food in our bodies and cleansing cells of toxins. Enzymes also help process metabolic functions and build up our immune system. Raw fruits and vegetables are loaded with enzymes to aid in the digestion of food, strengthen our immune systems, and cleanse our bodies of toxins.

Fresh fruit and vegetables when eaten raw and whole are nutritious, but they are even more beneficial when juiced. Some of the best nutrients are contained in the fiber of the fruit or vegetable, which just "passes through" the body. Juicing unlocks the nutrients, freeing them from the fiber, so that the nutrients are immediately absorbed into the bloodstream. Numerous books have been written that discuss the benefits of fresh vegetable and fruit juice. Visit our Web site for a listing of recent books that discuss the benefits and provide delicious recipes.

Adding a cup of fresh juice to your diet every day is vital to maintaining good health. Though there are more and more bottled vegetable juices on the market today, most of them lose a lot of their nutrients in the bottling process. It's best to

make your own juice, using fresh produce. There are many excellent juicers on the market today. Visit our Web site at www.healthconnex.com for a listing and reviews.

Staying healthy...

Continued from page 1

more tallied more doctor visits than residents of any other city. Surprisingly, Los Angeles was ranked as the 12 healthiest metro area.

If you want to maximize your chances of living a healthy life, move to Atlanta. Residents there reported the fewest health problems in a variety of categories. Kansas City is another healthy choice-workers there had the lowest rate of absenteeism due to sickness.

Run for Good Health

Running is one of the most effective methods of improving your cardiovascular system. Running also reduces body fat and helps you maintain a toned, lean physique. Some runners do it just for the sheer joy of being outside. Many runners claim that running boosts their self-esteem.

Of course, it's important to be patient to see these results. After all, every running stride that you take forces your body to absorb a huge impact, sometimes three times your body weight. You have to start slow, with reasonable goals, then gradually work up to greater distances and speeds. Many new runners make the mistake of running too fast and too soon. Doing this can cause aches and pains that make new runners give up before they have even started. Don't make this mistake. Start slowly and be patient. Over time you will see results and feel great!start gradually and be patient. ilt will all pay off in the end.

Working
with Graphics

Objectives

- ► **Plan an advertisement**
- ► **Change line weights and styles**
- ► **Crop a graphic**
- ► **Rotate an object**
- ► **Stack objects**
- ► **Create a shadow box**
- ► **Wrap text around a graphic**
- ► **Create a custom text wrap**
- ► **Create a polygon**
- ► **Use frames**
- ► **Use the Picture palette**
- ► **Design Workshop: Advertisements**

Graphics can add visual interest to a text-heavy publication, and can also help communicate a message or illustrate a point. PageMaker provides many tools to help you work with graphics. In this unit, you learn to crop and rotate graphics, manipulate the stacking order of objects, wrap text around graphics, draw shapes, and insert images from the Picture palette. The Atelier Gallery has hired Sara Norton to create a series of magazine ads announcing new exhibitions. Sara uses the graphic formatting features of PageMaker to enhance the final appearance of the ad.

Planning an Advertisement

Advertisements can have many different purposes. For example, some ads try to elicit an immediate response from a reader, while other ads aim to build awareness of a specific product or company. It is important that you determine the ultimate goal of your advertisement before you create it. Working with the gallery, Sara plans the first ad, as shown in Figure F-1. Sara decides to use pictures of the artist's work as the ad's foundation and to include a small amount of text in the ad. The advertisement will be in color because the ad will be placed in a magazine. Sara knows it's important to design the first ad so that it can be adapted for future ads she creates for the gallery.

Details

Keep the following guidelines in mind when planning an advertisement:

► **Build the ad around strong visual elements**

Large headlines or eye-catching images attract readers to an ad. Once an ad captures the reader's attention, it should then draw their interest to other aspects of the ad, such as more detailed information or a way to respond. Sara thinks her ad will have more impact if it shows the artist's work. She decides to place pictures of two of the artist's paintings in the top half of the ad. She also plans to make the artist's name stand out by using a large font size and bold formatting.

► **Organize the ad's layout**

Because print advertising is expensive, it might be tempting to put as much information as possible into an advertisement to justify its cost. However, too much information or a poor design confuses the reader. An effective ad has a simple message and is designed to be read from top to bottom, with the compelling headline or image at the top and specific details at the bottom. Sara will place graphics of the artist's work at the top of the page to draw the reader's attention. She will place information about the exhibit in a paragraph in the middle, and the art gallery contact information at the bottom. Sara plans to set the page size for the ad to be 5.25" wide and 7" tall, per the magazine's specifications for a quarter-page ad.

► **Visually separate the ad from other items on the page where it will appear**

With so much competing information in magazines, it is important to make your ad stand out on the page. Adding a border or white space around an ad visually separates it from competing ads and stories. Sara plans to use a curved border around her ad to help punctuate it on the page.

Encourage a quick response

► Similar to a flyer, an ad's main goal is to elicit a response from the reader. The reader should be given a clear course of action, such as a phone number to call for more information. In some advertisements, the price of the product or service is the motivating factor. Sara includes a sunburst that announces the opening date of the exhibit in her ad. She places the name of the artist in bold at the bottom of the ad, with the name and address of the Atelier Gallery below.

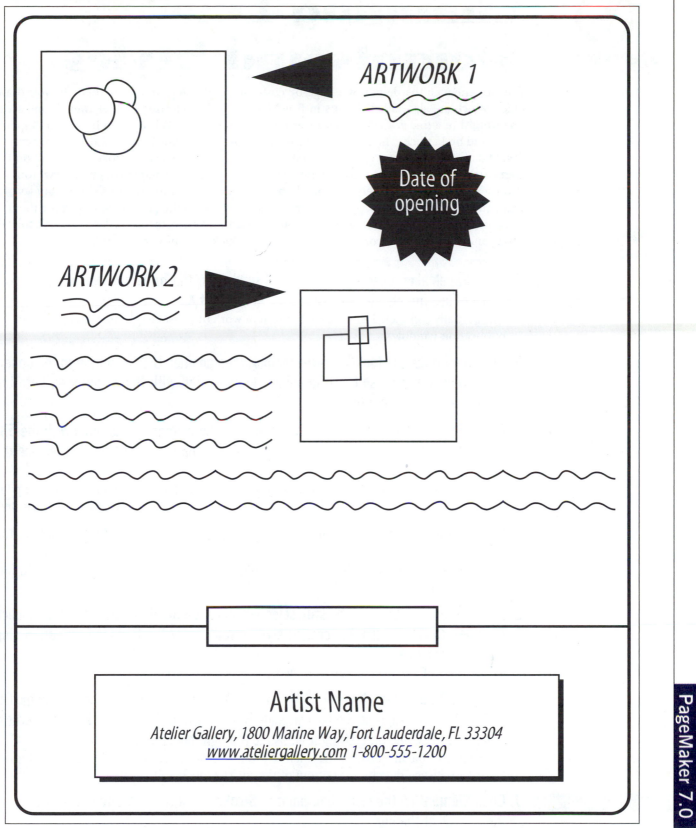

Changing Line Weights and Styles

You can enhance the design of a page by customizing the appearance of the lines you draw. Lines, which are also called **strokes** in PageMaker, are characterized by their weight and style. The **weight** of a line is its thickness, measured in points. A **point** is ½ of an inch, so a 72-point line would be 1" thick. The **style** of a line is its design, such as single, double, dashed, or reverse. PageMaker's default line style is a 1-point single line. You can use the Stroke command on the Element menu to change the line weight or line style of the lines and shapes you draw. You can also use the Rounded Corners command on the Element menu to convert the right angles of a shape into rounded corners. Sara has already placed the graphics and text for the first ad on the page. She now draws a border around the ad, and formats the border to give it a thicker appearance and rounded corners. She also draws a thick line above the artist's name.

Steps 1234

1. Start PageMaker, open the file **PM F-1.pmd** from the drive and folder where your Project Files are stored, then save it as **Art Exhibit Ad**

   The partially completed ad for an exhibition of work by artist Gregg Simpson appears in the publication window.

2. Click the **Rectangle tool** ▢ in the toolbox, then position the ✛ pointer in the upper-left corner of the ad so that the pointer guides align with the ⅛" mark on both the horizontal and vertical rulers

3. Drag to the lower-right corner of the ad so that the pointer guides align with the **5⅛"** mark on the horizontal ruler and the **6⅛"** mark on the vertical ruler, then release the mouse button

   A rectangle with a 1-point, single black line border is placed just inside the edges of the publication page. The selection handles around the border of the rectangle indicate it is selected.

4. Click **Element** on the menu bar, point to **Stroke**, then click the **2pt** single line on the Stroke menu

   The thickness of the stroke increases to 2 points. The Stroke menu includes standard line weights and styles.

5. Make sure the rectangle is still selected, click **Element** on the menu bar, click **Rounded Corners**, click the second style in row two of the Rounded Corners dialog box, then click **OK**

   The corners of the rectangle are rounded, as shown in Figure F-2.

6. Click the **Constrained-line tool** ⊢ in the toolbox, position the ✛ pointer on the left border of the rectangle so the pointer guide is aligned with the **5½"** mark on the vertical ruler, then click and drag straight across to the right border of the rectangle

   A new horizontal line dissects the small yellow rectangle above the artist's name, and creates a border between the top and bottom of the ad. The line is still selected.

QuickTip

To create a white line on a dark background, select the line, click Element on the menu bar, point to Stroke, then click Reverse.

7. Click **Element** on the menu bar, point to **Stroke**, click the **2pt** single line in the list, then deselect the line

   The weight of the stroke increases to 2 points, as shown in Figure F-3.

8. Click **File** on the menu bar, then click **Save** to save your changes to the publication

FIGURE F-2: 2-point border with rounded corners

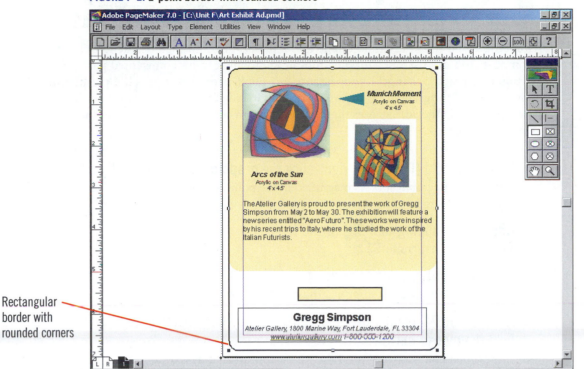

Rectangular border with rounded corners

FIGURE F-3: Ad with border and line added

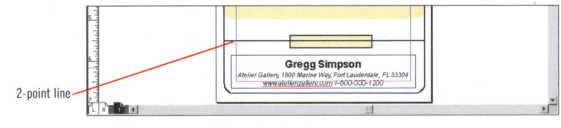

2-point line

CLUES TO USE

Creating custom lines

In addition to the standard line weights and styles available on the Stroke menu, PageMaker allows you to create custom lines, with weights between 0 and 800 points in thickness. To create a custom line, select the line or object you want to format, click Element on the menu bar, point to Stroke, then click Custom on the Stroke menu to open the Custom Stroke dialog box, shown in Figure F-4. In the dialog box, select a line style from the Stroke style list box, and then enter a point size in the Stroke weight text box. Make sure the Transparent background check box is checked if you want the blank spaces in a double, triple, dotted, or dashed line to be transparent rather than opaque. Check the Reverse check box if

you want the line to be white rather than black. When you have finished making your selections, click OK to close the dialog box and apply the custom line format to the selected line or shape.

FIGURE F-4: Custom Stroke dialog box

Custom Stroke	✕
Stroke style:	OK
Stroke weight: 2 points	Cancel
☑ Transparent background	
☐ Reverse	

Cropping a Graphic

Sometimes you might insert a graphic into a publication and then decide to only show a portion of it. You can use the Cropping tool in the toolbox to hide unwanted parts of a graphic. Cropping a graphic changes its appearance in a publication, but it does not permanently delete any portion of the graphic. ◄▬▬ Sara decides to hide the white space around the "Arcs of the Sun" painting in the ad. She uses the Cropping tool to cut the white space and then enlarges the cropped graphic.

Steps

This replaces Step 1.
1. Press and hold [Command] [Option], then click the graphic on the right side of the page

1. Press and hold **[Ctrl]**, then right-click the **graphic** on the right side of the page
The top of the publication is magnified in the publication window, with the Arcs of the Sun painting centered on the screen.

2. Click the **Cropping tool** ⊞ in the toolbox
The pointer changes to ⊄.

3. Click the **right graphic** to select it
Square selection handles appear around the Arcs of the Sun graphic.

4. Position the ⊄ pointer over the upper-right corner selection handle, then press and hold the **mouse button**
The pointer changes to ⤢ and the image appears in grayscale and is surrounded by a border, as shown in Figure F-5.

5. Drag ⤢ down and to the left to the upper-right corner of the painting, then release the mouse button
As you drag, the white border is removed from the top and right sides of the graphic.

6. Position ⤢ over the lower-left corner selection handle, then drag up and to the right to the lower-left corner of the painting
The white edge is cropped from the left and bottom edges of the graphic.

7. Click the **Pointer tool** ▶ in the toolbox, click the cropped graphic to select it, then drag the upper-right selection handle up and to the right approximately ⅛"
The image remains cropped as you enlarge it. The enlarged image contains no white space around it. Compare your screen to Figure F-6.

8. Save your changes to the publication

FIGURE F-5: Cropping a graphic

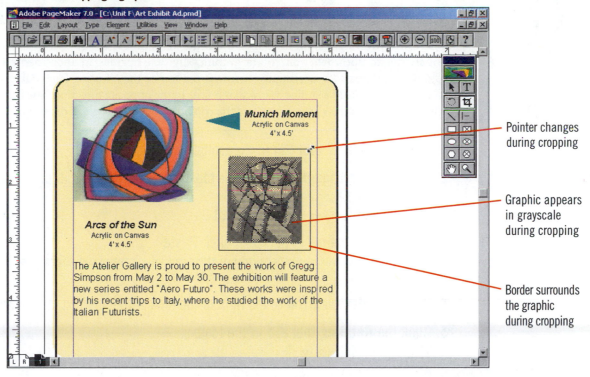

Pointer changes during cropping

Graphic appears in grayscale during cropping

Border surrounds the graphic during cropping

FIGURE F-6: Cropped and resized graphic

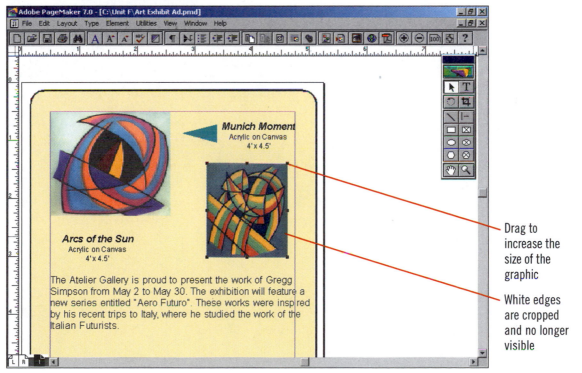

Drag to increase the size of the graphic

White edges are cropped and no longer visible

Rotating an Object

Sometimes you might want to change the angle of an object in your publication. The Rotating tool in the toolbox lets you rotate graphics by 360 degrees in increments of .01 degrees. Sara created the triangular arrow at the top of the ad using PageMaker's drawing tools. Now she wants to add a similar arrow that points in the opposite direction. She decides to copy and paste the existing arrow and then rotate the copied arrow to change its direction.

Steps

1. Click the **Pointer tool** in the toolbox if necessary

2. Click the **blue triangle arrow** at the top of the page to select it, click **Edit** on the menu bar, then click **Copy**
   The graphic is copied to the Clipboard.

3. Click **Edit** on the menu bar, then click **Paste**
   A copy of the arrow appears on top of the original arrow, offset slightly to the bottom right, and is selected.

4. Drag the **selected arrow** to the right of the Arcs of the Sun text, as shown in Figure F-7

5. Click the **Rotating tool** in the toolbox
   The pointer changes to ✳.

6. Position ✳ at the center of the selected arrow, click and drag the pointer to the arrow's **left-middle selection handle**, then release the mouse button
   The direction of the arrow is reversed, as shown in Figure F-8. As you drag with the ✳ pointer, a rotation lever follows the pointer from the starting point to the ending point to indicate the angle of rotation. You can rotate any line, text block, or other object using this method.

7. Save your changes to the publication

FIGURE F-7: Copy of the arrow moved to a new location

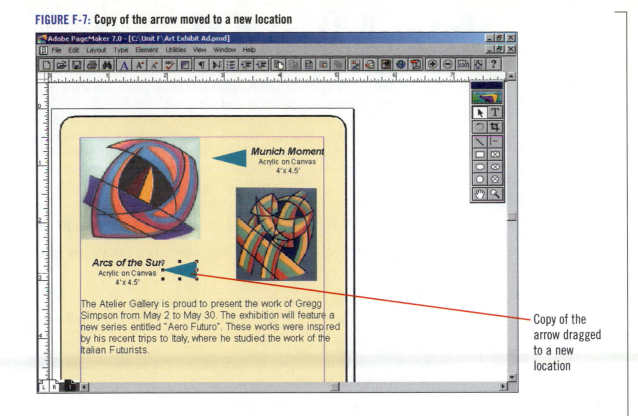

Copy of the arrow dragged to a new location

FIGURE F-8: Arrow rotated to the opposite direction

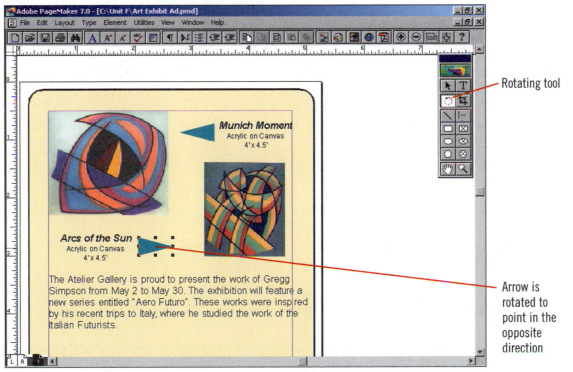

Rotating tool

Arrow is rotated to point in the opposite direction

Stacking Objects

You can layer graphics on top of each other in a publication to create interesting visual effects. Placing objects on top of other objects is called **stacking**. When you stack objects, they appear on the page in the order in which you placed them, with the first-placed object at the bottom (the back) of the stack, and the last-placed object on top (the front) of the stack. Figure F-9 shows a shadowed box effect you can create by stacking a white box on top of a black box. You can change the order of stacked objects using the Bring to Front, Bring Forward, Send Backward, and Send to Back commands. Sara wants to rearrange the objects in the ad so that the line she drew at the bottom of the page is underneath the yellow rectangle.

Steps

1. Scroll down so that the bottom half of the ad is visible in the publication window

2. Click the **Pointer tool** in the toolbox, then click the **yellow box** above the text "Gregg Simpson" to select it

3. Click **Element** on the menu bar, then point to **Arrange**
   The Arrange menu opens. Table F-1 describes the commands on the Arrange menu.

4. Click **Bring to Front**
   The stacking order of the line and the rectangle are changed so that the box is in front of the line, as shown in Figure F-10.

5. Save your changes to the publication

TABLE F-1: Commands on the Arrange menu

command	use to
Bring to Front	Move the selected object to the front of the stack of objects
Bring Forward	Move the selected object forward one layer in the stack of objects
Send Backward	Move the selected object back one layer in the stack of objects
Send to Back	Move the selected object to the back of the stack of objects

FIGURE F-9: Two objects stacked to create a shadow box

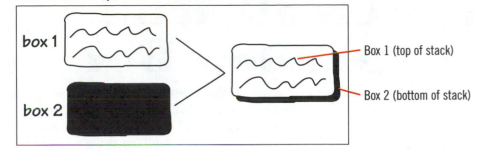

box 1

box 2

Box 1 (top of stack)

Box 2 (bottom of stack)

FIGURE F-10: Stacked objects with rectangle on top of line

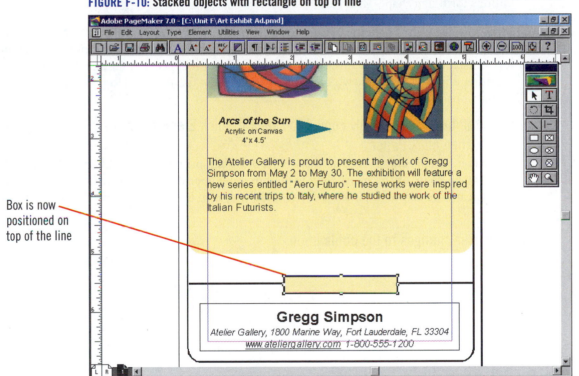

Box is now positioned on top of the line

Creating a Shadow Box

You can use PageMaker's stacking capabilities to create shadow boxes. A **shadow box** is a box with a drop shadow on two sides. To create a shadow box, you draw a box, copy the box, fill the copied box with black and then send it to the back of the stack. Sara creates a shadow box to make the contact information stand out at the bottom of the advertisement.

Steps 1 2 3 4

1. Click the **box** that surrounds the text "Gregg Simpson" and the address to select it, click **Edit** on the menu bar, then click **Copy**
   The box is copied to the Clipboard.

2. Click **Edit** on the menu bar, then click **Paste**
   A copy of the box appears on the page slightly below and to the right of the original box. The copy of the box is selected.

3. Click **Element** on the menu bar, point to **Fill**, then click **Solid**
   The box now appears in solid black, as shown in Figure F-11. The Fill menu also contains options for filling shapes with patterns.

4. Click **Element** on the menu bar, point to **Arrange**, then click **Send to Back**
   It might not seem as though anything changed, because the black box still appears to be on top. In fact, the black box is at the back of the stack, but it appears as though it is in front of the other objects because the white box has a transparent fill. You need to fill the original box with an opaque fill.

5. Click the **box** you originally copied to select it, click **Element** on the menu bar, point to **Fill**, then click **Paper**
   The paper fill appears as white on the screen, but when printed, objects filled with paper fill take on the color of the paper. The white box now appears on top of the black box, but underneath the text block, making it the middle layer in the stack. Compare your screen to Figure F-12.

6. Save your changes to the publication

FIGURE F-11: Copied box with black fill

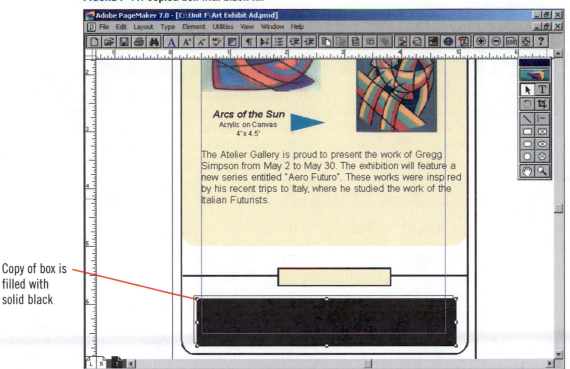

Copy of box is
filled with
solid black

FIGURE F-12: Completed shadow box

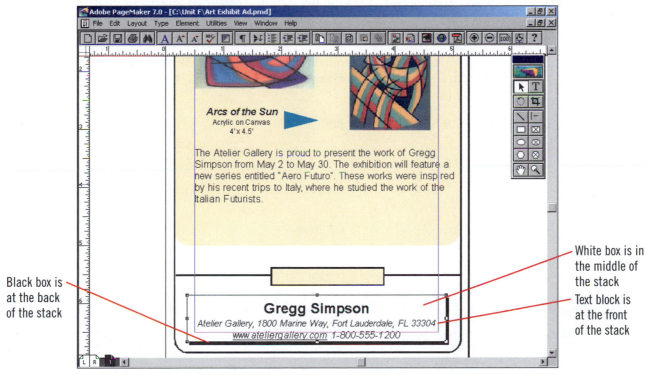

Black box is
at the back
of the stack

Arcs of the Sun
Acrylic on Canvas
4' x 4.5'

The Atelier Gallery is proud to present the work of Gregg
Simpson from May 2 to May 30. The exhibition will feature a
new series entitled "Aero Futuro". These works were inspired
by his recent trips to Italy, where he studied the work of the
Italian Futurists.

Gregg Simpson
Atelier Gallery, 1800 Marine Way, Fort Lauderdale, FL 33304
www.ateliergallery.com 1-800-555-1200

White box is in
the middle of
the stack

Text block is
at the front
of the stack

Wrapping Text Around a Graphic

You can create interesting visual effects by wrapping text around graphics. **Wrapping** means that text flows around an object rather than behind it or through it. You wrap text around a graphic by placing the graphic in a text block and then using the Text Wrap command to set the text wrapping options. Sara decides to create a more dramatic visual appearance by moving the Arcs of the Sun graphic down and wrapping the paragraph text around it.

Steps 1 2 3 4

1. Scroll so that the top half of the ad is visible in the publication window

2. Click the **Arcs of the Sun graphic** (the graphic on the right) to select it

3. Drag the graphic down so that its right edge is aligned with the right column guide and the bottom edge is aligned with the **4"** mark on the vertical ruler
   The graphic is placed on top of the text, with the text flowing behind it.

4. Click **Element** on the menu bar, then click **Text Wrap**
   The Text Wrap dialog box opens as shown in Figure F-13. You use the dialog box to select a wrap option and a text flow option, and to set the distance between the object and the wrapped text. Table F-2 describes the wrap and text flow options, each of which is represented by an icon in the dialog box.

QuickTip
You can wrap text only around graphic objects, not around another text block.

5. Click the **Rectangular wrap option icon** in the top row of the dialog box
   When you click the Rectangular wrap option icon, the Wrap-all-sides text flow icon is automatically selected in the second row of the dialog box. This means that PageMaker will flow the text around all four sides of the graphic. PageMaker sets the **standoff**, or the amount of blank space between the graphic and the wrapped text, to .167".

6. Click **OK**
   The paragraph text wraps around the graphic, as shown in Figure F-14. The dotted line borders that surround the edge of the graphic are the **standoff lines**, which indicate the boundaries for the wrapped text.

7. Save your changes to the publication

TABLE F-2: Text Wrap dialog box icons

icon	use to
	Flow text behind or in front of a graphic object, so that text does not wrap around the object
	Wrap text around the rectangular shape of a graphic object
	Wrap text around the irregular shape of a graphic object
	Flow the wrapped text to the top of the graphic object, and then continue the text at the top of the next column or page
	Flow the wrapped text to the top of the graphic object, and then continue the text at the bottom of the graphic object
	Flow the wrapped text around all four sides of the graphic object

FIGURE F-13: Text Wrap dialog box

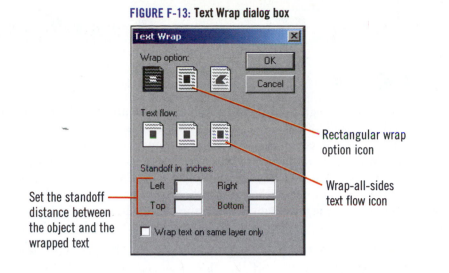

Set the standoff
distance between
the object and the
wrapped text

Rectangular wrap
option icon

Wrap-all-sides
text flow icon

FIGURE F-14: Text wrapped around graphic

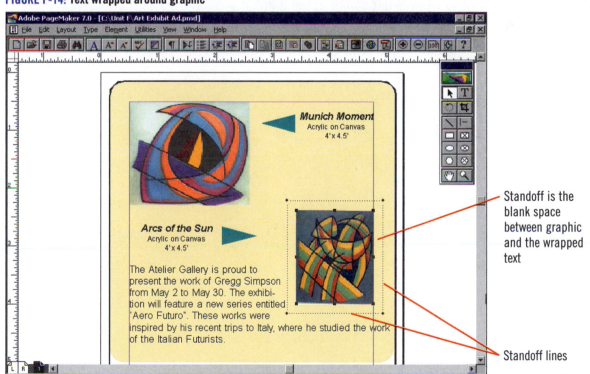

Standoff is the
blank space
between graphic
and the wrapped
text

Standoff lines

Creating a Custom Text Wrap

The standoff for a graphic object with text wrapped around it is indicated on the screen by the nonprinting standoff lines that appear when the object is selected. If you want to customize the standoff for an object by changing its measurement or shape, you can drag a definition point. **Definition points** are the diamond-shaped handles that appear at the corners of the standoff lines when a rectangular text wrapping style is applied to a graphic. You can add more definition points to a graphic by clicking anywhere on a standoff line. ✎═══ Sara adjusts the standoff lines so that the text wraps closer to the Arcs of the Sun graphic.

Steps 123 4

1. Select the **Arcs of the Sun graphic** if necessary, then click the **left standoff line** at the **3½"** mark on the vertical ruler, as shown in Figure F-15
   A new definition point appears on the standoff line at the point where you clicked.

QuickTip

To prevent text from being redrawn each time you adjust a standoff line, press and hold [Spacebar] as you create and move definition points.

2. Drag the new definition point right to the left edge of the graphic
   As you drag, the left standoff line bends to touch the left edge of the graphic, as shown in Figure F-16. Depending on the exact placement of your graphic and definition point, your text may wrap differently than the text in the figure.

3. Drag the **lower-left corner definition point** up and to the right until it meets the lower-left corner of the graphic
   The right side of the paragraph text now wraps closer to the graphic, as shown in Figure F-17.

4. Save your changes to the publication

FIGURE F-15: Adding a definition point to a standoff line

Click here to add a new definition point

Arcs of the Sun
Acrylic on Canvas
4' x 4.5'

The Atelier Gallery is proud to present the work of Gregg Simpson from May 2 to May 30. The exhibition will feature a new series entitled "Aero Futuro". These works were inspired by his recent trips to Italy, where he studied the work of the Italian Futurists.

FIGURE F-16: Dragged definition point

Dragged definition point

Arcs of the Sun
Acrylic on Canvas
4' x 4.5'

The Atelier Gallery is proud to present the work of Gregg Simpson from May 2 to May 30. The exhibition will feature a new series entitled "Aero Futuro". These works were inspired by his recent trips to Italy, where he studied the work of the Italian Futurists.

FIGURE F-17: Finished custom text wrap

Arcs of the Sun
Acrylic on Canvas
4' x 4.5'

The Atelier Gallery is proud to present the work of Gregg Simpson from May 2 to May 30. The exhibition will feature a new series entitled "Aero Futuro". These works were inspired by his recent trips to Italy, where he studied the work of the Italian Futurists.

Text wraps closer to the graphic after the standoff line is adjusted (your text might wrap differently)

Creating a Polygon

Art that shows the outline of an object is known as **line art**. PageMaker includes tools for creating your own line art or shapes. For instance, you can use the Polygon tool in the toolbox to create multisided objects or stars. The shapes you draw with the Polygon tool can have from three to 100 sides. ✎ Sara creates a star-shaped polygon with reverse text, intending it to resemble a stamp. She places it at the top of the ad to announce the opening date of the exhibition.

Steps

1. Scroll up so the top half of the publication is visible on your screen, click the **Polygon tool** ⬡ in the toolbox, then position the **+** pointer so the pointer guides align with the **1½"** mark on the vertical ruler and the **3"** mark on the horizontal ruler

Trouble?

Make sure to release the mouse button before you release [Shift]. This will ensure that the polygon is even on all sides.

2. Press and hold **[Shift]**, drag down and to the right to the **2¼"** mark on the vertical ruler, then release the mouse button
Pressing [Shift] as you drag creates a polygon with sides of equal length, as shown in Figure F-18. The number of sides in your polygon may be greater than six depending on your PageMaker settings.

3. Click **Element** on the menu bar, then click **Polygon Settings**
The Polygon Settings dialog box opens, as shown in Figure F-19.

4. Type **15** in the Number of sides text box, press **[Tab]** twice (*Macintosh Users: Press [Tab] only once*), type **20** in the Star inset text box, press **[Tab]**, then click **OK**
The polygon is changed to a 15-point star.

5. Click **Element** on the menu bar, point to **Fill**, then click **Solid**
The polygon is filled with solid black.

6. Click the **Text tool** ⊤ in the toolbox, click in the upper-left corner of the polygon, then drag down to the lower-right corner of the polygon to create a text block

MacintoshUsers

This replaces Step 7.
7. Click Type on the menu bar, click Character to open the Character Specifications dialog box, click Arial in the Font list, type 10 in the Size text box, click the Bold check box, click the Reverse check box, and then click OK

7. Click the **Character Specs button** Ⓐ on the toolbar to open the Character Specifications dialog box, click the **Font list arrow**, scroll up the Font list, click **Arial**, type **10** in the Size text box, click the **Bold check box**, click the **Reverse check box**, then click **OK**

8. Type **Opens May 2!**
The text appears in Arial, bold reverse type, according to the specifications you set in the Character Specifications dialog box. Notice that the text is left-aligned.

9. Select **Opens May 2!**, click **Type** on the menu bar, point to **Alignment**, click **Align Center**, then click outside the polygon to deselect the text
The text is now center aligned in the polygon and looks good. The finished publication is shown in Figure F-20.

10. Save your changes to the publication, print the publication, then close the file
The publication closes. PageMaker is still running.

FIGURE F-18: Six-sided polygon added to publication

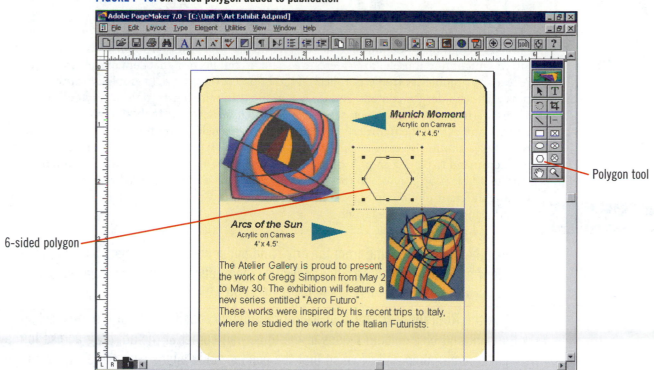

Polygon tool

6-sided polygon

FIGURE F-19: Polygon Settings dialog box

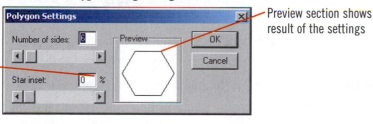

Preview section shows result of the settings

Value determines the angle at which the sides point toward the center of the shape

FIGURE F-20: Polygon with text block

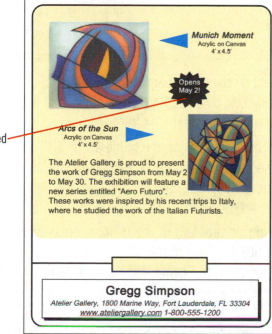

Arial 10-point bold type, center-aligned and reversed

Using Frames

If you are designing a publication that you plan to use over and over again with different content, you might find it useful to first create a standard publication that contains placeholders for the text and graphics. A **frame** is a special kind of object that can hold graphics or text and can act as a placeholder for content. You draw a frame using the frame tools in the toolbox. Once you draw a frame, you can attach content to it. When content is **attached** to a frame, it means that the content and the frame are joined together as a single object that can be moved, edited, or resized as a unit. You can attach content to a frame by typing text in the frame, by using the Place command to place a graphic or text file in the frame, or by using the Attach Content command to add text or graphics to the frame. Sara is creating an ad that will be used to promote different photography exhibitions at the Atelier Gallery. She decides to create a standard ad using frames for the layout.

Steps

1. Open the file **PM F-2.pmd** from the drive and folder where your Project Files are stored, save it as **Photo Exhibit Ad**, then maximize the publication window if necessary
   The partially completed ad opens in the publication window.

2. Click the **Rectangle frame tool** ⊠ in the toolbox, position ✛ at the intersection of the pink and blue column guides in the upper-left corner of the ad, drag across to the right column guide and down so that the pointer guide aligns with the **3"** mark on the vertical ruler, then release the mouse button
   A frame appears in the ad, as shown in Figure F-21. Notice that a 1-point, black line borders the frame. If you do not want the border to appear when you place text or graphics in the frame, you must remove it.

3. Click **Element** on the menu bar, point to **Stroke**, then click **None**
   The black border is removed and replaced with a nonprinting gray border.

4. Click **File** on the menu bar, click **Place**, click the Project File **Waves.jpg** in the list of files, verify that the **Within frame option button** is selected in the Place section of the dialog box, then click **Open** (*Macintosh Users: Click OK*)
   A dialog box appears, telling you the file size of the image and asking if you want to store it in your publication. Clicking Yes places a copy of the file in your publication. Clicking No links the file to the publication, without placing the actual file in the publication.

5. Click **Yes**
   A photograph of ocean waves is inserted in the frame and is left-aligned.

6. Click **Element** on the menu bar, point to **Frame**, click **Frame Options** to open the Frame Options dialog box, click the **Horizontal alignment list arrow**, click **Center**, then click **OK**
   The photograph is centered in the frame.

7. Position ✛ over the left column guide at the **3¼"** mark on the vertical ruler, then drag across to the right column guide and down so that the pointer guide aligns with the **4½"** mark on the vertical ruler
   A new frame appears below the first one.

8. Click the **Pointer tool** ▨ in the toolbox, press and hold **[Shift]**, click the frame you just drew, click the **text block** on the pasteboard, release **[Shift]**, click **Element** on the menu bar, point to **Frame**, then click **Attach Content**
   The text block now appears inside the frame, as shown in Figure F-22. The text block is attached to the frame, so that if you move the frame, the text block will move with it.

9. Save your changes to the publication, print the publication, then close the file

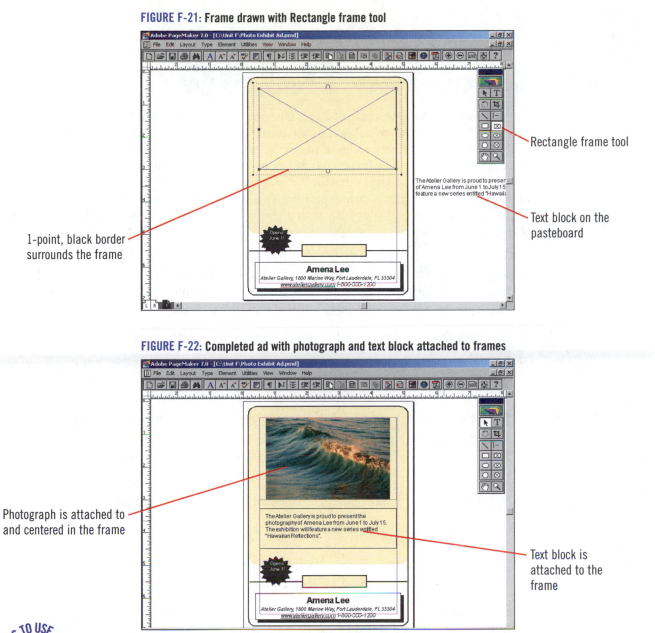

FIGURE F-21: Frame drawn with Rectangle frame tool

Rectangle frame tool

1-point, black border surrounds the frame

Text block on the pasteboard

FIGURE F-22: Completed ad with photograph and text block attached to frames

Photograph is attached to and centered in the frame

Text block is attached to the frame

Using text frames

For longer stories, you can place and thread text between multiple frames. To place text into multiple frames, press and hold [Shift], click each frame you want to use to select them, click File on the menu bar, and then click Place. Each selected text frame will have windowshade handles similar to normal text blocks, indicating that the frames are threaded. You can also place text in circular or polygon frames that you draw using the Ellipse frame tool or the Polygon frame tool, as shown in Figure F-23. You can enhance text frames with strokes and fills by selecting the frame, clicking Element on the menu bar, clicking Fill and Stroke, and then selecting from the options in the Fill and Stroke dialog box.

FIGURE F-23: Ellipse text frame

The Atelier Gallery is proud to present the photography of Amena Lee from June 1 to July 15. The exhibition will feature a new series entitled "Hawaiian Reflections".

Using the Picture Palette

You can enhance the appearance of a text-intensive publication by adding pictures. If you don't have any images of your own, you can use images that come with PageMaker. The PageMaker Content CD contains a wide range of photographs and **clip art** (ready-to-use line art) that you can use in your publications. To access these images, you need to insert the PageMaker CD in your CD drive. You view the images using the Picture palette, one of the plug-in palettes available from the Windows menu. ✐ Sara is creating an ad for an exhibition of nature photographs, but the gallery has not yet provided her with a graphic of the artist's work. In the meantime, she places an image from the Picture palette in the ad to use as a placeholder for the artist's work.

Steps 123 4

1. Open the file **PM F-3.pmd** from the drive and folder where your Project Files are stored, save it as **Nature Photography Ad**, then maximize the publication window if necessary
   The partially completed ad opens in the publication window.

2. Click **Window** on the menu bar, point to **Plug-in Palettes**, then click **Show Picture Palette**
   The Picture palette opens. You can use the Type and Category list arrows in the Picture palette to search for pictures of a certain type (clip art or images) in a specific category.

3. Click the **Type list arrow**, click **Images**, click the **Category list arrow**, then click **Nature & Landscapes**
   The Picture palette displays photographs (images) relating to nature and landscapes, as shown in Figure F-24.

4. Scroll down the Picture palette, then double-click the **Forest image** in the Picture palette
   The pointer changes to ⊠.

5. Click anywhere in the rectangular frame at the top of the publication
   The Forest image appears in the frame, as shown in Figure F-25. Notice it is left aligned.

6. Click **Element** on the menu bar, point to **Frame**, click **Frame Options**, click the **Horizontal alignment list arrow** in the Frame Options dialog box, click **Center**, then click **OK**
   The photograph is centered horizontally in the frame, as shown in Figure F-26.

7. Click **Window** on the menu bar, point to **Plug-in Palettes**, then click **Hide Picture Palette**
   The Picture palette closes.

8. Save your changes to the publication, print the publication, close the file, then exit PageMaker

FIGURE F-24: Picture palette showing Nature and Landscape images

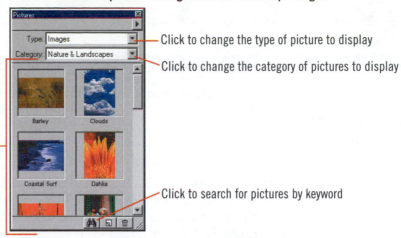

Click to change the type of picture to display

Click to change the category of pictures to display

Photographs (images) in the selected category

Click to search for pictures by keyword

FIGURE F-25: Ad with photograph from Picture palette attached to frame

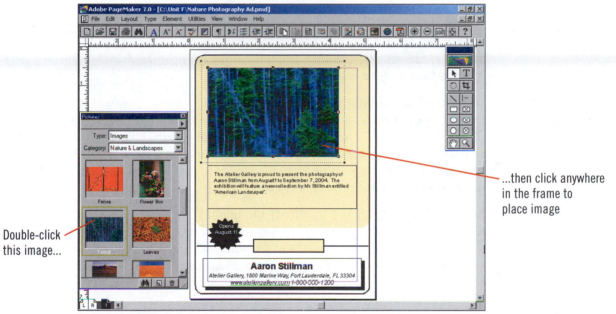

Double-click this image...

...then click anywhere in the frame to place image

FIGURE F-26: Forest image centered in frame

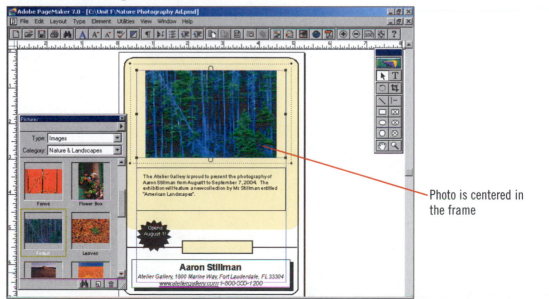

Photo is centered in the frame

Design Workshop: Advertisements

A successful advertisement should provide a clear course of action or form a positive image of a company or product. The first ad Sara created for the Atelier Gallery is shown in Figure F-27. Before presenting it to the client, Sara critiques her design.

Details

► Does the ad achieve its goal?

Graphics are the first things people see when looking at a page, followed by text. Because Sara placed the artwork of the artist in the ad, the reader forms an immediate impression of what the exhibit will be like. The art itself is a much more powerful draw to the reader than a paragraph describing the artist's work.

► Is the ad well-organized?

The ad is very simple: it contains two pieces of art, a short description of the exhibit, and information about where and when the exhibit will take place. Sara placed the graphics at the top to draw in the reader, a short paragraph describing the exhibit in the middle, and the contact information at the bottom. The starburst announcing the opening date is meant to generate excitement and impress the date upon the reader.

► Will the ad stand out on a magazine page?

Unless it is a full-page ad, a magazine ad can get lost in the crowd of other ads and stories. Sara realized her ad would lose impact in a magazine filled with other ads and competing messages, so she used minimal text and placed a border around the ad to separate it from the competing information on the page. By using a generous amount of white space, she achieved a simple, eye-catching ad that is free of too much detail.

► How will the color of the ad affect the impact?

Studies show a reader is more apt to view color objects on a page before black and white objects, so the colorful graphics and yellow background will help attract readers to Sara's ad. Of course, many successful ads do not use color. In the end, an ad's success is determined by its design, not by the amount of color used.

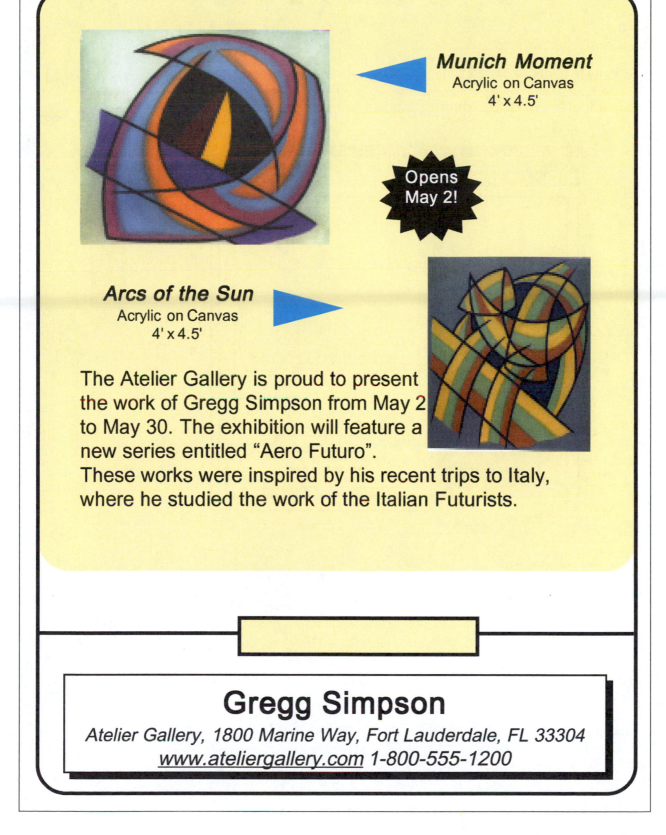

Practice

► Concepts Review

Label each element of the publication window shown in Figure F-28.

FIGURE F-28

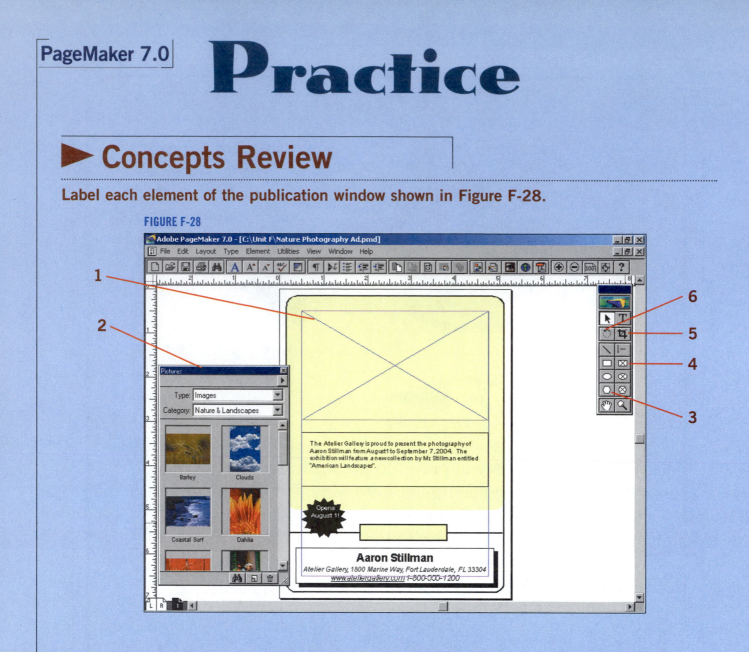

Match each term with the statement that best describes it.

7. Clip art
8. Definition point
9. Points
10. Standoff
11. Frame

a. Amount of space between a graphic and any wrapped text
b. An object that can hold text or graphics and can act as a placeholder
c. Diamond-shaped handle that appears at the intersection of two standoff lines
d. Unit of measurement for line widths and font sizes
e. Pictures that can be placed in a publication

12. **Which of the following should you NOT do when creating an ad?**
    a. Give the reader a clear course of action for responding.
    b. Use large headlines or an eye-catching graphic to attract the reader's attention.
    c. Visually separate the ad from other items on the page with a border or white space around the ad.
    d. Include as much information as you can fit in the ad.

13. **Which of the following statements about cropping is NOT true?**
    a. After you crop a graphic, you can resize it and maintain the cropping.
    b. Cropping only changes the way a graphic appears, it does not permanently delete any portion of a graphic.
    c. Cropping permanently deletes a portion of a graphic.
    d. You use the Cropping tool to crop a graphic.

14. **Which is NOT true about stacking objects?**
    a. Objects in a stack are stacked on the page in the order you placed them.
    b. You can change the order of stacked objects using the commands on the Arrange menu.
    c. The Send Backward command moves an object to the bottom of the stack.
    d. By default, the first object you place in a stack of objects is placed at the bottom of the stack.

15. **An object that can contain text or graphics and can act as a placeholder is called a:**
    a. Shadow box.   c. Text wrap.
    b. Frame.   d. Polygon.

16. **The standoff is represented by:**
    a. Blue lines around a selected graphic.
    b. Pink lines around a selected graphic.
    c. Square selection handles at the corners and sides of a selected object.
    d. A dotted border around the perimeter of a selected graphic.

17. **The default standoff for a rectangular text wrap is:**
    a. .167 points.   c. 1 inch.
    b. ½ inch.   d. .32 points.

18. **Which of the following statements is NOT true about frames?**
    a. They can contain text.
    b. They can contain graphics.
    c. You draw a frame using the Rectangle tool in the toolbox.
    d. Once a graphic is placed in a frame, text cannot be added to the frame.

▶ Skills Review

1. **Change line weights and styles.**
   a. Start PageMaker, open the file PM F-4.pmd from the drive and folder where your Project Files are stored, click OK if the PANOSE Font Matching Results dialog box opens, then save the publication as **Lobster Lounge 1**.
   b. Click the Rectangle tool in the toolbox, then position the pointer in the upper-left corner of the advertisement at the ¼" mark on both the horizontal and vertical rulers.
   c. Drag the pointer to the lower-right corner of the advertisement to the 5⅛" mark on the horizontal ruler and the 6⅞" mark on the vertical ruler.
   d. Using the Stroke command, change the line weight of the box you just drew to 2 points.
   e. Apply rounded corners to the box, choosing the most rounded style available in the Rounded Corners dialog box.
   f. Apply rounded corners to the box at the bottom of the ad that surrounds the contact information for Butch's Lobster Lounge. Choose the third style in the top row of the Rounded Corners dialog box.
   g. Use the Constrained-Line tool to draw a horizontal line from the left rectangular border to the right rectangular border at the 5⅜" mark on the vertical ruler. Your line should cut through the left facing point of the blue triangle.
   h. Change the line weight to 2 points for the line you just drew, then save your changes.

2. **Crop a graphic.**
   a. Click the Cropping tool in the toolbox, then select the shellfish graphic at the bottom of the ad.
   b. Crop the selected image so that only the lobster is showing.

c. Use the Pointer tool to increase the size of the cropped image by dragging its upper-right sizing handle up and to the right ¼".

d. Save your changes.

3. Rotate an object.

a. Using the Pointer tool, select the blue triangle at the bottom of the page.

b. Use the Copy and Paste commands to create a copy of the blue triangle.

c. Drag the copy of the triangle to the left of the original triangle.

d. Use the Rotating tool to rotate the copied triangle so that it is facing the opposite direction, with its narrowest point pointing to the right.

e. When the copied triangle is positioned perfectly in the opposite direction, click the Pointer tool, then drag the copied triangle so that its right-facing point is touching the left-facing point of the original triangle. The line you drew should cut both triangles evenly through the middle.

f. Save your changes.

4. Stack objects.

a. Using the Pointer tool, select the blue triangle on the right.

b. Use the Bring to Front command to place the selected triangle on top of the line. Now both triangles should appear on the top of the line.

c. Save your changes.

5. Create a shadow box.

a. Select the box at the bottom of the ad that surrounds the contact information, then use the Copy and Paste commands to create a copy of it.

b. Select the copy of the box if necessary, then fill it with Solid black fill.

c. Use the Send to Back command to send the selected box to the back of the stack.

d. Save your changes.

6. Wrap text around a graphic.

a. Select the lobster graphic.

b. Click Element on the menu bar, then click Text Wrap.

c. Select the Rectangular wrap option icon in the dialog box, and then click OK, accepting the default text flow and standoff settings.

d. Drag the graphic up and to the right so that its right edge is aligned with the right blue column guide and the top standoff line is positioned midway between "atmosphere" in the heading and the first line of paragraph text.

e. Save your changes.

7. Create a custom text wrap.

a. Select the lobster graphic if necessary.

b. Drag the upper-left definition point down and to the right so it is touching the upper-left corner of the blue water in the graphic.

c. Drag the lower-left definition point up and to the right so that it is touching the lower-left corner of the lobster tail. Notice how the text wraps closer to the graphic.

d. Click outside the graphic to deselect it, then save your changes.

8. Create a polygon.

a. Click the Polygon tool in the toolbox.

b. Position the pointer at the 4¼" mark on the vertical ruler and the left column guide.

c. Press and hold [Shift], then drag down and to the right so that the pointer is at the 1⅜" mark on the horizontal ruler and 5¼" mark on the vertical ruler.

d. Click Element on the menu bar, then click Polygon Settings.

e. Type **20** in the Number of sides text box, then press [Tab] twice to preview the multisided object. *(Macintosh Users: Press [Tab] once.)*

f. Type **15** in the Star inset text box, press [Tab] to preview the star inset, then click OK.

g. Using the Pointer tool, select the star, then fill it with Solid black fill.

h. Click the Text tool in the toolbox, then drag to create a text block that fills the polygon.

i. Click Type on the menu bar, click Character, select Impress BT or a different font if Impress BT is not available to you, select 12 points, bold, and reverse text, then click OK.

j. Type **10% off with this ad!** If the text is too large for the star, adjust the size of the text block, remove the bold formatting, or reduce the size of the text so that the text fits inside the star.

k. Save your changes.

9. **Use frames.**

a. Click the Rectangle frame tool in the toolbox, then position the pointer at the 4" mark on the vertical ruler and the 2" mark on the horizontal ruler.

b. Create a frame by dragging down and to the right so that the pointer aligns with the 4½" mark on the horizontal ruler and the 5⅛" mark on the vertical ruler, then release the mouse button.

c. Click the Pointer tool, press and hold [Shift], select the frame, then select the Thursday Night Jazz text block on the pasteboard.

d. Use the Attach Content command to attach the text block to the frame.

e. Compare your screen with Figure F-29, then save your changes.

f. Print the publication, then close the file.

10. **Use the Picture palette.**

a. Open the file PM F-5.pmd from the drive and folder where your Project Files are stored, click OK if the PANOSE Font Matching Results dialog box opens, then save the publication as **Lobster Lounge 2**.

b. Click Window on the menu bar, point to Plug-in Palettes, then click Show Picture Palette. *(Macintosh Users: Open the file Catalog.pdf from the PageMaker Content CD.)*

c. Use the Type and Category list arrows in the Picture palette to display clip art pictures in the Food & Dining category. *(Macintosh Users: Locate the clip art image of a fish in the Food & Dining category, then note its filename 0001252.ai.)*

d. Scroll down the list of clip art pictures, then double-click the graphic called Fish. *(Macintosh Users: Switch to PageMaker, open the Place document dialog box, navigate to the FoodDin folder within the Library folder on the PageMaker Content CD, click the file 0001251.ai, click OK, then click OK in the warning dialog box.)*

e. Click in the white space below the heading and slogan in the ad to place the clip art.

f. Reposition and resize the clip art so the ad is compelling.

g. Close the Picture palette. *(Macintosh Users: Close Acrobat Reader.)*

h. Save the publication, print it, close the file, then exit PageMaker.

▶ Independent Challenge 1

You work in the marketing department of Sunset Tours. Your manager has asked you to create a black and white advertisement promoting a trip to London. A sample advertisement is shown in Figure F-30.

a. Start PageMaker, then create a publication that is 6" tall and 9" wide, with default margins.

FIGURE F-29

FIGURE F-30

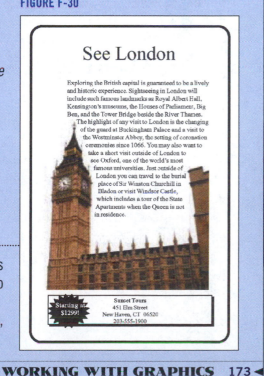

PageMaker 7.0

b. Place the graphic file Big Ben.tif, located in the drive and folder where your Project Files are stored, in the ad.

c. Place the text file PM F-6.doc, located in the drive and folder where your Project Files are stored, in the ad.

d. Increase the size of the Big Ben graphic so that it spans the width between the column guides (making sure to drag a corner sizing handle so as not to distort the picture).

e. Create a custom text wrap so that the text flows between the two towers in the graphic.

f. Place a rectangle at the bottom of the ad that spans the width between the column guides and is 1" high. Draw a text block inside the rectangle, and then type a fictitious address and phone number for Sunset Tours inside the text block. Format the text using a font, font style, and font size you think looks professional.

g. Create a shadow box for the rectangle you just drew at the bottom of the page.

h. Add the headline **See London** to the top of the ad.

i. Add a border around the ad, choosing a line width you think looks good.

j. Use the Polygon tool to draw a black starburst anywhere in the ad.

k. Draw a text block inside the starburst, format the text in Times New Roman 10-point reverse type, then type **Starting at $1299!** in the text block. Center-align the text.

l. Adjust the layout as necessary, then save the ad as **London Ad** to the drive and folder where your Project Files are stored.

m. Print the ad, close the file, then exit PageMaker.

▶ Independent Challenge 2

Clip three advertisements from a newspaper or magazine. Try to find ads that include graphics, borders, layered objects, and wrapped text. Evaluate the advertisements using the guidelines from the first lesson in this unit, and then write a brief critique of each ad, answering the following questions:

a. Which element of the ad attracts the reader's attention?

b. Do the graphics enhance the overall design of the advertisement, or do they detract from the ad's message?

c. Does the ad contain too much or too little information?

d. Is the organization of the ad effective?

e. Which elements of the ad make it stand out on the page?

f. What course of action does the ad offer the reader?

g. How could the ad be improved?

▶ Independent Challenge 3

Create an advertisement for a product of your choice. You can choose an existing product or create a new product. Sketch your ad on a piece of paper first to determine the layout of the text and graphics. The dimensions of the ad should be 7" x 10", and the ad should include at least one picture, a logo, a headline, a product description that wraps around one of the pictures, and a company name and address. You should use pictures from the Picture palette in your ad.

a. Start PageMaker, then create a publication that is 7" tall and 10" wide.

b. Place at least one picture from the Picture palette in your ad. *(Macintosh Users: Place a picture from the PageMaker Content CD.)* You can use images or clip art or both.

c. Add a text block with a headline and a text block describing the product. Wrap the text around a graphic in your ad. If appropriate, create a custom text wrap so that the text wraps closer to the graphic.

d. Create a company logo by drawing at least two polygon shapes and stacking them on top of each other in a visually appealing way. If you want, add a text block that contains the company name, and place it on top of the stacked polygons.

e. Add a text block to the ad that includes the company name and address.

f. Draw a rectangle around the ad to create a border. Format the line with a line width of 2 points. Apply rounded corners to the rectangle using a style of your choice.

g. When you are satisfied with the ad, save it as **Product Ad** to the drive and folder where your Project Files are stored.

h. Print the publication, close the file, then exit PageMaker.

e Independent Challenge 4

You work in the marketing department of Sea Breeze Cruises, a company that sells cruises to various destinations. The marketing director has assigned you the task of creating a quarter-page, color advertisement promoting one of the cruises. The dimensions of the magazine ad should be 6" x 9".

a. Open your browser, then use a search engine such as AltaVista (www.altavista.com) or Google (www.google.com) to search for information about cruises. Find a cruise destination that you will describe in the ad. For example, you might perform a search using the keyword **cruise**, and then find a Web page that describes a cruise to a Caribbean destination. You can also use Yahoo!, Excite, Infoseek, or another search engine.

b. Sketch your advertisement for the cruise company using the guidelines that you learned in this unit. Your sketch should include the following:
  • An appropriate headline
  • A paragraph of text that describes the cruise destination; this text should wrap around a graphic
  • At least one graphic; you can use a photograph or clip art graphic from the Picture palette
  • A logo for Sea Breeze Cruises
  • A text block for the company's contact information
  • A starburst that brings attention to a special offer
  • A border around the entire ad

c. Start PageMaker, then create a new publication with the dimensions 6" by 9".

d. Use story editor to write a brief paragraph describing your chosen destination, touching on two or three sight-seeing highlights, then place it in the ad.

e. Add a headline to the ad.

f. Add at least one image or clip art graphic from the Picture palette to illustrate your ad, cropping and resizing each graphic as necessary.

g. Wrap the paragraph text around the clip art or image you inserted. Create a custom text wrap so that the text wraps closely to the contours of the graphic, if appropriate.

h. Add a border around the ad, choosing a line weight that you think looks good.

i. Use the polygon tool to create a star shape with black fill. Type a message that brings attention to a special offer in the star and format it in reverse type.

j. Create a logo for Sea Breeze Cruises by drawing various shapes with the toolbox tools and then stacking them in a way that looks good. Make sure the text **Sea Breeze Cruises** appears somewhere in the logo.

k. Adjust the layout of your ad so that it is powerful and effective.

l. Save the publication as **Cruise Ad** to the drive and folder where your Project Files are stored.

m. Print the publication, close the file, then exit PageMaker.

▶ Visual Workshop

Create the ad shown in Figure F-31. Start by creating a new publication that is 7" by 10". Place the graphic file Paris.tif, found on the drive and folder where your Project Files are stored, and then crop and resize it as shown. Place the text file PM F-7.doc in the ad, and then create a custom text wrap so that the text flows close to the graphic as shown. Increase the size of the paragraph text to 14 points. To create the triangle, insert a three-sided polygon, and then rotate it so that one corner of the triangle points down, as shown. To create the starburst, create a polygon that has 15 sides and a 20% star inset. Draw a rectangular border with a line weight of 2 points around the entire ad. Save your ad as **Paris Ad** to the drive and folder where your Project Files are stored, then print a copy.

FIGURE F-31

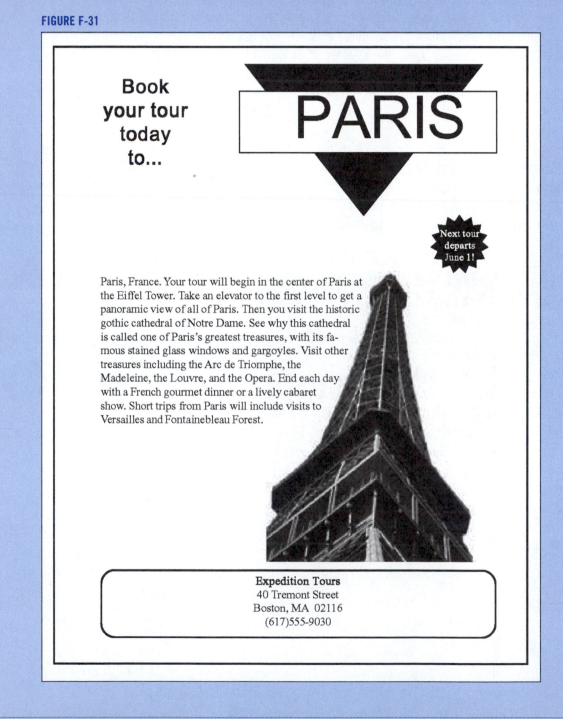

Formatting

Text

▶ **Plan a menu**

▶ **Set publication preferences**

▶ **Examine the Control palette in character view**

▶ **Examine the Control palette in paragraph view**

▶ **Format text using the Control palette**

▶ **Adjust the baseline**

▶ **Adjust text spacing**

▶ **Set character widths**

▶ **Set tabs**

▶ **Set indents**

▶ **Use the Bullets and numbering Plug-in**

▶ **Design Workshop: Menus**

This unit introduces you to more sophisticated text formatting features in PageMaker that can help you create professional and distinctive publications. You learn how to use the Control palette to format characters and paragraphs quickly. You also learn how to modify the spacing of text, change the width of characters, set tabs and indents, and add bullets and numbering to paragraphs, among other formatting options. The Windward Cafe in Maui, Hawaii, features a wide range of island specialties at family prices. The manager has hired Sara Norton to create a menu that can be modified easily as new specialties are available.

Planning a Menu

Creating a menu requires more thought and effort than simply copying a chef's recipes onto a piece of paper. No matter how simple or complex a menu's design, the menu is the final point of sale for a restaurant. A poorly planned and designed menu can confuse the customer and diminish sales. Menus usually include a lot of text, so it is helpful to take advantage of PageMaker's character and paragraph formatting features to enhance the menu's overall appearance. Sara received a list of items for the Windward Cafe menu from the manager, who highlighted the fact that the Seafood Combo brings the most profit because its perceived value is much greater than its actual cost. This information helps Sara decide where to place items as she designs the menu. Sara's sketch of the menu is shown in Figure G-1. She plans the menu to be a one-page publication.

Details

Keep the following guidelines in mind when planning a menu:

► **Determine the most important items on the menu**

Where you place items on the page directly affects how customers order from the menu. Certain areas of a page or spread are read before others. Areas read first are called **power points** because of their potential impact on the reader. Because the Seafood Combo is the most profitable item for the Windward Cafe, Sara will place it at the top of the center column. She will also place the Island Macadamia Nut Cream Pie at the top of the third column.

► **Organize menu items into categories**

The Windward Cafe menu items will be organized according to category, such as appetizers and entrees, and will flow from first course to beverages. To make each heading stand out and easy to read, Sara decides to increase both the space between characters and the character widths in the category headings.

► **Design the layout so the menu is easy to read**

Menus tend to include a large amount of information. By adjusting the character spacing of certain words, such as headings, you can "loosen" the text and make it easier to read. Formatting paragraphs with indents and tabs can also help organize the overall layout. Sara will use three columns for the five different types of menu items. She will place the entrees in the middle column so that they receive the most attention.

► **Produce menus on durable paper**

The Windward Cafe menus will remain on the tables, and will receive a lot of use from the high volume of customers. The menus will also experience extra wear and tear from the salt air, as part of the cafe is outside on the beach. Sara will ask her commercial printer to print the menus on a durable, 80-pound, light tan, card stock paper. She will also have the printer laminate the menus with a permanent plastic coating.

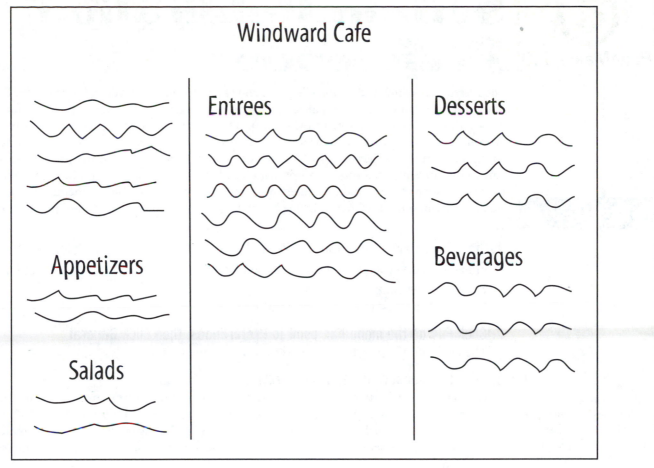

Setting Publication Preferences

The Preferences command on the File menu allows you to change the default settings for a publication. For example, you can change the system of measurement used on the horizontal and vertical rulers, determine the priority for saving a file (faster or smaller), change the way text displays in layout and story editor views, and improve the appearance of quotation marks and apostrophes, among other options. The changes you make to a publication's preferences apply only to the current publication. ✒ Sara has already begun her Windward Cafe menu and needs to change the publication's rulers from inches to picas. Sara also wants to use the Save Smaller option in the Preferences dialog box to help decrease the file size of her publication.

Steps

1. Start PageMaker, open the file **PM G-1.pmd** from the drive and folder where your Project Files are located, save it as **Windward Cafe**, then maximize the publication window if necessary
   The menu appears in the publication window.

2. Click **File** on the menu bar, point to **Preferences**, then click **General**
   The Preferences dialog box opens, as shown in Figure G-2.

MacintoshUsers

This replaces Steps 3 and 4.
3. Click the Measurements in list box, then click Picas
4. Click Vertical ruler in the list box, then click Picas

3. Click the **Measurements in list arrow**, then click **Picas**
   Changing the Measurements in setting changes the unit of measure used in the horizontal ruler in layout view. A **pica** is a unit of measurement equal to 12 points or about ⅙". In other words, six picas equal 1", and 12 points equal one pica. In PageMaker, pica measurement is denoted as 0p1, where the zero is picas and the one is points. Many commercial printers prefer to work in picas.

4. Click the **Vertical ruler list arrow**, then click **Picas**
   The unit of measure used in the vertical ruler will be picas. It is best to use one unit of measurement throughout a publication.

5. Click the **Smaller option button** in the Save option section
   Changing the Save option setting to Smaller tells PageMaker to make the file size as small as possible when you use the Save command to save the publication. The Faster Save option, saves the document quickly, but does not compact the file size.

QuickTip

You can change the default settings for all new publications by changing the preferences settings when no publications are open.

6. Click **OK**
   The dialog box closes and the new preferences settings are applied to the publication. Notice that the unit of measure used in the horizontal and vertical rulers has changed from inches to picas.

7. Click **File** on the menu bar, then click **Save** to save your changes to the publication

FIGURE G-2: Preferences dialog box

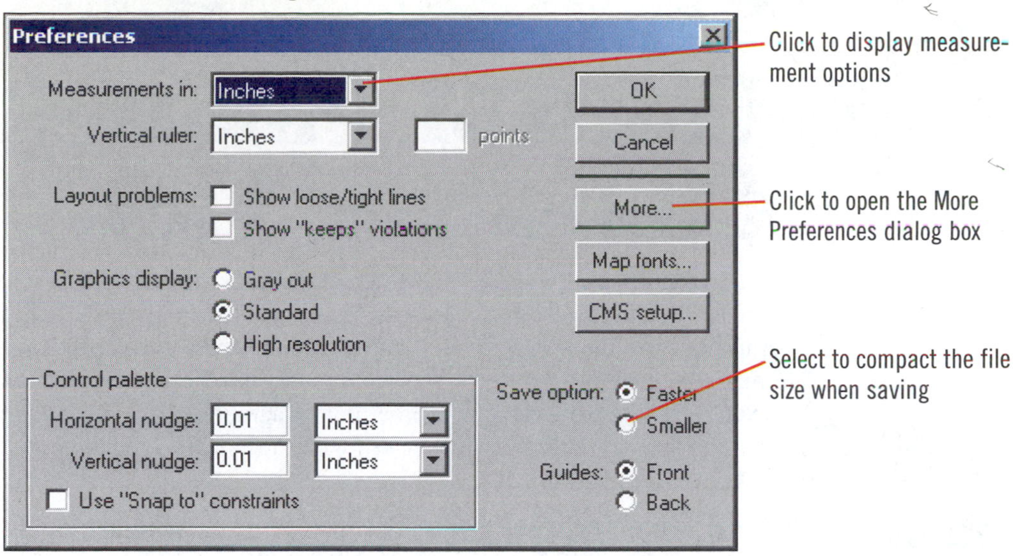

Click to display measurement options

Click to open the More Preferences dialog box

Select to compact the file size when saving

Setting more preferences options

To customize additional preferences settings in a publication, click More in the Preferences dialog box to open the More Preferences dialog box, shown in Figure G-3. In this dialog box, you can customize settings for working with text, story editor, graphics, and PostScript printing. For instance, you might have noticed PageMaker uses tick marks (" and ') for quotation marks and apostrophes. You can specify that PageMaker change the appearance of these tick marks to curly marks, or **typographer's quotes**, by selecting the Use typographer's quotes check box in the Text section of the dialog box. Also, if you use story editor often, you might want to change the default font or point size to one you find easier to read, or turn on the display of paragraph marks in story editor to make it easier to edit your text. You can change these settings in the Story editor section of the More Preferences dialog box.

FIGURE G-3: More Preferences dialog box

PageMaker 7.0

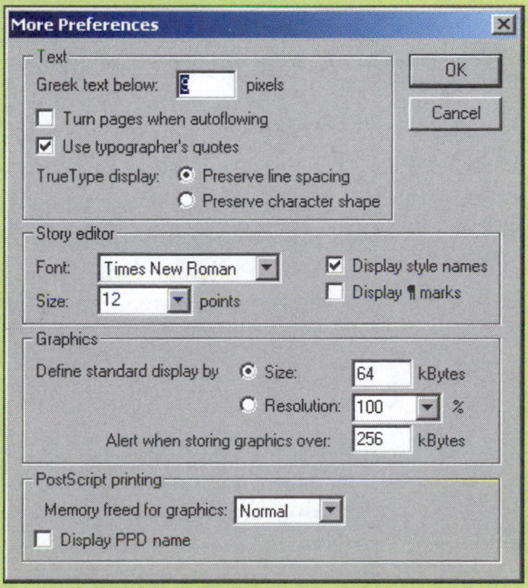

Examining the Control Palette in Character View

PageMaker often provides several different methods to accomplish the same task. For example, you can use the Character Specifications dialog box or the commands on the Type menu to format text. Another convenient tool for formatting text quickly is the Control palette, which includes different views, including character view and paragraph view. You use **character view** for formatting text, and **paragraph view** for formatting paragraphs. Sara opens the Control palette in character view, and familiarizes herself with the benefits of using it to format characters.

Steps

QuickTip

Press [Ctrl]['] to quickly show the Control palette in the publication window.

1. Click the **Text tool** T in the toolbox, click **Window** on the menu bar, click **Show Control Palette**, then click the **Character view button** T on the Control palette if necessary
   The Control palette opens in the publication window, as shown in Figure G-4. The settings shown on the Control palette in Figure G-4 are the default settings for PageMaker and the publication. If text is selected in your publication, the settings displayed in your Control palette might differ.

Details

Below are some of the benefits of using the Control palette and its character features:

► **Format characters quickly and easily**
   The Control palette provides the same functionality that is available in the Character Specifications dialog box or using the commands on the Type menu, however, it's faster to use the Control palette. The Control palette can be open all the time, giving you immediate access to buttons and list arrows for formatting characters. Table G-1 describes the character formatting options on the Control palette.

► **Move the Control palette anywhere in the layout or story editor view windows**
   You can move the Control palette anywhere in the publication window by clicking the solid bar below its close button and dragging it to a new location. You can also hide the Control palette by clicking the Close button, or by using the Hide Control Palette command on the Window menu.

QuickTip

To increase a nudge setting by a factor of 10, press [Shift] as you click a nudge button.

► **Change settings by precise measurements**
   Next to most Control palette options are little arrows called **nudge buttons** that allow you to make incremental changes to a setting by a preset measurement. When you click a nudge button, PageMaker immediately applies the new setting to the selected text. The amount by which the setting changes depends on the default unit of measurement for the publication. For example, the default nudge amount for inches is 0.01". You can change the default nudge setting using the Preferences dialog box. You can also change settings by a mathematical factor; for example, you can double the size of selected text.

CLUES TO USE

Adjusting settings by using mathematical adjustments

You can use the Control palette to perform simple arithmetic in any active numeric option by typing the numeric expression into the option's text box. For example, to increase a headline to three times its size, select the text, type "x3" in the Type size text box, and then click the Apply button.

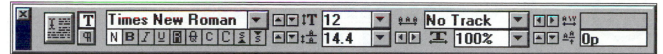

TABLE G-1: Control palette's character view buttons and options

button/box	option	use to
	Apply button	Apply the settings on the Control palette
	Paragraph view button	Change the Control palette to paragraph view
	Font list arrow	Change the font of the selected text
	Type style buttons	Apply normal, bold, italic, underline, reverse, and strikethrough type styles to the selected text
	Case buttons	Change the case of the selected text; the left button changes lowercase text to small capital letters, and the right button changes all selected text to uppercase letters
	Superscript/subscript buttons	Change the size and position of the selected text
	Type size options	Change the point size of selected text: type a value in the text box, use the nudge buttons, or use the list arrow to select a size
	Leading option	Adjust the leading of selected text: type a value in the text box, use the nudge buttons, or use the list arrow to select a size
	Track option	Adjust the tracking of the selected text
	Set width option	Change the width of the selected characters
	Kerning option	Adjust the kerning of the selected characters
	Baseline shift option	Raise or lower the baseline for the selected text

PageMaker 7.0

Examining the Control Palette in Paragraph View

Switching to paragraph view on the Control palette allows you to take advantage of the palette's options for setting paragraph formats, such as indents and tabs. Sara familiarizes herself with the benefits of using the Control palette to format paragraphs.

1. Click the **Paragraph view button** ¶ on the Control palette

   The Control palette changes to paragraph view, as shown in Figure G-5. Once again, the settings shown on the Control palette in Figure G-5 are the default settings for PageMaker and the publication. If text is selected in your publication, the settings displayed in your Control palette might differ.

Below are some of the benefits of using the Control palette and its paragraph features:

▶ **Format paragraph text quickly and easily**

The buttons available on the Control palette in paragraph view provide the same functionality as the Paragraph Specifications dialog box or the paragraph formatting commands on the Type menu, but it can be easier and faster to use the Control palette. Table G-2 describes the options on the Control palette in paragraph view. You can use the Control palette in paragraph view to set alignments, indents, styles, and other settings for one or more paragraphs.

▶ **Easily switch between character and paragraph view**

You can quickly switch between character view and paragraph view by clicking the Character view button **T** or the Paragraph view button **¶**, on the Control palette, making it easy to apply multiple format settings to text without having to use the menus.

FIGURE G-5: Control palette in paragraph view

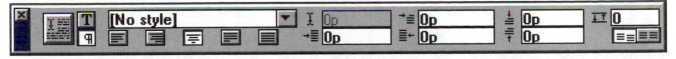

TABLE G-2: Control palette's paragraph view buttons and options

button/box	option	use to
	Apply button	Apply the settings on the Control palette
	Character view button	Change the Control palette to character view
[No style]	Paragraph style list arrow	Apply preset styles to the selected text
	Alignment buttons	Change the alignment of the selected text
0 in	Left indent option	Set the indent from the left margin
0 in	Right indent option	Set the indent from the right margin
0 in	First-line indent option	Set the indent for the first line of the selected paragraph(s) from the left margin
0 in	Space before option	Set the space above the beginning of the selected paragraph(s)
0 in	Space after option	Set the space below the last line of the selected paragraph(s)
0	Grid-size option	Set the size of the text grid to use when the Align-to-grid option is active
	Align-to-grid buttons	Vertically align the baselines of adjacent columns; the right button turns the option on and the left button turns it off
0 in	Cursor position indicator	Track the position of the cursor on the publication page

Formatting Text Using the Control Palette

You can format text and create special effects quickly using the Control palette. Once you drag place a text block, you can use the buttons on the Control palette to select the format settings to apply to the text, including font, size, alignment, and special effects such as reverse text and small capitals. Then, when you type text in the text block, all the formats you set will be applied to the text as you type it. Notice that not all text formatting features are available on the Control palette. For instance, if you want to change the size settings for small capitals, you need to use the Character Options dialog box. ✒ Sara adds the name of the cafe in reverse text to the black rectangle across the top of the page. She then applies small capitals to create an interesting visual effect.

Steps

1. Click the **Text tool** ⊤ in the toolbox if necessary, position ⊥ in the upper-left corner of the black rectangle, drag to the lower-right corner of the black rectangle, then release the mouse button

   After you release the mouse button, the insertion point appears at the top of the black rectangle in the center. Center alignment is the default alignment setting for new text blocks in this publication.

2. Click the **Character view button** ⊤ on the Control palette

   The Control palette appears in character view.

3. Click the **Font list arrow** on the Control palette as shown in Figure G-6, scroll up, click **Arial**, double-click **12** in the Type size text box, type **72**, click the **Reverse button** 🖪, then click the **Apply button** 🖽

   Any text you type will be formatted in 72-point Arial reverse text. Notice that the size of the insertion point increased because you increased the point size to 72.

Trouble?

Windows Users: If your screen display is not refreshed after typing Windward Cafe, click the Fit in Window button 🔲 on the toolbar.

4. Type **Windward Cafe**

   The format settings you applied on the Control palette are applied to the text as you type.

5. Click the **Pointer tool** ⬉ in the toolbox, then drag the Windward Cafe text block down so that the text is centered vertically in the black rectangle

   The name of the cafe is now centered horizontally and vertically in the rectangle, as shown in Figure G-7.

6. Click the **Text tool** in the toolbox, select **Windward Cafe**, then click the **Small caps button** 🄲 on the Control palette

   The lowercase text changes to capital letters that are smaller than regular capital letters. The cafe name might look better if the size of the small caps is reduced.

7. Click **Type** on the menu bar, click **Character**, then click **Options** in the Character Specifications dialog box

   The Character Options dialog box opens.

DesignTip

Small caps are effective only when text is 14 points or larger.

8. Type **50** in the Small caps size text box, click **OK**, then click **OK** in the Character Specifications dialog box

   The size of the small capital letters changes to become 50% the size of the first letter of each word, as shown in Figure G-8.

9. Deselect the text, then save your changes to the publication

FIGURE G-6: Font list on the Control palette

Character view button

Apply button

Reverse button

Font list arrow

Type size text box

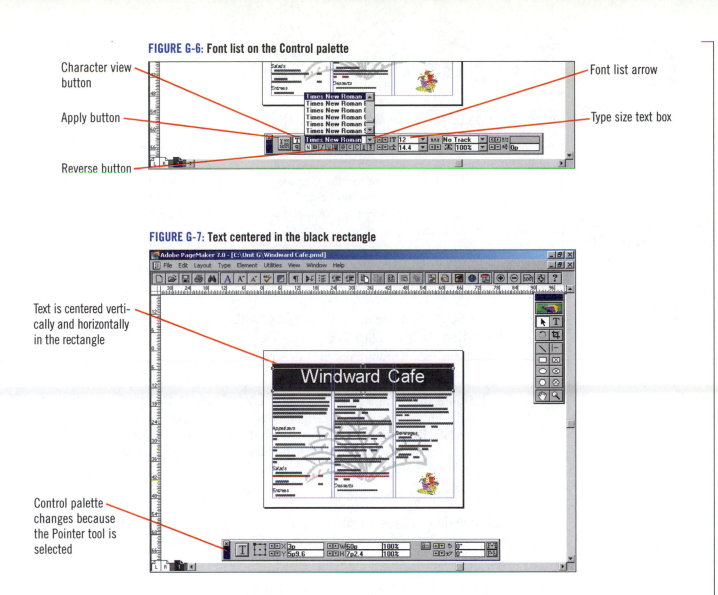

FIGURE G-7: Text centered in the black rectangle

Text is centered vertically and horizontally in the rectangle

Control palette changes because the Pointer tool is selected

FIGURE G-8: Cafe name with small caps applied

Small caps are 50% the size of the "W" and the "C"

Small caps button

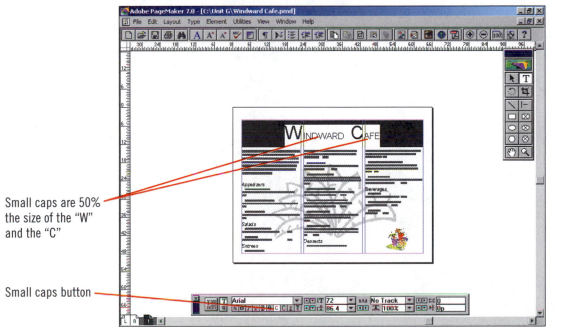

PageMaker 7.0

Adjusting the Baseline

You can also create special effects with text by adjusting its position on the baseline. The **baseline** is an imaginary line on which text rests, as shown in Figure G-9. Text can be moved above or below a baseline. You can use the Control palette in character view or the Character Options dialog box to shift the text above or below the baseline in increments as little as a tenth of a point. Sara uses the Control palette to shift the baseline of the small capital letters in the cafe name.

1. Select **indward** of the word "Windward," then click the **Actual Size button** [100] on the toolbar *(Macintosh Users: Click View on the menu bar, then click Actual Size)*

2. Double-click **Op** in the Baseline shift text box on the Control palette, type **Op6**, click the **Apply button** [▦], then click [100]

   Clicking the Actual Size button refreshes your screen. The selected text shifts up 6 points, as shown in Figure G-10.

3. Click the **Baseline shift nudge up button** on the Control palette six times, then click [100]

   You use the nudge buttons located to the left of the Baseline shift text box to move the baseline in small increments. Don't worry if the text does not show on your screen as you click, but notice that the setting in the Baseline shift text box changes each time you click. The setting in the Baseline shift text box is now 1p.

4. Deselect the text, then select **afe** of the word "Cafe"

5. Double-click **Op** in the Baseline shift text box on the Control palette, type **1p**, click [▦], then click [100]

   The baseline of the selected text is raised to 1 pica, as shown in Figure G-11.

6. Deselect the text, then save your changes to the publication

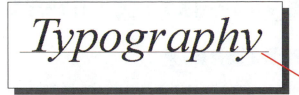

Imaginary line on which text rests

FIGURE G-10: Baseline shifted up six points

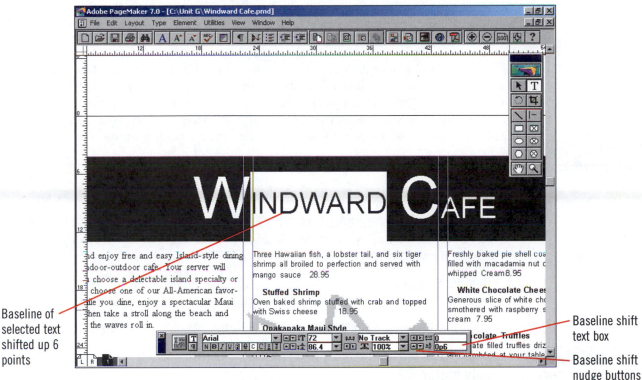

Baseline of selected text shifted up 6 points

Baseline shift text box

Baseline shift nudge buttons

FIGURE G-11: Baseline shifted up one pica

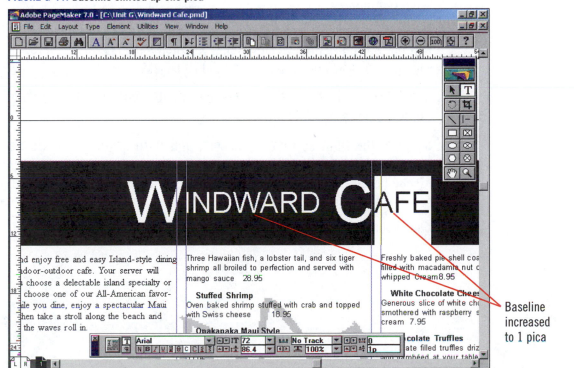

Baseline increased to 1 pica

Adjusting Text Spacing

You can adjust the space between words and letters to make text more readable or to improve the overall appearance of your publication. You change the distance between characters by adjusting the kerning or tracking. **Kerning** is the space between a pair of characters. Generally you adjust the kerning between two characters in an oddly-shaped letter pair, such as "WA" or "AY", but you can also adjust the kerning of a string of characters to create a special effect. You use the Kerning option on the Control palette to adjust the kerning of selected characters. **Tracking** is the space between two or more characters. You usually adjust tracking to improve the appearance of a block of text, such as a paragraph. You can change the tracking of selected text to make it looser or tighter by applying one of six predefined tracking settings using the Control palette or the Character Specifications dialog box. To maximize readability, it's generally best to apply loose tracking to small type and tight tracking to large type. ↠ Sara loosens the tracking of the paragraph text in the first column to make it easier to read. She also adjusts the kerning of the category headings in the menu to make them more eye-catching.

Steps 1 2 3 4

1. Scroll so that the first paragraph in the first column is visible on your screen

2. Select the entire paragraph, then click the **Track list arrow** on the Control palette
The Track list box opens as shown in Figure G-12. Table G-3 illustrates the difference between the six tracking options.

3. Click **Very Loose**
The space between each character in the paragraph increases, making the text easier to read.

4. Select the heading **Appetizers** below the paragraph text, scrolling if necessary

5. Double-click **0** in the Kerning text box on the Control palette, type **.25**, then click the **Apply button** ▦
The space between each letter in the Appetizers heading is increased, making the heading stand out more.

6. Scroll down the publication, select the heading **Salads**, double-click **0** in the Kerning text box on the Control palette, type **.25**, then click ▦
The space between the letters in the heading increases.

7. Scroll down, select the heading **Entrees**, double-click **0** in the Kerning text box on the Control palette, type **.25**, then click ▦

8. Scroll to the right so that the second and third columns are visible, then use the Control palette to adjust the kerning of the **Desserts** and **Beverages** headings to **.25**
All the headings now appear wider with the new kerning setting applied. Compare your screen with Figure G-13.

9. Save your changes to the publication

QuickTip

To remove all manual kerning from selected text, press [Ctrl][Alt][K].

FIGURE G-12: Track list on the Control palette

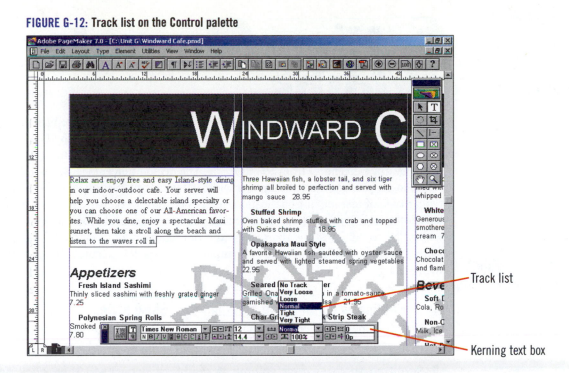

Track list

Kerning text box

FIGURE G-13: Kerning increased in the category headings

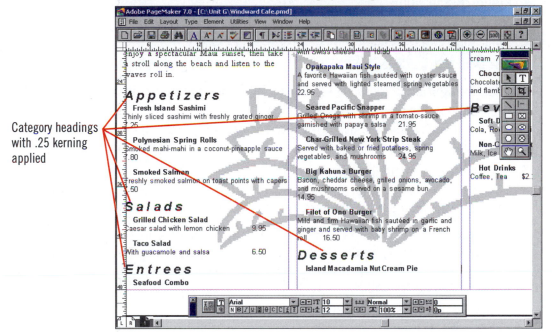

Category headings
with .25 kerning
applied

TABLE G-3: Examples of tracking

example	setting
This is an example of Tracking	No Track
This is an example of Tracking	Loose
This is an example of Tracking	Very Loose
This is an example of Tracking	Normal
This is an example of Tracking	Tight
This is an example of Tracking	Very Tight

Setting Character Widths

Sometimes you might want to make characters wider or narrower to achieve a particular visual effect. You can change the width of selected characters by changing the Horizontal scale percentage on the Control palette or in the Character Specifications dialog box. You can scale character width by any percentage from 5% to 250%. The default percentage is 100%. Table G-4 illustrates several examples of different character widths. If you want to adjust the character widths for a particular type of text in your publication, such as headings, you can save time by setting the character widths for a style. Sara decides the headings would look better if the characters were wider. She could adjust the character width of each heading individually, but it is faster to adjust all the category headings at once by changing the character spacing setting for the style applied to the headings.

Steps

1. Click **Window** on the menu bar, then click **Show Styles**
   The Style palette opens. Sara has created separate styles for the headings, item names, and item descriptions. The style applied to the headings is called Categories.

2. Scroll so that the first column is visible if necessary, then click anywhere in the **Appetizers** heading
   The Categories style is selected in the Styles palette.

3. Click **Type** on the menu bar, then click **Define Styles**
   The Define Styles dialog box opens.

4. Click **Categories** in the Style list box in the Define Styles dialog box, click **Edit**, then click **Char** in the Style Options dialog box
   The Character Specifications dialog box opens. Notice that Normal appears in the Horiz scale text box, indicating that there have been no changes made to the default character width settings.

5. Click the **Horiz scale list arrow**
   The Horizontal scale list opens, as shown in Figure G-14. You can select a Horizontal scale percentage from the list, or type a specific percentage in the Horiz scale text box.

6. Click **130**, then click **OK** to close each of the three dialog boxes
   Each character in every heading is wider, as shown in Figure G-15. Changing the Horizontal width setting for the Categories style changed the width of every character in the text to which the style is applied.

7. Save your changes to the publication

FIGURE G-14: Horizontal scale list

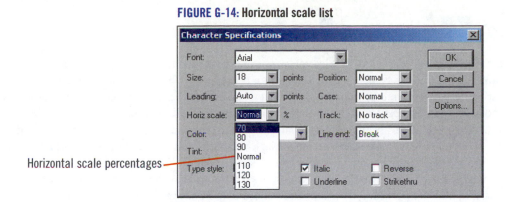

Horizontal scale percentages

FIGURE G-15: Wider character width applied to the Categories style

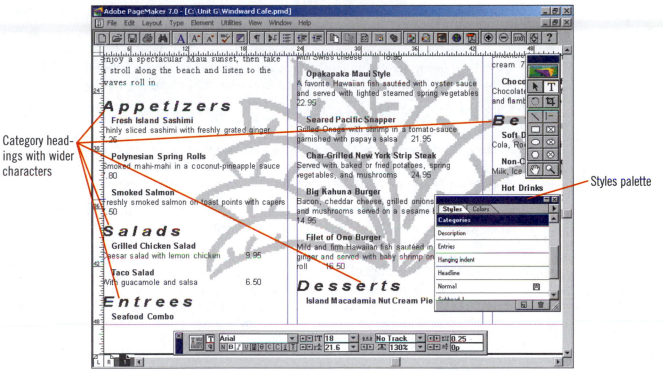

Category headings with wider characters

Styles palette

TABLE G-4: Examples of character widths

width setting	example
80%	The Windward Cafe
Normal	The Windward Cafe
130%	The Windward Cafe

Setting Tabs

Tabs are nonprinting characters that let you position text at specific locations within a text block. Tabs can help you create columns of text within a text block. When you enter the text for your publication, you insert a tab by pressing the Tab key. You can then use the Indents/Tabs dialog box to set positions for left, center, right, and decimal tabs so that all the tabs in the selected text or paragraph style will instantly align at the locations you set. You can also use the Indents/Tabs dialog box to insert a leader. **Leaders** are printing characters that repeat between tabbed items. Examples of leaders include repeated dots or dashes. ⬤ Sara has already inserted tabs before each price on the menu. She now wants to set a tab so that the prices right-align near the right margin, and are preceded by a dot leader. Sara could change the tabs for each description individually using the Indents/Tabs option on the Type menu. However, to save time, she decides to add a tab to the Description style.

Steps 1 2 3 4

1. Scroll so that column 2 is centered in the publication window

2. Click **Type** on the menu bar, then click **Define Styles**
   The Define Styles dialog box opens.

3. Click **Description** in the Style list box, click **Edit**, then click **Tabs** in the Style Options dialog box
   The Indents/Tabs dialog box opens, as shown in Figure G-16. It includes a small section of the ruler showing the default tabs. The indent markers on the ruler reflect the width of the active text block. Table G-5 describes the tab icons in the Indents/Tabs dialog box.

4. Click the **right tab icon** ⬇ in the dialog box, then click above the 18-pica mark on the ruler in the dialog box
   Clicking the tab area above the ruler sets a right-aligned tab. The exact position of the tab you placed appears in the Position text box. You can drag the tab to the right or left to adjust its position. Notice that the default tab positions were removed when you set the tab.

5. Drag the **right tab marker** from the 18-pica mark on the ruler to the 19-pica mark
   The measurement in the Position text box in the dialog box changes to 19p0, verifying the location of the tab at the 19-pica mark.

MacintoshUsers

This replaces Step 6.
6. Click the Leader list arrow in the dialog box

6. Click **Leader** in the dialog box
   A list of styles for tab leaders opens, as shown in Figure G-17. You can choose one of the styles from this list, or you can type any character in the Leader text box to create a custom tab leader. The character you type in the text box will repeat between tabs as a leader.

7. Click the **dotted line** in the Leader list, then click **OK** to close each of the three dialog boxes
   The prices right-align near the right margin, and dotted lines fill the space between the last word in each item description and the price, as shown in Figure G-18. The dotted lines indicate where tabs were inserted between the descriptions and the prices in the publication.

8. Save your changes to the publication

CLUES TO USE

Using the Indents/Tabs Position option

It can be difficult to drag a tab marker to a specific position on the ruler. The Position option in the Indents/Tabs dialog box allows you to set tabs at more precise locations than the ruler displays. To set a tab using the Position option, type the position of the tab in the Position text box, click Position, then click Add tab. You can also set tabs in increments by clicking Position, and then clicking Repeat tab.

FIGURE G-16: Indents/Tabs dialog box

Right tab icon

Left indent marker

Arrows indicate
default tab stops
at every pica

Click here to set a tab
at the 18-pica mark

Right indent marker

FIGURE G-17: Leader style options

Choose this leader style

Right tab at the
19-pica mark

FIGURE G-18: Tabs and leaders applied to the Description style

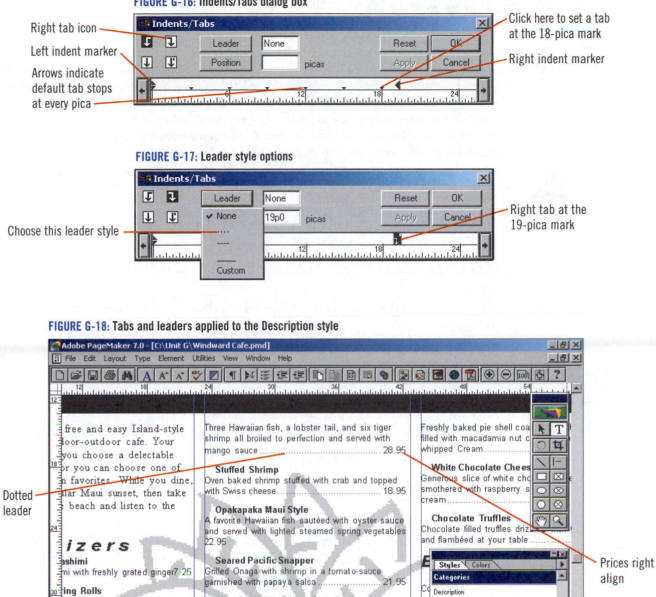

Dotted
leader

Prices right
align

TABLE G-5: Tab icons in the Indents/Tabs dialog box

tab icons	name	description
	Right tab	Sets a right-aligned tab
	Left tab	Sets a left-aligned tab
	Center tab	Sets a tab that centers text under it
	Decimal tab	Sets a tab aligned to a decimal point

Setting Indents

You can set indents within a text block to improve the look of your publication. An **indent** is a set amount of space between the first or last word in a line of text and the right or left margin. Indents let you move text inward from either the right or left margin without changing the original margin settings. You can change indents by using the Control palette, the Paragraph Specifications dialog box, or the Indents/Tabs dialog box. ✎ Sara wants to indent each of the menu description paragraphs so that the menu items stand out from their descriptions. Once again, she adjusts all the paragraphs at once by editing the Description style. She also wants to set a first line indent for the welcome paragraph in the first column. She didn't create a style for the welcome paragraph, so she uses the Control palette in paragraph view to set the indent.

Steps

1. Click **Type** on the menu bar, then click **Define Styles**

   The Define Styles dialog box opens.

2. Click **Description** in the Style list box, click **Edit**, then click **Tabs** in the Style Options dialog box

   The Indents/Tabs dialog box opens. Table G-6 describes the indent icons in the Indents/Tabs dialog box.

   MacintoshUsers

   This replaces Step 3.
   3. Drag the left indent marker to the right until 2 appears in the Position text box

3. Drag the **left indent marker** ▶ to the right until **2p0** appears in the Position text box

   Make sure you drag the lower half of ▶, so that both triangles move as a single unit. The left indent marker is positioned as shown in Figure G-19.

4. Click **OK** to close each of the three dialog boxes

   All the menu item descriptions are now indented 2 picas from the left, as shown in Figure G-20.

5. Scroll to display the welcome paragraph at the top of the first column, then click the welcome paragraph

   Before applying an indent to a paragraph, you must place the insertion point inside the paragraph.

6. Click the **Paragraph view button** ¶ on the Control palette, double-click **0p** in the First-line indent text box on the Control palette, type **4p**, then press **[Enter]**

   A four-pica indent looks too extreme for this short paragraph.

7. Double-click **4p** in the First-line indent text box, type **2**, then press **[Enter]**

   The first line of the paragraph is now indented 2 picas, and looks better, as shown in Figure G-21.

8. Save your changes to the publication

TABLE G-6: Indent icons in the Indents/Tabs dialog box

indent icons	description
◤	First-line indent
▶	Left indent
◀	Right indent

FIGURE G-19: Left indent marker dragged to a new location

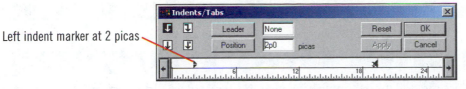

Left indent marker at 2 picas

FIGURE G-20: Indents applied to the Description style

2-pica left indent applied to the Description style

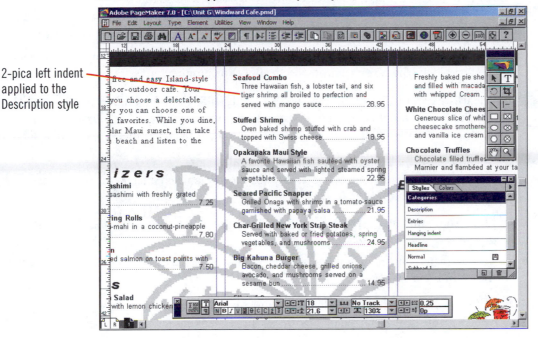

FIGURE G-21: First line of paragraph indented 2 picas

First line indented 2 picas

Paragraph view button

Control palette in Paragraph view

First-line indent text box

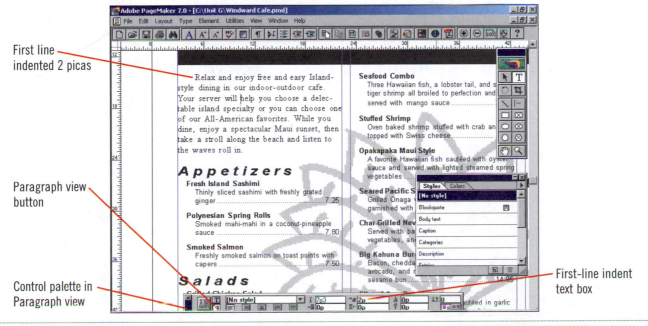

Using the Bullets and Numbering Plug-in

You can use the Bullets and numbering plug-in to create visually attractive lists that have numbers or bullets. A **bullet** is a small picture, usually a dot, used to identify an item in a list. You can add bullets or numbers to consecutive paragraphs, to all paragraphs with a specific style, to every paragraph in a story, or to only selected paragraphs. ▰▰▰▰▰ Sara wants to add a flower bullet to identify each menu item. To do this, she modifies the Entries style to include a bullet. The Entries style is the style used for the name of each menu item.

Steps

1. Click I in the menu item name **Seafood Combo** in the second column
   In order to use the Bullets and numbering plug-in, the insertion point must be placed inside the text block where you want to add the bullet or number.

QuickTip

If you make a mistake while using the Bullets and numbering plug-in, use the Revert command on the File menu to open the last saved version of the current file.

2. Click **Utilities** on the menu bar, point to **Plug-ins**, then click **Bullets and numbering**
   The Bullets and numbering dialog box opens, as shown in Figure G-22. You can select any bullet in the Bullet style section, or click Edit to see a list of all characters that can be used as a bullet.

3. Click **Edit** in the Bullets and numbering dialog box
   The Edit bullet dialog box opens. It displays the available characters for the selected font, in this case, Times New Roman.

Trouble?

Select a different font and bullet character if Wingdings is not available to you.

4. Click the **Font list arrow** *(Macintosh Users: Click the Font list box)*, then click **Wingdings**
   The characters in the dialog box change to show the characters for the Wingdings font, as shown in Figure G-23.

5. Click the **flower character** located in row 6, column 12
   The Example box in the dialog box shows the flower character.

6. Click **OK**
   The Edit bullet dialog box closes. The Bullets and numbering dialog box now includes the flower character among the bullet styles.

MacintoshUsers

This replaces Step 7.
7. Click the All those with Style option button, click the All those with Style list box, click Entries, then click OK

7. Click the **All those with style option button** in the Range section, click the **All those with style list arrow**, click **Entries**, then click **OK**
   The flower bullet is automatically applied to the beginning of each paragraph formatted with the Entries style, as shown in Figure G-24.

8. Close the Styles palette, save your changes, print the publication, close the file, then exit PageMaker

FIGURE G-22: Bullets and numbering dialog box

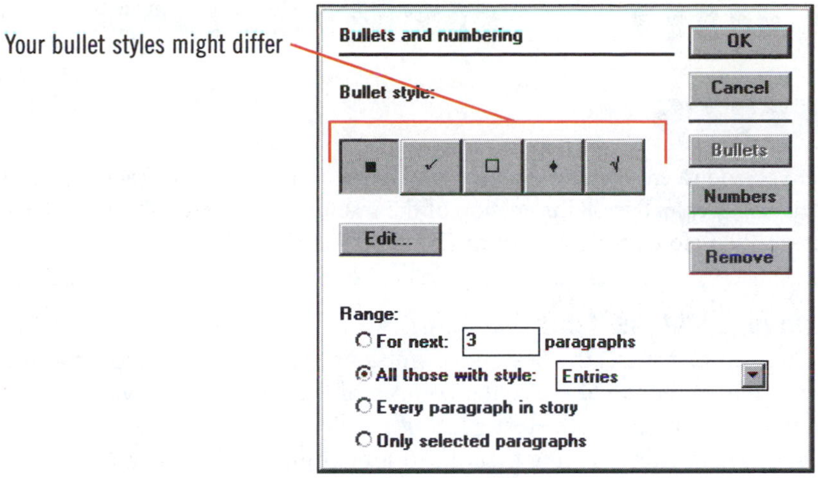

Your bullet styles might differ

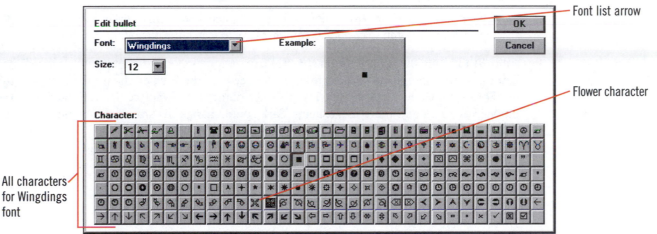

FIGURE G-23: Edit bullet dialog box

Font list arrow

Flower character

All characters for Wingdings font

FIGURE G-24: Flower bullet applied to paragraphs with Entries style

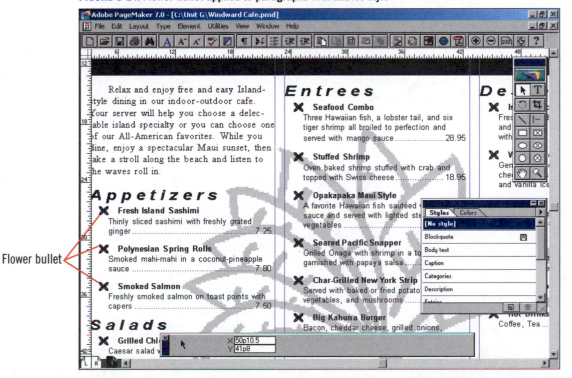

Flower bullet

Design Workshop: Menus

A menu needs to provide a creative, concise listing of a restaurant's fare. The menu needs to feature certain selections and give an overall impression of the restaurant. The completed menu is shown in Figure G-25. Before showing it to the client, Sara critiques her design.

Details

► Does the menu highlight the items it should?

According to Sara's information, the Seafood Combo needed to be featured prominently. She placed this menu item at the top of the center column of the menu. Other ways to highlight the menu item could include reversing the text, placing a bullet or other icon next to the menu item to give it special treatment, or changing the font to something much bolder. No one way is correct. Usually, a few different techniques can work well together to produce the desired result.

► Is the menu well-organized?

Sara separated the menu into five sections to help customers select items quickly. She also placed all of the entrees in one column so customers wouldn't have to search the menu for more selections.

► What other improvements can Sara make?

Sara can easily change menu items to meet the needs of the chef, or change the menu seasonally. For example, during Thanksgiving, a turkey dinner could replace the Seafood Combo. To add variety or to add more menu items, Sara could change the size of the menu or possibly rotate the orientation so the menu is tall instead of wide.

Windward Cafe

Relax and enjoy free and easy Island-style dining in our indoor-outdoor cafe. Your server will help you choose a delectable island specialty or you can choose one of our All-American favorites. While you dine, enjoy a spectacular Maui sunset, then take a stroll along the beach and listen to the waves roll in.

Appetizers

✖ **Fresh Island Sashimi**
Thinly sliced sashimi with freshly grated ginger 7.25

✖ **Polynesian Spring Rolls**
Smoked mahi-mahi in a coconut-pineapple sauce 7.80

✖ **Smoked Salmon**
Freshly smoked salmon on toast points with capers 7.50

Salads

✖ **Grilled Chicken Salad**
Caesar salad with lemon chicken 9.95

✖ **Taco Salad**
With guacamole and salsa.............................. 6.50

Entrees

✖ **Seafood Combo**
Three Hawaiian fish, a lobster tail, and six tiger shrimp all broiled to perfection and served with mango sauce 28.95

✖ **Stuffed Shrimp**
Oven baked shrimp stuffed with crab and topped with Swiss cheese 18.95

✖ **Opakapaka Maui Style**
A favorite Hawaiian fish sautéed with oyster sauce and served with lighted steamed spring vegetables 22.95

✖ **Seared Pacific Snapper**
Grilled Onaga with shrimp in a tomato-sauce garnished with papaya salsa 21.95

✖ **Char-Grilled New York Strip Steak**
Served with baked or fried potatoes, spring vegetables, and mushrooms 24.95

✖ **Big Kahuna Burger**
Bacon, cheddar cheese, grilled onions, avocado, and mushrooms served on a sesame bun 14.95

✖ **Filet of Ono Burger**
Mild and firm Hawaiian fish sautéed in garlic and ginger and served with baby shrimp on a French roll 16.50

Desserts

✖ **Island Macadamia Nut Cream Pie**
Freshly baked pie shell coated with chocolate and filled with macadamia nut custard topped with whipped Cream................................ 8.95

✖ **White Chocolate Cheesecake**
Generous slice of white chocolate cheesecake smothered with raspberry sorbet and vanilla ice cream 7.95

✖ **Chocolate Truffles**
Chocolate filled truffles drizzled with Grand Marnier and flambéed at your table 10.50

Beverages

✖ **Soft Drinks**
Cola, Root Beer, Lime, Orange $2.50

✖ **Non-Carbonated Beverages**
Milk, Ice Tea, Juices $2.50

✖ **Hot Drinks**
Coffee, Tea $2.25

Practice

► Concepts Review

Label each element of the publication window shown in Figure G-26.

FIGURE G-26

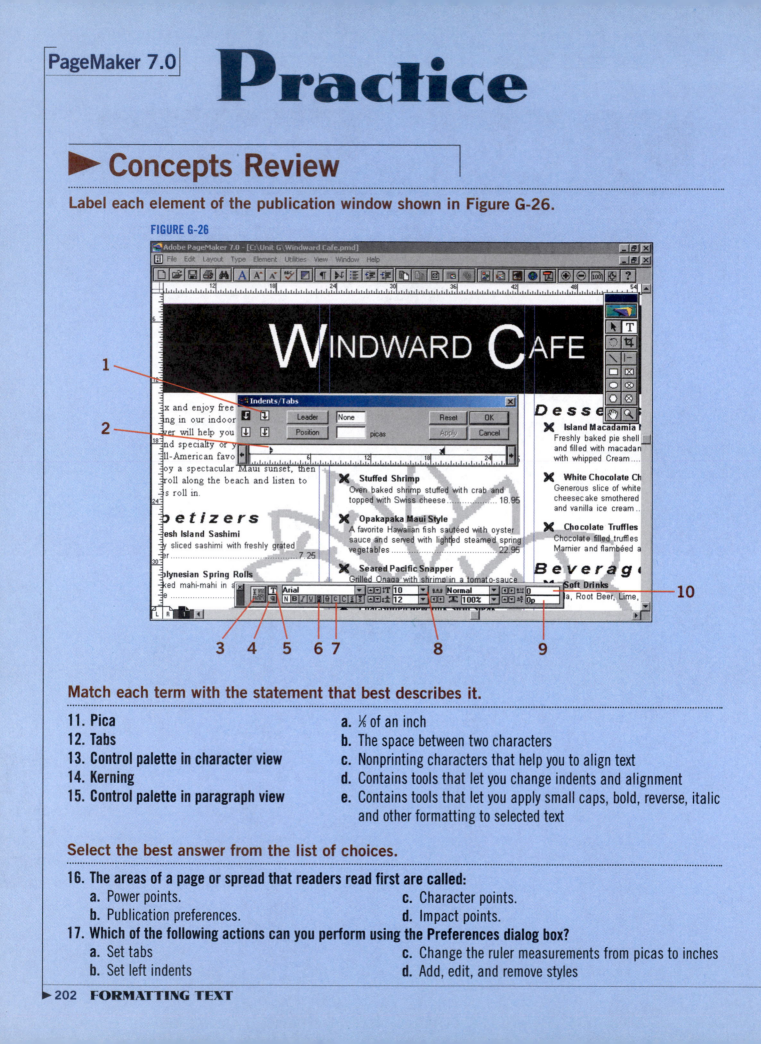

Match each term with the statement that best describes it.

11. Pica
12. Tabs
13. **Control palette in character view**
14. Kerning
15. **Control palette in paragraph view**

a. ⅙ of an inch
b. The space between two characters
c. Nonprinting characters that help you to align text
d. Contains tools that let you change indents and alignment
e. Contains tools that let you apply small caps, bold, reverse, italic and other formatting to selected text

Select the best answer from the list of choices.

16. **The areas of a page or spread that readers read first are called:**
   a. Power points.
   b. Publication preferences.
   c. Character points.
   d. Impact points.
17. **Which of the following actions can you perform using the Preferences dialog box?**
   a. Set tabs
   b. Set left indents
   c. Change the ruler measurements from picas to inches
   d. Add, edit, and remove styles

18. **The imaginary line on which text rests is the:**
    a. Guide.
    b. Track.
    c. Margin.
    d. Baseline.

19. **The Track option on the Control palette lets you:**
    a. Adjust the spacing between lines of text.
    b. Tighten or loosen the space between characters.
    c. Adjust the width of characters.
    d. Adjust the baseline.

20. **The Kerning option on the Control palette lets you:**
    a. Adjust the space between a pair of characters.
    b. Adjust the baseline.
    c. Change the text size.
    d. Set the tracking for paragraphs.

21. **A repeated pattern between tabs is called a(n):**
    a. Tab stop.
    b. Leader.
    c. Indent.
    d. Bullet.

22. **A set amount of space between the first or last word in a line of text and the left or right margin is called a(n):**
    a. Tab.
    b. Indent.
    c. Leader.
    d. Tab stop.

23. **Which of the following tasks is NOT possible to do using the Control palette in character view?**
    a. Apply a font to selected text
    b. Center align selected text
    c. Increase the font size of selected text
    d. Apply small capitals formatting to selected text

24. **Which of the following tasks is NOT possible to do using the Control palette in paragraph view?**
    a. Set a left indent
    b. Set a first-line indent
    c. Right align selected text
    d. Apply bold formatting

25. **Character width can be set using the:**
    a. Character Specifications dialog box.
    b. Control palette in paragraph view.
    c. Font menu.
    d. Paragraph Specifications dialog box.

▶ Skills Review

1. **Set publication preferences.**
    a. Start PageMaker, open the file PM G-2.pmd from the drive and folder where your Project Files are stored, click OK if the PANOSE Font Matching Results dialog box opens, then save the file as **Bistro Menu**.
    b. Open the Preferences dialog box.
    c. Change the Measurements in and Vertical ruler settings to picas.
    d. Change the Save option to Smaller.
    e. Click More to open the More Preferences dialog box.
    f. In the Text section, select the Use typographer's quotes check box.
    g. Click OK in each dialog box to close it.
    h. Save the publication.

2. **Format text using the Control palette.**
    a. Click the Text tool in the toolbox, then select the text Bob's Bistro at the top of the publication page.
    b. Change the view to Actual Size.
    c. Open the Control palette in Character view.
    d. Increase the font size of the selected text to 72 points.
    e. Apply small caps formatting to the selected text.
    f. Open the Character Specifications dialog box, then click Options to open the Character Options dialog box.
    g. Set the small caps size to 70.
    h. Click OK to close each dialog box, then save the publication.

3. **Adjust the baseline.**

   a. Select ob's in the word Bob's.

   b. Change the baseline of the selected text to 0p8 using the nudge up button on the Control palette.

   c. Deselect the text, then select istro in the word Bistro.

   d. Change the baseline to 0p8 for the selected text.

   e. Save the publication.

4. **Adjust text spacing.**

   a. Select the heading Bob's Bistro.

   b. Use the Control palette to change the tracking to Very Loose.

   c. Select the heading Appetizers, then use the Control palette to set the kerning to .30.

   d. Adjust the kerning to .30 for the headings Salads, Beverages, and Entrees, scrolling down as necessary.

   e. Save the publication.

5. **Set character widths.**

   a. Open the Define Styles dialog box, then select the Category style.

   b. Click Edit, then click Char to open the Character Specifications dialog box.

   c. Adjust the horizontal scale to 120.

   d. Click OK to close each dialog box, then save the publication.

6. **Set tabs.**

   a. Open the Define Styles dialog box, then select the Descriptions style.

   b. Click Edit, then click Tabs to open the Indents/Tabs dialog box.

   c. Set a right tab marker at the 16-pica mark on the ruler.

   d. Select the dotted line leader style.

   e. Click OK to close each dialog box.

   f. Open the Define Styles dialog box, select the Appetizer item style, click Edit, then click Tabs.

   g. Set a right tab marker at the 16-pica mark on the ruler, select the dotted line leader style, then click OK to close each dialog box.

   h. Save the publication.

7. **Set indents.**

   a. Open the Define Styles dialog box.

   b. Select the Descriptions style, click Edit, then click Tabs.

   c. Drag the left indent marker to the 1 pica mark, then click OK to close each dialog box.

   d. Save the publication.

8. **Use the Bullets and numbering plug-in.**

   a. Scroll up, then click anywhere in the Blackened Chicken heading.

   b. Click Utilities on the menu bar, point to Plug-ins, then click Bullets and numbering.

   c. Select a bullet style of your choice.

   d. In the Range section, click the All those with style option button, select the Item style, then click OK to close the dialog box.

   e. Change the view to Fit in Window, then compare your screen with Figure G-27.

   f. Save your publication, print a copy, close the file, then exit PageMaker.

FIGURE G-27

BOB'S BISTRO

Appetizers   Entrees

Tomato & Mozzarella.................. 7.95
Escargot 6.95
Jalapeno Poppers 7.95
Assorted Tapas for 2 .... 12.95

- **Blackened Chicken**
  A Creole blend of spices baked into an 8 oz. chicken breast. Served on a bed of red beans and rice with jambalaya and a house vegetable on the side. 12.95

- **Marinated Grille**
  Our 8 oz. chicken breast marinates in light Italian dressing for 24 hours before grilling. Served on a kaiser roll with french fries or baked potato on the side. 14.95

Salads

Grilled Chicken Caesar Salad 5.95
Chef Salad 5.95
Spinach & Tomato Salad 4.75
House Salad 2.50

- **Cowboy Dinner**
  A 14 oz. New York Strip Steak marinated in Jack Daniels and flame-grilled to perfection. Served with baked potato, house vegetable and salad. 18.95

- **Surf & Turf**
  An 8 oz. sirloin steak and a half pound of shrimp join forces. Served with baked potato, house vegetable, and salad 18.95

Beverages

Coffee, Tea 1.25
Juice (Cranberry or Orange) 2.00
Bob's Bistro Punch 3.00

- **Scallops**
  A lemon butter sauce engulfs a generous portion of white scallops 16.95

- **Shrimp**
  A guaranteed pound and a half of headless shrimp served on ice with lemon and homemade cocktail sauce 16.95

- **Swordfish**
  Meaty, grilled swordfish served with new potatoes and house vegetable 16.95

► Independent Challenge 1

Antonio Romano, the owner of Antonio's Pizza Place, has hired you to create a new menu for the restaurant. Antonio wants the menu to be a single wide page with three columns. He wants to list the appetizers and salads in the first column, the pizzas and different toppings in the middle column, and the weekend specials in the third column. The clientele is mostly college students and young adults, so the design needs to appeal to a 20-something audience.

a. Create a rough sketch of the menu that contains the following elements: a headline for the name of the restaurant, headings for Appetizers, Salads, Pizzas, Toppings, and Weekend Specials, and one piece of appropriate clip art.

b. Start PageMaker, create a new 8½" × 11" document with wide orientation, then save it as **Pizza Place Menu** to the drive and folder where your Project Files are stored. Use the Preferences dialog box to change the ruler measurements to picas, and choose the Save Smaller option.

c. Create column guides for three columns. Create a headline for the name of the restaurant at the top of the page. Use the Control palette to format the text so that it looks compelling.

d. Place the text for the menu items in the three columns under the restaurant name. The text for the menu items is contained in the following three files, located in the drive and folder where your Project files are stored: PM G-3.doc (for column 1 items), PM G-4.doc (for column 2 items), and PM G-5.doc (for column 3 items).

e. Use the Control palette to format the category headings, choosing a font, font style, and font size that looks good. Apply small caps to the headings, then use the Character Options dialog box to adjust the small caps size to 60%.

f. Apply Very Loose tracking to the headings, adjust the kerning for each of the headings to .1 pica, then change the horizontal scale of the headings to 120%. Use paragraph view of the Control palette to center the headings.

g. Format a single menu item so that it looks good, then create a style called **Item**. Apply the Item style to the other menu items.

h. Edit the Item style to set a tab at an appropriate place on the ruler for the prices. Choose a dotted leader to run between each menu item and its price.

i. In column 2, apply appropriate formatting to the Topping and Small/Large subheadings.

j. In column 3, apply formatting to the special The Romano Lode so that it stands out and looks good. Create a style called **Special** based on this formatting. Apply the Special style to both The Romano Lode and The Casi Romano.

k. Add a bullet to the Special style.

l. Add an appropriate piece of clip art somewhere on the menu using the Picture palette or the PageMaker Content CD.

m. Use your PageMaker skills to format the Weekend Specials column so that this information stands out from the rest of the menu. For instance, you might want to draw a shaded rectangle around these items and then use the Arrange/Send to Back command to place it behind the text.

n. Adjust the formatting of the menu so that it looks professional, save your publication, print a copy, close the file, then exit PageMaker.

▶ Independent Challenge 2

Collect three menus from local restaurants. Critique the menus using the design guidelines you learned in this unit:

- Does the menu adequately use the power points? What is the first thing you see when you look at the menu?
- Does the overall design organize the menu items in a simple, easily understood format?
- Does the menu contain too much text? If so, is there too much text because of the number of items on the menu or because of the item descriptions?
- Does the menu offer too many choices? Studies show restaurant guests look at a menu for 1.5 minutes. Can you make your choices easily in this time frame?

Re-create one of the menus using the techniques learned in this unit. Use the Control palette as much as possible for both character and paragraph formatting modifications.

a. Start PageMaker, create a new publication, then save it as **Copied Menu** to the drive and folder where your Project Files are stored.

b. Set an appropriate paper size and orientation for the menu, then set the following preferences: change the measurement system to picas, choose the Save Smaller option, and set typographer's quotes.

c. Enter the text and illustrate the menu with a clip art graphic, if appropriate. Use the [Tab] key to insert tabs between each menu item and its associated price.

d. Use the Control palette to set the font, size, type style, kerning, tracking, baseline, and the horizontal scale of the text so that the menu headings resemble the real menu as much as possible.

e. Format the menu items, descriptions, specials, and so forth, and create styles for each type of text.

f. Set tabs and indents as appropriate, and use tab leaders between menu items and prices, if appropriate.

g. Adjust the formatting so the menu looks good, save your changes, print a copy, close the file, then exit PageMaker.

▶ Independent Challenge 3

You are opening a new restaurant offering your favorite cuisine. Take a few minutes to determine the name of your restaurant, the type of restaurant it is, the kind of food you serve, and the kind of clientele you want to attract. Your restaurant can be anything from a four-star establishment that caters to business executives to a family pancake house.

a. Sketch your menu.

b. Start PageMaker, then create a new publication using your sketch as a guide. Save your publication as **My Restaurant Menu** to the drive and folder where your Project Files are stored.

c. Modify the publication preferences to use the pica measurement system, the Save Smaller option, and typographer's quotes.

d. Enter the text for your menu. Either enter original text, or use the text from the following files, found on the drive and folder where your Project Files are stored: PM G-6.doc (appetizers and salads), PM G-7.doc (entrees), and PM G-8.doc (desserts and beverages). Modify this text to suit the menu offerings for your restaurant.

e. Use the Control palette to format the menu text. Choose fonts, font styles, and font sizes that make the menu attractive and readable. Adjust the kerning, tracking, baseline, and horizontal scale to make the headings stand out. Create styles for the different categories of text in the menu (such as heading, item, description, and so forth).

f. Use the [Tab] key to insert a tab between each menu item and its price, then use the Indents/Tabs dialog box to position the tabs and add leaders.

g. Add a clip art graphic or graphics to the menu using an image (or images) from the Picture palette or the PageMaker Content CD.

h. Adjust the formatting of the menu, save it, print the menu, close the file, then exit PageMaker.

e Independent Challenge 4

You work for a design firm in London. Your boss has asked you to create a new menu for a well-known restaurant in the city. The restaurant manager has requested that the design be black and white, as the menus get so much use that they must be reprinted often. She also told your boss that their printer requires that the publication be submitted in picas.

a. Open your browser, then use a search engine such as Infoseek (www.infoseek.com) to search for information on a restaurant located in London. You should be able to find a restaurant that offers some or all of the menu items on the World Wide Web. If not, be prepared to make up some of your own dishes and be sure to include the prices. You can also use Yahoo!, Excite, AltaVista, or another search engine.

b. Once you find a restaurant and menu, download or print the menu, then sketch a new menu design.

c. Create a new publication in PageMaker, choosing appropriate dimensions for your publication based on your sketch.

d. Set your menu's preferences to pica measurements.

e. Enter the text in the publication, placing headings according to your sketch. You can use story editor if you wish, or enter the text in a word processor and then place it in your publication.

f. Use the Control palette to format the text. Format at least one item in small caps and adjust the baseline to create an interesting effect.

g. Create styles for the different parts of the menu, as appropriate. Apply any fonts and formatting that you wish, however, you must adjust the tracking and horizontal scale for at least two styles in a way that makes the menu look great.

h. Insert tabs before each price in the publication, then add dotted tab leaders to separate your descriptions from the prices.

i. Indent each of the menu description paragraphs so they look good.

j. Add a bullet to one of the styles in the menu.

k. Save your menu as **London Menu** to the drive and folder where your Project Files are stored, print a copy, close the file, then exit PageMaker.

▶ Visual Workshop

Open the file PM G-9.pmd from the drive and folder where your Project Files are stored, and enhance it to create the menu shown in Figure G-28. Format the restaurant name as shown, using 36-point Arial bold. Format the welcome paragraph in 14-point Times New Roman bold, and apply Very Loose tracking to it. Edit the Category style to include 24-point Arial bold, Very Loose tracking, and a Horizontal scale of 130. Edit the Description style to include 14-point text, a 2-pica left indent, and a right tab at the 19-pica mark with a dotted leader, as shown. Edit the Entree Item style and the Dessert and Beverage Item style to include 14-point bold Arial, and add a bullet to the Entree Item style. Place the graphic and text boxes as shown, save the publication as **Neptune Lounge** to the drive and folder where your Project Files are stored, then print a copy.

FIGURE G-28

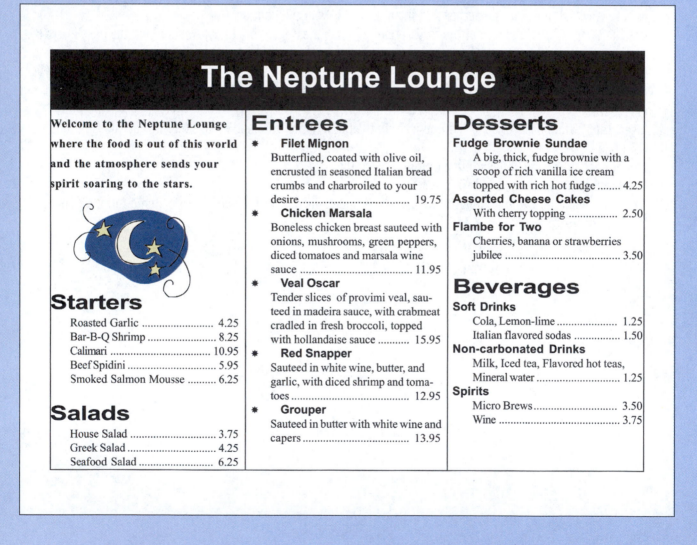

PageMaker 7.0

Unit H

Using Advanced Graphics

Objectives

- Plan a poster
- Examine the Control palette in object view
- Link a graphic to a publication
- Scale a graphic
- Place an inline graphic
- Modify an inline graphic
- Skew an object
- Reflect an object
- Change an object's link
- Use layers
- Use image control
- Design Workshop: Posters

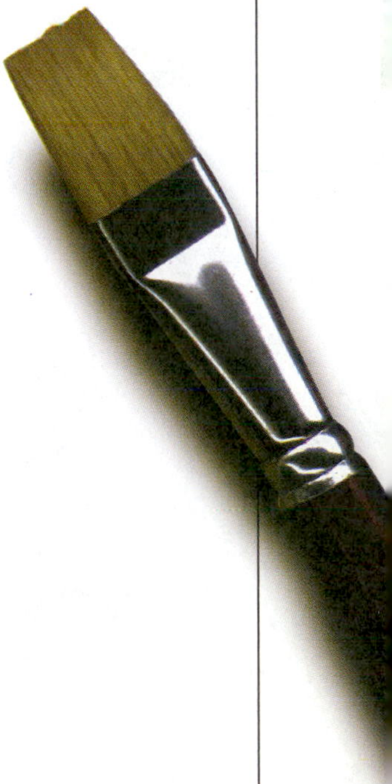

PageMaker's advanced graphics capabilities allow you to create special effects with graphics. In this unit, you learn how to use the Control palette in object view to modify graphics quickly and precisely. You also learn how to link a graphic to a publication, how to improve the appearance of black-and-white images, and how to work with layers. The Watsonville Chamber Music Society has hired Sara Norton to create several posters advertising their spring and summer concert series.

PageMaker 7.0

Details

Planning a Poster

Posters follow many of the same rules as other advertising publications, but on a larger scale. Posters usually contain large, color graphics and bold type. Although full-color posters can be expensive, they are often worth the expense because they can create an instant and lasting impact on viewers. Sara's first poster for the Watsonville Chamber Music Society will advertise a concert performance by Riviera Strings, a world-renowned string quartet from the French Riviera. Sarah's sketch for the poster is shown in Figure H-1.

Keep the following guidelines in mind when planning a poster:

► Create a proof version of the poster

A **proof version** is a smaller, less costly version of the final poster. Because posters are expensive to produce, Sara decides to first create an 8" × 14" proof version. After Sara is satisfied with her proof version of the poster, she will send her PageMaker file to a commercial printer, who will create another proof to make sure the printing equipment can produce the correct color output. Once Sara approves this proof version, the commercial printer will print the poster at the final 24" × 42" dimensions.

► Use colorful, striking graphics

Posters are meant to be on display. Whether tacked up on a wall or placed in a frame, posters have a longer life span than most other forms of advertising. For a successful design, use graphics or photography that is pleasing and memorable. Sara will use a striking photograph of the French Riviera, where the group originates. The photo dominates Sara's sketch of the poster.

► Use bold text in a unique way

If you plan to use text on your poster, it should be large and bold so it jumps out at the viewer. Sara will feature the words "Riviera Strings" in bold type on the poster. She will then add a clip art graphic of a violin between the two words to create an interesting visual effect.

► Use paper stock that is durable

The type of paper you choose for your poster depends on your budget and your goal for the longevity of the posters. The thicker the paper, the longer the posters will last. Sara decides to use a 60-pound glossy paper so that the posters communicate a sense of elegance and quality.

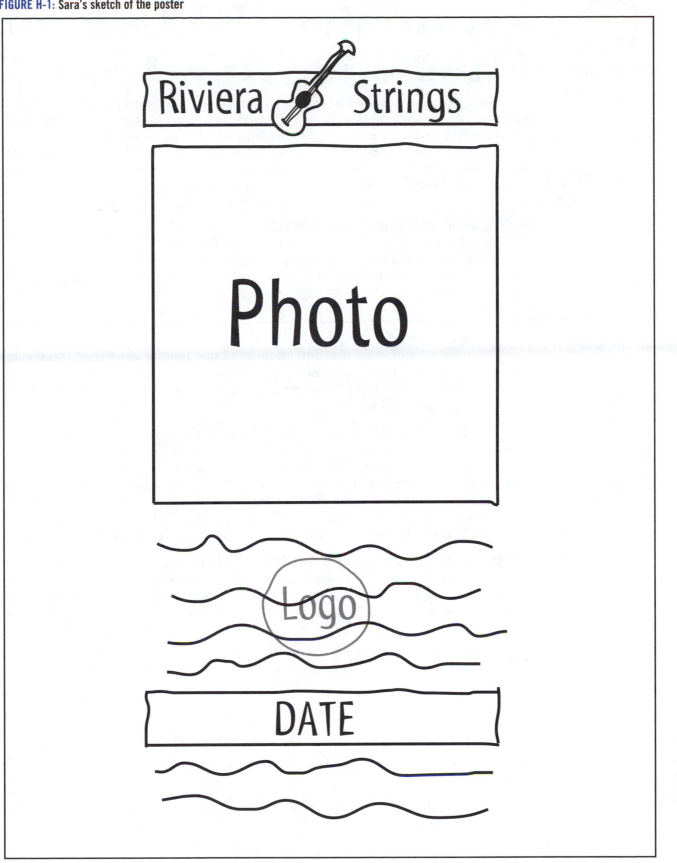

Examining the Control Palette in Object View

The Control palette can appear in character view, paragraph view, and object view. **Object view** gives you the ability to create unique effects with graphic images and to size, position, or transform them easily and uniformly. To **transform** an object means to change its appearance by rotating, skewing, or reflecting it. Figure H-2 shows the Control palette in object view. Before Sara begins her poster, she reviews the benefits of using the Control palette in object view to modify graphics.

Details

► Reflect, skew, and rotate graphic objects

The Control palette in object view gives you the ability to reflect, skew, and rotate graphic objects. When you **reflect** an object, you flip it from top to bottom or from right to left. When you **skew** an object, you stretch the object at an angle, giving it a distorted appearance. When you **rotate** an object, you change the angle at which it appears. The Control palette allows you to skew or rotate an object by nudging it or by entering a precise angle measurement.

► Size, scale, and position objects with precision

You can rely on the rulers and your own judgment to size, scale, or move graphics using the mouse. However, using the Control palette, you can enter exact measurements for sizing, scaling, and positioning graphic objects, or you can use the nudge buttons to change the size and position of an object by increments.

► Size, position, and transform objects using a specific reference point

When you modify an object using the Control palette, you must choose a side, a corner, or the center of the object to serve as the **reference point**. You select a reference point by using the **Proxy** on the Control palette, a graphical representation of the selected object, as shown in Figure H-3. When you reflect, skew, rotate, or scale a graphic, the reference point you select remains fixed as you transform or size the object. In addition, the X and Y coordinates that appear on the Control palette reflect the position of the reference point for the selected object.

► Rotate, reflect, and position multiple objects at once

You can rotate, reflect, or position multiple objects at one time using the Control palette, allowing you to modify graphics quickly and easily. Note, however, that you cannot scale or skew more than one object at a time.

FIGURE H-2: Control palette in object view

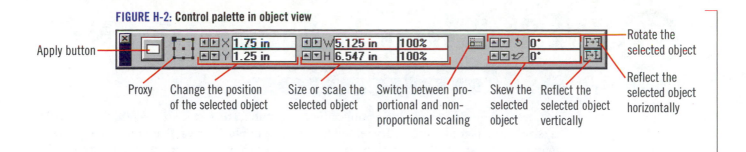

Apply button

Proxy   Change the position   Size or scale the   Switch between pro-   Skew the   Reflect the   Reflect the
         of the selected object   selected object   portional and non-   selected   selected object   selected object
                                                      proportional scaling   object   vertically   horizontally

Rotate the
selected object

FIGURE H-3: The reference point on the Proxy

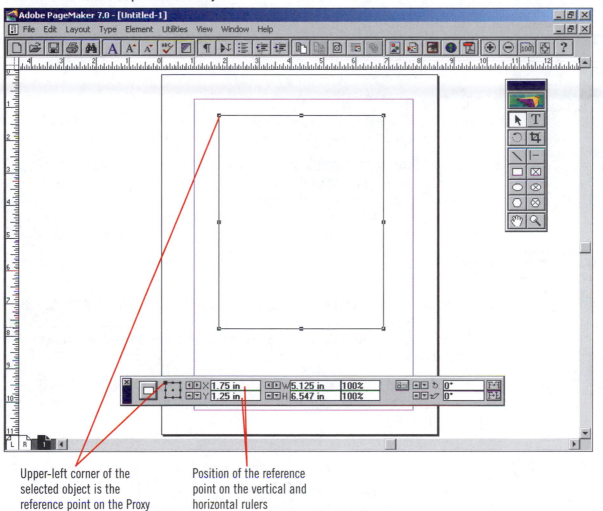

Upper-left corner of the   Position of the reference
selected object is the   point on the vertical and
reference point on the Proxy   horizontal rulers

Linking a Graphic to a Publication

Each time you place a graphic in a publication, your publication's file size increases by the original size of the placed graphic. Therefore, the size of a publication can balloon to a huge size if it has a lot of graphics. You can minimize the file size of your publication by linking a graphic to the publication when you place it, rather than storing a copy of the graphic in the publication. When you link a graphic, it is important to store the original source graphic file in the same location as your PageMaker publication file, so that the linked file will appear when you open the publication. If you do not store the original file in the same location as the publication, the graphics will not appear in the publication. Sara decides to minimize the size of the poster file by linking the graphics to the publication.

Steps

Trouble?

Click OK if the PANOSE Font Matching Results dialog box opens.

1. Start PageMaker, open the file **PM H-1.pmd** from the drive and folder where your Project Files are stored, save it as **Concert Poster**, then maximize the publication window if necessary
The partially completed poster opens in the publication window.

QuickTip

To change the default link options for all new publications, change the settings in the Link Options: Defaults dialog box when no publications are open.

2. Click **Element** on the menu bar, then click **Link Options**
The Link Options: Defaults dialog box opens, as shown in Figure H-4. You use this dialog box to change the link option defaults for the current publication.

3. Click the **Store copy in publication check box** in the Graphics section to deselect it
Turning off the option ensures that placed graphics are stored outside the publication, but are linked to the publication. Notice that when you choose to link placed graphics, the Update automatically option turns on. This ensures that if the original source file is modified, the linked graphic in the publication will be updated automatically.

4. Click **OK**
The Link Options: Defaults dialog box closes.

QuickTip

Turning off the Store copy in publication option only affects the graphic objects you place in the future; it does not affect graphic objects previously placed in a publication.

5. If necessary, click **Window** on the menu bar, then click **Show Control Palette**
The Control palette appears in object view. Notice that as you drag the pointer across the publication window, the values in both the Position X and Y text boxes change to reflect the exact position of the pointer.

6. Click **File** on the menu bar, click **Place**, select the graphic file **CapFerat.jpg** from the drive and folder where your Project Files are stored, then click **Open** *(Macintosh Users: Click OK)*
The pointer changes to ⊠.

Trouble?

If you have trouble placing the figure exactly in the correct position, place it as closely as you can, then enter the exact measurements in the X and Y text boxes on the Control palette.

7. Move ⊠ to the upper-left corner of the publication, position the pointer so that the pointer guides align with the **1.25"** mark on the horizontal ruler and the **1"** mark on the vertical ruler, then click
The photograph appears on the publication page with its upper-left corner positioned at the 1.25" mark on the horizontal ruler and the 1" mark on the vertical ruler. The Control palette shows the measurements 1.25 in the X text box and 1 in the Y text box, as shown in Figure H-5.

8. Click **File** on the menu bar, then click **Save** to save your changes to the publication
Although the photo appears in the publication, it is linked to the publication and is not saved as part of the publication file.

FIGURE H-4: Link Options: Defaults dialog box

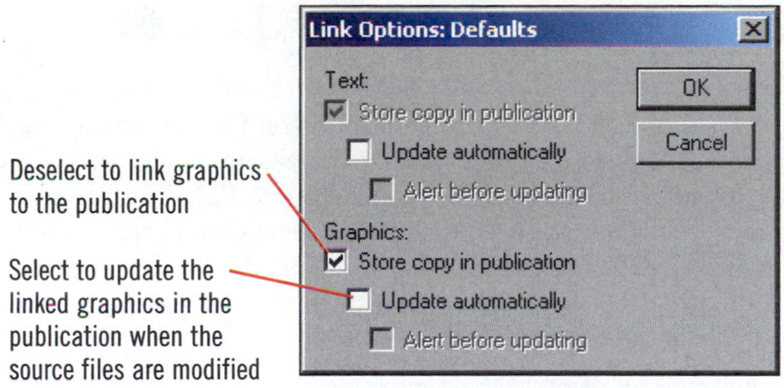

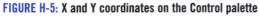

Link Options: Defaults
Text:
Store copy in publication
Update automatically
Alert before updating
Graphics:
Store copy in publication
Update automatically
Alert before updating
OK
Cancel
Deselect to link graphics to the publication
Select to update the linked graphics in the publication when the source files are modified

FIGURE H-5: X and Y coordinates on the Control palette

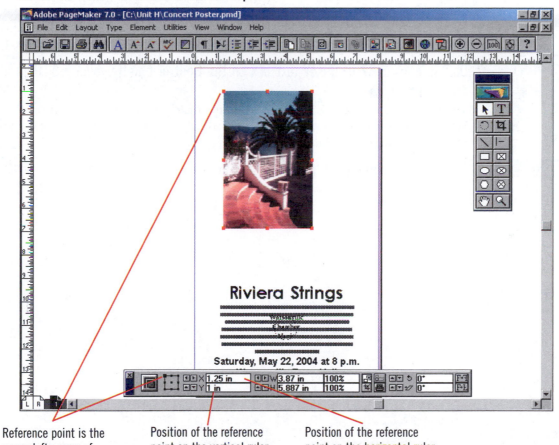

Adobe PageMaker 7.0 - [C:\Unit H\Concert Poster.pmd]
File Edit Layout Type Element Utilities View Window Help
Riviera Strings
Saturday, May 22, 2004 at 8 p.m.
X 1.25 in
Y 1 in
W 3.87 in
H 5.887 in
100%
100%
0°
0°
Reference point is the upper-left corner of the photo
Position of the reference point on the vertical ruler
Position of the reference point on the horizontal ruler

Scaling a Graphic

When a graphic is selected, the Control palette displays the coordinates of the reference point, the dimensions of the graphic, and the percentage of its current size in relation to the original. Using the Control palette you can **scale** an object by decreasing or increasing its dimensions either proportionally or nonproportionally. You can also use the Control palette to crop a graphic. Table H-1 describes the buttons on the Control palette used to scale and crop graphics. Sara wants to increase the size of the photo while maintaining its proportions. She uses the Control palette to increase the width to 5.5", and then lets PageMaker automatically determine the proportional height.

Steps

Trouble?

If the upper-left reference point is not selected on the Proxy, click it to select it.

1. Select the **photograph**, if necessary

The red selection handles indicate the graphic is selected. Notice on the Control palette that the upper-left reference point is selected on the Proxy. This corner of the graphic will remain anchored as the photo is resized.

2. Click the **Proportional scaling off button** ⊞ on the Control palette

Clicking the Proportional scaling off button changes the button to the Proportional scaling on button ⊞. When ⊞ is active on the Control palette, any change you make to one dimension of the graphic will automatically adjust the other dimension so that the graphic is enlarged or reduced proportionally. This button is a **toggle button**, which means that you use it to turn proportional scaling on and off.

3. Double-click **3.87** in the W text box on the Control palette, type **5.5**, then click the **Apply button** ▣

The photograph is now 5.5" wide and approximately 8.4" high, as shown in Figure H-6. When you changed the width of the photograph, PageMaker automatically scaled the height of the photograph to maintain its original proportions.

4. Deselect the graphic, then save your changes to the publication

QuickTip

To restore a graphic to its original dimensions, type 100 in the size percentage text boxes on the Control palette.

Using the Control palette to crop a graphic

You can use the Control palette in object view to crop a graphic with precision. With the graphic selected, click the Cropping button ⊞ on the Control palette, then select a reference point on the Proxy. The reference point remains fixed as you crop the graphic, so, for example, if you want to crop a graphic from the right, select a reference point on the left side of the graphic. Once you have selected a reference point, enter new height and/or width measurements for the graphic in the Height and Width text boxes on the Control palette, and then click the Apply button to crop the graphic. When you are finished cropping, click the Scaling button in the Control palette to turn off the crop feature.

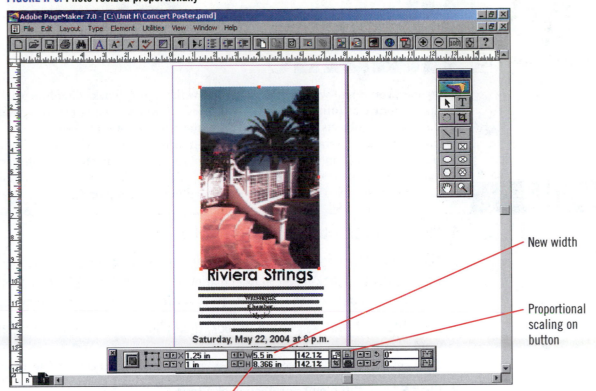

New width

Proportional scaling on button

Height is automatically adjusted to maintain the photo's original scale

TABLE H-1: Control palette scaling and cropping options

button	name	use to
	Scaling button	Size a graphic proportionally or nonproportionally
	Proportional scaling on	Size a graphic to any percentage of its original dimensions; a toggle button
	Proportional scaling off	Size the height and width of a graphic independently; a toggle button
	Printer resolution scaling button	Scale a graphic to match the resolution of the target printer
	Cropping button	Conceal part of a graphic

PageMaker 7.0

Placing an Inline Graphic

Sometimes, you might want to place a graphic within a text block. Graphics placed within text blocks are known as **inline graphics**. In the previous units, the graphics you placed were independent of other objects and you could move them freely within the layout view. Inline graphics, however, are part of a line of text and remain within the text block in which they are placed. You move an inline graphic by moving the text block or by moving the text within the text block. Sara wants to personalize the headline "Riviera Strings" by adding an inline graphic of a violin. Before she does this, she moves the headline to the top of the poster.

Steps

1. Click the Riviera Strings text block to select it

2. Make sure the upper-left reference point is selected in the Proxy on the Control palette, double-click **9.281** in the Position Y text box, type **.25**, then press **[Enter]**
   The text block moves to the top of the page, above the photograph, as shown in Figure H-7.

3. Click the **Text tool** [T] in the toolbox, then click to the left of the letter "S" in the word "Strings"
   The Control palette changes to character view because you clicked the Text tool.

4. Click **File** on the menu bar, then click **Place**
   The Place dialog box opens.

5. Select the file **Violin.jpg** from the drive and folder where your Project Files are stored, then verify that the **As inline graphic option button** is selected in the Place section of the dialog box
   Because the Text tool is active when you opened the Place dialog box, PageMaker assumes you want to place an inline graphic, so the As inline graphic option button is selected by default in the dialog box. If the Pointer tool had been active, the As independent graphic option button would have been selected by default.

6. Click **Open** (*Macintosh Users: Click OK*)
   The violin graphic appears between "Riviera" and "Strings" at the location of the insertion point in the text block. Notice that the photograph is now covering the headline and graphic slightly. Placing the inline graphic in the text block made the text block taller.

7. Click the **Pointer tool** [↖] in the toolbox, click the **photograph** to select it, make sure the upper-left reference point is selected in the Proxy, double-click **1** in the Position Y text box, type **1.5**, then press **[Enter]**
   The photo is now repositioned below the text block so that it no longer covers the violin graphic, as shown in Figure H-8.

8. Save your changes to the publication

FIGURE H-7: Text block moved above photograph

Upper-left corner of the text block aligns with the .25" mark on the vertical ruler

Upper-left corner is the reference point

Apply button changes depending on the selected object

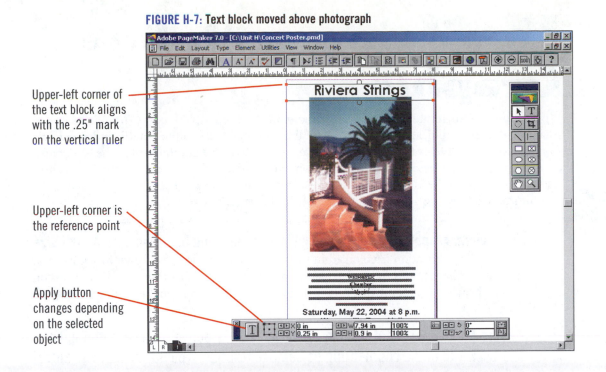

FIGURE H-8: Violin inline graphic

Inline graphic

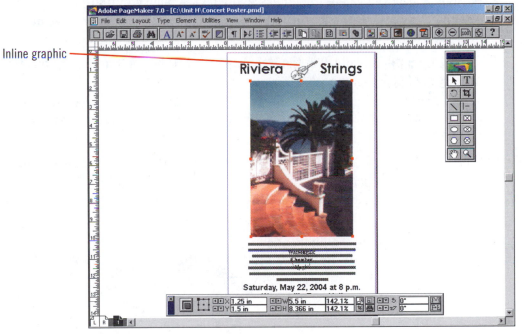

Advantages and disadvantages of using inline graphics

One advantage of using an inline graphic is that it allows you to keep related text and graphics together so that when you move the text block, the graphic moves with the text. This is particularly useful for figures with captions. One disadvantage of using an inline graphic is that when you enter or delete text from the text block, the graphic moves as the text flow changes; therefore the graphic continuously moves during editing. Another disadvantage is that you cannot move the graphic independently of the text. Finally, you cannot wrap text around an inline graphic.

Modifying an Inline Graphic

When you move or rotate a text block that contains an inline graphic, the graphic moves or rotates with the text block. However, you can also manipulate an inline graphic independently from the text block. For example, you can size and rotate an inline graphic within the line of text, or you can adjust the baseline position of an inline graphic independently of the line of text. Sara resizes the violin graphic to make it 80% of the original size. She then adjusts the graphic's baseline position to center it vertically in the text block.

Steps 1234

1. Click the **violin graphic** to select it, click **View** on the menu bar, then click **Actual Size**
   The top of the publication is enlarged in the publication window, as shown in Figure H-9. Notice the Baseline shift option has replaced the Proxy and the Position X and Y options on the Control palette. The Control palette displays only options that can be used to modify the selected object.

> **Trouble?**
>
> If you get an error message, check that you typed 80 in the Width percentage text box and not in the Width text box (containing the measurement "in").

2. Make sure the **Proportional scaling on button** ⊡ is active on the Control palette, double-click **100** in the Width sizing percentage text box, type **80**, then press **[Enter]**
   The violin is resized to 80% of its original size, as shown in Figure H-10.

3. Position ▸ over the violin, then press and hold the mouse button
   The pointer changes to ↕ allowing you to move the graphic either up or down in relation to the baseline.

4. Drag ↕ up until **0** displays in the Baseline shift text box on the Control palette, then release the mouse button
   The violin is now resting on the baseline and looks much better. However, it is positioned closer to "Strings" than to "Riviera" and would look better still if the blank space after Riviera is removed.

> **MacintoshUsers**
>
> This replaces Step 5.
> 5. Click directly to the left of the Violin graphic with the Text tool, and then press [Delete]

5. Click the **Text tool** T in the toolbox, click after Riviera, then press **[Delete]** to remove the extra space
   The inline graphic is now centered between the words in the headline text, as shown in Figure H-11.

6. Save your changes to the publication

CLUES TO USE

Spacing around inline graphics

By simply pressing [Spacebar], you can add space between text and an inline graphic. Another way to control the horizontal space between text and inline graphics is to use indents and tabs. You can control the vertical space between paragraph text and an inline graphic by changing the leading. Whenever you place an inline graphic, PageMaker applies an autoleading format to it that is different from the paragraph's leading, creating odd line spacing in the paragraph. To make the line spacing consistent in a paragraph that includes an inline graphic, you can either reduce the size of the inline graphic or increase the leading of the paragraph.

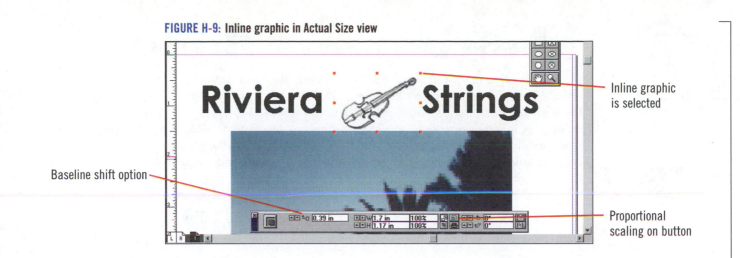

FIGURE H-9: Inline graphic in Actual Size view

Inline graphic is selected

Baseline shift option

Proportional scaling on button

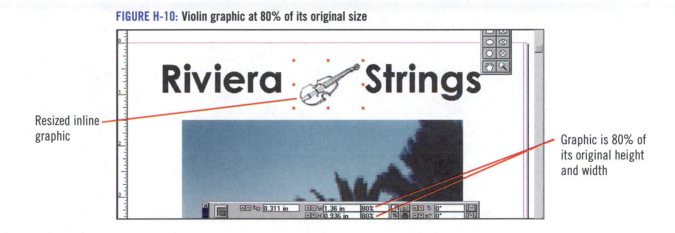

FIGURE H-10: Violin graphic at 80% of its original size

Resized inline graphic

Graphic is 80% of its original height and width

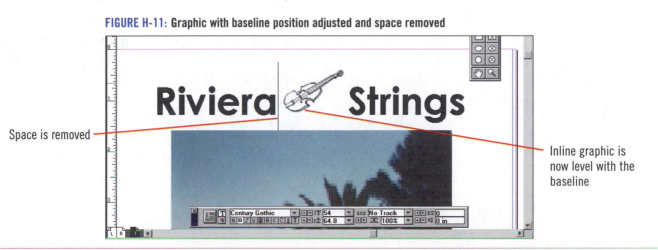

FIGURE H-11: Graphic with baseline position adjusted and space removed

Space is removed

Inline graphic is now level with the baseline

Skewing an Object

When you skew, or distort, an object's horizontal dimensions, you can create an interesting visual effect. Skewing an object stretches it at an angle, giving it a distorted appearance. Using the Skew text box on the Control palette in object view, you can skew a graphic horizontally by 85 degrees in either direction. You cannot skew an object's vertical dimensions. ✎ Sara wants to add a skewed box to the top of the poster. Before she draws the box, she sets up vertical ruler guides and turns on the Snap to Guides option, so that it will be easier to draw the box to exact measurements.

Steps 1234

1. Click **View** on the menu bar, point to **Zoom To**, click **50% Size**, then scroll if necessary so the top half of the poster is displayed in the publication window

2. Drag a **vertical ruler guide** to the **.5"** mark on the horizontal ruler, then drag a second **vertical ruler guide** to the **7.5"** mark on the horizontal ruler

3. Click **View** on the menu bar, then verify that a check mark appears next to **Snap to Guides** on the View menu; if a check mark does not appear, click **Snap to Guides**
   Turning on the Snap to Guides option gives the ruler guides a "magnetic" effect, making it easier to align items to the guides.

4. Click the **Rectangle tool** ▢ in the toolbox, then position the **+** pointer at the **.5"** mark on the vertical and horizontal rulers

5. Drag **+** down and to the right until the pointer guides align with the **7.5"** mark on the horizontal ruler and the **1.25"** mark on the vertical ruler, then release the mouse button
   As you drag, notice that the right edge of the rectangle snaps to the ruler guide at the 7.5" mark. The rectangle appears as shown in Figure H-12. Notice the rectangle's dimensions in the Control palette.

6. Click **Element** on the menu bar, then click **Fill and Stroke**
   The Fill and Stroke dialog box opens, as shown in Figure H-13.

7. Click the **Fill list arrow**, click **Solid**, click the **Color list arrow** in the Fill section, click **Black**, click the **Tint list arrow** in the Fill section, click **20**, click the **Stroke list arrow**, click **None**, then click **OK**
   The rectangle is filled with a grey tint, a 20% shade of black. There is no line around the rectangle.

QuickTip

To skew an object to the left, enter a negative measurement in the Skew text box.

8. Double-click **0+** in the Skew text box on the Control palette, type **25**, then press **[Enter]**
   The rectangle is skewed 25% to the right, as shown in Figure H-14. You can skew an object in .01% increments.

9. Click **Element** on the menu bar, point to **Arrange**, click **Send to Back**, then save your changes to the publication
   The skewed rectangle moves behind the headline and the inline graphic.

FIGURE H-12: Rectangle with exact measurements shown in the Control palette

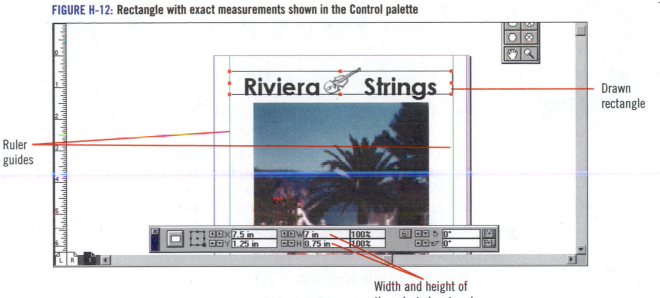

Ruler guides

Drawn rectangle

Width and height of the selected rectangle

FIGURE H-13: Fill and Stroke dialog box

Select a fill pattern, color, and tint

Select a stroke weight, style, color, and tint

Fill and Stroke			
Fill: None	Stroke: 1pt	OK	
Color: None	Color: Black	Cancel	
Tint: 100 %	Tint: 100 %		
☐ Overprint	☐ Overprint		
	☑ Transparent background		
	☐ Reverse		

FIGURE H-14: Rectangle skewed 25%

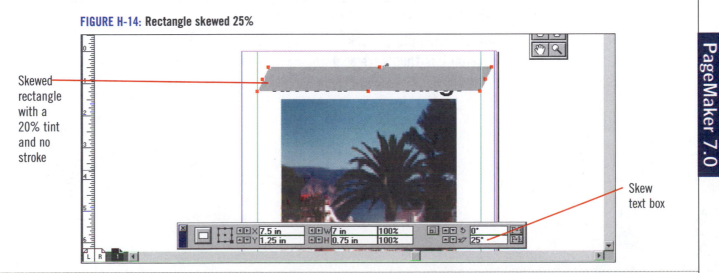

Skewed rectangle with a 20% tint and no stroke

Skew text box

Reflecting an Object

You can also use the Control palette in object view to reflect an object either vertically or horizontally. Sara wants to create a visual link between the top and bottom headlines in the poster. She decides to create a copy of the skewed box behind the headline, reflect the copy, and then place it behind the phone number at the bottom of the poster.

1. Click the **Pointer tool** in the toolbox, click the **skewed rectangle** to select the Riviera Strings text block, press and hold **[Ctrl]** (*Macintosh Users: Press [Command]*), then click the **skewed rectangle** again to select the rectangle
   Pressing [Ctrl] as you click stacked objects allows you to select the next layer down in the stack.

2. Click **Edit** on the menu bar, click **Copy**, click **Edit** on the menu bar, then click **Paste**
   A copy of the skewed rectangle appears on top of the headline.

QuickTip

To remove skewing or reflecting from an object, select the object, click Element on the menu bar, then click Remove Transformation.

3. Click the **Vertical reflecting button** on the Control palette, click **View** on the menu bar, then click **Fit in Window**
   The copy of the skewed rectangle reflects vertically, and appears as a mirror image of the original, as shown in Figure H-15.

4. Position the pointer over the title bar on the left side of the Control palette, then drag the Control palette to the middle of the page
   The Control palette is now out of the way.

Trouble?

If you have trouble positioning the object, type 7.5 in the X text box on the Control palette, type 12.25 in the Y text box, then click the Apply button.

5. Drag the **reflected skewed rectangle** over the Saturday May 22 headline so that the top pointer guide aligns approximately with the **12.25"** mark on the vertical ruler and the far-left corner aligns with the **ruler guide**
   The skewed rectangle covers the date and time of the concert, as shown in Figure H-16.

6. Click **Element** on the menu bar, point to **Arrange**, then click **Send to Back**
   The rectangle moves behind the text block. It would look better if it did not overlap the text below the date and time.

7. Click the **Proportional scaling on button** on the Control palette so that the Proportional scaling off button appears, select **0.75** in the Height text box, type **.5**, then press **[Enter]**
   The skewed rectangle is now ¼ of an inch shorter and no longer overlaps the text below, as shown in Figure H-17. Because the Proportional scaling off button is active, the width of the rectangle remained the same when you changed the height. The two skewed rectangles provide a visual link between the top and bottom of the poster.

8. Drag the **Control palette** back to the bottom of the publication window above the horizontal scroll bar, then save your changes to the publication

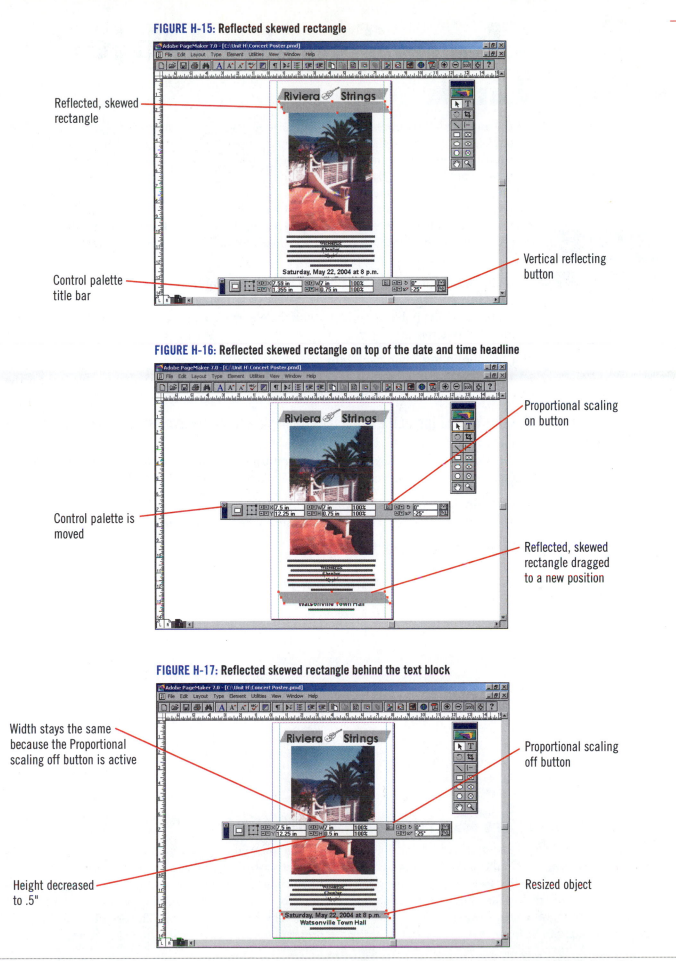

FIGURE H-15: Reflected skewed rectangle

Reflected, skewed rectangle

Control palette title bar

Vertical reflecting button

FIGURE H-16: Reflected skewed rectangle on top of the date and time headline

Control palette is moved

Proportional scaling on button

Reflected, skewed rectangle dragged to a new position

FIGURE H-17: Reflected skewed rectangle behind the text block

Width stays the same because the Proportional scaling off button is active

Proportional scaling off button

Height decreased to .5"

Resized object

Changing an Object's Link

When you place linked graphics in your publication, PageMaker automatically creates a link from the publication to the graphic's source file. You can use the Links Manager dialog box, which lists the source files of every graphic placed in your publication, to monitor and control object linking in your publication. The violin graphic that Sara inserted has a white background, making it look as if a white box surrounds it. Sara obtained a different version of the violin graphic with a transparent background that she thinks will look much better. To replace the graphic in the publication with the newer version, she uses the Links Manager dialog box to change the source file for the graphic so it is linked to the file with the transparent background.

Steps

QuickTip

If a plus sign appears in front of a filename, it indicates the source file for the graphic has been modified. To update the graphic in the publication, select the filename in the Links Manager dialog box, then click Update.

1. Click **File** on the menu bar, then click **Links Manager**

The Links Manager dialog box opens, as shown in Figure H-18. It lists the graphic files that are linked to the publication, along with the file type for each file and the page on which the linked object appears.

2. Click **Violin.jpg**, then click **Info**

The Link Info:…jpg dialog box opens. The folder containing the Violin.jpg file is the active folder. You use this dialog box to change the source file for a linked graphic.

3. Click **Violin2.jpg** in the list of files, then click **Open** (*Macintosh Users: Click Link, then click Yes*)

The Link Info dialog box closes and you return to the Links Manager dialog box. Notice the filename has changed from Violin.jpg to Violin2.jpg in the list of linked files.

4. Click **OK**

The violin graphic appears without a white box in the publication, as shown in Figure H-19.

5. Save your changes to the publication

Importing files using Publish and Subscribe

You can import text or graphics created in different applications using PageMaker's Publish and Subscribe feature. When you use this feature, the application program used to create a file, called the **publishing application program**, creates a separate file called an **edition**, which can be imported, or subscribed to, by other application programs, including PageMaker. The subscribed editions are automatically updated when changes occur in the original publishing edition. You can also edit an edition placed in your publication by double-clicking it. The original publishing program opens, allowing you to make changes.

FIGURE H-18: Links Manager dialog box

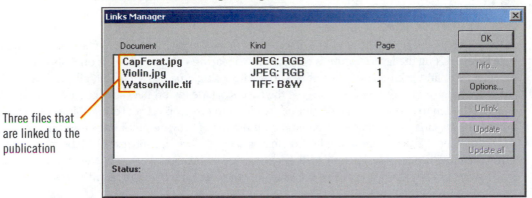

FIGURE H-18: Links Manager dialog box

Three files that are linked to the publication

FIGURE H-19: New violin graphic linked to publication

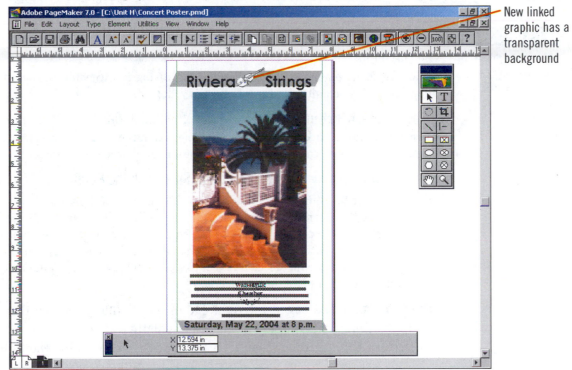

New linked graphic has a transparent background

Using Layers

You can design a page by placing all the objects directly on the page, or you can place objects on multiple **layers**. Using the layers feature is comparable to placing groups of objects onto sheets of transparency film, and then stacking the sheets to create a single page. By default, all publications are created with a single layer, but you can use the Layers palette to add new layers. A layer can be temporarily hidden to allow you to make fine adjustments to other objects in your publication. The total number of the layers you create for a publication is limited only by the amount of RAM (memory) on your computer.  Sara would like to create a separate layer for the text block below the photo. This will allow her to hide the layer so that she can easily increase the size of the logo underneath. Placing this text in a layer also means she can show the client the publication with or without text.

1. Click **Window** on the menu bar, then click **Show Layers**

   The Layers palette opens. You use the Layers palette to create, edit, organize, and delete layers in the publication. The top layer always appears at the top of the palette. At the moment, the Layers palette displays only the default layer, which is indicated by a red square. Any objects placed on this layer display red selection handles when selected. Having color-coded handles makes it easy to identify which layer a particular object is on.

QuickTip

If you want to use a different color, click the Color list arrow, then select a color.

2. Click the **right arrow** ▶ on the Layers palette to open a menu, then click **New Layer** on the menu

   The New Layer dialog box opens. You use this dialog box to name and select a color for the new layer. The default color for this layer is yellow.

3. Type **Concert text** in the Name text box, then click **OK**

   The new yellow Concert text layer is now selected in the Layers palette, making it the **target layer**. Any new objects added to the publication are placed on the target layer.

4. Click **View** on the menu bar, click **Actual Size**, click the **Pointer tool** ▶ in the toolbox, then click the **paragraph text block** below the photo, scrolling down if necessary

   The red selection handles around the text box indicate it is part of the default layer. The default layer now becomes the target layer in the Layers palette, as shown in Figure H-20. Notice the small red box that appears to the right of the default layer name on the Layers palette. You can move the selected object to a different layer in the publication by dragging this box to a different layer in the palette.

5. Drag the **small red box** at the right end of the [Default] layer on the Layers palette up to the **Concert text** layer on the Layers palette

   The color of the selection handles on the text block changes to yellow, the color of the Concert text layer, as shown in Figure H-21. This text box is now on a separate layer from the other objects in the publication.

6. Click the **eye icon** 👁 to the left of the Concert text layer on the Layers palette

   Clicking the eye icon hides the layer, as shown in Figure H-22. With the text block hidden, it is easier to modify the logo.

7. Click the **Watsonville Chamber Music logo** to select it, then click the **center reference point** in the Proxy on the Control palette

8. Make sure the **Proportional scaling on button** ⬚ is active on the Control palette, select **80%** in the Width sizing percentage box, type **100**, then click the **Apply button** ▦

   The logo is enlarged.

9. Click the **far-left empty square** in the Concert text layer on the Layers palette, where the eye icon used to be, then save your changes to the publication

   The Concert text layer is no longer hidden, and the text block reappears on top of the logo.

FIGURE H-20: Layers palette

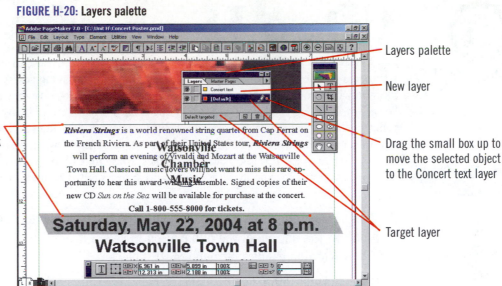

Layers palette

New layer

Drag the small box up to move the selected object to the Concert text layer

Target layer

Red selection handles indicate the text block is on the default layer

FIGURE H-21: Text block moved to the Concert text layer

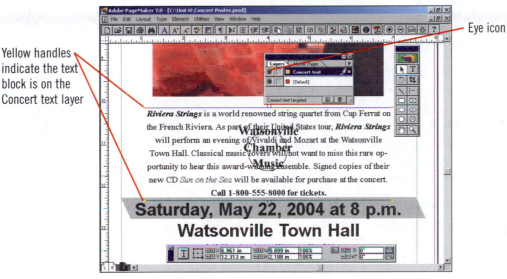

Eye icon

Yellow handles indicate the text block is on the Concert text layer

FIGURE H-22: Poster with Concert text layer hidden

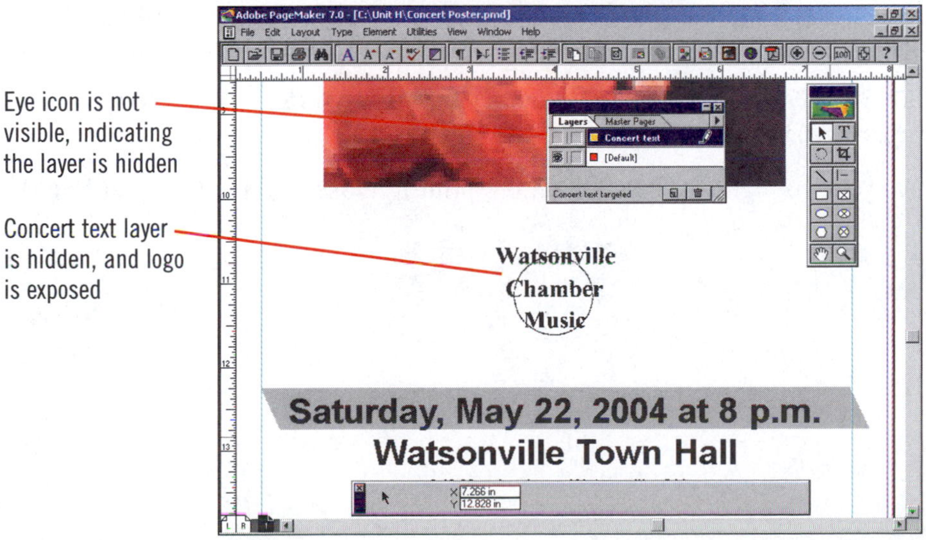

Eye icon is not visible, indicating the layer is hidden

Concert text layer is hidden, and logo is exposed

PageMaker 7.0

Using Image Control

PageMaker's **image control** feature lets you alter or enhance the appearance of grayscale and line art images in your publication. Using image control is like having access to a photographic darkroom in which you can lighten and adjust the contrast of black-and-white photographs and images. For example, using the Image Control dialog box, you can lighten images so they can be printed behind text or graphics, or you can adjust the contrast between light and dark in an image to make it more compelling. Note that you cannot alter color images using image control. The logo behind the paragraph text is too dark and makes it hard to read the paragraph. Sara decides to adjust the lightness of the logo so that it is lighter and appears faded behind the paragraph.

Steps

MacintoshUsers

This replaces Steps 3–6.
3. Click Window on the menu bar, then click Show Colors
4. Verify that the logo is still selected, click 100% in the Tint box on the Colors palette, then type 20%
5. Close the Colors palette
Resume at Step 7.

1. Click the **Pointer tool** ![pointer] in the toolbox, if necessary, then click the **paragraph text block** at the bottom of the publication to select it
   Yellow selection handles surround the text block.

2. Click the **eye icon** for the Concert text layer on the Layers palette, then click the **Watsonville Chamber Music logo** to select it
   Red selection handles surround the logo.

3. Click **Element** on the menu bar, point to **Image**, then click **Image Control**
   The Image Control dialog box opens, as shown in Figure H-23. Table H-2 describes the options available in the Image Control dialog box.

4. Drag the scroll box next to the Lightness text box to the right until approximately **80** appears in the Lightness text box
   You can also click the scroll arrows on either side of the Lightness scroll bar to increase or decrease the Lightness percentage by 1%, or type a percentage in the Lightness text box. Notice that the Apply button in the Image Control dialog box becomes active when you adjust a setting. You can click Apply to preview the new image settings in the publication before clicking OK to apply them.

5. Click **Apply** in the Image Control dialog box
   The logo is faded in the publication and appears in gray.

6. Click **OK**
   The new lightness setting is applied to the logo.

7. Click the **far-left empty square** in the Concert text layer on the Layers palette, where the eye icon used to be
   The paragraph text appears on top of the logo and is now much easier to read, as shown in Figure H-24.

8. Click **Window** on the menu bar, then click **Hide Layers**
   The Layers palette closes.

9. Save your changes to the publication, print it, close the file, then exit PageMaker

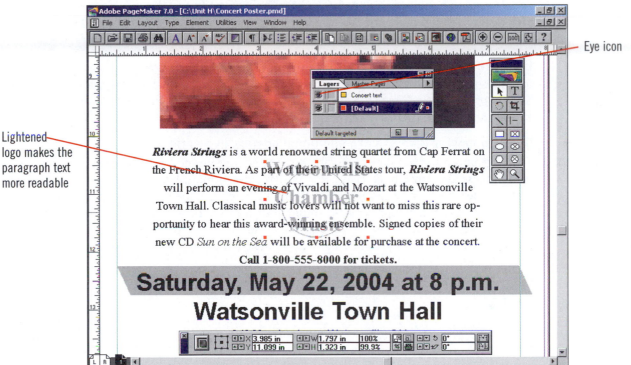

Lightness scroll box

Default button; click to restore the default settings

Apply button; click to preview the settings

FIGURE H-24: Logo with 80% lightness applied

Eye icon

Lightened logo makes the paragraph text more readable

TABLE H-2: Image Control options

option	use to
Lightness	Adjust the percentage of lightness in an image; the greater the percentage, the lighter the image
Contrast	Make the objects in the image darker or lighter in relation to the background; the higher the contrast percentage, the greater the contrast and the blacker the image; the lower the percentage, the lower the contrast and the more gray the image
Printing parameters	Change the halftone settings for an image; specify a line screen for special effects and override the printer defaults for screen angle and number of lines per inch

PageMaker 7.0

Design Workshop: Posters

Each poster Sara creates for the Watsonville Chamber Music's concert series needs to attract attention and to make a positive statement that motivates people to buy tickets. The first poster Sara created is shown in Figure H-25. Before showing the poster to the client, Sara critiques her design.

Details

▶ Do the graphics add to the overall effect of the poster?

Sara used a photograph of the French Riviera to showcase the chamber orchestra's home country. The large photograph grabs the viewer's attention and conveys a sense of elegance to potential ticket buyers. In addition, the violin graphic helps make the top headline jump out at the viewer. Sara could have added color to the violin graphic to further enhance it.

▶ Is the message clear?

People need to be able to read the information on a poster from a distance, so it is important to choose the font and point size carefully. When Sara reproduces this poster at full size, the body copy will be nearly 30 points, which is almost a half inch. This is perfect for Sara's needs.

▶ Does the headline's shadow effect enhance the poster?

Sara uses skewed and reflected boxes to link the headline at the top with the information at the bottom of her poster. The skewed box creates a unique effect, but Sara could have improved the appearance by adding color to the shaded, skewed boxes.

▶ Does the poster lend itself to additional posters in a series?

The large photo and headline can easily be changed to accommodate other musical groups. Sara plans to use the same basic layout for posters advertising other concerts sponsored by the Watsonville Chamber Music group. For the inline graphic in the top headline, Sara plans to use a well-known icon that represents the sound of each group. For example, for a jazz ensemble she can use a saxophone, and for an orchestra she can use a trumpet. For the photo, she plans to showcase scenery from the featured group's home country or city.

Riviera Strings is a world renowned string quartet from Cap Ferrat on the French Riviera. As part of their United States tour, **Riviera Strings** will perform an evening of Vivaldi and Mozart at the Watsonville Town Hall. Classical music lovers will not want to miss this rare opportunity to hear this award-winning ensemble. Signed copies of their new CD *Sun on the Sea* will be available for purchase at the concert.

Call 1-800-555-8000 for tickets.

Saturday, May 22, 2004 at 8 p.m.
Watsonville Town Hall

348 Meadow Lane, Watsonville, OH

Practice

▶ Concepts Review

Label each element of the publication window shown in Figure H-26.

FIGURE H-26

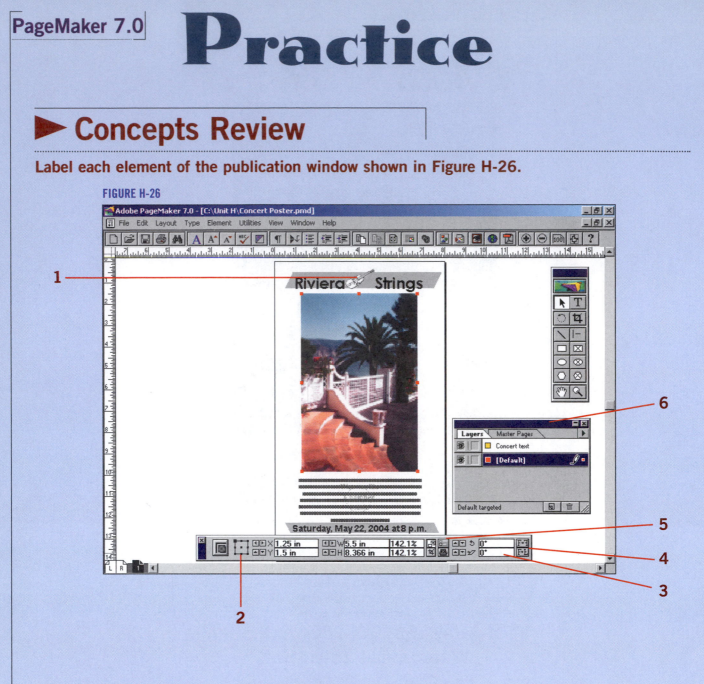

Match each term with the statement that best describes it:

7. **Reflected graphic**   a. A collection of objects in a publication
8. **Proxy**   b. Graphic that has been flipped to create its mirror image
9. **Skewed graphic**   c. A graphical representation on the Control palette of the selected object
10. **Inline graphic**   d. Graphic that is part of a text block
11. **Layer**   e. Graphic that has been stretched horizontally

12. **Which of the following can you NOT do using the Control palette in object view?**
    a. Reflect an object
    b. Skew an object
    c. Rotate multiple objects at once
    d. Change the height and width of multiple objects at once

13. **Which dialog box can you use to minimize the file size of a publication?**
    a. Links Manager
    b. Link Options: Defaults
    c. Image Control
    d. Save As
14. **If you increase the width of an object, which of the following items must be displayed on the Control palette in order for PageMaker to automatically resize the object's height?**
    a. Proportional scaling on button
    b. Proportional scaling off button
    c. Baseline shift text box
    d. All of the above
15. **Which of the following is NOT true of inline graphics?**
    a. When you move a text block that contains an inline graphic, the graphic moves with it.
    b. You can adjust the baseline position of an inline graphic.
    c. You can move an inline graphic independently from a text block.
    d. You cannot wrap text around an inline graphic.
16. **Which of the following dialog boxes would you use to replace a linked black-and-white graphic with a color graphic?**
    a. Links Manager
    b. Place
    c. Link Options: Defaults
    d. Image Control
17. **Which of the following dialog boxes would you use to darken a black-and-white line art image?**
    a. Links Manager
    b. Fill and Line
    c. Link Options
    d. Image Control
18. **What color are the selection handles of objects contained in the default layer of a publication?**
    a. Yellow
    b. Blue
    c. Red
    d. Green

▶ Skills Review

1. **Link a graphic to a publication.**
   a. Start PageMaker, open the file PM H-2.pmd from the drive and folder where your Project Files are stored, click OK if the PANOSE Font Matching Results dialog box opens, then save the file as **Audition Poster**.
   b. If the Control palette is hidden, show it.
   c. Click Element on the menu bar, then click Link Options.
   d. In the Link Options: Defaults dialog box, deselect the Store copy in publication check box, then click OK.
   e. Open the Place dialog box, select the file Russia.tif from the drive and folder where your Project Files are stored, then click Open *(Macintosh Users: Click OK)*.
   f. Position the pointer so the pointer guides align with the 3" mark on the vertical and horizontal rulers, then click to place the graphic.
   g. Save the publication.

2. **Scale a graphic.**
   a. Select the graphic.
   b. If necessary, click the Proportional scaling off button on the Control palette so that the Proportional scaling on button appears.
   c. Using the Width sizing text box, change the width of the photograph to **2.75** in.
   d. Click the Apply button.
   e. Save the publication.

3. **Place an inline graphic.**
   a. If necessary, scroll so the bottom of the page is visible.
   b. Click the Text tool in the toolbox.
   c. Click between the words Fall and Auditions to place the insertion point.
   d. Open the Place dialog box, then select the graphic file Piano.jpg from the drive and folder where your Project Files are stored.
   e. Make sure the As inline graphic option button is selected in the Place dialog box, then click Open *(Macintosh Users: Click OK).*
   f. Save the publication.

4. **Modify an inline graphic.**
   a. Click the Pointer tool in the toolbox, then select the piano inline graphic.
   b. Verify that the Proportional scaling on button is showing on the Control palette, change the width of the graphic to **1** in, then click the Apply button.
   c. Drag the inline graphic up until approximately .2 in displays in Baseline shift text box on the Control palette. Don't be concerned if your baseline shift value is not exactly .2 inches.
   d. Use the [Spacebar] or [Backspace] key to adjust the spacing of the text and inline graphic so that it looks good.
   e. Save the publication.

5. **Skew an object.**
   a. Position a horizontal ruler guide so that it is flush with the top of the capital letters in the Fall Auditions headline.
   b. Position a second horizontal ruler guide so that it is flush with the bottom of the letters in the Fall Auditions headline.
   c. Click the Rectangle tool in the toolbox.
   d. Position the pointer at the intersection of the top ruler guide and the .5 inch mark on the horizontal ruler.
   e. Drag down and to the right to the intersection of the bottom ruler guide and the 1.75 inch mark on the horizontal ruler to create a rectangle that is 1.25 inches wide.
   f. Double-click the value in the Skew text box, type **30**, then click the Apply button.
   g. Click Element on the menu bar, then click Fill and Stroke.
   h. In the Fill and Stroke dialog box, change the Fill to Solid, change the Fill Color to Cyan, change the Fill Tint to 50%, change the Stroke to None, then click OK.
   i. Save your publication.

6. **Reflect an object.**
   a. Click the Pointer tool, select the skewed rectangle, click Edit on the menu bar, then click Copy.
   b. Click Edit on the menu bar, then click Paste.
   c. Reflect the selected skewed rectangle horizontally.
   d. Change the reference point on the Proxy to the upper-left corner.
   e. Drag the reflected skewed rectangle to the other side of the word Auditions, and position it so that the top and bottom align with the horizontal ruler guides and the value in the X position text box is approximately 6.5.
   f. Remove the horizontal ruler guides.
   g. Save the publication.

7. Change an object's link.

   a. Select the piano inline graphic.

   b. Open the Links Manager dialog box.

   c. With the Piano.jpg file selected in the dialog box, click Info.

   d. In the Link Info dialog box, select the file Music.jpg from the drive and folder where your Project Files are stored, then click Open (*Macintosh Users: Click Link, then click Yes*).

   e. Click OK to close the Links Manager dialog box.

   f. Save the publication.

8. Use layers.

   a. Open the Layers palette if necessary.

   b. Click the right arrow on the Layers palette, then click New Layer.

   c. In the New Layer dialog box, create a layer called **Audition text**, then click OK.

   d. Select the text block below the Fall Auditions headline.

   e. Move the text block to the Audition text layer by dragging the small red box on the Layers palette.

   f. Hide the Audition text layer by clicking the eye icon next to the layer in the Layers palette.

   g. Select the Burlington Arts Council logo that was behind the paragraph text, select the center reference point on the Proxy if necessary, change the Y position to **.75**, then click Apply.

   h. Scroll up if necessary so that the top of the publication is visible in the publication window.

   i. Verify that the Proportional scaling on button is active on the Control palette, change the width of the graphic to **1**, then click the Apply button.

   j. Display the Audition text layer by clicking the far-left empty square to the left of the layer on the Layers palette.

   k. Save the publication.

9. Use Image control.

   a. Select the Burlington Arts Council logo at the top of the publication.

   b. Click Element on the menu bar, point to Image, then click Image Control. (*Macintosh Users: Open the Colors palette.*)

   c. In the Image Control dialog box, change the Lightness to 20%, then click OK. (*Macintosh Users: Make sure the logo is still selected, then change the Tint value to 20%.*)

   d. Close all open palettes, save the publication, then compare your completed publication with Figure H-27.

   e. Print the publication, close the file, then exit PageMaker.

FIGURE H-27

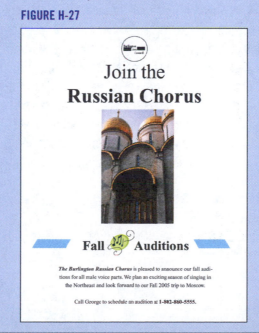

▶ Independent Challenge 1

You volunteered to create a poster to help your local theater promote its fall production. Your budget is small, so you create the poster on 8.5" × 11" paper.

a. Decide what play to promote. It can be a modern comedy, a Shakespearean tragedy, a Broadway classic, or an original play with a fictional title.

b. Create a sketch of the poster that includes a headline with the play title, a graphic illustrating the topic of the play, a short paragraph with a brief description of the production, and the date, time, and location of the play. Include an inline graphic in the play title.

c. Start PageMaker, then create a new 8.5" × 11" publication.

d. Using your sketch as a guide, add the text for the play title headline, the short paragraph describing the production, and the date, time, and location of the play.

e. Format the text with fonts, font styles, and font sizes to create an eye-catching, effective design.

f. Add an appropriate clip art graphic to the poster. The graphic should illustrate something about the play. Use graphics from the Picture palette, the PageMaker Content CD, or another source.

g. Add an inline graphic to the play title. Use the file Apple.bmp, found on the drive and folder where your Project Files are stored, as a placeholder graphic if you don't have a more appropriate graphic to use.

h. Enhance the poster by drawing a shape, filling it with a color and tint of your choice, and then skewing it. Create a copy of the shape, then reflect the copied shape. Position both shapes on the poster to create a compelling design.

i. Add a layer to the publication called **Art**, then move the independent graphic to the new layer. Add another layer called **Text**, then move the text block containing the paragraph text to this layer.

j. Save the publication as **Play Poster** to the drive and folder where your Project Files are stored, print a copy, close the publication, then exit PageMaker.

▶ Independent Challenge 2

Find two posters, one with an effective design and one with a design that could be improved. Critique the posters using the design guidelines you learned in this unit.

a. Find a poster that you think is especially effective, and write a brief critique. Comment on how the message of the poster is presented, explain how the graphics enhance the message, and describe how the special effects, if any, are used to enhance the design or attract the reader.

b. Find a poster that you think is poorly designed, and write a brief critique. What message is the poster trying to communicate and why does it fail to deliver that message successfully? Do the graphics and the formatting of the text in the poster enhance its message or detract from it? How could the poster be improved?

c. Using your critique of the poorly designed poster, sketch a new design for the poster that communicates the message more effectively. In your sketch, include at least one graphic and a skewed and reflected shape.

d. Start PageMaker, then create a new publication with the dimensions you require for your redesigned poster.

e. Using your sketch as a guide, add the text and graphics to the publication. You can use graphics from the Picture palette, the PageMaker Content CD, or your own graphics.

f. Use the Control palette to adjust the elements of the poster until you are satisfied that the poster looks compelling and delivers a strong message.

g. Save the publication as **Redesigned Poster** to the drive and folder where your Project Files are stored, print the publication, close the file, then exit PageMaker.

▶ Independent Challenge 3

Create a poster for an event of your choosing. It could be a grand opening of a new store or restaurant, a bake sale to raise money for a school trip, a sporting event, or any other event you want.

a. Create a sketch for your poster that includes the following elements: a headline announcing the event; a brief paragraph describing the event; the date, time, and location of the event; and a graphic illustrating the event.

b. Start PageMaker, then create a new publication that is 8" × 14".

c. Place the text in the publication, positioning each text block so that the information is logical and easy to read.

d. Format the text so that the headline and other information stand out and the remaining text is easy to read from a distance. Use no more than two fonts in the publication.

e. Place appropriate graphics from the Picture palette or the PageMaker Content CD in the poster. Adjust the placement and size of each graphic using the Control palette in object view.

f. Add at least one skewed or reflected shape to the poster.

g. Add a new layer to the publication, then move the independent graphics to this layer.

h. Save the publication as **Event Poster** to the drive and folder where your Project Files are stored, print it, close the file, then exit PageMaker.

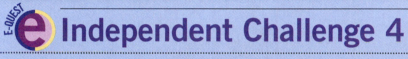 Independent Challenge 4

A local travel agency has hired you to create a poster promoting tour packages to a foreign destination. The poster will be posted all over the campus of a local community college, so it needs to attract the attention of college students. Before you create your poster, you need to research a destination so that your poster can feature highlights of the trip.

a. Open your browser, then use your favorite search engine to search the World Wide Web for information about a foreign country or city. For example, you might go to the AltaVista search engine at www.altavista.com and enter keywords such as **sightseeing attractions in Beijing, China** to perform your search. You can also use Yahoo!, Excite, Google, or another search engine.

b. Write down three sightseeing attractions that the tour group will visit, and list the name and address of a hotel where the tour group will stay.

c. Create a sketch of the poster that includes the following: a headline that announces the tour destination; a graphic illustrating something about the destination; a paragraph describing the hotel and three highlights of the trip; the dates and price of the trip; and the name, address, and phone number of the travel agency.

d. Start PageMaker, then create an 8" × 14" proof version of the poster in PageMaker using your sketch as a guide.

e. Place the text for the headline, the paragraph text, the dates and price of the tour, and the name, address, and phone number of the travel agency.

f. Place the graphics in your publication. You can use images downloaded from the Web or graphics from another source.

g. Use the Control palette in object view to adjust the placement and sizing of the graphics.

h. Enhance the design by adding at least one skewed shape to the poster.

i. Create a new layer called **Poster graphics**, then place all the graphics for the publication in this layer.

j. Save the publication as **Tour Poster** to the drive and folder where your Project Files are stored, print it, close the file, then exit PageMaker.

▶ Visual Workshop

Create the poster shown in Figure H-28 as an 8.5" × 11" publication. Use the Project File PM H-3.doc, found on the drive and folder where your Project Files are stored, for the paragraph text, and create the other text blocks from scratch. Format the headline in 72-point Impact, format the paragraph text in 18-point Arial, and format the name and address information at the bottom in Arial. For the guitar graphic, place the file Guitar.jpg, found on the drive and folder where your Project Files are stored, then create a reflected copy and place it as shown. Create the triangles by creating a three-sided polygon and rotating them to the angles shown. For the small triangles, create one triangle, make a reflected copy, then place it as shown. Save the publication as **Guitar Lessons Poster** to the drive and folder where your Project Files are stored, then print a copy.

FIGURE H-28

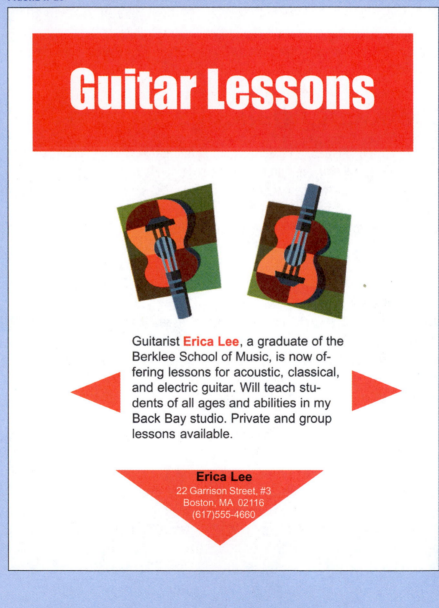

Adding
Color and Using Mail Merge

Objectives

- ▶ **Plan a brochure**
- ▶ **Apply color to text and graphics**
- ▶ **Plan color use in PageMaker**
- ▶ **Use a color library**
- ▶ **Create a new color**
- ▶ **Apply spot colors**
- ▶ **Edit a color and create a tint**
- ▶ **Trap colors**
- ▶ **Create color separations**
- ▶ **Save for a service provider plug-in**
- ▶ **Set up a data merge**
- ▶ **Run a data merge**
- ▶ **Design Workshop: Brochures**

In this unit you learn how to create colors and apply colors to graphical elements and text, how to edit colors and produce tints, how to create color separations that can be used by a commercial printer, and how to save a publication for a service provider. You also learn how to use the data merge feature to create several copies of a publication, each addressed to a different customer. Arcadia Tours has contracted with Sara Norton to create a brochure about the company's new range of tours to Tuscany. She will also use data merge to create envelopes for sending the brochure.

PageMaker 7.0

Planning a Brochure

Brochures come in all sizes and styles. **Informational brochures** include detailed information about a product or service. For example, a 10-page color brochure distributed by a car dealership includes large, colorful pictures of several cars, along with detailed explanations of each car's features. A **teaser brochure**, in contrast, is designed to encourage the recipient to request more information (usually in the form of another, more detailed, brochure) about a product or service. Teaser brochures do not include a lot of text—they depend on graphics and color to make the viewer want to find out more. Sara needs to create a teaser brochure that announces the one- and two-week, theme-based tours to Tuscany offered by Arcadia Tours. This brochure will be mailed to people who have already taken a tour with Arcadia Tours and may be interested in the new range of Tuscany tours. To design the color brochure, Sara considers the following guidelines:

Details

▶ **Determine the purpose of your brochure**

If you plan to create a teaser brochure, you don't want to include too much information. Instead, you rely on dramatic pictures and other graphics to attract the reader's interest. If you plan to create an informational brochure, you need to find unique ways of presenting the information and accompanying graphics so that the reader can easily comprehend the information. Elements to consider include page size, paper quality, and the layout of the text with relation to the graphics. Sara decides to create a teaser brochure to advertise the Tuscany tours offered by Arcadia Tours. She makes this decision for two reasons. First, the company can determine how many of their former customers were satisfied enough with their first tour to purchase another one. Second, the company's follow-up brochure is large and expensive to produce. Arcadia Tours would prefer to send this brochure only to customers who are likely to purchase a tour.

▶ **Be creative with the size of the brochure**

Most designers experiment with paper size and the way the paper folds when they begin the design process. One of the most popular brochure sizes is a vertical three-panel, two-fold brochure based on a letter-size (8½" × 11") page. You can be creative and try horizontal folds, varied paper sizes, or even a folder-type brochure with one-page handouts. Sara decides to make a four-panel, three-fold brochure based on a legal page size of 8½" × 14".

▶ **Be consistent with other marketing materials**

Brochures describing a single product or service should maintain consistency with other corporate brochures. The Arcadia Tours logo placed in the brochure will help provide a consistent corporate identity. Sara develops a layout for the brochure that could be easily replicated for future brochures that highlight any of the destinations covered by Arcadia Tours.

▶ **Include a point of response**

A teaser brochure should provide readers with a point of response such as a phone number, Web site address, or e-mail address. Some brochures also include a reply card that readers can mail back to the company to receive more information. Sara includes a perforated cutoff, self-mailer in her brochure. When customers receive the brochure, they can detach the mailer, fill in the required information, then send it back to Arcadia Tours.

Figures I-1 and I-2 show Sara's sketches of the teaser brochure.

FIGURE I-1: Sara's sketch of the outside panels (Page 2)

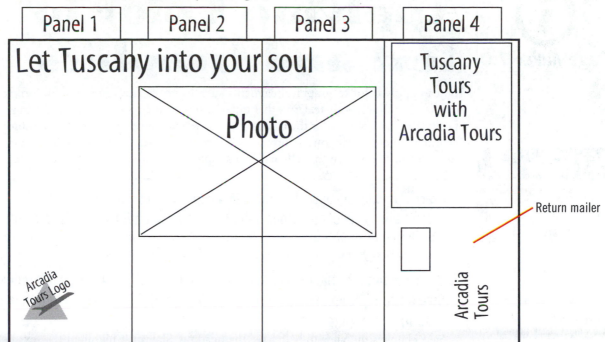

| Panel 1 | Panel 2 | Panel 3 | Panel 4 |

Let Tuscany into your soul

Photo

Tuscany Tours with Arcadia Tours

Return mailer

Arcadia Tours Logo

Arcadia Tours

FIGURE I-2: Sara's sketch of the inside panels (Page 3)

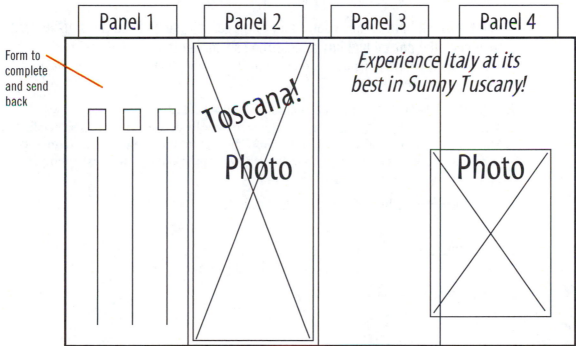

| Panel 1 | Panel 2 | Panel 3 | Panel 4 |

Form to complete and send back

Toscana!

Photo

Experience Italy at its best in Sunny Tuscany!

Photo

PageMaker 7.0

Applying Color to Text and Graphics

You can apply color to graphical elements such as boxes and lines. In addition, you can apply colors to headlines, body text, or other types of text. You apply colors to text using the Character Specifications dialog box or the Colors palette. Sara wants to add red color to the word "Toscana!" that appears on the brochure's front panel when it is folded. She then wants to add blue color to the box on the self-mailer that appears on the brochure's back panel.

Trouble?

Click Continue and Close if a warning appears.

1. Start PageMaker, open the file **PM I-1.pmd** from the drive and folder where your Project Files are located, then save the file as **Arcadia Tours Brochure**
   Notice that this publication includes three pages, but contains information only on pages 2 and 3 so that you can see both pages of the brochure at the same time.

MacintoshUsers

This replaces Step 2.
2. Click Actual Size on the View menu, click the Text tool, then drag [TIF] over Toscana!

2. Click **Toscana!** at the top of the panel on page 3 with to select it, click the **Actual Size button** on the toolbar, click the **Text tool** in the toolbox, then drag over **Toscana!** to highlight it
   Sara changes the view to better see the heading. She must highlight the text before she can apply color to it. Sara will use the Character Specifications dialog box to apply the red color.

MacintoshUsers

This replaces Step 3.
3. Click Character on the Type menu, click the Color list, scroll down the list of colors, then click Red

3. Click the **Character Specs button** on the toolbar, click the **Color list arrow**, scroll down the list of colors, then click **Red**
   By default, you can replace black with red, blue, green, cyan, magenta, or yellow.

4. Click **OK**, then click the **Pointer tool** in the toolbox to deselect the text
   The text is now red, as shown in Figure I-3.

5. Use the scroll bars to move down and to the left so you can see the self-mailer box, then click the **dotted line box** around the self-mailer information
   Sara wants to apply the blue color only to the dotted lines that make the box. She leaves the color inside the box white.

6. Click **Window** on the menu bar, then click **Show Colors**
   The Colors palette appears in the publication window. By default, the Colors palette includes Blue, Cyan, Green, Magenta, Red, and Yellow. You can modify these colors, add new colors, and remove colors that you don't want to use in your publication. For a description of all the options on the Colors palette, see Table I-1.

7. Click the **Line button** on the Colors palette
   See Figure I-4.

8. Click **Blue** on the Colors palette
   The dotted line changes to blue. Sara is satisfied with the color.

9. Save the publication

FIGURE I-3: Applying color to text

Red color applied to Toscana!

FIGURE I-4: Colors palette

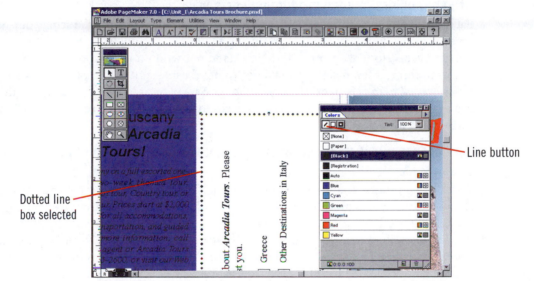

Line button

Dotted line box selected

TABLE I-1: Colors palette options

option	description
[Paper]	Indicates the color of the paper you are using
[Black]	Indicates one of the process colors (black prints over all other colors)
[Registration]	Indicates the percentage of each of the colors in your publication
	Indicates the color model is RGB (Red, Green, Blue)
	Indicates the color model is CMYK (Cyan, Magenta, Yellow, Black)
	Indicates that the color is a spot color
	Indicates that the color uses multiple inks
Tint 100%	Indicates if the color is a tint by showing the percentage of color
	Opens the Color Options dialog box to edit the currently selected color
	Removes the currently selected color from the Colors palette and from the publication

PageMaker 7.0

Planning Color Use In PageMaker

When you create a PageMaker publication that you plan to send to a commercial printing press, you need to consider the two types of color that you can use in a publication: spot colors and process colors. A **spot color** uses one specific ink to create a color. For example, to create green using spot colors, you use one of PageMaker's online color libraries to specify the green that suits your publication. Color libraries are "industry standards" for creating specific colors. **Process colors** are made from four basic colors combined in percentages to create other colors. The four basic colors are **Cyan** (C) (a shade of blue), **Magenta** (M) (a shade of red), **Yellow** (Y), and **Black** (K). The use of process colors is commonly referred to as **CMYK**. Most color publications you see, including this book, are printed using process colors. Sara needs to create color separations that can be given to a commercial printer. Figure I-5 shows how one of the pages of the brochure appears as color separations. Sara uses the following guidelines when deciding to use spot colors or process colors or both:

Details

▶ ### Use spot colors to keep production costs low
Each time you use a different color, you add to the overall cost of producing your publication. If you are on a limited budget for producing a publication, adding one spot color adds the extra impact needed to make your publication stand out without adding excessive costs. A publication with three or fewer colors should be produced using spot colors. Spot colors are also sometimes needed to match an exact color. Although Sara plans to use process color for this brochure because it includes photographs, she still needs to use a spot color to exactly match the lavender color in the Arcadia Tours logo.

▶ ### Use process colors to produce a greater variety of colors and to reproduce photographs
When using process colors, you pay for four inks, CMYK, but you can create a wide variety of colors. Process colors must be used to produce color photographs. Process colors should also be used if you need to create a publication with four or more spot colors. The process colors can be used to create the specified spot color; however, you need to be aware that most commercial printers don't guarantee that process colors will create an exact match to an "industry standard" or predefined library color. Sara needs to use process colors in her brochure because she is using color photographs.

QuickTip

If you wish to print a color photograph in your publication, you must use CMYK process colors to create the wide variety of colors in the photograph. If you use process colors in your publication, you can also use process colors to create your own specific spot colors.

▶ ### Use both spot and process colors to give you the most flexibility
Using spot and process colors together in a publication is the most expensive method for printing a publication. However, using both color methods gives you the most flexibility to produce a publication that contains the specific colors you want. You can print color photographs and also specify an exact spot library color for a graphical element such as a company logo. In order to create the most attractive and stunning brochure possible, Sara uses both spot and process colors in the Arcadia Tours brochure.

FIGURE I-5: Color separations of a publication page

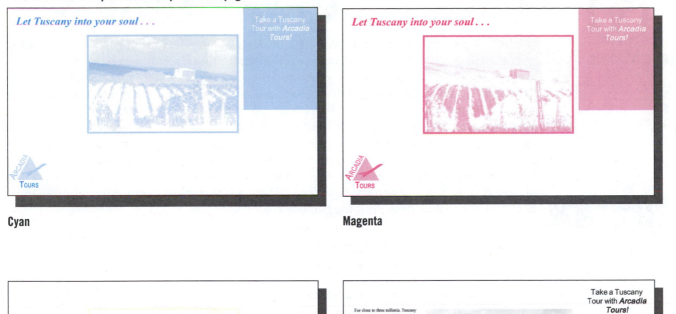

Cyan

Magenta

Yellow

Black

CLUES TO USE

Using commercial printers

Because printing a color publication is costly, make sure you discuss with a printing representative the colors you plan to use and whether the printing company has the appropriate equipment and time to handle the job. After you give your PageMaker publication to the printing company, the printing company creates a film copy for each spot color used. The film copy for each spot color is known as a *separation*. Each film separation is then used to make printing plates. The plates are placed directly onto the printing press to make impressions on the paper in the publication. In color printing, each color ink has its own set of plates and the paper passes through each plate once. For four-color process printing, four plates are created and each paper receives four passes of color. Since each ink is an additional cost, four-color printing is more complex and more costly than one- or two-color printing. However, the commercial printer can create a wide variety of different colors using a four-color process.

Using a Color Library

One of the greatest challenges in printing is matching colors in your PageMaker publication with the color of the final output from a commercial printer. Color representation can vary between monitors and even vary on different days using the same monitor. Several companies have developed color matching systems that are used by designers and printing companies as standards to print consistent colors. PageMaker supports several color matching systems, which are stored as color libraries in the Define Colors dialog box. See Table I-2 for a list of PageMaker color libraries. Sara recreated the Arcadia Tours logo in PageMaker so she could have more control over the colors in the logo. The triangle shape is filled with a specific color in the Pantone Matching System (PMS). The color is known as Pantone color 530. Sara wants to add this color to the Colors palette. When this publication is sent to the commercial printer, a separate ink will be required to print the Pantone color 530.

Steps 1 2 3 4

1. Click **Utilities** on the menu bar, then click **Define Colors**
   The Define Colors dialog box opens.

2. Click **New**, then click the **Libraries list arrow**
   A list of PageMaker's color libraries appears.

3. Scroll down and click **PANTONE® Coated**
   The Color Picker dialog box opens for the PANTONE® Coated library. To choose a Pantone color, you can scroll through the list or type a specific Pantone number in the text box. The designer who originally created the Arcadia Tours logo used the spot color Pantone color 530 for the triangle shape. Sara wants to use the exact color for the logo in this brochure.

4. Drag ℑ over the text in the PANTONE CVC text box, then type **530**
   An attractive lavender color is highlighted in the color window, as shown in Figure I-6. The color on your monitor might not match exactly the color shown in the figures in this book.

5. Click **OK**
   See Figure I-7. Notice PANTONE 530 CVC automatically appears in the text box. Sara closes the dialog box so she can apply the color to the logo.

6. Click **OK** twice

7. Use the scroll bars to move to the far left to display the **Arcadia Tours logo** on page 2, click the **triangle** in the logo with ⬉, then click the **Both button** ⊠ on the Colors palette
   Sara wants to add Pantone color 530 to both the line and the fill of the triangle.

8. Click **PANTONE 530 CVC** on the Colors palette
   PageMaker changes the color of the triangle from white with a black border to the spot color Pantone 530, as shown in Figure I-8.

9. Deselect the triangle, then save the publication

FIGURE I-6: Pantone 530 shown in the Color Picker dialog box for the PANTONE® Coated library

FIGURE I-7: New color selected in the Color Options dialog box

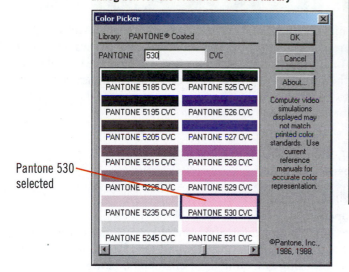

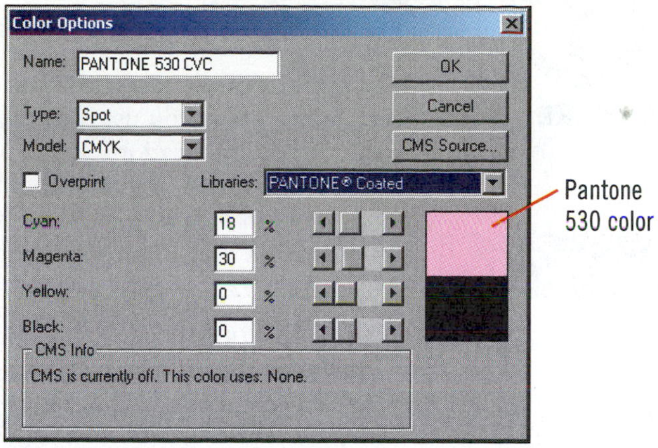

Pantone 530 selected

Pantone 530 color

FIGURE I-8: Logo with new color applied

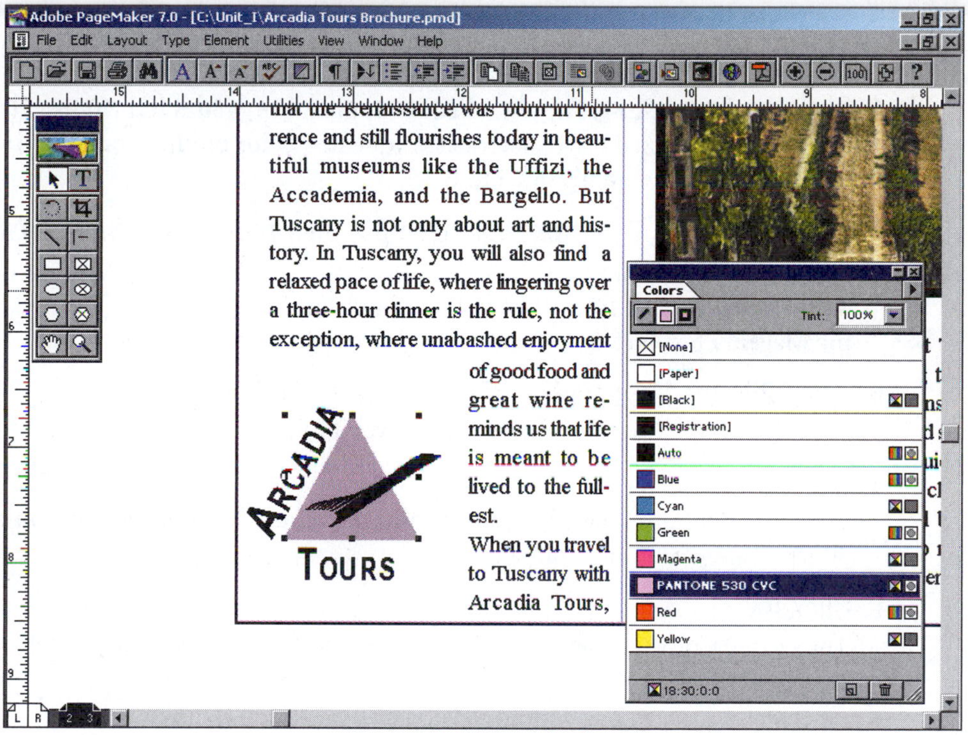

TABLE I-2: A sample of PageMaker's color matching libraries

library name	type	number of colors
Dainippon	Spot	1280
TOYO	Spot	1050
PANTONE	Process	3006
PANTONE	Spot	736
Focoltone	Process	763
Trumatch	Process	2093

ADDING COLOR AND USING MAIL MERGE

Creating a New Color

When using process colors, you can mix the four CMYK colors to create any color you want. To create a new color, you use the Define Colors dialog box. The color you create is available only to the current publication. ✒️ In addition to the spot color Sara used for the triangle, she needs to use process colors so that the commercial printer can print color photographs in the publication. In addition, she wants to create an additional spot color to enhance the text in the company logo. Sara uses process colors to create the new spot color.

Steps

1. Click **Utilities** on the menu bar, then click **Define Colors**
   The Define Colors dialog box opens.

2. Click **[None]** in the Colors list box, then click **New**
   The Color Options dialog box opens. Sara needed to click "None" to clear the previously selected color settings in order to create a new color. She wants to create and name a purple color to apply to the text in the logo and to the boxes around the photos. You can customize the name to your preference, using any number of characters. However, the new color name must be unique. You cannot use a name such as "Blue" or "Red" already listed in the Color Palette.

3. Type **Purple** in the Name text box
   This name identifies the new color that you are creating by using process colors.

   MacintoshUsers

   This replaces Step 4.
   4. Click the Type list, click Process, click the Model list, then click CMYK

4. Click the **Type list arrow**, click **Process**, click the **Model list arrow**, then click **CMYK**
   With CMYK selected, PageMaker bases your new color on the four components of process colors: Cyan, Magenta, Yellow, and Black.

5. Double-click the **Cyan text box**, type **80**, then press **[Tab]** twice *(Macintosh Users: Press [Tab] only once)*
   See Figure I-9. PageMaker displays an example of the color you are creating, then highlights the Magenta text box. Sara decides to add magenta to make the purple color she wants.

6. Type **60** in the Magenta text box, then press **[Tab]** once
   See Figure I-10. The color changes from cyan to purple.

7. Click **OK**
   The Color Options dialog box closes and the Define Colors dialog box reopens. Notice that "Purple" appears in the Colors list box.

8. Click **OK**
   The Define Colors dialog box closes. Purple is added to the Colors palette.

FIGURE I-9: Cyan added to the new color

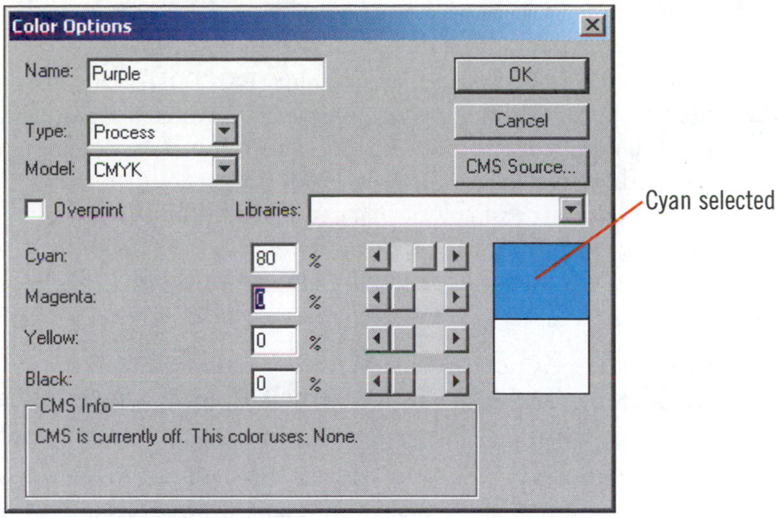

Cyan selected

FIGURE I-10: Cyan and Magenta combined to create the new color

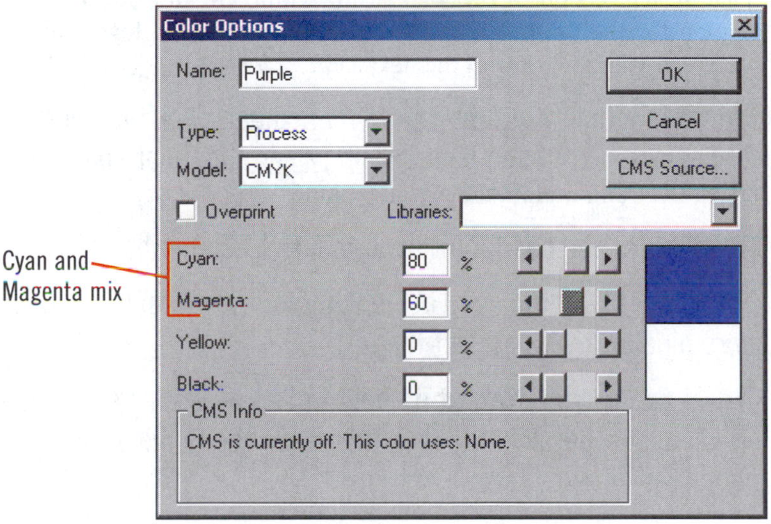

Cyan and
Magenta mix

Using process colors to create Pantone colors

You can mix process colors to create Pantone colors. If you have a Pantone swatch book, you can determine the percentage of the process colors needed to create a Pantone color. The only disadvantage is that some commercial printers won't guarantee that mixing process colors will exactly match the Pantone color.

PageMaker 7.0

Applying Spot Colors

Earlier, you applied a specific spot color (PANTONE 530 CVC) to the Arcadia Tours logo. When the brochure is printed by the commercial printer, a separate ink called Pantone 530 is used to print the spot color in the brochure. The four process colors (Cyan, Magenta, Yellow, and Black) are used to create all of the other color images in the brochure, including the purple spot color created with process colors. Sara will be charged for five colors; however, she will not be charged for the purple spot color created using the process colors. She now decides to apply colors to both the text and graphics in her brochure. First she adds the new purple color to the text in the Arcadia Designs logo.

Steps

1. Click the **Text tool** T in the toolbox, drag I over the word **Arcadia** in the logo, click **Purple** on the Colors palette, then click outside the highlighted area

   See Figure I-11. The word "Arcadia" now appears in the newly created Purple color. Note that when you first apply color to text and drawn objects, they may not appear fully colored, or may appear cut off. Once you change the view, however, PageMaker redraws the objects and they display correctly.

2. Highlight the word **Tours**, click **Blue** on the Colors palette, then click outside the highlighted area

   Sara applies the default Blue color to the logo.

3. Click the **Pointer tool** in the toolbox, click the **airplane graphic**, then click **Purple** on the Colors palette

   Sara's PageMaker version of the logo is now complete and the colors match her ongoing identity plan for the use of the logo. Any distortion in the logo will disappear when you switch to Fit in Window view in the next step.

   > **MacintoshUsers**
   >
   > This replaces Step 4.
   > **4.** Click Fit in Window on the View menu, click the photo of the vineyard on page 2 to select it, click the Line button on the Colors palette, then click Purple

4. Click the **Fit in Window button** on the toolbar, click the photo of the **vineyard** on page 2 to select it, click the **Line button** on the Colors palette, then click **Purple**

   The color of the frame around the vineyard photo is Purple.

5. Click the photo of the **castle** in the bottom right corner of page 3, then click **Purple**

6. Click T, drag I over the text **Let Tuscany into your soul...** on page 2, click **Blue** on the Colors palette, then deselect the text

7. Drag I over **Experience Italy at its best in Sunny Tuscany!** on page 3, click **Blue** on the Colors palette, deselect the text, then save the publication

   The publication appears as shown in Figure I-12.

FIGURE I-11: Purple added to text

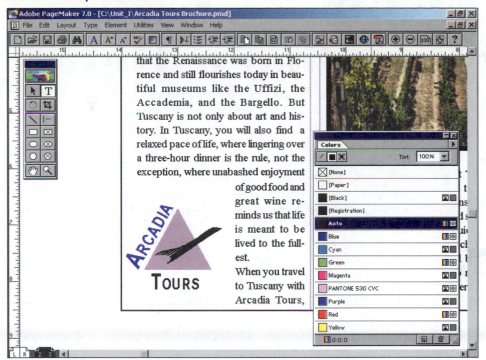

FIGURE I-12: Colors added to publication

Blue applied to text

Logo includes both purple and blue text

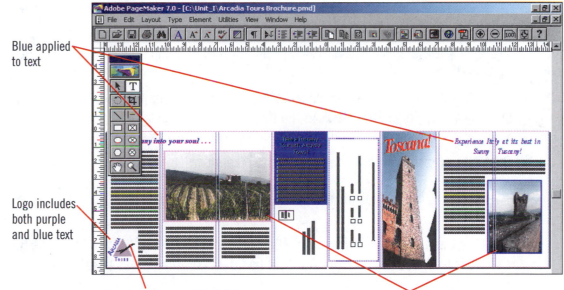

Purple airline graphic matches the purple in the frames

Purple added to picture frames

CLUES TO USE

Applying colors to imported graphics

You can apply a color to imported grayscale TIFF, EPS, or PIC file formats. Color TIFF files imported in a PageMaker publication print in their original colors, even if you apply a color to the image. To apply a color to an imported graphic, select the image, then choose the color from the Colors palette. If you decide to return the graphic image to its original colors, click [Registration] on the Colors palette.

Editing a Color and Creating a Tint

You use the Define Colors dialog box to edit a color. After the color is edited, PageMaker automatically changes the color wherever you applied it in the publication. When you import an EPS image in your publication, PageMaker automatically adds the image spot colors to PageMaker's Colors palette. A **tint** is a new color based on a percentage of a color you created or based on one of PageMaker's default colors. When you use only spot colors in your publication, tints can save money because the commercial printer uses only one ink to create the original color as well as the tint. Tints appear on the Colors palette with a percent sign (%) in front of the CMYK or RGB color square. ✒ Sara doesn't think the shade of purple is the color she wants, so she plans to lighten the Purple color by decreasing the amount of cyan and adding some yellow. Sara then wants to lighten the color of the box behind the text in the fourth panel on page 2 by creating a new blue tint.

Steps 1 2 3 4

1. **Click the photo of the vineyard on page 2 to select it, then double-click Purple in the Colors palette**
   The Color Options dialog box opens with the new Purple color selected.

2. **Use the scroll bar to decrease the Cyan percentage to 30**
   See Figure I-13. Notice that the color in the top half of the preview box has changed. The bottom half of the preview box remains the original color. Sara is still not satisfied with the appearance of the color. She refers to a color chart that gives formulas for mixing colors to create new colors and determines that she needs to add yellow to make the color a richer purple.

   > **QuickTip**
   > To remove a fill color from an object, select the object, click Element on the menu bar, point to Fill, then click None.

3. **Double-click the Yellow text box, type 10, press [Tab] once, then click OK**
   The Color Options and Define Color dialog boxes close and PageMaker automatically updates the frame color boxes behind the photo and the fill color of the plane.

4. **Click Utilities on the menu bar, click Define Colors, click [Paper] in the Color list box, click New, then type 30% BLUE in the Name text box**
   Sara names the tint color with the percentage she plans to use of the original color.

5. **Click the Type list arrow, then click Tint (Macintosh Users: Choose Tint in the Type list box)**
   The bottom half of the dialog box changes to display only the color selected in the Base Color list box.

6. **Click the Base Color list arrow, click Blue (Macintosh Users: Choose Blue in the Base Color list box), double-click the Tint text box, type 30, then press [Tab]**
   See Figure I-14.

7. **Click OK twice**
   The Color Options and Define Colors dialog boxes close, and "30% BLUE" appears on the Colors palette. A "%" appears on the right edge of the color's entry on the Colors palette to indicate that the color is a tint.

8. **Click the Both button ▣ on the Colors palette, click the blue box surrounding the text box in the fourth panel on page 2, then click 30% BLUE on the Colors palette**
   The fill and line colors change from 100% BLUE to 30% BLUE, as shown in Figure I-15. Sara is pleased with the new color.

9. **Save the publication**

FIGURE I-13: Cyan reduced in the Color Options dialog box

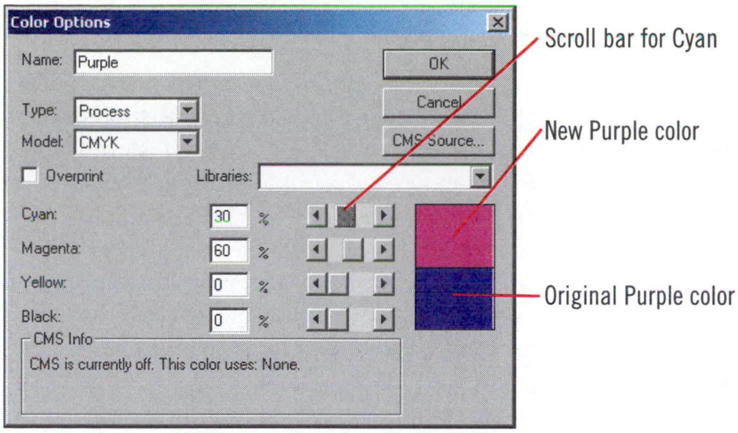

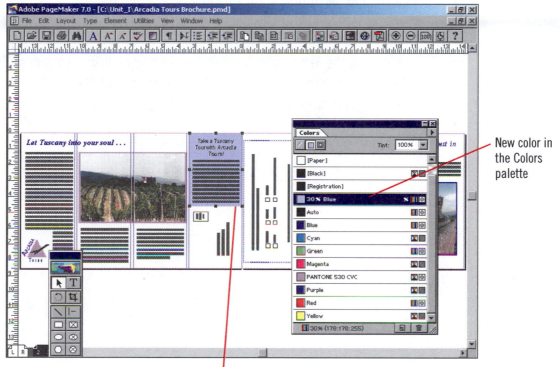

Scroll bar for Cyan

New Purple color

Original Purple color

FIGURE I-14: 30% BLUE tint created

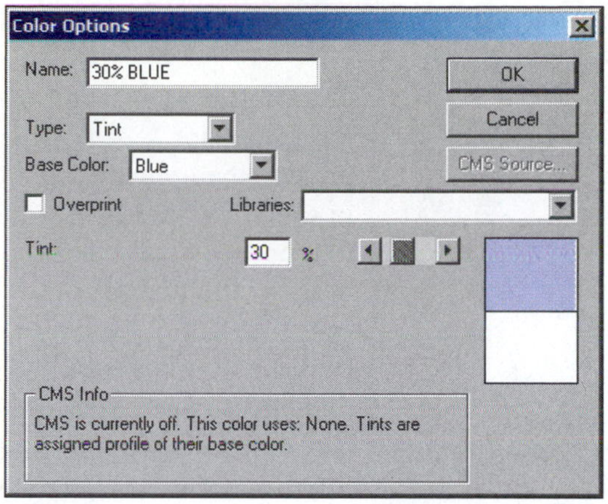

FIGURE I-15: Publication enhanced with edited colors and tints

New color in the Colors palette

The 30% BLUE provides an attractive background for the text and the tint unites the blue headlines in the brochure

CLUES TO USE

Applying tints using the Colors palette

A second type of color tint, created using the Colors palette, is an object-level tint. To create an object-level tint, select the desired object to be filled with the color tint, click the desired color on the Colors palette, click the Tint percentage list arrow on the Colors palette, then click the desired percentage tint. You can use this method to quickly apply tint color. If you are using a specific tint color numerous times in your publication, you might want to choose to create a new color tint so that the defined tint color always appears on the Colors palette.

Trapping Colors

Trapping is a technique used to compensate for the gaps that can appear between colors when creating color separations. The gap between colors is called misregistration. **Misregistration** occurs when one or more of the colors in a multiple-color process (like CMYK) is not printed in exact alignment with the other colors. Figure I-16 shows an example of the misregistration that occurs when colors are printed out of registration and the results obtained when the trapping feature is applied. In the Trapping Options dialog box, you can enable PageMaker to apply trapping automatically on the different objects in your publication. Trapping is used only on color separations, and you do not see any results of trapping on the screen. However, the effects do appear on the color separations. Trapping affects only text and graphic objects that are created using PageMaker. Imported graphics and photographs are not affected by the trapping options. Sara wants to make sure she enables trapping to ensure that the Arcadia Tours logo prints in registration.

Steps

1. Click **File** on the menu bar, point to **Preferences**, then click **Trapping**
   The Trapping Preferences dialog box opens.

2. Click the **Enable trapping for publication check box**
   By selecting this option, you instruct PageMaker to automatically apply trapping to all objects in your publication.

3. Double-click the **Trap width Default text box**, type **.005** then press **[Tab]**
   The default trap measurement is used for all colors except black.

4. In the Black width text box, type **.01**, as shown in Figure I-17

5. Click **OK**
   The dialog box closes. You cannot see the effects of enabling the trapping options on the screen. However, you do see the effects when creating color separations at a commercial printer.

6. Close the Colors palette, then save your publication

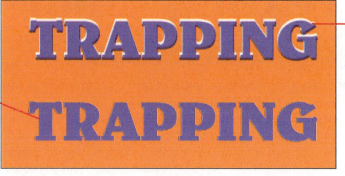

Colors not aligned correctly, resulting in undesirable white gaps

PageMaker compensates for possible misregistration, eliminating gaps

FIGURE I-17: Settings selected in the Trapping Preferences dialog box

Trapping Preferences

Trapping settings
☑ Enable trapping for publication

Trap width
Default: .005 inches
Black width: 0.01 inches

Trapping thresholds
Step limit: 10 %
Centerline threshold: 100 %
Trap text above: 23.9 pts

☐ Traps over imported objects

Black attributes
Black limit: 100 %
Auto-overprint black:
☑ Text below 24 pts
☐ Strokes
☐ Fills

OK
Cancel
Ink setup...

CLUES TO USE

Editing color in an EPS image

When you place a color EPS file in a publication, PageMaker imports all colors stored in the image onto the Colors palette. The colors appear on the Colors palette with an EPS graphic place icon symbol **PS** positioned in front of the newly imported color.

Imported colors can be converted from spot colors to process colors, or you can modify a spot color. Process colors that are part of an EPS file cannot be edited in PageMaker.

Creating Color Separations

Separations are printouts on paper or film, one for each of the four process colors. If you used spot colors, PageMaker prints out a separation for each spot color applied to your publication. When you create color publications, PageMaker lets you print separations from the Print Document dialog box that your commercial printer uses to apply color to your publication. Sara wants to print separations of the brochure to proof it before sending it to the commercial printer for printing on legal size paper. By printing the separations, Sara can make sure the graphic objects and text blocks have been assigned the correct spot or process colors.

Steps 1 2 3 4

1. Click **File** on the menu bar, then click **Print**

2. If you are using a PostScript printer, click **Paper**
   The Print Paper dialog box opens.

> **Trouble?**
> You might need to click Advanced in the Print dialog box to see options for printing on legal-size paper.

3. If you are using a non-PostScript printer, click **Setup**, select **Legal** in the Paper Size list box if your printer accepts legal size paper or select **Letter** if your printer holds only letter size paper, click **OK**, click **OK** again, then continue with **Step 6**

4. If you have a printer capable of printing on legal-size paper, make sure **Legal** appears in the Size list box in the Paper section; if you can print only on letter-size paper, select **Letter** in the Size list box

5. Click the **Center page in print area check box**
   PageMaker reduces the legal-size pages to fit on smaller paper and centers the information on the page you print.

> **Trouble?**
> You might need to click Options in the Print dialog box to see printing options.

6. Click the **Printer's marks** and **Page information check boxes** if they are not already selected
   Printer's marks are the cropping and registration marks used by commercial printers to line up separations on the printing press and then to trim the print job to the final size after it's printed. **Page information** adds the filename, date, and separation name to the bottom of each separation page.

7. In the Scale section, click the **Reduce to fit option button** if it's not already selected
   The Reduce to fit option reduces the brochure to fit on whatever paper size you chose in Step 3 or 4. See Figure I-18.

8. Click **Color**
   The Print Color dialog box opens, as shown in Figure I-19. Notice the small "X" next to each of the four process colors.

> **Trouble?**
> If PageMaker displays the message "All links may not print as expected," click Print Pub to continue. If your printer is not able to print the publication because of low memory, save a version of the publication without the photographs and then try printing again.

9. Click the **Separations option button**, scroll down the Separations color list box to display PANTONE 530 CVC, click **PANTONE 530 CVC**, click the **Print this ink check box**, click **Print**, then save the publication
   PageMaker sends the file to the specified printer one separation at a time, starting with the cyan plate and ending with the Pantone 530 plate. A total of five separations print for page 2, and four separations print for page 3 (because you applied no PANTONE 530 CVC to page 3).

FIGURE I-18: Print Paper dialog box

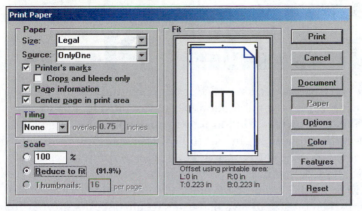

FIGURE I-19: Print Color dialog box

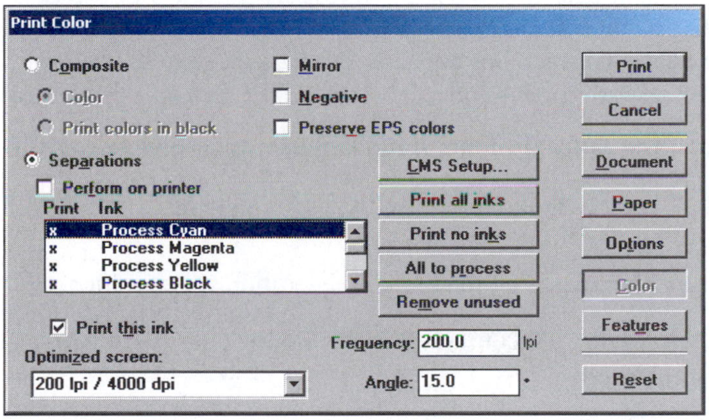

PageMaker 7.0

Saving for a Service Provider Plug-In

Once you have printed a proof copy of a publication, then made any final changes required, you are ready to send the publication to a service provider for full-color printing. You use the **Save for Service Provider Plug-in** to copy the publication file, all the linked image files, the fonts used in the publication, and any other files required to print your document. The plug-in also prompts you to fix any broken links and then generates a report of all the information that your service provider requires in order to print the publication. You can use the plug-in to check a PageMaker publication or a PostScript file created with PageMaker. Sara uses the service provider plug-in to save all the files required for the Arcadia Tours brochure. She then sends the PageMaker file, all accompanying files, and the service provider plug-in report to the service provider who is printing the brochure.

Steps

1. Click **Utilities** on the menu bar, click **Plug-ins**, then click **Save For Service Provider**
   The Save for Service Provider dialog box opens.

2. Click **Preflight pub**
   Sara has chosen to send the publication as a PageMaker file instead of a PostScript file to the printer.

Trouble?

If you do not have a PostScript printer, a warning may appear. Click OK in response to the warning.

3. Click **Yes** if a Save warning appears *(Macintosh Users: Click Continue)*
   In a few moments, Sara learns that both the fonts and the links are okay for printing or creating a package for a service provider. See Figure I-20. If a font was incorrect or a link was broken, a red x icon would appear in place of the green check mark icon. Sara can now choose to print the publication or save it in a package for the service provider.

4. Click **Package**
   The Save As dialog box appears. *(Macintosh Users: The Package dialog box opens.)* Sara wants the package report to open as soon as she's saved the publication and its associated files.

5. Click the **Auto open package report check box** to select it

6. Click the **Save In list arrow**, select a new location in which to store the files, then click **Save**
   PageMaker copies all the files to the location you specified.

7. When saving is complete, click **Close**, click **Window** on the menu bar, then click **Report.pmd**

8. Click the **Actual Size button** [100] on the toolbar *(Macintosh Users: Click Actual Size on the View menu)*, then scroll to view the Document, Link, and Font information
   See Figure I-21. Sara can print and send this report to the service provider.

9. Click the **Print button** [🖨] on the toolbar *(Macintosh Users: Click Print on the View menu)*, click **Print**, close the Report window without saving, then close the publication

FIGURE I-20: Save for Service Provider dialog box

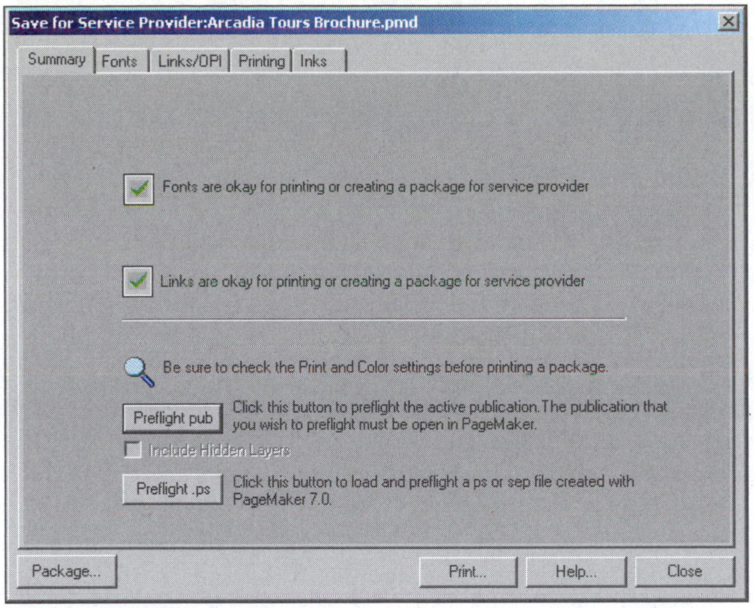

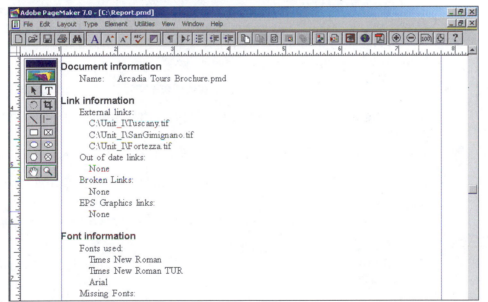

FIGURE I-21: Document, Link, and Font information in the Publication report

Sending files to a service provider

You can send a publication to a service provider as the original PageMaker file or you can send it as a PostScript file. You send a PageMaker file when you want the service provider to have access to the publication in order to make any final changes, to check print settings, or to perform other prepress tasks. You send a PostScript file when you want to retain total control over the final output. When you send a PostScript file, you must ensure that the print settings you've selected are correct. You need to consult with your service provider to determine the best option for sending your publication.

Setting Up a Data Merge

You use the data merge function to combine information from two sources so that you can create several new versions of a publication. For example, you can create a set of form letters, mailing labels, or envelopes. To create a data merge, you need the data source file and the target publication. The **data source file** contains the information that varies from publication to publication and the **target publication** is the PageMaker document that includes placeholders for the variable data and all the other text and graphics that remain the same in each merged publication. To set up a data merge, you first determine where **variable data** should appear in the target publication. You then create a data source in a spreadsheet or database program and save the file as a comma-delimited text file. A **comma-delimited text file** separates each data field with a comma instead of a tab. Next, you insert fields from the Data Merge palette into the target publication. A **field** represents a unit of variable information. For example, a typical data source containing names and addresses could include a separate field for each recipient's name, street address, state or province, and postal code. All the fields required for one recipient are called a **record**. Arcadia Tours plans to send some of the brochures to a selection of former customers. ⬛ Sara creates an envelope in a PageMaker publication that she can merge with the names and addresses of customers who will receive a copy of the brochure.

Steps 123 4

1. Open the file **PM I-2.pmd** from the drive and folder where your Project Files are located, click **OK** if necessary, then save the file as **Arcadia Tours Envelope**
   A text box containing "Customer Address" appears in the middle of the envelope publication that also includes the Arcadia Tours logo and return address. Sara needs to replace the text in this text box with fields for the data merge.

2. Click the **Text tool** T , select **Customer Address**, then press **[Delete]**

3. Click **Window** on the menu bar, click **Plug-in Palettes**, then click **Show Data Merge Palette**
   The Data Merge palette opens, where you can select the file containing the data for the merge.

4. Click the **right arrow** ▶ at the top right of the Data Merge palette, then click **Select Data Source**
   The folder containing the publication appears in the Select Data Source dialog box.

Trouble?

If the PM I-3.csv file is not listed, navigate to the drive and folder where your project files are stored.

5. Click **PM I-3.csv**, then click **Open**
   The three fields included in the data source file appear in the Data Merge palette, as shown in Figure I-22.

6. Click **Name** in the Data Merge palette, then press **[Enter]**
   The field called "Name" is inserted in the text box and the insertion point is on the next line, where the address should go.

7. Click **Address1** in the Data Merge palette, press **[Enter]**, then click **Address2** in the Data Merge palette
   The three data fields appear in the text box as shown in Figure I-23.

8. Save the publication

FIGURE I-22: Data fields listed in the Data Merge palette

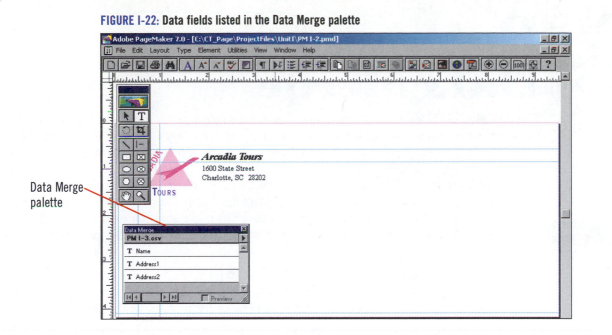

Data Merge palette

FIGURE I-23: Data fields inserted in the publication

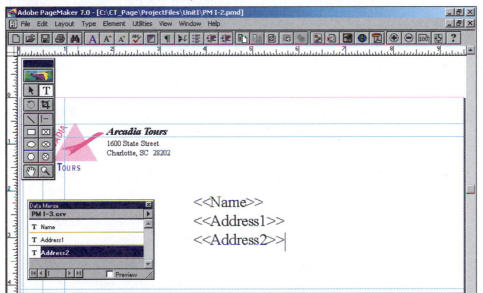

Creating a data source file

You can create a data source file in a spreadsheet application such as Microsoft Excel, a database program such as Microsoft Access, or in PageMaker. To create a data source in a spreadsheet or database program, enter each field as a column name, enter the data for each record on a separate row, then use the program's Save As feature to save the file as a comma-delimited text file. To create a data source in PageMaker, click the Text tool, enter each field name followed by a comma and no space (for example, Name,Address1,Address2), press Enter, then type the data for each record followed by a comma and no space. You then save the text block as a text file by selecting the text in the text block, clicking File, Export, Text, then entering a filename.

Running a Data Merge

The final step in the data merge process is to merge the target publication with the data source to create as many copies of the target publication as you need. You can either merge a publication with every entry, or you can choose to merge only a few of the records with the target publication. Typically you have a large data source and want to merge a publication with just some of the records in it, but for this lesson you merge the publication with every entry in the data source. You should always preview a few of your merged publications before printing them. Sara previews each of the merged envelopes to make sure the names and addresses appear correctly. She then runs the merge and prints envelopes for two of the customers.

Steps

1. Click the **Preview check box** on the Data Merge palette
   The first name and address in the data source file appears, as shown in Figure I-24. Sara wants to increase the width of the text box and reduce the font size of the text.

2. Click the **Pointer tool** ▶, click the text box, drag the top right corner handle to the right until the second line no longer wraps, click the **Text tool** T, select the text, then change the font size to **14 pt**

3. Click the **right arrow** ▶ at the bottom of the Data Merge palette once
   The record for Joseph Trelawney appears.

4. Click ▶ at the bottom of the Data Merge palette to preview the next record and then the final record
   The data from each of the records looks fine.

5. Click ▶ at the top of the Data Merge palette, then click **Merge Records**
   Sara can choose to merge all the records or just a selection of records. She wants to merge only records 1 and 3.

6. Click the **Ranges option button**, then type **1,3** as shown in Figure I-25

7. Click **OK**
   A new publication containing two envelopes appears. You can click the page numbers at the bottom of the screen to view each envelope.

8. Print the envelopes on plain paper (or on envelopes if you have them), close the publication without saving it, click the **Preview option button** on the Data Merge palette to deselect it, then close the Data Merge palette
   The next time Sara needs to print some envelopes, she can run the data merge again. She never needs to save each individual merged publication.

9. Save and close the publication, then exit PageMaker

FIGURE I-24: Data for Madelaine Watson

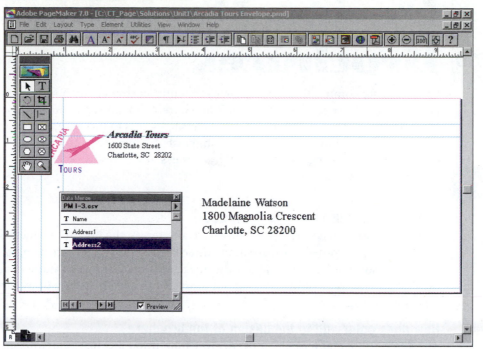

FIGURE I-25: Merge Records dialog box

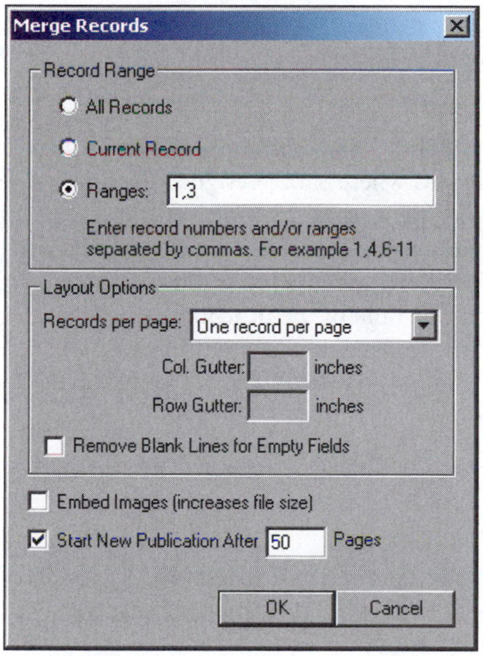

PageMaker 7.0

Design Workshop: Brochures

Brochures are commonly used to provide potential customers with information about a company's products or services. As such, a brochure is intended to educate. By using color in a brochure effectively, you can help get the message across to the reader. Color should be used to enhance information, to help readers distinguish differences, or to unite the commonalities of the information being presented. ✎ Let's review Sara's completed brochure design, shown in Figure I-26.

Details

► Does the brochure educate the reader?

Although Sara plans on using this brochure as a teaser, the brochure educates as it entices. In the brochure, customers learn about the three kinds of Tuscany tours being offered by Arcadia Tours and some information about the attractions of Tuscany. Customers also discover that they can obtain more information about tours to Tuscany and to five other destinations if they send away for it.

► How does color add to the design of the brochure?

Although Sara could have designed the brochure using just black ink, the effect of the photos of Tuscany would not be the same. If members of Sara's target audience have been to Tuscany, color photos may spur their memories of past vacations better than black and white photos. Customers who have not yet visited Tuscany are likely intrigued enough by the beauty in the photos to want to find out more information. Aside from including the three photographs, Sara uses color quite conservatively. She avoids splashing it onto every text block or every part of white space.

► Does the paper size and folding technique help or hinder the design?

Sara's design using standard legal-size paper is relatively common in the printing industry. She will have no problems finding an economical way to print the brochure. The folds of the brochure are also simple. The longest measurement is folded in half and then folded in half again.

► Does the brochure make it easy for potential customers to respond?

Potential response is where Sara's design really pays off. One flap of the brochure includes the mailing address of the company on one side and the reply card on the reverse side. Sara saves money and makes responding easier for customers. How? Sara can have the printing company add a perforation along the fold line so the customer can separate the card easily from the rest of the brochure. The bulk of the brochure stays intact for the customer, and the response card is mailed back to Arcadia Tours.

FIGURE I-26: Sara's completed brochure

Let Tuscany into your soul . . .

For close to three millenia, Tuscany has produced to some of the world's greatest artists. Today, visitors to one of Italy's most blessed provinces can find superb examples of Estruscan art in the museums of Florence and Volterra, Roman ruins at every turn, massive medieval fortresses, and exquisitely decorated Romanesque churches. Great masterpieces by Michelangelo, Leonardo da Vinci, Botticelli, and Raphael remind us that the Renaissance was born in Florence and still flourishes today in beautiful museums like the Uffizi, the Accademia, and the Bargello. But Tuscany is not only about art and history. In Tuscany, you will also find a relaxed pace of life, where lingering over a three-hour dinner is the rule, not the exception, where unabashed enjoyment of good food and great wine reminds us that life is meant to be lived to the fullest.

When you travel to Tuscany with Arcadia Tours,

you are free to enjoy all that Tuscany has to offer without needing to worry about finding accommodations, getting from one place to another, and selecting the best restuarants. Our guides take care of it all! You'll stay in charming, family-run hotels and travel by minibus. Our tours are limited to no more than 20 people, so you'll never feel like

you're part of a conventional bus tour. And you will never need to worry about food! Great restaurants abound throughout Tuscany and our guides know most of them. How about gnocchi baked in gorgonzola cheese or fettucine tossed with fresh basil and garlic? You won't go hungry. We guarantee it!

Take a Tuscany Tour with *Arcadia Tours!*

Enjoy Tuscany on a full escorted one-week or two-week themed tour. Choose an Art tour, Country tour, or Hill Town tour. Prices start at $2,000 per person for all accommodations, dinners, transportation, and guided tours. For more information, call your travel agent or Arcadia Tours at 1-800-555-2600, or visit our Web site at www.arcadiatours.com*.*

Place Stamp Here

Arcadia Tours
1600 State Street
Charlotte, SC 28202

Yes! Send me more information about *Arcadia Tours*. Please check the destinations that interest you.

☐ Tuscany   ☐ France   ☐ Greece
☐ Spain   ☐ Portugal   ☐ Other Destinations in Italy

Please detach and mail back to Arcadia Tours to receive more information.

Toscana!

Experience Italy at its best in Sunny Tuscany!

Arcadia Tours offers one- and two-week theme-based tours in Tuscany. You can choose from three themes: art tours, hill town tours, and country tours. Each of our tours is accompanied by an expert guide who provides you with a wealth of information and experience based around the chosen theme *and* makes sure you have ample time to soak up the wonderful Tuscan atmosphere. The Art tours focus on the museums and churches in Florence and Siena, while the Hill Town tours lead you through the twisting cobbled streets of charming medieval towns such as San Gimignano with its famous towers and Montalcino with its unsurpassed wine. Country tours focus on relaxation. You stay at a farm deep in the Tuscan countryside and spend your days ambling or cycling along quiet country roads.

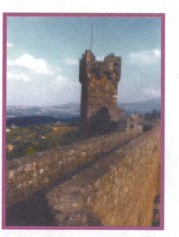

Practice

► Concepts Review

Label each of the publication window elements shown in Figure I-27.

FIGURE I-27

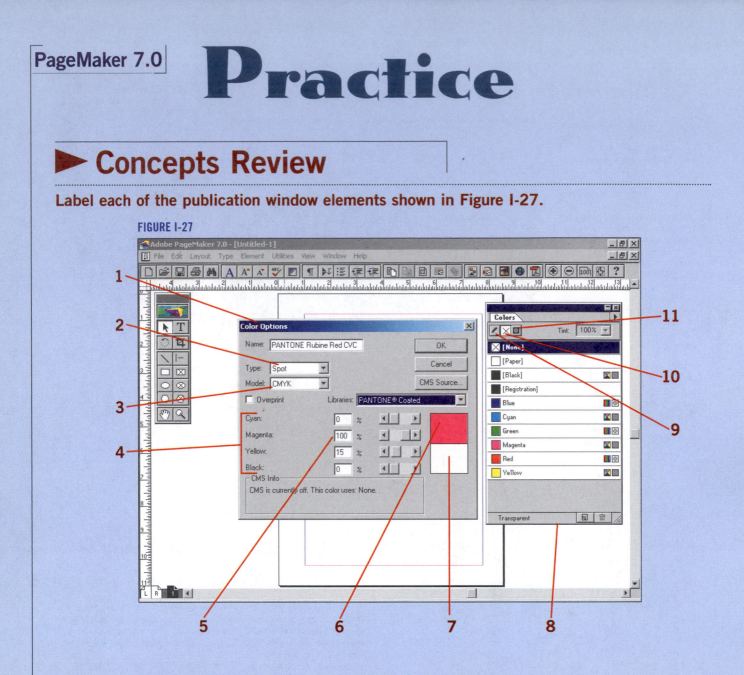

Match each of the terms with the statement that describes its function.

12. **Process colors**
13. **Spot color**
14. **Tint**
15. **Color library**
16. **Separations**
17. **Field**
18. **Trapping**

a. Based on a specific color ink
b. Printouts on paper or film of each color used for commercial printing of publications
c. PageMaker's storage for color matching systems
d. The four main colors used in combinations to create many other colors
e. Compensate for misregistration
f. A new color based on a percentage of another color
g. Unit of variable information used in a data merge

Select the best answer from the list of choices.

19. **Which of the following is true about brochures?**
    a. Brochures can be used as teasers to entice the reader to find out more information.
    b. The standard brochure size is 8" × 10".
    c. All brochures include some sort of self-mailer as the point of response.
    d. Teaser brochures are generally multiple-page documents loaded with details about a company's products or services.

20. **The four process colors are:**
    a. Cyan, magenta, yellow, and red.
    b. Cyan, magenta, green, and yellow.
    c. Cyan, magenta, yellow, and black.
    d. Red, yellow, blue, and black.

21. **Which of the following statements best describe a spot color?**
    a. A spot color is made from four basic colors combined in percentages.
    b. A spot color is made from one color defined as a percentage.
    c. A spot color is created from one specific ink.
    d. A spot color uses CMYK.

22. **Colors can be applied to:**
    a. Text.
    b. Graphical elements.
    c. Lines.
    d. All of the above

23. **Tints are based on:**
    a. Color matching systems.
    b. Process colors.
    c. Black.
    d. Color libraries.

24. **The purpose of a color matching system is to create:**
    a. Colors that display vibrantly on a color monitor.
    b. Color separations.
    c. Process colors.
    d. Consistent color representation between monitors and print output.

25. **Color separations are:**
    a. Previews of final color composite output.
    b. Printouts on paper or film of process colors.
    c. Printouts on paper or film of spot colors.
    d. Both b and c

PageMaker 7.0

26. Which of the following tasks is **NOT** performed by the service provider plug-in?
   a. Copies linked image files
   b. Copies fonts
   c. Fixes broken links
   d. Prompts for broken links

27. What are the two information sources required for a data merge?
   a. Variable data and target data
   b. Data source file and variable data
   c. Data source file and fields
   d. Target publication and data source file

28. From what menu do you select the Data Merge palette?
   a. File
   b. Window
   c. Insert
   d. Element

▶ Skills Review

1. Apply color to text and graphics.
   a. Start PageMaker and open the file PM I-4.pmd from the drive and folder where your Project Files are located, accept any warnings, then save the file as **Chicago Meeting**.
   b. Open the Define Colors dialog box.
   c. Click [Paper] in the Colors list box, then click New.
   d. In the Color Options dialog box, make sure CMYK is selected.
   e. Change the value for Cyan to 100.
   f. Change the value for Magenta to 50.
   g. Change the value for Yellow to 100.
   h. Name the color **Forest Green**, then close the Color Options and Define Colors dialog boxes.

2. Use a color library.
   a. If necessary, display the Colors palette in the publication window.
   b. Select the horizontal box around the word Speaker in the upper-left corner on page 2.
   c. Change both the line and the fill for the Speaker text box to Forest Green.
   d. Select the vertical box intersecting the box on the far right side of page 2.
   e. Apply the Forest Green color to both the line and the fill of the selected box, then deselect it.
   f. Select the vertical box to which you just applied the color.
   g. Click [Registration] on the Colors palette to return the object to its original color.
   h. Apply the Forest Green color to both the line and the fill of all horizontal boxes on page 2 and in the left two columns on page 3.

3. Create a new color.
   a. Open the Define Colors dialog box.
   b. Select Forest Green in the Color list, then click Edit.
   c. Reduce the Magenta percentage to 30%.
   d. Close the Color Options and Define Colors dialog boxes.
   e. Make sure your new color is automatically applied to all objects set to that color.

4. **Apply spot colors.**
   a. Open the Define Colors dialog box.
   b. Click [Paper] in the Color list box, then click New.
   c. Select the PANTONE Coated library.
   d. In the Pick Colors dialog box, select the color named Rubine Red.
   e. Click OK twice.
   f. Click New to create a second color.
   g. Select the PANTONE Coated library again.
   h. Name the new color **3955** to select that color.
   i. Click OK three times to close the Define Colors dialog box.
   j. Scroll down the Colors palette to see the new Pantone colors that you added.

5. **Edit a color and create a tint.**
   a. Select the headline text inside the Forest Green box in the upper-left corner on page 2.
   b. Apply the PANTONE 3955 CVC color on the Colors palette to the text.
   c. Repeat Steps a and b above to apply the PANTONE 3955 CVC color to all headline text inside Forest Green boxes.
   d. Apply the Rubine Red color to the text Advertising Professionals – Chicago Chapter on the front panel of the brochure.
   e. Open the Define Colors dialog box.
   f. Click New.
   g. Change the color Type to Tint.
   h. Select Forest Green in the Base Color list box.
   i. Change the value in the Tint text box to 50%.
   j. Name the color **50% Forest Green**.
   k. Click OK twice.
   l. Apply the new 50% Forest Green color to all vertical boxes in the brochure and to the black box on the front panel.

6. **Trap colors.**
   a. Open the Trapping Preferences dialog box.
   b. Enable trapping for this publication.
   c. Change the Trap width Default to .005.
   d. Change the Black width to .011.
   e. Click OK.

7. **Create color separations.**
   a. Open the Print dialog box.
   b. If you are using a PostScript printer, click Paper. If you are using a non-PostScript printer, go to Step e.
   c. Click the Center page in print area check box.
   d. Click the Reduce to fit option button.
   e. Click Color.
   f. Click the Separations option button.
   g. Add the PANTONE 3955 CVC color to the list of inks to print.
   h. Click Print.
   i. Save your publication.

8. Save for service provider plug-in.

a. Start the Save For Service Provider plug-in.

b. Select Preflight pub.

c. Click Yes in response to the Save warning.

d. Click Package.

e. Click the Auto open package report check box to select it.

f. Click the Save In list arrow, select a new location in which to store the files, then click Save.

g. When saving is complete, click Close, then switch to the Report.pmd file.

h. View the Document, Link, and Font information.

i. Print a copy of the report, close the Report window, then close the publication.

9. Set up a data merge.

a. Open the file PM I-5.pmd from the drive and folder where your Project Files are located, click OK if necessary, then save the file as **AP Envelope**.

b. Delete Customer Address.

c. Show the Data Merge palette.

d. Click the right arrow at the top right of the Data Merge palette, then click Select Data Source.

e. Open the PM I-6.csv data source.

f. Add the Name field from the Data Merge palette, then press [Enter].

g. Add the Address1 field from the Data Merge palette, press [Enter], then add the Address2 field from the Data Merge palette.

h. Save the publication.

10. Run a data merge.

a. Preview the first record.

b. Preview the remaining three records.

c. Merge all the records.

d. Change the Record Range so that records 1 and 2 are merged.

e. Click OK.

f. Print the envelopes on plain paper (or on envelopes if you have them), close the publication without saving it, deselect the Preview option button on the Data Merge palette, then close the Data Merge palette.

g. Save and close the publication, then exit PageMaker.

▶ Independent Challenge 1

You work for Paradise Tours in the Young Audience Tours division. You have decided to create a teaser brochure that can be sent to all of the company's customers who are between the ages of 18 and 24 to announce new spring break trips to Hawaii. The purpose of the brochure is to encourage readers to send back an attached mailer for more information. The brochure is to be printed using four-color process inks and include photos and color elements to enhance the overall message of the brochure.

a. Plan and sketch the brochure design.

b. Open a new publication and determine the size, shape, and possible ways to incorporate a reply card. Use either letter- or legal-size paper and a three- or four-panel format.

c. Place in the brochure the Hawaii-related photos called Hawaii1 and Hawaii2, located in the drive and folder where your Project Files are located.

d. Add headlines and copy for the brochure, then apply color to text where appropriate. If necessary, you can use the Word document, HawaiiText, located in the drive and folder with your Project Files, for text describing the tour to Hawaii. Supplement the text with additional information about cost and dates where appropriate.

e. Create a spot color using the process colors. Apply the color to the headlines.

f. Create an additional spot color using one of PageMaker's color libraries. Apply the color to appropriate graphical elements included in your brochure.

g. Create color separations for each of the process colors. Be sure to include a separation for each additional spot color.

h. Include a text box that contains your name.

i. Save the brochure as **Hawaii Brochure**, then print a copy.

▶ Independent Challenge 2

You work for a landscaping company called GreenArt Gardeners that occasionally sends promotional materials to selected customers. The company is quite small and does not have preprinted stationery on hand. You have been asked to create an envelope in PageMaker that includes a colored logo for the company, and then to create a data source file containing the names and addresses of five customers. You will then merge the envelope file with the data source file and print three of the envelopes. You start by selecting an envelope template from PageMaker's selection of predefined templates.

a. In PageMaker, click Window on the menu bar, click Plug-in Palettes, then click Show Template Palette. *(Macintosh Users: Insert the PageMaker Content CD and open the Letters palette. Choose one of the envelope options and click OK. Resume at Step c.)*

b. Click the Category list arrow, click Business Sets, then select the Business Set shown in Figure I-28 below.

FIGURE I-28

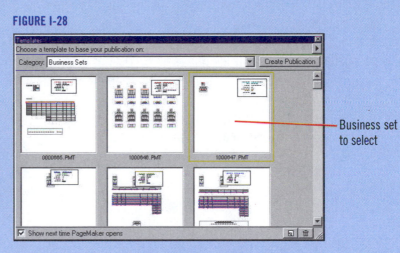

Business set to select

c. Click Create Publication, then click OK if a font message appears.

d. Delete the objects on the publication, then save it as **GreenArt Envelopes**.

e. Use the Circle tool and Text tool to create the simple logo shown in Figure I-29. Note that you need to select black for the lines around the circle and for the text. In the Color palette defined for the template, Black is set at a 40% tint. You need to restore Black to 100%.

f. Delete the four PANTONE colors currently listed in the Colors palette. (*Hint*: To delete a color, click it, then drag it to the Delete icon, which appears as a trash can, at the bottom of the Colors palette.)

g. Create a new spot color using the PANTONE 359 CVC color from the PANTONE® Coated library.

h. Fill the circle with the new spot color.

i. Save the publication, then start a new publication in a new window.

j. Create a text block containing the text entries shown in Figure I-30. Note that you must separate each entry with a comma and include no spaces between entries. For entries that include commas (such as Seattle, WA) you need to enclose the entry in quotation marks, e.g., "Seattle, WA 98121", as shown in Figure I-30.

FIGURE I-29

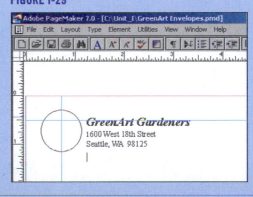

PageMaker 7.0

k. Select all six lines of text, click File on the menu bar, click Export, then click Text.

l. Enter **GreenArt Data** as the filename, then click Save.

m. Save the publication as **GreenArt Data**, then close it.

n. In the Envelope publication, show the Data Merge palette, select the GreenArt Data source, click the Text tool, then add and enhance the three fields in the center of the envelope.

o. Preview the record for Ellen Madison, then compare the completed envelope to Figure I-31.

p. Print the envelopes for Kevin (record 2), Lana (record 3), and Donald (record 5). Write your name on each envelope.

q. Close and save the publication.

FIGURE I-30

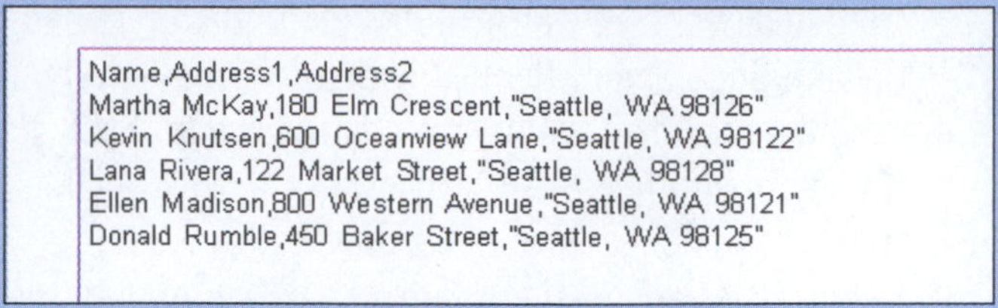

Name,Address1,Address2
Martha McKay,180 Elm Crescent,"Seattle, WA 98126"
Kevin Knutsen,600 Oceanview Lane,"Seattle, WA 98122"
Lana Rivera,122 Market Street,"Seattle, WA 98128"
Ellen Madison,800 Western Avenue,"Seattle, WA 98121"
Donald Rumble,450 Baker Street,"Seattle, WA 98125"

FIGURE I-31

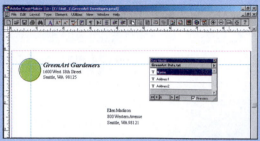

▶ Independent Challenge 3

You work for a small but promising software company called Digital Art Media Ltd, located in your home town. The president, Mr. John McGraw, has asked you to create a brochure for three new software packages: Great Travel Destinations, Maps of the World, and Gardening Encyclopedia. This brochure will serve as a teaser.

a. Create a vertical three-panel, two-fold brochure.

b. Place frames for text and graphics into the publication. If you wish, fill the frames with appropriate text and photographs or simply identify them as TEXT or PHOTO.

c. Create colors that can be applied to text and drawn graphic designs. Use one color from the Pantone® Coated library.

d. Create a tint, then apply it in your design.

e. Include your name somewhere on the brochure.

f. Save the publication as **CD-ROM Brochure**, then print a copy of the brochure.

ⓔ Independent Challenge 4

You work for a travel agency that is offering cruises to Alaska in conjunction with a major cruise ship company. You have been given the job of creating a teaser brochure that describes the cruise and some of the sites and scenes along the way.

a. Search the World Wide Web for information on cruises to Alaska.

b. Using the information that you find, create a sketch of both the inside and outside panels of your brochure following the guidelines that you learned in this unit. Be sure to include a logo for the travel agency and a return mailer or point of response.

c. Create a brochure in PageMaker from your sketch. If you wish, you can use the Alaska1, Alaska2, and Alaska3 photos located in the drive and folder where your Project Files are located or you can add your own photos. Add your own headlines and text from the information that you have found on the World Wide Web.

d. Use color to add to the design of the brochure. Create a new spot color from the four process colors and also from a predefined library color. Apply these colors to different elements in your brochure.

e. Edit the spot color that you created from the four process colors.

f. Create a tint from one of PageMaker's default colors and use it as the background color for a text block in the publication.

g. Create color separations for your brochure, being sure to first turn on the Trapping option.

h. Include your name somewhere on the brochure.

i. Critique your final brochure to make sure that it achieves its purpose.

j. Save the brochure as **Alaska Brochure**, then print it.

PageMaker 7.0

▶ Visual Workshop

Create the tri-fold brochure shown in Figure I-32. This brochure advertises trips offered by Arcadia Tours to Provence in France. If you wish, open and adapt the brochure you created to advertise the Tuscany tours. Use the photo files Provence1, Provence2, and Provence3 and the Word file FranceText, all located in the drive and folder where your Project Files are located. Create a tint of 30% yellow for Provence!, create a tint of 50% cyan for the colored box on page 2, create cyan-colored, 8-pt frames for the photograph of the village and the photograph of the pathway, create a new process color called Dark Green that consists of 100% cyan and 80% yellow, apply the Dark Green color to the two headlines, fill the airplane graphic in the logo with 100% cyan, then fill the triangle in the logo with the spot color called PANTONE® Coated 130 CVC. Save the publication as **Provence Brochure**, then print a copy.

FIGURE I-32

Working
with Long Publications

- ▶ **Design an index**
- ▶ **Add index entries**
- ▶ **Use index keyboard shortcuts**
- ▶ **Use the index shortcut menu**
- ▶ **Create a cross-reference**
- ▶ **Set index format**
- ▶ **Generate an index**
- ▶ **Edit an index**
- ▶ **Create a table of contents**
- ▶ **Add a drop cap**
- ▶ **Use the Build Booklet plug-in**
- ▶ **Design Workshop: Books with TOCs and Indexes**

PageMaker provides the tools required to easily add an index and a table of contents to your publication. In this unit, you learn how to mark the text in stories that you want to be included in an index, how to use shortcuts for identifying text included in the index, how to edit index entries, how to create cross-references, and how to generate an index. In addition, you learn how to create a table of contents and how to use the Drop cap and Build Booklet plug-ins. ✒ A group of tour operators in Vancouver, British Columbia, has hired Sara to create a small booklet of tourist information about Vancouver that can be distributed to visitors. Sara creates an index and a table of contents for the 18-page booklet.

Designing an Index

When you are planning a publication with many pages, you should consider adding an index to help your readers find specific information in your document. You can create a comprehensive index, or you can create an index based on major topics, or **key words**. When sketching her design for the booklet index, shown in Figure J-1, Sara used the following guidelines to help her create an effective index.

▶ Determine your readers' need for an index

Long publications containing a great many technical terms and concepts generally need to be supplemented by a comprehensive index that readers can use to quickly locate specific information. Publicity or marketing publications that are relatively short generally require only an index of key words. Sara is working on a brief publication designed to publicize the sites and attractions in Vancouver, so she creates an index that contains key words.

▶ Provide alternative methods for finding keywords in an index

When designing an index, you need to take into consideration the different ways readers might use the index to find a specific topic. For example, you can add cross-reference index entries to provide readers with an expanded number of ways to find information. A reader looking for information about hotels in Vancouver may look under "A" for "accommodations." There, they could find a cross-reference to "Hotels." Under the Hotels entry, readers could then find a list of all the specific hotel properties discussed in the booklet. Sara adds several cross-references to the index.

▶ Formatting index pages

Many publications end with indexes that consist of numerous pages of closely spaced text. You can break up the monotony of these pages by adding graphic designs or photographs and by selecting a multiple-column format. Sara formats the index in two columns.

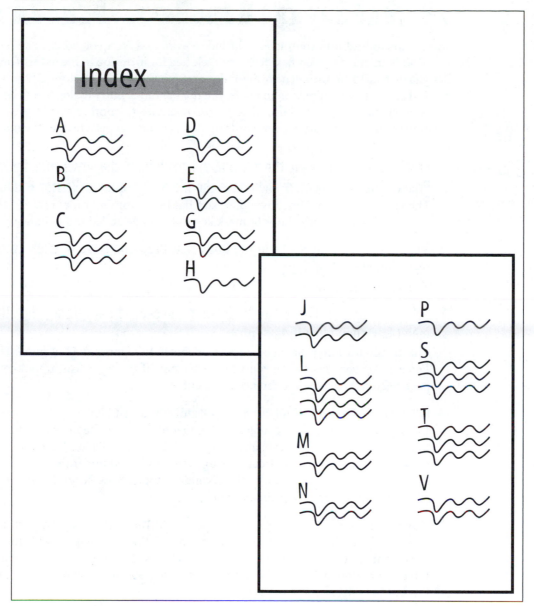

Unit J

PageMaker 7.0

Adding Index Entries

You use the Index Entry command to include a word or a group of words in an index. This command adds an index marker next to the text selected for inclusion in the index. The **index marker** designates text to be included in the index and is visible only in story editor. Once you have marked all the text required for an index, you use the Index Entry dialog box to determine if each index entry has a page reference or is a cross-reference to another entry. Sara begins creating the index by marking key words in the first story on page four of the publication.

Steps 1 2 3 4

QuickTip

Windows Users: After launching PageMaker, you need to close the Templates palette.

1. Start PageMaker, open the file **PM J-1.pmd** from the drive and folder where your Project Files are located, then save the file as **Vancouver Visitor Guide**
   The visitor guide for Vancouver that Sara has been working on appears in the publication window. She uses story editor to mark key words to be added to the index.
2. Move to **page 4**, click [pointer tool] in the **body text block** on page 4, click **Edit** on the menu bar, then click **Edit Story**
   The text block opens in story editor.
3. Select the text **Anthropology Museum** in the second paragraph, click **Utilities** on the menu bar, then click **Index Entry**
   The Add Index Entry dialog box opens, as shown in Figure J-2. (*Macintosh Users: The Index Entry dialog box opens.*) You must first determine if the topic "Anthropology Museum" is a page reference or a cross-reference index entry.
4. Make sure the **Page reference option button** is selected
   In the Topic section of the dialog box, you identify topics to be indexed. You can also choose to add subcategories to create a more detailed index. See Figure J-3 for an example of secondary and tertiary topics. Secondary topics are indented under the primary topic, and tertiary topics are indented under the secondary topic. Sara decides that the Anthropology Museum index entry is a primary topic.
5. Make sure the **Current page option button** in the Page range section is selected
   Sara could enter a different page range option, so that the index would show a longer page range, but for this booklet, she decides to make the page reference the first page where the topic is mentioned. The final option in this dialog box allows you to format the page number, but Sara decides not to use this option.
6. Click **OK**
   The dialog box closes and PageMaker inserts an index marker in front of the word "Anthropology."
7. Click **Story** on the menu bar, then click **Close Story**
8. Save the publication

FIGURE J-2: Add Index Entry dialog box

Selected index topic

Description of
page range

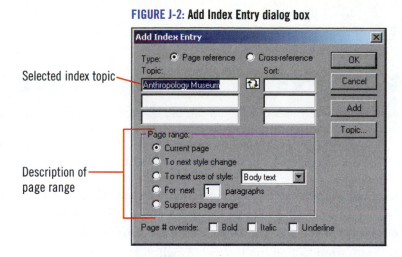

FIGURE J-3: Example of primary, secondary, and tertiary topic index

Primary
index topics

Secondary topics

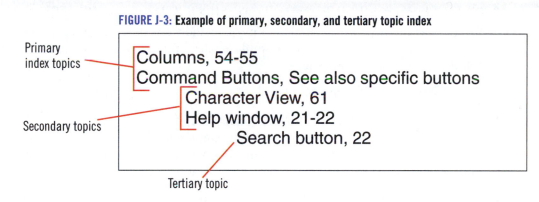

Columns, 54-55
Command Buttons, See also specific buttons
Character View, 61
Help window, 21-22
Search button, 22

Tertiary topic

Sorting index topics

You can work in the Index Entry dialog box to sort topics alphabetically by the spelling entered in the Sort text boxes. However, the topic appears in the index as it is spelled in the Topic text box. Figure J-4 shows an example where "St. Louis" is entered in the Topic text box and "Saint Louis" is typed in the Sort text box. When the index is generated, the index entry is printed as "St. Louis" in the index, but it is sorted as "Saint Louis" because of the sort specification entered in the Sort text box.

FIGURE J-4: Example of topic sort

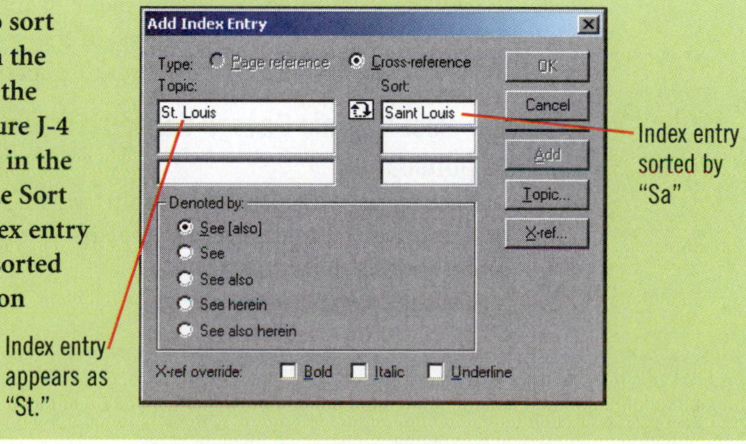

Index entry
sorted by
"Sa"

Index entry
appears as
"St."

Using Index Keyboard Shortcuts

Once you understand how to index topics, you can use shortcuts that allow you to quickly add index items. You can use keyboard shortcuts to mark index entries in the publication window. Using keyboard shortcuts saves you time; however, you cannot see index markers because you are working in the publication window instead of story editor. You can also use a keyboard shortcut to index a person's proper name so that it is sorted by last name first. Sara uses index shortcuts to quickly index important topics that she wants to include in the index.

Steps

1. Move to page 6 of the publication, click the body text block on page 6, then click the Actual Size button 🔲 on the toolbar to switch to actual size (*Macintosh Users: Click Actual Size on the View menu*)

> **MacintoshUsers**
>
> In steps that instruct you to press [Ctrl] + another key, [Ctrl] is the equivalent of [Command]. For example, in Step 3 below, press [Command] [Y] in place of [Ctrl] [Y] to open the Index Entry dialog box.

2. Click the **Text tool** 🇹 in the toolbox, select the text **Stanley Park**, then press **[Ctrl][Y]**
   The Add Index Entry dialog box opens, as shown in Figure J-5. (*Macintosh Users: The Index Entry dialog box opens.*)

3. Click **OK** to accept the index entry, deselect the text, then press **[Ctrl][E]**
   You can use the [Ctrl][E] keystrokes to move to and from story editor. In story editor, an index marker appears in front of the word "Stanley." You want to continue using the keyboard shortcut to select index topics.

4. Press **[Ctrl][E]** to exit story editor

5. Select the word **Gastown**, then press **[Ctrl][Shift][Y]**
   Although you can't see it, an index marker is automatically inserted in front of the word "Gastown." Using [Ctrl][Shift][Y] to index terms accepts the default settings in the Add Index Entry dialog box. The topic is also automatically added as a primary index topic.

6. Repeat Step 5 to index the following entries on pages 7, 8, and 9: **Capilano Canyon Suspension Bridge**, **Granville Island**, and **Grouse Mountain**

7. Press **[Ctrl][E]** to enter story editor again
   The story appears in the story editor. The index topics selected using the keyboard shortcuts have been marked with index markers, as shown in Figure J-6.

> **MacintoshUsers**
>
> To insert a nonbreaking space, press [Option] [Spacebar].

8. Exit story editor, move to **page 4** in the publication, click ▶ on **page 4**, enter story editor, click after **Captain** in the second paragraph, delete the current space, then press **[Ctrl][Shift][H]** to insert a nonbreaking space
   Sara needs to index the proper name "Captain George Vancouver," but she wants it to appear as "Vancouver, Captain George" in the completed index. Since the name consists of three words, she first inserts a nonbreaking space between "Captain" and "George."

9. Select **Captain George Vancouver**, press **[Ctrl][Alt][Y]**, exit story editor, then save the publication
   Sara uses [Alt] instead of [Shift] so that PageMaker places an index marker in front of "Captain," and the entry appears in the index as "Vancouver, Captain George" and references page 4.

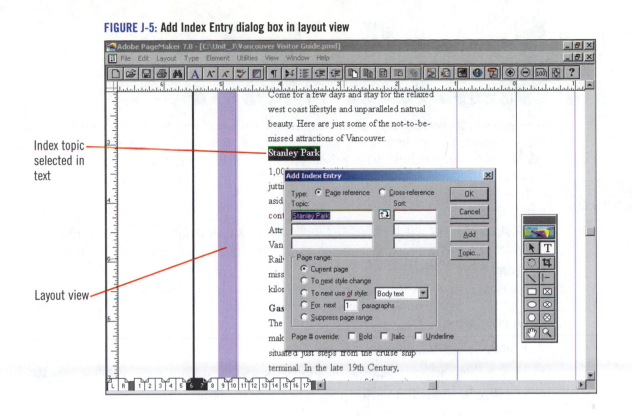

Index topic
selected in
text

Layout view

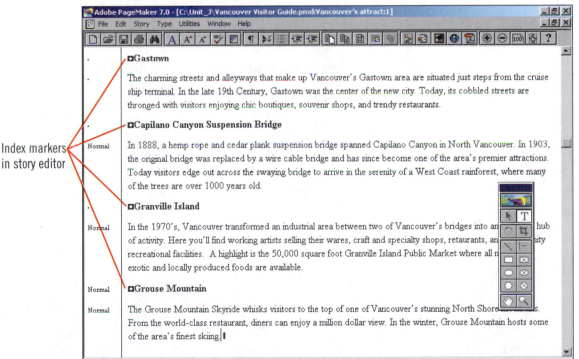

Index markers
in story editor

Using the Index Shortcut Menu

In addition to keyboard shortcuts, you can use the Change command shortcut in story editor. This command allows you to index all occurrences of words or phrases with one command. Sara wants to create a secondary-level reference for each of the beaches in Vancouver underneath the primary index reference "Beaches: Vancouver." She begins by using a keyboard shortcut to open the Add Index Entry dialog box.

1. Move to **page 11**, click 🖰 on the **body text block** on page 11, switch to story editor, select the text **English Bay** in the third paragraph, press **[Ctrl][Y]**, then click the **Promote/Demote button** 🔁

   See Figure J-7. Notice that the phrase "English Bay" is now displayed in the second Topic text box. The insertion point is flashing inside the first Topic text box prompting you to type a primary reference.

2. Type **Beaches: Vancouver**, then click **OK**

3. Click Ⅰ at the beginning of the story, click **Utilities** on the menu bar, then click **Change**

   The Change dialog box opens where Sara can index all the occurrences of "University of British Columbia."

4. Type **University of British Columbia** in the Find what text box, press **[Tab]**, type **^;** (caret and semicolon) in the Change to text box, then click the **All stories option button**

   Sara has entered the information required to index all occurrences of the phrase "University of British Columbia." See Figure J-8.

5. Click **Change all**

   PageMaker adds every instance of "University of British Columbia" to the index.

6. Click the **Close button** in the Change dialog box, then exit story editor

7. Save and close your publication

FIGURE J-7: Topic moved in the Add Index Entry dialog box

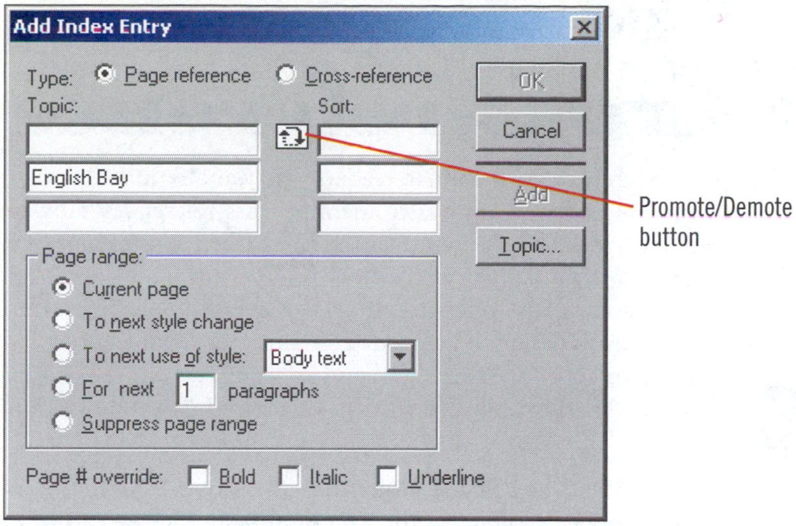

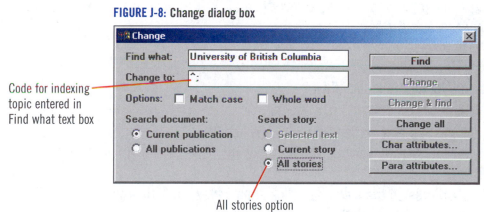

Add Index Entry

Type: ● Page reference ○ Cross-reference

OK

Topic: Sort:

Cancel

English Bay

Add

Topic...

Page range:
○ Current page
○ To next style change
○ To next use of style: Body text
○ For next 1 paragraphs
○ Suppress page range

Page # override: ☐ Bold ☐ Italic ☐ Underline

Promote/Demote button

FIGURE J-8: Change dialog box

Code for indexing topic entered in Find what text box

Change

Find what: University of British Columbia   Find

Change to: ^;   Change

Options: ☐ Match case ☐ Whole word

Change & find

Search document: Search story:

Change all

● Current publication   ○ Selected text

Char attributes...

○ All publications   ○ Current story

Para attributes...

○ All stories

All stories option button selected

Creating a Cross-reference

Cross-references are helpful to readers who want to find related or additional topics. You use the Add Index Entry dialog box to identify cross-references. However, unlike primary references, PageMaker does not generate an index marker to indicate a cross-reference. As a result, the placement of your cursor in the story is irrelevant when creating a cross-reference. ✎ Sara wants to add a cross-reference to help readers find pertinent information. She opens a version of the Visitor's Guide that already contains most of the entries required for the index and adds a cross-reference for "North Vancouver." She wants to remind readers that they can find additional information about North Vancouver in the Cycling section of the guide.

Steps

1. Open the file **PM J-2.pmd** from the drive and folder where your Project Files are located, then save the file as **Vancouver Visitor Guide Complete**
   The publication is nearly complete with most of the index selections selected.

2. Click **Utilities** on the menu bar, then click **Index Entry**
   The Add Index Entry dialog box opens. Remember, because a cross-reference does not generate an index marker, you do not need to place the insertion point before the phrase "North Vancouver" in the publication.

3. Click the **Cross-reference option button** if necessary
   Notice that the bottom half of the dialog box changed. See Figure J-9.

4. Type **North Vancouver** in the Topic text box, then click **X-ref**
   The Select Cross-Reference Topic dialog box opens. See Figure J-10.

5. Click the **Topic section list arrow**, then click **C** (*Macintosh Users: Choose C in the Topic section list box*)
   The index entries beginning with the letter "C" appear in the Level 1 list box so that Sara can locate the "Cycling" entry she created earlier. See Figure J-11.

6. Click **Cycling**, then click **OK**
   The dialog box closes.

7. Click the **See also option button**, then click **OK**
   Make sure you select the See also option and not the See [also] option. This selection determines how the cross-reference appears in the index.

MacintoshUsers

This replaces Step 8.
8. Click Utilities on the menu bar, click Show Index, and choose N in the Index section list box

8. Click **Utilities** on the menu bar, click **Show Index**, click the **Index section list arrow**, scroll down, then click **N**

9. Verify that **See also Cycling** appears next to the North Vancouver entry, click **OK**, then save the publication

FIGURE J-9: Cross-reference option button selected

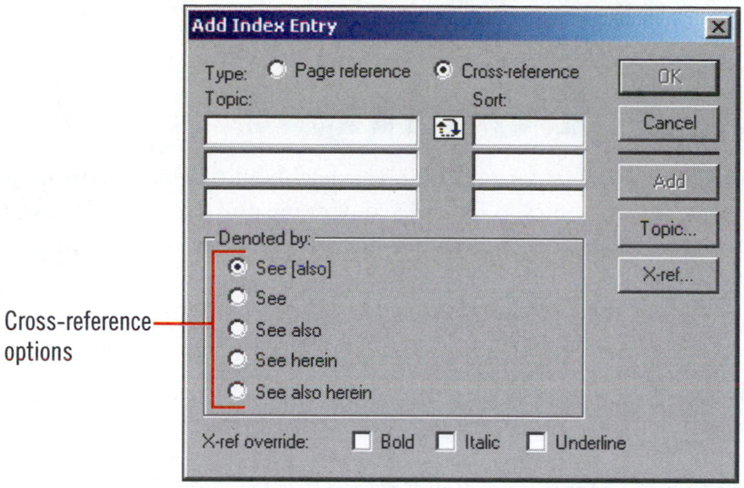

Cross-reference
options

FIGURE J-10: Select Cross-Reference Topic dialog box

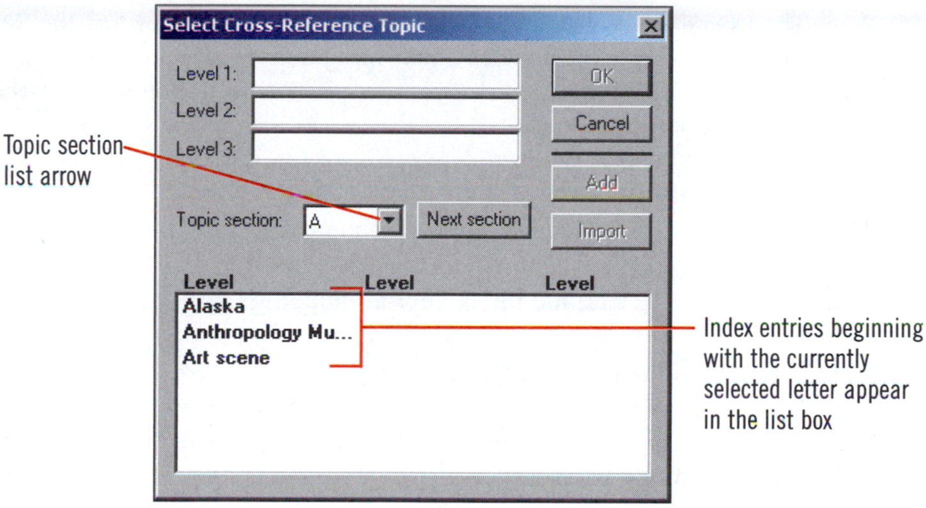

Topic section
list arrow

Index entries beginning
with the currently
selected letter appear
in the list box

FIGURE J-11: Index list box for the letter C

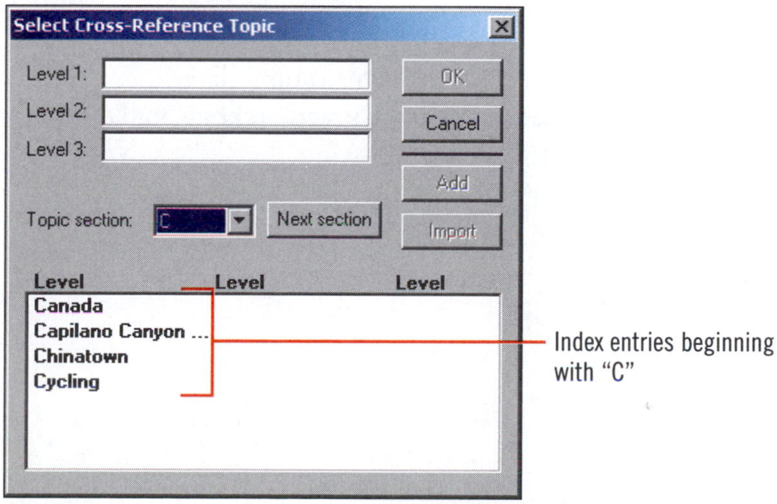

Index entries beginning
with "C"

Setting the Index Format

Table J-1 describes the various format options available in the Index Format dialog box. After you have identified all the topics to be indexed, you use the Create Index command to format the index information. You can specify how index entries are arranged in the index, and you can also change the paragraph style applied. Sara is ready to format the index with a two-column format that includes section headings.

Steps

1. **Move to page 16 in the publication**
   The index starts on page 16 and extends to page 17.

2. **Click Layout on the menu bar, click Column Guides, type 2 in the Number of columns text box for both the Left and Right pages, as shown in Figure J-12, then click OK**
   Pages 16 and 17 show two columns on each page.

3. **Click Utilities on the menu bar, then click Create Index**
   The Create Index dialog box opens. See Figure J-13. Notice that the Remove unreferenced topics option is selected at this time. This option removes any unreferenced topics for which entries were deleted or for which a topic was removed if an index marker was deleted. Sara leaves this option turned on.

4. **Click Format**
   The Index Format dialog box opens, as shown in Figure J-14.

5. **Make sure the Include index section headings check box is selected**

6. **Click the Run-in option button**
   Notice the example at the bottom of the dialog box. When Run-in is selected, as opposed to Nested, the subentries for an index entry run together in one paragraph, and each subentry is separated by a semicolon.

7. **Click the Nested option button**
   After examining the options for displaying the index, Sara decides she prefers the Nested format. The remaining text boxes are used to enter other index format specifications. These specifications determine how PageMaker enters characters and spaces to separate parts of your index entries.

8. **Click OK to close the Index Format dialog box**
   The Create Index dialog box appears again. In the next lesson, you generate the index.

FIGURE J-12: Column Guides dialog box

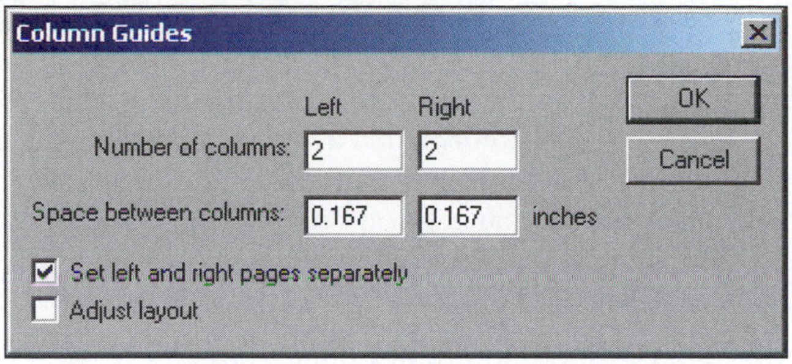

FIGURE J-13: Create Index dialog box

You do not need to enter a title here because a title already appears on the publication page in a separate text block

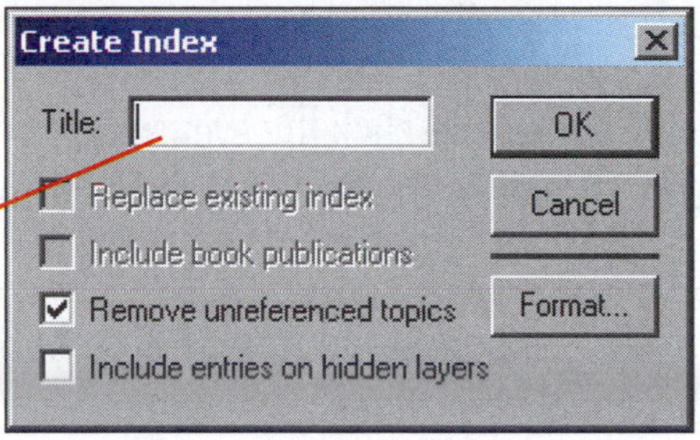

FIGURE J-14: Index Format dialog box

Shows selected format style

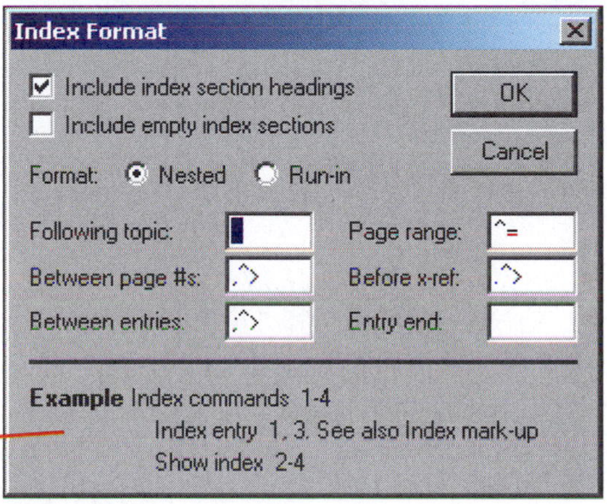

TABLE J-1: Index Format options

option	description
Following topic	Space used to separate the topic and the page number; the default is two spaces
Between page #s	Space used to separate multiple page references; the default is an en space (a space equal to the width of the "n" character)
Between entries	Character used to separate level entries in a run-in format or character used to separate cross-references; the default is a semicolon and en space
Page range	Character used to separate first and last page references in a series; the default is a dash
Before x-ref	Character that appears before a cross-reference; the default is a period and en space
Entry end	Character that appears at the end of every entry in a nested format or following the last cross-reference in the topic; the default is no character

Generating an Index

After setting the format for an index, you can generate it and insert it into your publication. PageMaker creates the index information as a new story that you can place in your publication as you would any other story. If you continue to add or to edit index entries, then you must regenerate the index for the changes to appear in the placed index story. ✎ Sara places the index on the last two pages of the publication.

1. Click **OK** to close the Create Index dialog box

   The manual text flow pointer ▦ appears in the publication window indicating that you need to place the new index story.

2. Move ▦ to the left margin guide even with **2** on the vertical ruler bar on **page 16**, press **[Shift]** and click, but do not release [Shift]

3. Continue to hold **[Shift]**, and click ▯ even with **2** on the vertical ruler bar in the **second column** on **page 16** and in the **first** and **second columns** on **page 17** to finish placing the story

4. Click on **page 16**, then click the **Actual Size button** ▦ on the toolbar (*Macintosh Users: Click Actual Size on the View menu*)

   See Figure J-15. The newly generated index is displayed in the publication.

5. Save the publication

FIGURE J-15: Index generated using Create Index command

Section

Primary
entry

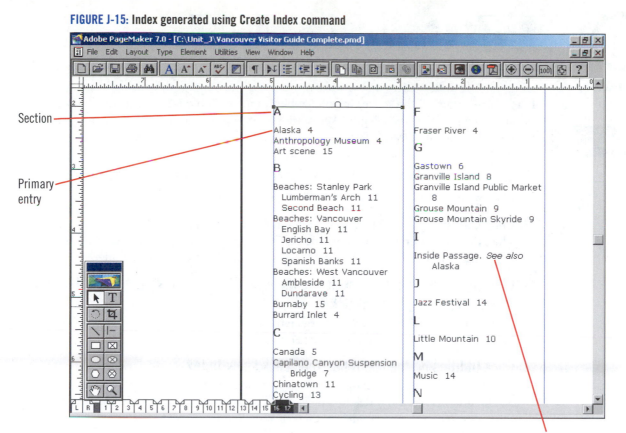

Cross-reference

Special index paragraph styles

PageMaker automatically creates special index paragraph styles and applies them to the index story when you generate an index, as shown in Figure J-16. These styles can be edited using the same method you use to change normal styles. The names of index styles should not be changed because PageMaker looks for the original index style names each time you regenerate an index.

FIGURE J-16: Styles palette with the index styles

Styles
generated
based on
formatting
options

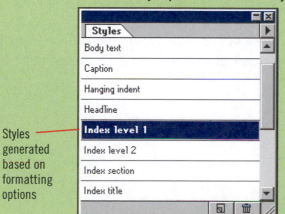

Editing an Index

After reviewing the index, you can edit index entries by selecting the specific index entry and using the Edit Index Entry dialog box. You can use the Show Index dialog box to edit all the index entries from all the stories in your publication. See Table J-2 for a detailed description of the special codes used when PageMaker cannot locate a publication page. ✒️ After reviewing the index she just created, Sara wants to edit several index references.

Steps 1234

1. Move to **page 14**, click the **body text block**, press **[Ctrl][E]**, then select just the **index marker** in front of the word **Jazz** in the first paragraph

2. Click **Utilities** on the menu bar, then click **Index Entry**
   The Edit Index Entry dialog box opens. The entry includes only the words "Jazz Festival" and not the words "Vancouver International," which Sara wants to include.

3. Click Ⅰ in the Topic text box before the word "Jazz", type **Vancouver International**, press **[Spacebar]**, then click **OK**
   The dialog box closes. When Sara regenerates the index, this index entry will be corrected to read "Vancouver International Jazz Festival."

4. Click **Utilities** on the menu bar, then click **Show Index**
   The Show Index dialog box opens, which you use to edit any index entry in the publication. See Figure J-17. You can delete index entries using the Show Index dialog box by selecting the index item you want to delete, then clicking Remove.

   MacintoshUsers

   This replaces Step 5.
   5. Choose W in the Index section list box, click Whistler Ski Resort in the Index section list box, then click Edit

5. Click the **Index section list arrow**, scroll down and click **W**, click **Whistler ski resort** in the Index section list box, then click **Edit**

6. Click Ⅰ in the Topic text box after the word "Whistler," type a hyphen (-), type **Blackcomb**, click **OK** twice, then press **[Ctrl][E]** to exit story editor
   The name of the ski area near Vancouver is not "Whistler ski resort" but rather "Whistler-Blackcomb ski resort." The changes Sara has made to the index won't be visible until she regenerates and views the index.

7. Move to **page 16**, click **Utilities** on the menu bar, then click **Create Index**
   The Create Index dialog box opens. Notice that new options are now available.

8. Make sure the **Replace existing index check box** is selected, then click **OK**
   PageMaker automatically replaces the index with the new index.

9. Verify that *See also* **Cycling** appears under the entry for North Vancouver and that the edited entries for **Vancouver International Jazz Festival** and **Whistler-Blackcomb ski resort** appear

10. Click the **Fit in Window button** 🔳 on the toolbar (*Macintosh Users: Click Fit in Window on the View menu*), compare the completed index to Figure J-18, then save the publication

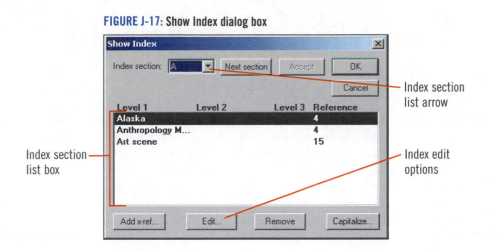

Index section list arrow

Index section list box

Index edit options

FIGURE J-18: Completed index

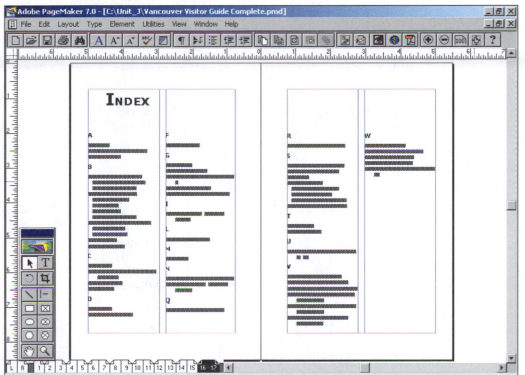

TABLE J-2: Index special characters

character	description
LM	Left master page
RM	Right master page
PB	Pasteboard
UN	Unplaced story in story editor
OV	Text outside of text blocks in layout view
?	Text included in a page range that has changed

PageMaker 7.0

Creating a Table of Contents

You can use PageMaker to automatically generate a table of contents (TOC) for your publication. Designing a TOC is as important as designing the index; however, it is generally less work since you have already created the main headings by the time you generate the TOC. You select styles or individual paragraphs for the TOC, and use the Create TOC command on the Utilities menu. PageMaker searches for the paragraphs you selected for the TOC and creates the TOC text block that you can then place in your publication. ✐ Sara uses the Create TOC command to generate a table of contents.

Steps 1 2 3 4

1. **Move to page 3, click Type on the menu bar, click Define Styles, click Headline in the Style list box, then click Edit**

   The Style Options dialog box opens. Sara needs to select the styles to be included in the table of contents. She decides to include the Headline style so that every story with a headline appears in the TOC.

2. **Click Para, click the Include in table of contents check box, then click OK three times**

   Choosing Paragraph tells PageMaker to identify what page the story appears on in the publication.

3. **Click Utilities on the menu bar, then click Create TOC**

   The Create Table of Contents dialog box opens. See Figure J-19. You can choose to enter a title for the table of contents in this dialog box or you can leave the title text box blank if the publication page already includes a title.

4. **Make sure that the Page number after entry option button is selected and that the ^t code appears in the Between entry and page number text box, then click OK**

   The code "^t" tells PageMaker to insert a tab between the text and page number. The dialog box closes and PageMaker generates the table of contents. The manual text flow pointer ▤ appears indicating that you can place the TOC.

5. **On page 3, click ▤ at the left margin guide even with 2 on the vertical ruler bar**

   The table of contents is inserted on page 3.

6. **Click Window on the menu bar, then click Show Styles**

7. **Press [Ctrl] (Macintosh Users: Press [Command] and click TOC Headline), click TOC Headline on the Styles palette to open the Style Options dialog box, click Char, click in the Size text box and type 16, then click OK twice**

   The font size of the table of contents headings is reduced to 16 pt. Note that the headlines themselves are not affected, since you changed the TOC Headline style, not the Headline style.

MacintoshUsers

This replaces Step 8.
8. Select the text (Contents and the dots and 3), press [Delete], place the insertion point in front of Vancouver, then press [Delete] again to move Vancouver up one line

8. **Click the Text tool T, select Contents and the dots and 3 following it in the table of contents list, then press [Delete] twice to delete the text and the blank line below it**

   The first entry in the table of contents is "Contents" because the heading "Contents" at the top of page 3 is formatted with the Headline style. However, Sara does not want to include an entry for "Contents" in the table of contents.

9. **Click the Close button on the Styles palette, then save the publication**

   The modified table of contents appears, as shown in Figure J-20.

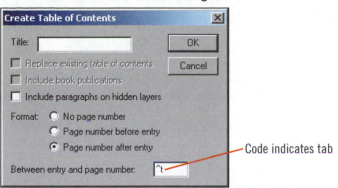

Code indicates tab

FIGURE J-20: Modified table of contents

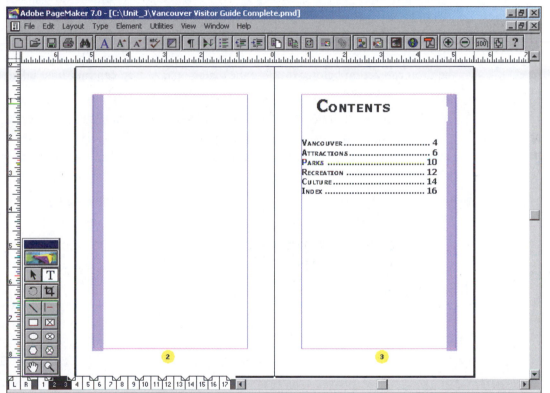

CLUES TO USE

Marking individual paragraphs to be included in a TOC

You can add more stories or select individual paragraphs to include more items within a table of contents. To add an individual paragraph to the table of contents, click T within the paragraph you want included, click Type on the menu bar, then click Paragraph. The Paragraph Specifications dialog box opens. Click the Include in table of contents check box, then click OK. Click the Create TOC command on the Utilities menu, then click OK in the Create Table of Contents dialog box to regenerate the TOC with the new paragraph.

Adding a Drop Cap

Many publications use a design feature called a drop cap. A **drop cap** is the first letter in a story that is enlarged and lowered so the top of the letter is even with the first line of text and the base of the letter drops next to the rest of the paragraph. You determine the size of the drop cap based on how many lines you want it to descend into the paragraph. The Drop cap command is a PageMaker plug-in. Sara wants to add a drop cap to the first paragraph of the page 4 story to help the story stand out on the page.

Steps

MacintoshUsers

This replaces Step 1.
1. Move to page 4, click the body text block on page 4, and then click Actual Size on the View menu

1. Move to **page 4**, click [cursor], click the **body text block** on page 4, then click the **Actual Size button** [100]

2. Click the **Text tool** [T] in the toolbox, then click [I-beam] anywhere within the first paragraph

3. Click **Utilities** on the menu bar, point to **Plug-ins**, then click **Drop cap**
   The Drop cap dialog box opens. See Figure J-21.

4. Type **4** in the Size text box, then click **Apply**
   Sara wants the drop cap to descend four lines into the paragraph. The Apply button previews the drop cap action before you close the dialog box. A drop cap four lines tall appears next to the first paragraph.

5. Drag the Drop cap dialog box down if necessary so you can see the drop cap inserted at the beginning of paragraph 1 on page 4
   Sara decides that 4 lines are too much. She must remove the drop cap and then insert a new one that drops fewer lines.

6. Click **Remove**, select **4** in the Size text box, type **2**, then click **Apply**
   The new size looks fine.

7. Click **Close**, then click anywhere in the story to deselect the drop cap
   The modified drop cap appears as shown in Figure J-22.

8. Save the publication

FIGURE J-21: Drop cap dialog box

FIGURE J-22: Drop cap placed in first paragraph

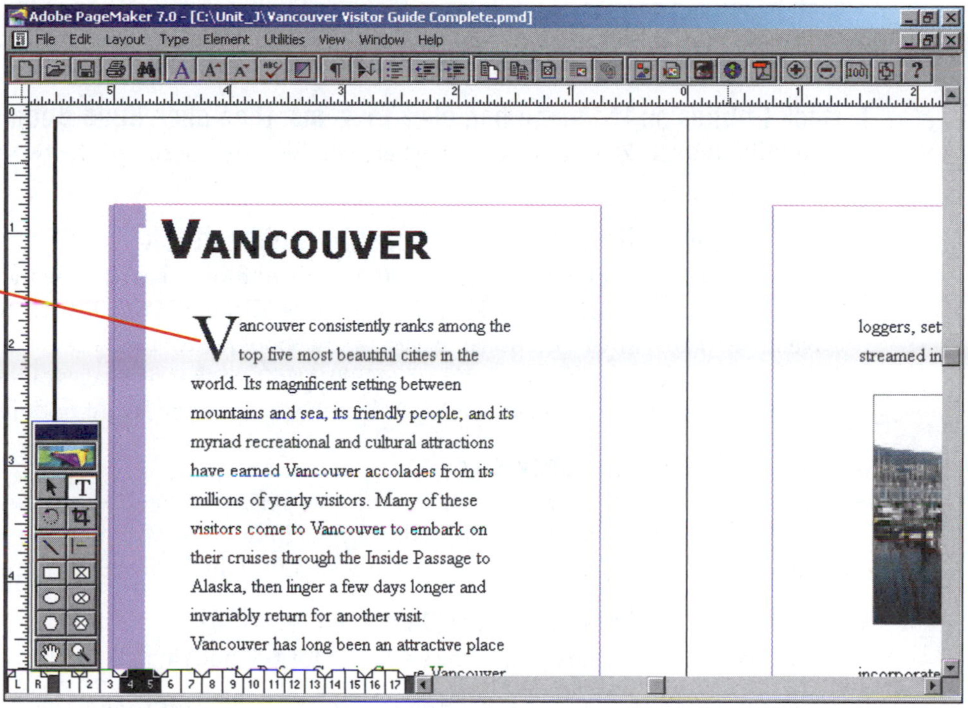

Drop cap is
two lines tall

Creating pull quotes

A **pull quote** is a small amount of text enlarged within a story to catch the reader's attention. To create a pull quote, click the Text tool pointer in the text that you want to use for the pull quote, copy the text you want to use for the pull quote, paste the text as a text block where you want the pull quote to appear in the publication, click Type on the menu bar, click Paragraph, then click Rules. In the Rules dialog box, you can add a fine line above and below a specified paragraph of text. The rule lines set off the text from the rest of the story. Then increase the size of text in the new paragraph so it stands out from the body text. See Figure J-23. You attach lines to a paragraph of text so that the lines stay attached to the paragraph and flow with that paragraph if the text is modified.

FIGURE J-23: Pull quote feature

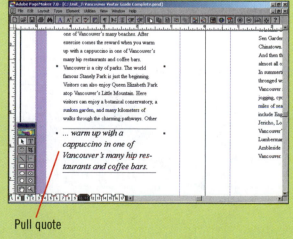

Pull quote

Using the Build Booklet Plug-in

You use the Build Booklet plug-in to arrange a publication so that it can be printed as multiple-page spreads. Each multiple-page spread (for example, pages 2 and 3) prints on a single sheet, called an **imposition**, that is then folded into the completed booklet. Figure J-24 shows how the Build Booklet plug-in organizes pages created sequentially in PageMaker into a series of multiple-page spreads that can be printed and then folded into a completed publication. ✏️ Sara wants to use the Build Booklet plug-in to print a copy of the publication that she can send directly to the printer.

Steps

1. **Click Utilities on the menu bar, click Plug-ins, then click Build Booklet**
   The Build Booklet dialog box opens, where you identify the size of the two-page spread. See Figure J-25.

2. **Click the Layout list arrow, then click 2-up saddle stitch**
   Sara selects a layout option that requires a multiple of four pages because the pages are paired and then printed back to back. The current publication contains 17 pages. Therefore, PageMaker adds three additional pages to the booklet to reach 20, a multiple of four. PageMaker also changes the spread size to 11.00×8.50" so that two pages of the 5×8.50" booklet can be printed on each page. Table J-3 describes each of the layout options.

3. **Click the Use creep check box**
   Sara needs to select a creep measurement appropriate for a 20-page booklet printed on glossy paper. **Creep** occurs when the edges of the folded sheets do not line up exactly. Sheets toward the middle of a booklet can stick out slightly, which creates an unprofessional look.

4. **Double-click the Total creep text box, then type 0.01**
   Sara is satisfied with the options she's selected for the booklet.

5. **Click OK, then click Yes** (*Macintosh Users: Click OK and then click Save*)
   The current document is saved and closed, and then the plug-in builds the booklet. In a few seconds, the completed booklet is created.

6. **Maximize the publication window, move to page 5, then reduce the width of the text block in column 1 so that none of the text appears in the purple rectangle**
   See Figure J-26. Page 16 appears as the left page and page 5 appears as the right page. When the booklet is printed and folded, the pages appear in the correct positions.

7. **Save the publication as Vancouver Visitor Guide Booklet, print a copy, then exit PageMaker**

TABLE J-3: Build Booklet layouts

layout	description
None	A new publication is created, but the pages are not rearranged and the spread size is not changed; the page arrangement and page size can be adjusted automatically and new pages inserted
2-up saddle stitch	Double-sided pages are folded once and then fastened along the fold; the first page is printed on the same sheet as the last page, the second page is printed on the same sheet as the second-to-last sheet, and so on
2-up perfect bound	A series of folded booklets are created and then bound with adhesive along the spine; the number of pages per booklet is specified and then PageMaker calculates the number of booklets required
2-, 3-, 4-up consecutive	Sets of 2, 3, or 4 pages are combined side-by-side on a single page to create multiple-page spreads; this layout is also used to create 2-, 3-, and 4-panel brochures

FIGURE J-24: Using the Build Booklet plug-in

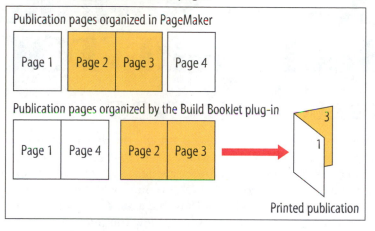

FIGURE J-25: Build Booklet dialog box

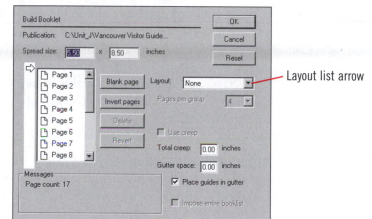

FIGURE J-26: Pages 16 and 5 formatted for printing

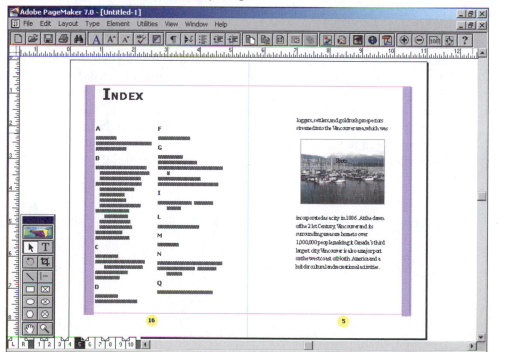

Design Workshop: Books with TOCs and Indexes

A book's table of contents (TOC) is usually the first place a reader looks after viewing the book's cover. It is important to include a TOC so that the reader can quickly glance at the overall contents of the publication. After viewing the table of contents, a reader's next search might be in the publication's index. As a result, you should also consider including an index in your publication so that readers can quickly find a topic they wish to view. As you found out in this unit, PageMaker provides the tools that allow you to quickly create a TOC and an index. The Vancouver Visitor Guide TOC and index pages are shown in Figure J-27. Let's review Sara's design.

Details

► Does the visitor guide table of contents and index give enough information?

The publication's TOC and index are the reader's road map for your book. You must know your target audience in order to determine how information should be included in the TOC and the index. Readers prefer a more detailed TOC and index for most technical manuals; however, for marketing books, the TOC and index must quickly capture the reader's attention. For these books, the TOC should include only the main topics and the index should include key words. Since Sara's Vancouver Visitor Guide is a marketing piece, she included only the stories with headlines in her table of contents, and she used key words to create the index.

► Does the text format make the index easy to read?

Sometimes the type size of a publication's index is much smaller than the text used in the body of the publication in order to reduce the total number of pages. However, this practice is not recommended since the size of text in an index must be large enough to be read by everyone in your target audience. PageMaker gives you many different index formats to improve the readability of the index. You can include index section entries, which help break up the consecutive index entries. By selecting a nested format, you can separate each subentry in a new paragraph. In addition, you can enter a space or special characters following each topic, between page numbers, between page ranges, before cross-references, and/or at the end of an entry. Sara added section headings and used the nested format to improve the readability of the index.

► Does the overall layout of the index encourage the reader to view the index?

Many indexes, especially multiple-page indexes, encourage readers to quickly bypass the pages. However, if you add photos, graphics, or small boxed stories, you can capture your reader's attention, causing the reader to read these objects. You could also add related material in a colored or gray-shaded, boxed, sidebar story. An example would be adding a list of all the phone numbers listed in the book, or a listing of all the important figures included in the publication. Sara will add a photo of Vancouver to fill the blank spot on the last page of the index.

CONTENTS

3

INDEX

PageMaker 7.0

Practice

► Concepts Review

Label each of the publication window elements shown in Figure J-28.

FIGURE J-28

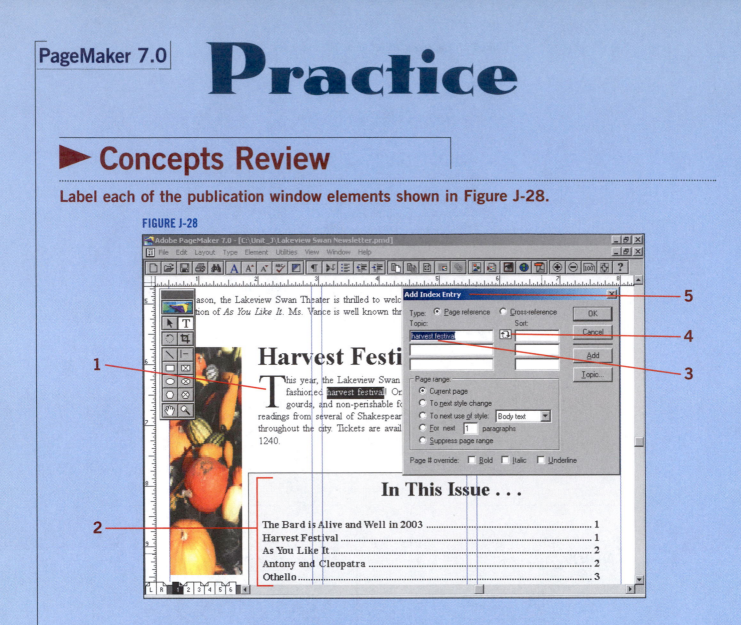

Match each of the terms with the statement that describes its function:

6. **Pull quote**
7. **Index entry**
8. **Cross-reference**
9. **Drop cap**
10. **Show index**

a. Information used to find related or additional topics
b. Allows you to edit commands on all index entries
c. A word or group of words to be included in the index
d. First letter in a story that is enlarged
e. Text enlarged within a story to catch the reader's attention

11. **You can use the Index Entry command to perform which of the following tasks?**
    a. Add headlines to the table of contents
    b. Set cross-references
    c. Remove unneeded index entries
    d. All of the above

12. **Which of the following statements is true about a cross-reference?**
    a. A cross-reference can be created in the layout view.
    b. A cross-reference is added to an index using the Index Entry command.
    c. Both a and b
    d. None of the above

13. **To generate an index:**
    a. Click Edit on the menu bar, select an element, then click Generate Index.
    b. Click Utilities on the menu bar, then click Create Index.
    c. Click the Promote/Demote button in the Cross-reference dialog box.
    d. Both b and c

14. **Which of the following is an option in the Index Format dialog box?**
    a. Edit the type, style, and size of the index
    b. Format space separating multiple page references
    c. Add an index title
    d. All of the above

15. **The Show Index command allows you to:**
    a. Generate the index.
    b. Use edit commands on all index entries.
    c. Display all of the indexed topics.
    d. Both b and c

16. **Which of the following statements about drop caps is NOT true?**
    a. The Drop cap command is a PageMaker plug-in.
    b. Drop caps can be used only in the first paragraph of a story.
    c. A drop cap can drop six lines into the paragraph.
    d. All of the above

17. **To add lines above and below a pull quote, which dialog box do you use?**
    a. Rules
    b. Pull quote
    c. Line and fill
    d. Either a or c

18. **The 2-up saddle stitch layout requires a publication to be formatted in multiples of which number?**
    a. Three pages
    b. Two pages
    c. Six pages
    d. Four pages

▶ Skills Review

1. **Add index entries.**
    a. Start PageMaker, open the file PM J-3.pmd from the drive and folder where your Project Files are located, click OK to accept any warnings, then save the file as **New World Airlines Information**.
    b. Move to page 4, click the body text block on page 4, then enter story editor.
    c. Select the text New World Airlines in the first paragraph.
    d. Open the Index Entry dialog box.
    e. Click the Page reference option button, if necessary, to select this option.
    f. Click the Current page option button in the Page range section.
    g. Close the Index Entry dialog box, exit story editor, then save the publication.

2. **Use index keyboard shortcuts.**
    a. Move to page 6, select the word Caribbean in the first paragraph, then use the [Ctrl][Y] keystrokes to add the word to the index.
    b. Use the [Ctrl][Shift][Y] keystrokes to add the text **San Juan** in the first paragraph to the index, without opening the Index Entry dialog box.

    c. Repeat the previous step to index the following entries: Puerto Rico, St. Thomas, Virgin Islands, frequent flyer miles (all in the first paragraph), Charlotte Amalie in the second paragraph, and Sunset Tours in the fourth paragraph.

    d. Select the text Michelle Snow under the subheading Fly To The Caribbean.

    e. Use the [Ctrl][Alt][Y] keystrokes to add the text to the index so that it will appear as **Snow, Michelle**, then save the publication.

3. Use the index shortcut menu.

    a. Move to page 8, then enter story editor for the story on page 8.

    b. Click Utilities on the menu bar, then click Change.

    c. Type **New World Airlines** in the Find what text box, press [Tab], then type **^;** (caret and semicolon only) in the Change to text box, click the All stories option button, click Change all, then click the Close button in the Change dialog box.

    d. In the third paragraph, select the text Eagle Club restaurants, then press [Ctrl][Y].

    e. Click the Promote/Demote button, type **Eagle Flight Program** inside the first Topic text box, then click OK.

    f. Close story editor, close any other open story editor windows, then save the publication.

4. Create a cross-reference.

    a. Open the Index Entry dialog box.

    b. Click the Cross-reference option button.

    c. Type **SkyCar** in the Topic text box.

    d. Click X-ref.

    e. Click the Topic section list arrow, then click E. (*Macintosh Users: Click the Topic Section list box.*)

    f. Click Eagle Flight Program, then click OK.

    g. Click the See also option button, then click OK.

    h. Save the publication.

5. Generate an index.

    a. Move to page 13.

    b. Open the Create Index dialog box.

    c. Type **Wings Index** in the Title text box.

    d. Click Format.

    e. Make sure the Include index section headings check box is selected.

    f. Click the Nested option button if it is not already selected.

    g. Close the Index Format dialog box, then close the Create Index dialog box.

    h. Press [Shift], position the text flow pointer at the left margin on page 13 even with 2 on the vertical ruler bar, click and then continue placing the text on the pages.

    i. Move to page 13, show the Define Styles dialog box, change the font size of the Index Title style from 30 pt to 20 pt, then save the publication.

6. Edit an index.

    a. Move to page 9, enter story editor for the story under the headline Bonuses Await On Special Trips, then select the index marker in front of the word South in the first paragraph.

    b. Open the Index Entry dialog box. (*Macintosh Users: Open the Edit Index Entry dialog box.*)

    c. Position the insertion point in the Topic text box after the word "South," press [Spacebar], type **Korea**, then click OK.

    d. Click Utilities on the menu bar, then click Show Index.

    e. Click the Index section list arrow (*Macintosh Users: Click the Index Section list box*), click S, click Sunset in the Index entry list box, then click Remove.

    f. Close the Show Index dialog box, then close story editor.

    g. Move to page 13, then generate the index.

    h. Save the publication.

7. Create a table of contents.

    a. Move to page 3.

    b. Show the Define Styles dialog box.

    c. Scroll to and click Reg. Headline in the Style list box, then click Edit.

    d. Click Para, click the Include in table of contents check box, then click OK three times.

    e. Click Utilities on the menu bar, click Create TOC, then type **Table of Contents** in the Title text box.

    f. Click the Page number after entry option button in the Format section if it is not already selected.

    g. Make sure ^t appears in the Between entry and page number text box, then close the dialog box.

    h. Place the TOC at the left margin approximately 1" below the top of the page.

    i. Click Window on the menu bar, then click Show Styles.

    j. Press [Ctrl], click the TOC Reg. Headline on the Styles palette, then change the font size to 16 pt.

    k. Click the Close button on the Styles palette, then save the publication.

8. Add a drop cap.

    a. Move to page 4, click View on the menu bar, then switch to Actual Size view.

    b. Click the Text tool pointer anywhere in the first paragraph of the story.

    c. Click Utilities on the menu bar, point to Plug-ins, then click Drop cap.

    d. Type **2** in the Size text box if necessary, then click Apply.

    e. Click Close, then click anywhere in the story to deselect the drop cap.

    f. Save the publication.

9. Use the Build Booklet plug-in.

    a. Click Utilities on the menu bar, click Plug-ins, then click Build Booklet.

    b. Select the 2-up saddle stitch layout.

    c. Make sure the Use creep check box is selected, then change the creep measurement to 0.01.

    d. Click OK to run the plug-in.

    e. Save the publication as **New World Airlines Information Booklet**, print a copy, close the document then exit PageMaker.

▶ Independent Challenge 1

As the investment manager for Reno Investors Group Inc, you need to create a report for your investors that describes the performance of all investments. You decide that a booklet publication best conveys the information. To make the booklet more user-friendly, you have decided to add an index and a table of contents. In addition, you enhance the appearance of the report by adding a drop cap at the beginning of each of the main sections.

    a. Open the file PM J-4.pmd from the drive and folder where your Project Files are located, then save the file as **Reno Investors Group Information**.

    b. On page 1, index the following two topics: Reno Investors Group Plan Summary and group funds.

    c. Move to pages 4 and 5, then use the Change command to index all occurrences of Reno Investors Group in the publication.

    d. Using keyboard shortcuts, start at the top of story editor, then index the following topics: Guaranteed Investment contracts, Bank Investment contracts, FDIC, Vanguard Institutional Index Fund, and The Wall Street Journal.

    e. Create cross-references for Guaranteed Investment contracts to Fixed Income Fund, and Bank Investment contracts to Fixed Income Fund.

    f. Create an index on page 10. Name the index **Plan Summary Index**.

    g. Reduce the font size of the Index title style to 18 pt.

    h. Edit your index using the Show Index command, then delete the index entry for Standard.

    i. Move to page 3 to create a TOC. Name the TOC **Plan Summary Contents**.

    j. Change the font size of the TOC title style to 26 pt and remove the Plan Summary Index entry from the TOC.

   k. Add a drop cap dropped 2 lines in the first paragraph under the Investment Fund Report headline on page 4 and also in the first paragraph under the Fund Performance headline on page 9.

   l. Save the publication, then use the Build Booklet plug-in to create a 2-up saddle stitch booklet with a 0.01 creep.

   m. Save the new booklet as **Reno Investors Group Booklet**, then print a copy.

► Independent Challenge 2

Earth Wise Cosmetics manufactures and distributes a complete range of bath and beauty products that have been made with all-natural ingredients. Their products are selling well, so now Earth Wise Cosmetics is looking for partnership opportunities. You've been asked to complete a proposal for setting up a partnership with Eco-Spa, a company that owns two salons in southern France. The proposal currently consists of a title page and three pages of text and pictures. You will add and then modify a table of contents.

   a. Open the file PM J-5.pmd from the drive and folder where your Project Files are located, then save the file as **Partnership Proposal**.

   b. In the maroon horizontal rectangle on page 1, insert a table of contents with default settings.

   c. Reduce the width of the text block so that it fits within the rectangle.

   d. Open the Styles palette.

   e. Change the color of the TOC Title to Paper and the size to 24-point, change the color of the TOC Headline to Paper and the size to 18-point, then change the color of the TOC Subhead 1 to Paper and the size to 14-point.

   f. Double-click TOC Headline in the Styles palette to open the Style Options dialog box, click Tabs, select the leader style of your choice, click above 5.25" on the ruler bar in the Indents/Tabs dialog box to set the tab at 5.25", click OK, then click OK. If the TOC entries do not fill the space attractively, change the tab setting.

   g. Repeat the procedure to set tabs for the TOC Subhead 1 style.

   h. Modify the positioning of the various text blocks on page 1 of the proposal and increase the size of the maroon rectangle so that page 1 appears as shown in Figure J-29.

   i. Save the publication, then print a copy.

FIGURE J-29

► Independent Challenge 3

Several art galleries in Portland, Oregon are holding an Art Festival. The owner of one of the galleries has written a report that describes the festival and the galleries participating in it. Now you need to complete the report by creating an index. First, you'll mark text for inclusion in the index and then you insert and format the index.

   a. Open the file PM J-6.pmd from the drive and folder where your Project Files are located, then save the file as **Art Festival Report**.

   b. Go to page 3 of the publication, enter story editor, then mark the following entries for inclusion in the index:

Text	Special Directions
Bellevue Art Gallery	
Charlotte Reed	Sub-topic under the main topic Gallery Owners
Jason Chow	Sub-topic under the main topic Gallery Owners
Uma Ralston	Sub-topic under the main topic Oregon Artist of the Year

(continued)

Text	Special Directions
Pacifica Galleria	
Celebrity Art Auction	
Marisol Quinn	Sub-topic under the main topic Gallery Owners
Grand Paintathon	
Children's Art Fair	
Gallery Artists Shows	
Juried Art Competition	
Lantern Parade	
Merchant Window Displays	
Art Raffle	
Art Supplies Fair	
artist and curator talks	

c. Insert a new page at the end of the publication, then format the left page with two columns.

d. Create an index at the top of column one.

e. Open the Styles palette, then change the font of the Index title style to Century Gothic or a similar font.

f. Change the font of the Index Section style to Arial and the font size to 18-point.

g. Change the font size of the Index Level 1 and Index Level 2 styles to 14-point.

h. Modify height of column 1 so that the finished index spans two columns, as shown in Figure J-30.

i. Save the publication, then print a copy.

FIGURE J-30

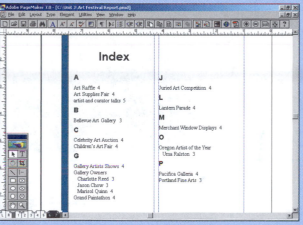

Independent Challenge 4

As the marketing manager for a major airline, you have been asked to create a visitor's guide for potential visitors to Chicago, one of the airline's most popular destinations. In order to complete this independent challenge, you need to design the layout for the guide, place the stories, then add an index and table of contents (TOC).

a. Search the World Wide Web for information on Chicago's major tourist attractions.

b. Using PageMaker, create a 16-page, double-sided publication with the dimensions 5.5" by 8.5" with .5" margins.

c. On page 1 of the publication, create an attractive cover that includes the text Chicago Visitor's Guide.

d. Add page numbers to every page in the guide except page 1, then draw frames for text and illustrations on pages 4 to 14.

e. Fill at least three of the frames with information that you find on the World Wide Web about attractions in Chicago.

f. Make a sketch of your index, using the guidelines that you learned in this unit. Index all of the important subjects and names in your guide using story editor and shortcuts in the publication window.

g. Create at least two cross-references for your index.

h. Generate your index, review it for any mistakes or changes that you would like to make, then edit your index to make these changes.

i. Create a TOC for your guide, then place it on page 3 of the publication. Edit the styles of the TOC.

j. Add drop caps to your publication.

k. Review the design of your TOC and index.

l. Save the publication as **Chicago Guide**, and then print it.

m. Use the Build Booklet plug-in to create a booklet of the publication. Experiment with different layouts before selecting the one that presents the booklet in an easy-to-print format.

n. Save the booklet as **Chicago Booklet**, then print a copy.

► Visual Workshop

Open the file PM J-7.pmd from the drive and folder where your Project Files are located. Create an index and table of contents (TOC), as shown in Figure J-31. Save the publication as **Fitness First News**, then print it.

FIGURE J-31

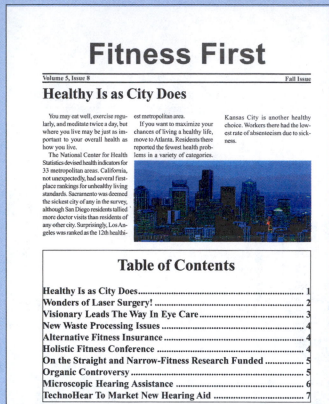

Fitness First

Volume 5, Issue 8   Fall Issue

Healthy Is as City Does

You may eat well, exercise regularly, and meditate twice a day, but where you live may be just as important to your overall health as how you live.

The National Center for Health Statistics devised health indicators for 33 metropolitan areas. California, not unexpectedly, had several first-place rankings for unhealthy living standards. Sacramento was deemed the sickest city of any in the survey, although San Diego residents tallied more doctor visits than residents of any other city. Surprisingly, Los Angeles was ranked as the 12th healthiest metropolitan area.

If you want to maximize your chances of living a healthy life, move to Atlanta. Residents there reported the fewest health problems in a variety of categories.

Kansas City is another healthy choice. Workers there had the lowest rate of absenteeism due to sickness.

Table of Contents

Index

PageMaker 7.0

Publishing

Electronically

Objectives

- ► Review file formats used for electronic viewing
- ► Plan a Web site
- ► Set up a publication for a Web site
- ► Create a navigation scheme with hyperlinks
- ► Format hyperlinks
- ► Create hyperlinks to URLs and e-mail addresses
- ► Export a PageMaker publication to an HTML file
- ► Modify an HTML file in PageMaker
- ► Create a PDF file
- ► Use Acrobat Reader to view a PDF file
- ► Add a PDF file to a Web site
- ► Design Workshop: Web Sites

In previous units you learned how to create different kinds of publications that eventually ended up in a final paper format for distribution to your intended audience. In this unit you will learn how to produce a publication that can be viewed electronically on the World Wide Web. You will also learn how to save a publication as a PDF file that can be distributed and viewed by anyone using a Macintosh, Windows, or Unix operating system, or that can be downloaded from the World Wide Web. ▬▬ Twin Peaks Resort in Whistler, British Columbia, has asked Sara to create a simple Web site that describes the resort and its facilities.

PageMaker 7.0

Reviewing File Formats Used for Electronic Viewing

In the early 1980s, Adobe started the desktop publishing revolution by introducing PageMaker as a means for creating and producing high-quality, camera-ready publications. In the 1990s, PageMaker pioneered two features for creating publications: the export HTML function and the export to PDF function. Both features allow you to create publications that can be viewed and distributed electronically on the Internet. You use PageMaker's Export HTML function to create an HTML file from an existing PageMaker publication. As a result, you can create Web pages from your PageMaker publications. You can also convert a PageMaker publication into a PDF file, which can be shared by users regardless of their computer platform. ✒️ Sara investigates both options in more detail.

Details

HTML and the World Wide Web

► **HTML** (Hypertext Markup Language) is a computer language used to create files known as **Web pages** that can be viewed on the World Wide Web. The **World Wide Web**, also known as the **Web** or WWW, allows users to graphically interface with the Internet. The **Internet** is a network of millions of interconnected computers worldwide. A **graphical interface** is one in which the computer user interacts with the computer by clicking pictures, icons, and words rather than typing commands.

► To view Web pages, users need Internet access and a software program called a **Web browser**. Popular Web browsers are Netscape Navigator and Microsoft Internet Explorer.

► To create Web pages, you need to know HTML, or you need to have a program that inserts HTML code for you as you insert and format text and graphics. In PageMaker, the **HTML Author** feature translates a publication into a new file that uses HTML. This feature therefore allows you to create Web pages without knowing HTML. A set of Web pages is called a **Web site**, and a **home page** is the first page viewed on a Web site. A home page can be the first of many hundreds of pages that make up a Web site. Figure K-1 shows an example of a home page.

PDF

► You can easily convert any PageMaker publication into a PDF file. **PDF** stands for portable document file. A publication saved in a PDF format retains all page designs and layouts created in PageMaker and can be viewed and printed on most computer platforms, such as a PC or a Mac. See the PDF file shown in Figure K-2. Once you have converted a PageMaker publication into a PDF file, you view the publication in Acrobat Reader, a program included with PageMaker 7.0 and widely available for download over the Web.

► The PDF file shown in Figure K-2 is displayed in Acrobat Reader. In this program, you can view the publication in various magnifications, show thumbnails of the various pages in the publication along the left side of the window, and click bookmarks to navigate through the document. You can print a PDF file, distribute it electronically, or you can include a link to it on your Web site. A visitor to your Web site can click the link, download the PDF file, and then view it in Acrobat Reader.

FIGURE K-1: An example of a home page on the World Wide Web

FIGURE K-2: PDF file displayed in Acrobat Reader

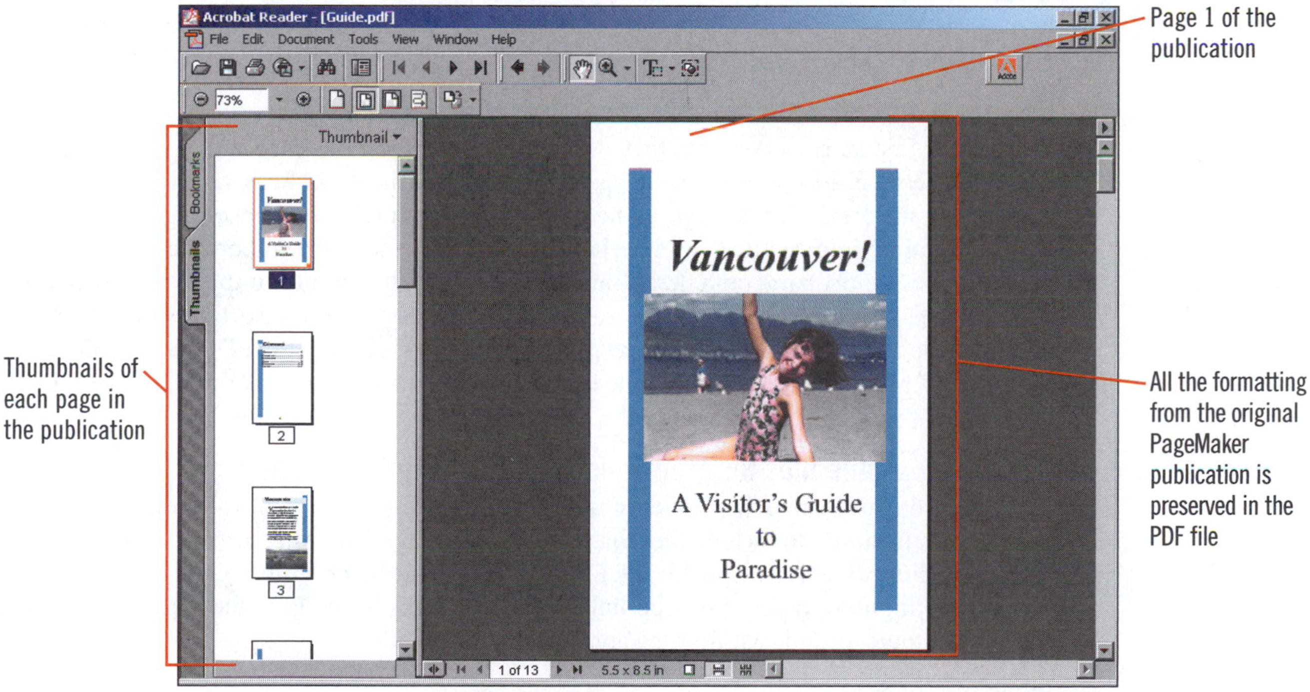

Page 1 of the publication

Thumbnails of each page in the publication

All the formatting from the original PageMaker publication is preserved in the PDF file

Planning a Web Site

An effective Web site should instantly capture the attention of your target audience and convey useful information. Users should be able to find the information they want quickly and easily by using hypertext links. **Hypertext links** (or **hyperlinks**) are specially formatted blocks of text or graphics that a user can click to open other Web pages within a Web site or to move to other parts of the current Web page. A hyperlink can also open a page on another Web site located anywhere on the World Wide Web. When planning a Web site, you need to consider what information to include on the home page, because it is the first page that readers see when they open the Web site. You then need to consider what information should be available through hypertext links. Twin Peaks Resort in Whistler, British Columbia, has hired Sara to create a simple Web site that describes the resort and its facilities. Sara makes a sketch of the Web site. See Figure K-3. She uses the following guidelines to design the Web site:

Details

► Use graphic images discretely

An effectively designed Web site uses images to enhance the content, not to overwhelm it. If too many large complex graphics are used on a Web site, the site may load too slowly. Instead of waiting for the graphics to appear, many users simply click the browser's Back button and go find another Web site. Sara decides to keep the home page of the Web site simple by including only one color picture of a skier.

► Develop a clear navigation scheme

Users need to be able to navigate around the Web site quickly and easily. At the very least, each page in a Web site should include a link back to the home page. Ideally, each page should also include links to the major sections of the Web site. The Web site that Sara is designing consists of only three pages. Sara creates a navigation scheme that contains hyperlinks to the three pages in the Web site: the home page, the Tours page and the Facilities page. Figure K-4 shows the navigation scheme of the finished Web site. Each of the underlined items in the navigation scheme in the left column of each page is a link. For example, when users click the Facilities link on the home page, the Facilities page appears, and when they click the home link on the Tours page, the home page appears.

► Use headings and minimize text

When users first access a Web site, they do not want to be overwhelmed by a screen full of text. A simple Web site, such as the one being developed for Twin Peaks Resort, should list the contents of the site on the home page, along with short descriptions that encourage them to want to find out more information—and perhaps even contact the resort to book accommodations. Sara includes a short paragraph describing the resort, plus hyperlinks to the two other pages in the Web site. One page describes the tour packages offered by the resort and the other page describes the resort facilities. The home page also includes a link to the PDF file containing the Vancouver Visitor's Guide. The PDF file is not considered a page in the Web site since it opens in a different program; only a link to the PDF file appears in the Web site.

► Use downloadable files for graphic images or long publications

Some users do not wish to spend a lot of time reading a computer screen. To accommodate these users, you can choose to include files that can be downloaded and then printed. Sara's Web site includes a link to a downloadable PDF file for the Vancouver Visitor Guide. The PDF file includes both photographs and hyperlinks. The hyperlinks in the PDF file assist the reader to move from topic to topic within the Vancouver Visitor Guide.

► Allow for feedback

A Web site should provide users with the means to request more information about the products or services described on the Web site. Sara includes a link to a screen that allows users to send an e-mail that either requests further information or a response from the Marketing Department at Twin Peaks Resort.

FIGURE K-3: Sara's diagram of the Twin Peaks Resort Web site

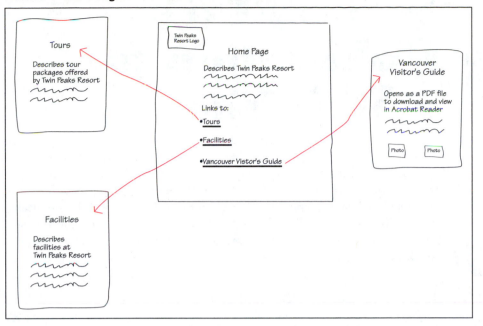

FIGURE K-4: Web site navigation scheme

Navigation scheme includes links to each of the three pages in the Web site and appears on each of the three pages

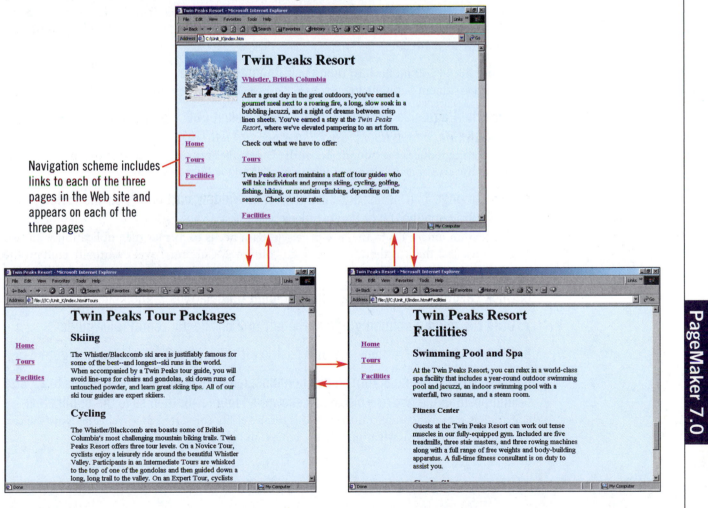

Setting Up a Publication for a Web Site

If you decide to use a PageMaker publication as the basis for a Web site, you first need to set up the PageMaker publication for viewing on a Web browser. By so doing, you make sure that you are working within parameters that approximate the size and shape of a window in a Web browser. You can choose from several sizes of Web browsers, depending on how you'd like the completed Web site to appear. ✒ Sara has already created a publication containing the information about Twin Peaks Resort that she wants to appear in the Web site. The publication consists of three pages in 8½" x 11" format. Sara needs to open the publication, select one of the Web browser document setups, and then format the publication in two columns.

Steps 1 2 3 4

1. Start **PageMaker**, open the file **PM K-1.pmd** from the drive and folder where your Project Files are located, then save the file as **Twin Peaks Resort Web Site**
   This document contains the three pages that are included in the Twin Peaks Resort Web site.

2. View the three pages in the publication to get an idea of its contents
   The first page of the publication contains general information about Twin Peaks Resort, the second page contains information about the tours offered by Twin Peaks Resort, and the third page describes some of the resort's facilities. Text on both the second and the third page is already formatted.

3. Click **File** on the menu bar, then click **Document Setup**
   In the Document Setup dialog box, you can select an appropriate page size for a Web page.

4. Click the **Page size list arrow**, scroll down, select **600 × 450 Browser – large**, then click **OK** (*Macintosh Users: Click the Page size list box*)
   This setting reduces the boundaries of the PageMaker publication so that one page approximates the size of a Web browser window set at 600 × 450 resolution.

5. Move to page 1, if necessary, click the **Fit in Window button** 🔲 on the toolbar, then scroll up to see the top of the text block
   The text no longer fits in the new page size. Sara needs to format the publication with two columns, and then fit the text block into column 2. Column 1 will eventually contain the Web site's navigation scheme.

6. Click **Layout** on the menu bar, click **Column Guides**, type **2**, then click **OK**

7. Drag the **middle column guide** to the left to **2** on the horizontal ruler guide

8. Click the **text block**, then size and position it in column 2, as shown in Figure K-5

9. Move to pages **2 and 3**, turn on **two columns**, reduce column 1 on both pages to **2"**, size and position the two text blocks, as shown in Figure K-6, then save the publication
   Sara has set up the publication so that it can be easily converted to a Web site. Now she can go on to create the navigation scheme in the left column.

FIGURE K-5: Text block sized and positioned on page 1

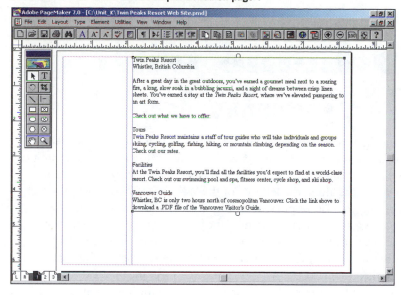

FIGURE K-6: Text blocks sized and positioned on pages 2 and 3

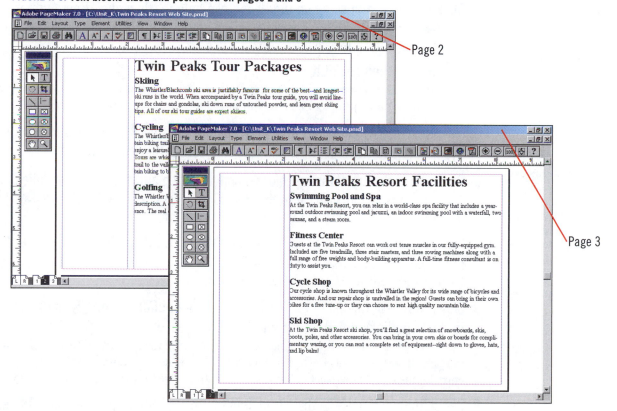

Page 2

Page 3

Creating a Navigation Scheme with Hyperlinks

A navigation scheme contains links to the main pages of a Web site. Most navigation schemes include a link to the home page plus links either to the remaining pages in the Web site, or to major sections of the Web site, if the Web site is very large. Many Web sites display the navigation scheme along the left side of the Web browser window, although the top and bottom of the window are also popular locations for a navigation scheme. The key requirement for an effective navigation scheme is consistency. Users should be able to quickly identify where on the Web page they need to click to navigate from page to page. Two steps are required to create links in PageMaker. First, you must create an **anchor**, which is the location that appears when the link is clicked. Then, you must associate or connect the link text with the anchor. The link text, which is the text the user clicks in order to jump to the anchor, is called the **source**. Sara first creates an anchor at the top of each of the three pages in the publication, and then she types the link text in the left column and connects it with the appropriate anchor.

Steps

1. Click **Window** on the menu bar, then click **Show Hyperlinks**
   You use the Hyperlinks palette to create anchors and allocate sources.

2. Move to **page 1**, click the **Text tool** T, then click to the left of **T** in **Twin** at the top of the text block

3. Click the **right arrow** ▶ on the Hyperlinks palette, then click **New Anchor**
   The New Anchor dialog box opens. By default, the anchor is called Anchor1. Sara can choose to type the name of the anchor.

4. Type **Home**, then click **OK**
   The anchor is now set up, so that when a user clicks the home link (which you set up in a moment), the user jumps to this anchor at the top of page 1, the home page.

5. Move to **page 2**, click T at the top of the text block on page 2, click ▶ on the Hyperlinks palette, click **New Anchor**, type **Tours**, then click **OK**

6. Click T at the top of the text block on page 3, then add a new anchor called **Facilities**
   The three new anchors appear in the Hyperlinks palette, as shown in Figure K-7. Now Sara is ready to create the text that links to the three anchors.

7. Move to **page 1**, click T in the **left column** toward the top of the page, then type the three entries shown in Figure K-8
   Each of these entries is a hyperlink to an anchor.

8. Select **Home** in the list of text entries, click the **Anchor button** ⚓ to the left of **Home** in the Hyperlinks palette, then click **OK**
   As you create the navigation scheme, you are identifying many sources. To save time, you accept the default source number, which is Source4. A "4" is used because you are creating the fourth entry for the Hyperlinks palette. The first three entries were the three anchors, which you renamed.

9. Select **Tours**, click ⚓ to the left of **Tours** in the Hyperlinks palette, click **OK**, repeat the procedure to create a source for the Facilities anchor, then save the publication
   The Hyperlinks palette now appears as shown in Figure K-9.

QuickTip

You can increase the size of the Hyperlinks palette when you have many links in a publication, allowing you to view all the entries at one time.

FIGURE K-7: Three new anchors in the Hyperlinks palette

HyperLinks

⚓ Home

Anchor button

⚓ Tours

⚓ Facilities

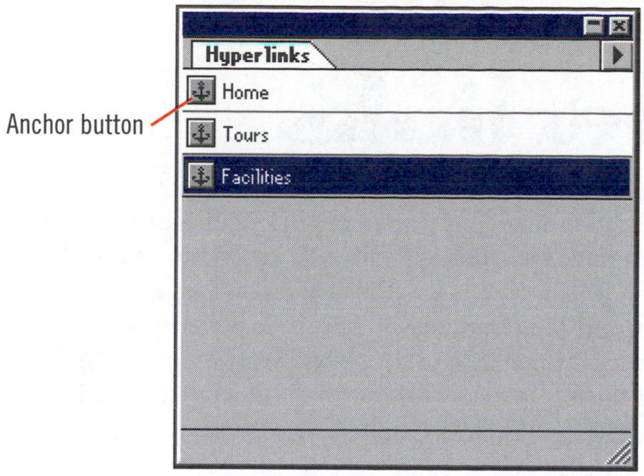

FIGURE K-8: Text entries for the navigation scheme

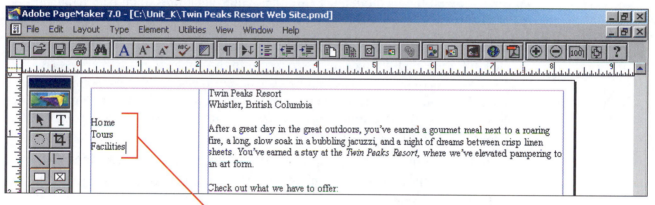

Adobe PageMaker 7.0 - [C:\Unit_K\Twin Peaks Resort Web Site.pmd]

File   Edit   Layout   Type   Element   Utilities   View   Window   Help

Home
Tours
Facilities

Twin Peaks Resort
Whistler, British Columbia

After a great day in the great outdoors, you've earned a gourmet meal next to a roaring
fire, a long, slow soak in a bubbling jacuzzi, and a night of dreams between crisp linen
sheets. You've earned a stay at the *Twin Peaks Resort*, where we've elevated pampering to
an art form.

Check out what we have to offer:

Text entries in column 1

FIGURE K-9: Anchors and sources in the Hyperlinks palette

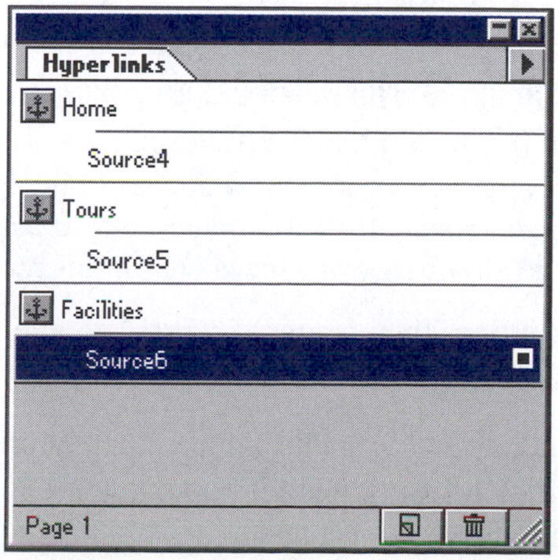

HyperLinks

⚓ Home

    Source4

⚓ Tours

    Source5

⚓ Facilities

    Source6

Page 1

Formatting Hyperlinks

In PageMaker, you use the Hand tool 👋 from the toolbox to view hyperlinks. If you are exporting a PageMaker publication containing hyperlinks to HTML pages for viewing on the World Wide Web, you generally format the hyperlinks so that users know they can be clicked. Most hyperlinks in Web pages on the World Wide Web are underlined and displayed in a text colored differently than regular text. ✎ Sara uses the Hand tool to view the hyperlinks on page 1 of the publication. She then creates a new style for hyperlink text and applies the style to the list of links in the navigation scheme. Finally, she copies the formatted set of links to the other two pages in the publication.

Steps

1. Click the **Hand tool** 👋 in the toolbox

   The three hyperlinks are outlined in blue, as shown in Figure K-10. Sara decides to test the hyperlinks.

2. Click the **Tours** hyperlink to verify that you jump to the Tours page, return to **page 1**, test the **Facilities** link, then return to **page 1**

   The links work fine.

3. Click **Type** on the menu bar, click **Define Styles**, click **New**, then type **Hyperlink**

   The new style will be called "Hyperlink."

4. Click **Char**, select **Bold**, **Underline**, and the **Blue text color**, as shown in Figure K-11, click **OK**, then click **OK** twice more to return to the publication

   The new Hyperlink style is bold, underlined, blue text. Note that applying this style to text in a publication does not turn the text into a hyperlink, but it makes the text look like a standard Web link. To avoid confusing people using your Web site, you should not apply this style to text that you haven't set up as a link.

5. Click **Window** on the menu bar, click **Show Styles**, click the **Text tool** T, select **Home** in column 1, click **Hyperlink** in the Styles palette, then apply the Hyperlink style to **Tours** and **Facilities**

   Now the hyperlinks on the home page are formatted correctly.

6. Click the **Pointer tool** ↖, click the text box containing the three hyperlinks to select it, click **Edit** on the menu bar, click **Copy**, move to **page 2**, click **Edit** on the menu bar, click **Paste**, move to **page 3**, then click **Edit**, **Paste** again

   When creating a navigation scheme for a Web site, you save time by creating and formatting the navigation scheme on the home page and then copying it to all the remaining pages in the Web site.

7. Return to **page 1**, click T, select **Tours** in the main text on **page 1**, click the **Tours anchor button** in the Hyperlinks palette, click **OK**, apply the Hyperlink style, then create and format a hyperlink for **Facilities**

   Notice that several new sources now appear in the Hyperlinks palette. These sources were created when you copied the list of hyperlinks to pages 2 and 3 of the publication. You are now able to "go anywhere from anywhere" in this publication.

8. Deselect **Facilities**, then compare **page 1** to Figure K-12

   The hyperlinks are formatted correctly.

9. Click 👋, click one of the **Tours** links, click **Facilities** on the Tours page, click **Home** on the Facilities page, then save the publication

   The navigation scheme is complete.

FIGURE K-10: Hyperlinks displayed on page 1

Hyperlinks are highlighted

Hand tool

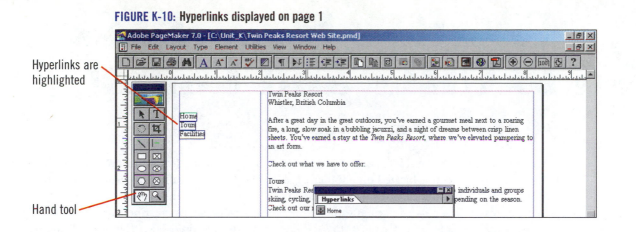

FIGURE K-11: Formatting for Hyperlink style

Blue font color selected

Bold selected

Underline selected

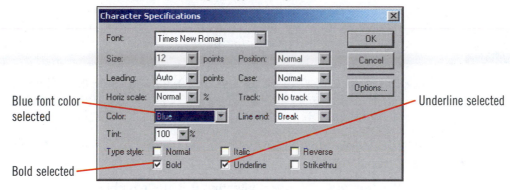

FIGURE K-12: Formatted hyperlinks on page 1

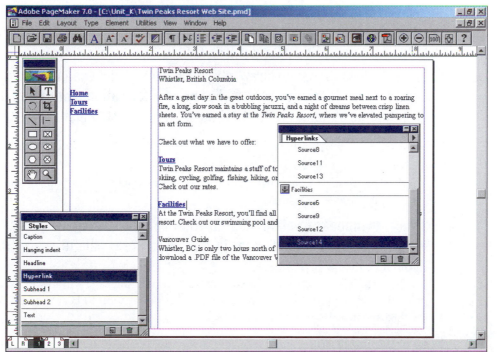

Creating Hyperlinks to URLs and E-mail Addresses

In the previous two lessons, you learned how to create hyperlinks that moved from one page of a publication to an anchor located on another page. In addition to creating hyperlinks to anchors within a publication, you can create hyperlinks to other Web sites on the World Wide Web and to e-mail addresses. Table K-1 describes some of the options available for creating hyperlinks. A link to a Web site is made by entering "http://" followed by the required URL (Uniform Resource Locator) into the New URL dialog box. A **URL** is the Web site address of the Web site to which you are linking. A link to an e-mail address is made by entering "mailto:" followed by the required e-mail address into the New URL dialog box. Sara decides to include a link from the text "Whistler, British Columbia" at the top of page 1 to a Web page that provides general information about Whistler. She also adds a link to an e-mail address at the bottom of page 1. When visitors to the Web site click on the e-mail link, a new e-mail message window appears. Users can then send an e-mail right from the Web browser to request additional information about Twin Peaks Resort.

Steps

1. Click the **right arrow** ▶ on the Hyperlinks palette, then click **New URL**
   The New URL dialog box opens, where you can enter the URL of a Web site that includes general information about Whistler, BC.

2. Type **http://www.whistler.com** as shown in Figure K-13, then click **OK**
   You've created the anchor.

3. Click the **Text tool** T, select **Whistler, British Columbia** at the top of page 1, click the **URL button** 🖳 next to **http://www.whistler.com** in the Hyperlinks palette, click **OK**, then click **Hyperlink** in the Styles palette
   The link is created and formatted.

4. Click the **Hand tool** 🖑, click **Whistler, British Columbia** to test the link, then when the Web browser appears, maximize the Web browser window, if necessary
   In a few seconds, the Whistler.com Web site should appear in your default Web browser. Figure K-14 shows the Web site in the Internet Explorer Web browser.

5. Close the Web browser window, click T, click at the end of the last paragraph on page 1, press **[Enter]** twice, type **For more information call us at 1-800-555-7800 or e-mail us at:**, press **[Enter]**, then type **twinpeaks@whistler.ca**

6. Click ▶ on the Hyperlinks palette, click **New URL**, type **mailto:twinpeaks@whistler.ca**, as shown in Figure K-15, then click **OK**
   The URL is entered as an anchor in the Hyperlinks palette, but you still need to set up the text on page 1 as a hyperlink.

7. Select **twinpeaks@whistler.ca** at the bottom of page 1, click 🖳 next to **mailto:twinpeaks@whistler.ca** in the Hyperlinks palette, click **OK**, then click **Hyperlink** in the Styles palette
   The hyperlink to a Web site address opens a new mail message window in your default e-mail program after you have exported the PageMaker publication to HTML pages and then viewed the pages in a Web browser.

8. Save the publication

FIGURE K-13: New URL dialog box with URL entered

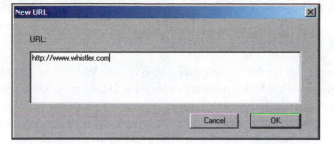

FIGURE K-14: Web site in the Web browser window

FIGURE K-15: New URL dialog box with e-mail address entered

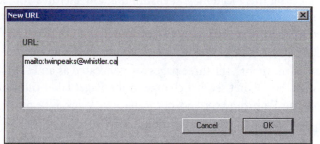

TABLE K-1: URL types

type	description
http://	Precedes the URL of a Web site on the World Wide Web; for example, you would enter http://www.course.com to create a hyperlink to the home page for Course Technology
mailto:	Precedes the e-mail address of a company or individual
ftp://	Precedes the URL of a site containing files to download; FTP stands for File Transfer Protocol
file://	Precedes the filename of a document contained on the user's computer; for example, you would enter file://C:/Tours.htm to create a hyperlink to a file called Tours.htm that is stored on the C: drive

Exporting a PageMaker Publication to an HTML File

After you create the basic layout and design of your Web site in PageMaker, you use HTML Author to identify which PageMaker pages are exported as HTML files. You can assign more than one PageMaker page to an HTML file. As a result, you can create your entire Web site in one PageMaker publication. Sara has already chosen to create the entire three-page Web site in one PageMaker publication. Now she needs to associate all three pages in the PageMaker publication with a single HTML file she is calling index.htm. She calls the file "index" because that is a standard filename for the first page in a Web site to be loaded when a user comes to the site on the World Wide Web.

Steps

1. Click **File** on the menu bar, point to **Export**, click **HTML** to open the Export HTML dialog box, then click **Untitled1**

   The three PageMaker pages in the current publication are listed, as shown in Figure K-16. Sara needs to assign a name to the HTML document file she will create.

2. Click **Edit**

   The Export HTML: Edit Contents window appears, where you can name the HTML document, choose which pages to include in the file, and choose a background graphic.

3. Type **Twin Peaks Resort** in the Document Title text box

   This document title is the name that appears in the title bar above the top of the page on the World Wide Web. This name should not be confused with the filename (index.htm) for the file that Sara will create later for the HTML file that she exports.

4. Click **Done**

   The Export HTML dialog box opens. All three pages in the PageMaker publication are included in the HTML page called Twin Peaks Resort.

5. Click **Document** in the Export Files to Location section, navigate to the location where you save files for this book, type **index** in the File Name For HTML Document text box, then click **OK**

   The name and location of the HTML file to be created are displayed in the Export Files To Location section.

6. Click **Graphics**, then select the same location as you selected for the index file

   By selecting this location, you ensure that any pictures you add to the Web site are stored in the same folder as the index.htm file. When working with files that are used in Web pages, you need to make sure that every file associated with the Web site is saved in the same location.

7. Click **Export HTML**

   In a few moments, the three pages are generated as an HTML file that you can view in a Web browser. You won't see any change in the PageMaker publication.

8. Open the Web browser you normally use, click **File** on the menu bar, click **Open**, click **Browse**, navigate to the location where you saved the index file, click **index.htm**, click **Open**, click **OK**, then maximize the Web browser if necessary

   The new Web site appears in the Web browser, as shown in Figure K-17. The links are now purple because in earlier lessons you clicked on them to test them. In the Web browser, a link that has been followed changes color.

9. Click **Tours** in the navigation scheme, click **Facilities**, then click **Home** to test the navigation scheme; click **Whistler, British Columbia** on page 1 to test that link; click the **Back button** on the Web browser to return to the Twin Peaks Resort Web site, then scroll to and click **twinpeaks@whistler.ca** at the bottom of page 1 to test the e-mail link

   A new e-mail messaging window opens similar to Figure K-18.

10. Close the e-mail message window (don't save changes if prompted), then return to the PageMaker publication, but leave your browser open

FIGURE K-16: Export HTML dialog box

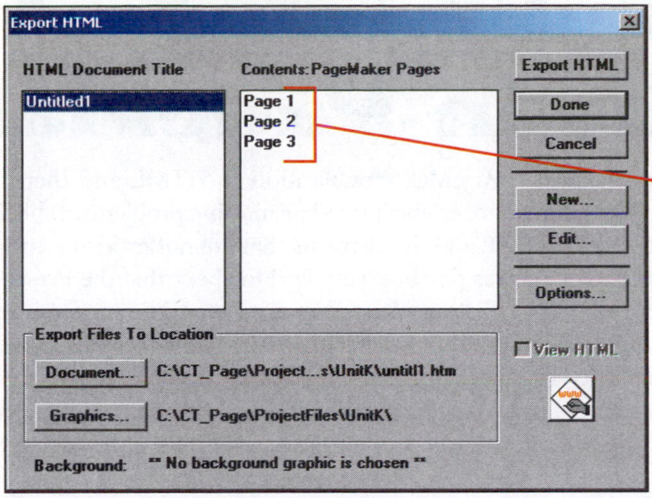

Export HTML

HTML Document Title

Untitled1

Contents: PageMaker Pages

Page 1
Page 2
Page 3

Export HTML
Done
Cancel
New...
Edit...
Options...

☐ View HTML

PageMaker pages associated with the HTML document

Export Files To Location

Document...   C:\CT_Page\Project...s\UnitK\untitl1.htm

Graphics...   C:\CT_Page\ProjectFiles\UnitK\

Background: ** No background graphic is chosen **

FIGURE K-17: Web site displayed in the Web browser

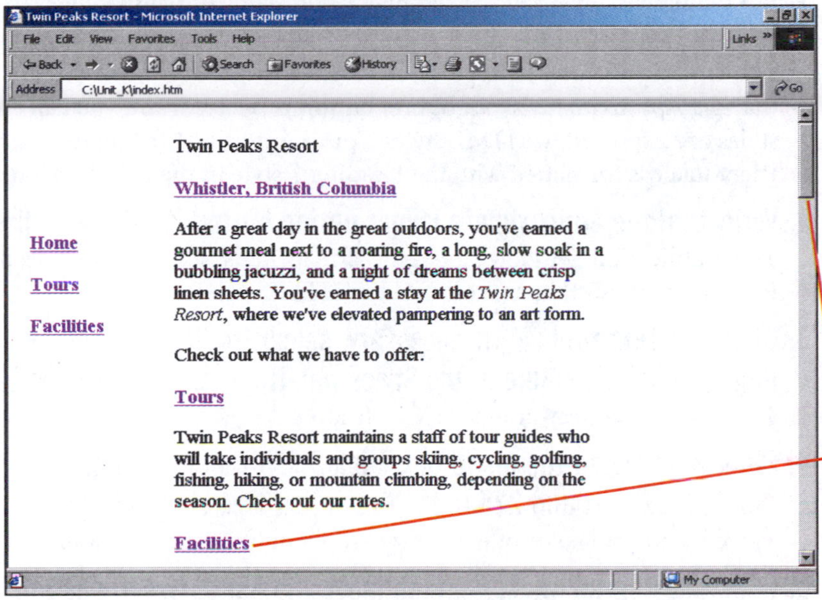

Twin Peaks Resort - Microsoft Internet Explorer

File   Edit   View   Favorites   Tools   Help   Links »

Back · Search Favorites History

Address   C:\Unit_K\index.htm   Go

Twin Peaks Resort

Whistler, British Columbia

Home

Tours

Facilities

After a great day in the great outdoors, you've earned a gourmet meal next to a roaring fire, a long, slow soak in a bubbling jacuzzi, and a night of dreams between crisp linen sheets. You've earned a stay at the *Twin Peaks Resort*, where we've elevated pampering to an art form.

Check out what we have to offer:

Tours

Twin Peaks Resort maintains a staff of tour guides who will take individuals and groups skiing, cycling, golfing, fishing, hiking, or mountain climbing, depending on the season. Check out our rates.

Facilities

My Computer

Users can scroll down to view more information or they can use the hyper-links

---

FIGURE K-18: E-mail messaging window

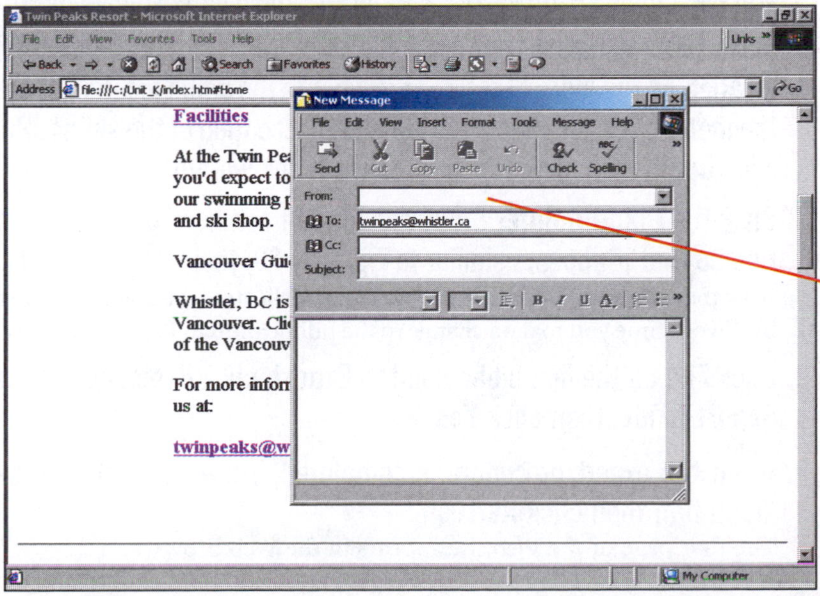

Twin Peaks Resort - Microsoft Internet Explorer

File   Edit   View   Favorites   Tools   Help   Links »

Back · Search Favorites History

Address   file:///C:/Unit_K/index.htm#Home   Go

Facilities

At the Twin Pe
you'd expect to
our swimming p
and ski shop.

Vancouver Gui

Whistler, BC is
Vancouver. Clic
of the Vancouv

For more infor
us at:

twinpeaks@w

New Message

File   Edit   View   Insert   Format   Tools   Message   Help

Send   Cut   Copy   Paste   Undo   Check   Spelling

From:

To: twinpeaks@whistler.ca

Cc:

Subject:

My Computer

Your e-mail address or the e-mail address associated with the computer you are using appears here

PageMaker 7.0

Modifying an HTML File in PageMaker

When you export a PageMaker publication to HTML and then view the HTML file in a Web browser, you often discover unexpected formatting problems. Table K-2 describes the elements that are exported to HTML and the elements that are not exported to HTML. To ensure that as many elements are retained as possible, you need to check that the Preserve Approximate Layout option in the Export HTML Options dialog box is selected. You may also need to make some adjustments to the PageMaker publication so that it appears correctly as an HTML file. ✐ Sara checks the Export HTML Options dialog box and then modifies the PageMaker publication. She then formats selected text on page 1 with a PageMaker style that is easily converted to an HTML style and changes the background color of all the pages in the publication. Finally, she adds a picture of a skier to page 1 because Twin Peaks Resort is first and foremost a ski resort.

Steps

1. In PageMaker, click **File** on the menu bar, point to **Export**, click **HTML**, click **Twin Peaks Resort**, then click **Options**

   The Options dialog box appears, as shown in Figure K-19. In this dialog box, you can check that the Approximate layout option button is selected, and you can check which PageMaker styles are exported to HTML styles. For example, text formatted with the Headline style in PageMaker is formatted with the Heading 1 style in the HTML document.

2. Verify that the **Approximate layout option button** is selected, click **OK**, then click **Done**

   The publication window appears. Sara formats some of the headings on page 1 with PageMaker styles that are converted to HTML styles.

3. Click the **Text tool** T if necessary, select the text **Twin Peaks Resort** at the top of page 1, click **Headline** in the Styles palette, then deselect the text

   This text will appear in the HTML Heading 1 style in your Web browser.

4. Click **Window** on the menu bar, click **Show Colors**, double-click **Paper**, enter **200** in the Red text box and **225** in the Green text box, click **OK**, then close the Colors palette

   The background color of every page in the publication is now an attractive light blue.

5. Click the **Pointer tool** ▶, then move the list of hyperlinks in column 1 down so the top of the list is at **2** on the vertical ruler bar

   You need to make some space available for the picture you are inserting.

6. Make sure you have a copy of the file **skiing.JPG** from your Project Files saved in the same location as the index.htm file (or move it to the same location, if necessary), click **File** on the menu bar, click **Place**, navigate to the location of the **skiing.JPG** file, click **skiing.JPG**, click **Open**, then click **Yes** in response to the warning

7. Click the **Place pointer** ⊠ at the top left corner of **page 1**, modify the size of the picture so that it appears similar to Figure K-20, then save the publication

   Now that you've modified the PageMaker publication, you need to export it again as an HTML file. Every time you make a change to the publication in PageMaker, you need to export it again.

8. Click **File** on the menu bar, point to **Export**, click **HTML**, click **Twin Peaks Resort**, click **Export HTML**, then click **Yes**

9. When the export procedure is completed, show the Web browser, click **View** on the menu bar, then click **Refresh**

   The first page of the Web site appears in the Web browser.

Approximate layout
option button is
checked by default

Styles in PageMaker
with their HTML
equivalents

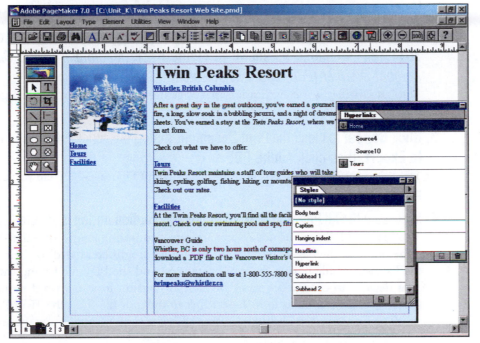

TABLE K-2: PageMaker elements exported to HTML

element	exported to HTML	not exported to HTML
Graphics	Imported pictures are exported to HTML as .jpg or .gif files	Graphics drawn in PageMaker are not exported to HTML, with the exception of single horizontal lines drawn with the Line tool
Text	Character-level attributes such as bold, italic, underline, and type color are exported to HTML	Type attributes such as font, type size, leading, horizontal scale, tracking, kerning, outline and shadow type styles, and indent and tab positions are not preserved in HTML
Page Layout	Columns are exported as tables; however, use a limited number of columns in the PageMaker publication for best results	Objects that have been rotated, skewed, or flipped in PageMaker revert to their original state in HTML; overlapping objects in PageMaker may not appear correctly in HTML; nonrectangular text wrap shapes are not exported; masked objects are unmasked in HTML

PageMaker 7.0

PageMaker 7.0

Creating a PDF File

You can easily create a PDF file from any PageMaker publication. When you select Adobe PDF from the Export menu, PageMaker generates a PostScript file and then uses a program called Acrobat Distiller to convert the PostScript file to a PDF file. **PostScript** is a language used for printing documents and is the standard for desktop publishing. The PDF file can then be read in Acrobat Reader on any computer, retaining the formatting and layout of the original publication. Both the Acrobat Distiller and Acrobat Reader applications are included with your installation of PageMaker 7.0. Web site designers sometimes include a link to a PDF file on a Web site instead of formatting the contents of the file in HTML, especially when the file is long and is intended for printing. Users can then click the link to the PDF file, and then view and print it in its original form. Sara wants her Web site to include a link to a PDF file containing the Vancouver Visitor's Guide. Her first task is to convert the PageMaker publication containing the Visitor's Guide into a PDF file.

Steps

1. **Return to PageMaker, open the file PM K-2.pmd from the drive and folder where your Project Files are located, then save the file as Vancouver Visitors Guide to the location you saved the other files for this unit**
   This publication contains 13 pages and includes a table of contents. Each of the entries in the table of contents becomes a hyperlink when the publication is converted to a PDF file.

2. **Click File on the menu bar, click Print, then check to ensure that Acrobat Distiller 3011.104 is entered as shown in Figure K-21 (*Macintosh Users: Confirm that the Acrobat Distiller (PPD) option is selected in the PPD text box*)**
   Acrobat Distiller is the application that PageMaker uses to convert the PageMaker publication to a PDF file.

3. **Click Cancel to close the Print Document dialog box, click File on the menu bar, point to Export, then click Adobe PDF**
   The PDF Options dialog box appears, as shown in Figure K-22. Here you can choose which pages to export.

4. **Make sure the All Pages in Current Publication option button is selected, then click Export**
   The Export PDF Save As dialog box appears, prompting you to save the PDF file with the same name as the PageMaker file. The two files are differentiated by their extensions, with the PageMaker file having the .pmd extension and the PDF file having the .pdf extension. Sara decides to change the name of the .pdf version to a one-word name containing no spaces because she plans to include a link to the .pdf file from the Twin Peaks Resort Web site. The filename of a file linked from a Web site cannot contain any spaces.

5. **Type Guide, then click Save**
   If you get a message that "Saving the PostScript output failed," close the dialog box and the next one, and then repeat Step 5. In a few moments, the Acrobat Reader program opens, and the publication appears in the Acrobat Reader window. You may get a message saying, "When you create a PostScript file, you have to send the host fonts. Please go to the Acrobat Distiller printer properties, Adobe PDF Settings page, and turn OFF the option 'Do not send fonts to Distiller'." If so, click the Start button, click Printers and Faxes, right-click the Acrobat Distiller icon, click Properties, click Printing Preferences, click the Adobe PDF Settings tab, make sure the Do not send fonts to Distiller check box is deselected, click OK twice, then close the Printers and Faxes window.

6. **Click the Zoom list arrow on the Acrobat Reader toolbar, then click Fit in Window**
   The publication appears in the Acrobat Reader window, as shown in Figure K-23.

A different printer probably appears on your system

Print Document

Printer: IBM 4039 LaserPrinter PS on LPT1:

PPD: Acrobat Distiller 3011.104

Copies: 1

☐ Collate
☐ Reverse
☐ Proof

Acrobat Distiller entered in the PPD text box

Pages
⦿ All
○ Ranges: 1-
☐ Ignore "Non-Printing" setting

Print: Both Pages
☐ Reader's spreads
☐ Print blank pages

Book
☐ Print all publications in book
☐ Use paper settings of each publication

Orientation

Print
Cancel

Document
Paper
Options
Color
Features
Reset

PDF Options

PDF Style: [On Screen]

General | Doc. Info | Hyperlinks | Articles/Bookmarks | Security

Distiller Settings
Job Name:
Edit Job Options...

Pages
○ All Pages in Book
⦿ All Pages in Current Publication
○ Ranges 1-

Enter page numbers and/or ranges separated by commas.
For example: 1, 4, 6-11

Page Size(s): Same as current publication

Printer
Style: Acrobat
☑ Check for PageMaker printer style conflicts

☐ Embed Tags in PDF (for accessibility and reflow)

Export...
Cancel
Save Style...
Delete Style...
Add Style...

Zoom list arrow

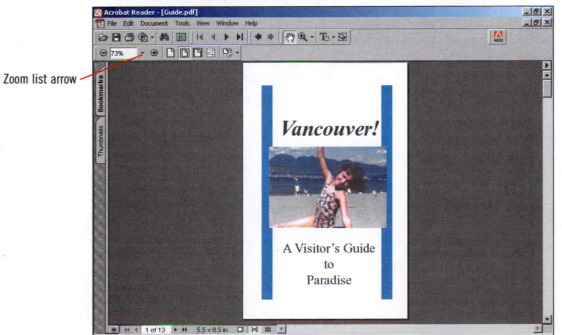

PageMaker 7.0

Using Acrobat Reader to View a PDF File

You use Acrobat Reader to view and print PDF files. A PDF file can be viewed or printed on any computer platform (such as a PC or a Mac) as long as you have that platform's version of Acrobat Reader. When you open the PDF file, you will notice that all page formats, layouts, colors, and graphics are retained from the original file. The viewer cannot alter any of the pages in the PDF file, further ensuring that the file remains as you intended. ✒ Sara wants to check how the publication appears in Acrobat Reader. She first decides to view thumbnails of the pages in the visitor's guide. A **thumbnail** is a miniature version of each page in the publication.

Steps 1 2 3 4

1. Click the **Show/Hide Navigation Pane button** 🖼 on the toolbar if necessary
   The navigation pane opens along the left side of the Acrobat Reader window.

2. Click the **Thumbnails tab** at the left side of the Acrobat Reader window, if necessary, click the **Thumbnail list arrow** at the top of the Navigation pane, then click **Small Thumbnails**
   Small thumbnails of the first several pages in the publication appear in the navigation pane, as shown in Figure K-24.

3. Scroll down the Thumbnails window to view the 13 pages in the publication

4. Scroll up to view page 2, then click the **page 2 thumbnail**
   The Contents page appears. The original Contents page was created in PageMaker using the Table of Contents feature. When a page containing a table of contents is exported to a PDF file, each TOC entry becomes a hyperlink.

5. Click **Attractions** in the table of contents to test that link
   The Attractions page appears. Sara can also check all the bookmarks in the Bookmarks tab.

6. Click the **Bookmarks tab** at the left side of the navigation pane to show the list of bookmarks in the publication
   The list of bookmarks is the same as the list of entries in the table of contents.

7. Click **Culture** in the Bookmarks list
   The page describing cultural activities in Vancouver appears, as shown in Figure K-25.

8. Close the Acrobat Reader file, then in PageMaker, close the Vancouver Visitors Guide publication
   The PageMaker version of the Twin Peaks Resort Web site is again the active document.

Show/Hide
Navigation
Pane button

Thumbnail
list arrow

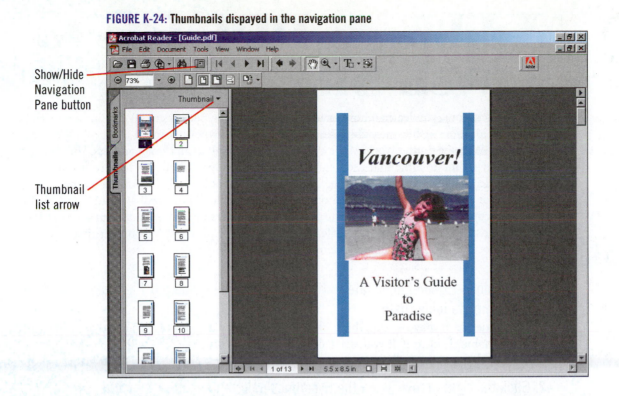

FIGURE K-25: Culture page

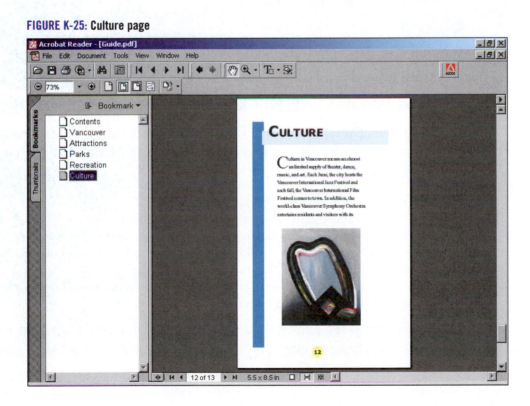

PageMaker 7.0

Adding a PDF File to a Web Site

In previous lessons, you learned how to add three kinds of hyperlinks to a Web site: a hyperlink to another location within the publication or Web page, a hyperlink to the URL of a Web page on another Web site on the World Wide Web, and a hyperlink to an e-mail address. You can also include a hyperlink to a file that users might want to download, such as a picture, a sound file, or a PDF file. When a visitor to the Web site clicks the link to the PDF file, the file is downloaded to the visitor's own computer. The visitor can then open the file in Acrobat Reader and read it or print a copy. Sara returns to the PageMaker version of the Twin Peaks Resort Web site and adds a link to the Guide.pdf file she created in the previous lesson. Her first step is to verify the location of the Guide.pdf file on her system.

Steps 1234

1. In Windows Explorer, navigate to the location of the **Guide.pdf** file, then write down the complete folder path
   The folder path may be something like C:\ followed by a series of folders and ending with the filename Guide.pdf. If you saved all files to a floppy disk, the path will begin with A:\. You need to know the exact path in order to create a hyperlink to the file in PageMaker.

2. Click the **right arrow** ▶ on the Hyperlinks palette, then click **New URL**
   In the New URL dialog box, you need to enter the location of the Guide.pdf file.

3. Type **file://**, then type the path of the Guide.pdf file
   See Figure K-26. Here the path is C:\Unit K\Guide.PDF. You enter a different path, depending on where you saved the Guide.pdf file.

4. Click **OK**

5. Click the **Text tool** T, select the text **Vancouver Guide**, then click the **URL button** next to the file URL in the Hyperlinks palette

6. Click **OK**, then apply the **Hyperlink style** to the selected text

7. Save the publication, export it to HTML, click **Yes** to replace the current index.htm file, wait until the export process is complete, switch to the Web browser, click **View** on the menu bar, then click **Refresh**

8. Click **Vancouver Guide** on page 1
   If the URL has been entered correctly, the Vancouver Guide file should open as shown in Figure K-27. If the Vancouver Guide link does not work, return to the PageMaker publication, then modify the file URL by clicking it in the Hyperlinks palette, clicking the right arrow, then clicking Edit URL. You may need to check the correct path in Windows Explorer. Each time you make a change to the URL, make sure you save the publication, export it again to HTML, and then refresh the browser before testing the link.

9. Click your browser's **Back button**, print a copy of the Web page from the browser, close the Web browser, close the publication in PageMaker, then exit PageMaker

Path you enter after file:// will probably be different

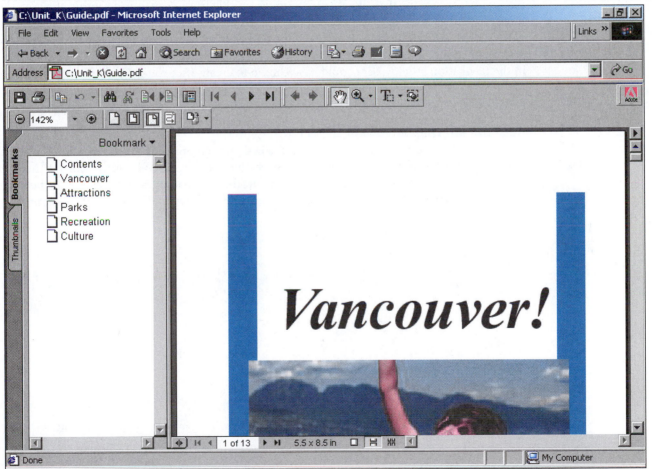

PageMaker 7.0

Design Workshop: Web Sites

PageMaker 7.0

The World Wide Web is one of the most exciting technologies to emerge in recent years. The potential benefit for individuals and businesses is almost unlimited. The challenge for Web site designers is to create unique, easy-to-use Web sites that capture the attention of users without overwhelming them. The Twin Peaks Resort Web site is the first site that Sara has designed using PageMaker. The completed site appears as shown in Figure K-28. Let's review Sara's Web page design.

Details

▶ ### Does the Web site capture the reader's attention?

Sara favors a clear, uncluttered design that includes just one picture. On her home page, Sara also includes a blue background color, which is attractive and appropriate for a Web site that advertises a ski resort. The background color is light enough to enhance the site without making the text difficult to read.

▶ ### Is the Web site easy to use?

Besides capturing the reader's attention, the Web site must be easy to use. Sara has created a simple navigation scheme that allows users to move quickly from page to page within the Web site. In the Twin Peaks Resort Web site, all three pages are actually contained on one HTML page because Sara converted all three pages of the PageMaker publication into a one-page Web site. Users can choose to scroll down the page to see all the contents or they can use the hyperlinks in the navigation scheme. Sara could have chosen to create a separate HTML file for each of the three pages in the publication; however, she decided that this very simple Web site would be best contained on one HTML page exported directly from one set of pages in PageMaker.

▶ ### Does the information benefit the reader?

You can have the best looking Web site, but if you do not give readers the information they need, they will go to the next Web site. Sara believes she has included useful information on the Twin Peaks Resort Web site. Readers can find out about the tour packages and facilities at the resort and then can check out information about Vancouver by downloading the PDF file containing the Vancouver Visitors Guide.

Address C:\Unit_K\index.htm | Go

Twin Peaks Resort

Whistler, British Columbia

After a great day in the great outdoors, you've earned a gourmet meal next to a roaring fire, a long, slow soak in a bubbling jacuzzi, and a night of dreams between crisp linen sheets. You've earned a stay at the *Twin Peaks Resort*, where we've elevated pampering to an art form.

Home

Check out what we have to offer:

Tours

Tours

Facilities

Twin Peaks Resort maintains a staff of tour guides who will take individuals and groups skiing, cycling, golfing, fishing, hiking, or mountain climbing, depending on the season. Check out our rates.

Facilities

At the Twin Peaks Resort, you'll find all the facilities you'd expect to find at a world-class resort. Check out our swimming pool and spa, fitness center, cycle shop, and ski shop.

Address file:///C:/Unit_K/index.htm#Tours | Go

Twin Peaks Tour Packages

Home

Skiing

Tours

Facilities

The Whistler/Blackcomb ski area is justifiably famous for some of the best--and longest--ski runs in the world. When accompanied by a Twin Peaks tour guide, you will avoid line-ups for chairs and gondolas, ski down runs of untouched powder, and learn great skiing tips. All of our ski tour guides are expert skiers.

Cycling

The Whistler/Blackcomb area boasts some of British Columbia's most challenging mountain biking trails. Twin Peaks Resort offers three tour levels. On a Novice Tour, cyclists enjoy a leisurely ride around the beautiful Whistler Valley. Participants in an Intermediate Tours are whisked to the top of one of the gondolas and then guided down a long, long trail to the valley. On an Expert Tour, cyclists experience some of the most gnarley mountain biking to be found on the face of this or any other planet!

Golfing

The Whistler Valley includes a world championship golf

Address file:///C:/Unit_K/index.htm#Facilities | Go

Twin Peaks Resort
Facilities

Home

Tours

Swimming Pool and Spa

Facilities

At the Twin Peaks Resort, you can relax in a world-class spa facility that includes a year-round outdoor swimming pool and jacuzzi, an indoor swimming pool with a waterfall, two saunas, and a steam room.

Fitness Center

Guests at the Twin Peaks Resort can work out tense muscles in our fully-equipped gym. Included are five treadmills, three stair masters, and three rowing machines along with a full range of free weights and body-building apparatus. A full-time fitness consultant is on duty to assist you.

Cycle Shop

Our cycle shop is known throughout the Whistler Valley for its wide range of bicycles and accessories. And our repair shop is unrivalled in the region! Guests can bring in

Start | Inbox - Outlook Ex... | Microsoft PowerPoi... | index.htm - Micr... | 9:10 PM

PageMaker 7.0

Practice

► Concepts Review

Label each of the publication window elements shown in Figure K-29.

FIGURE K-29

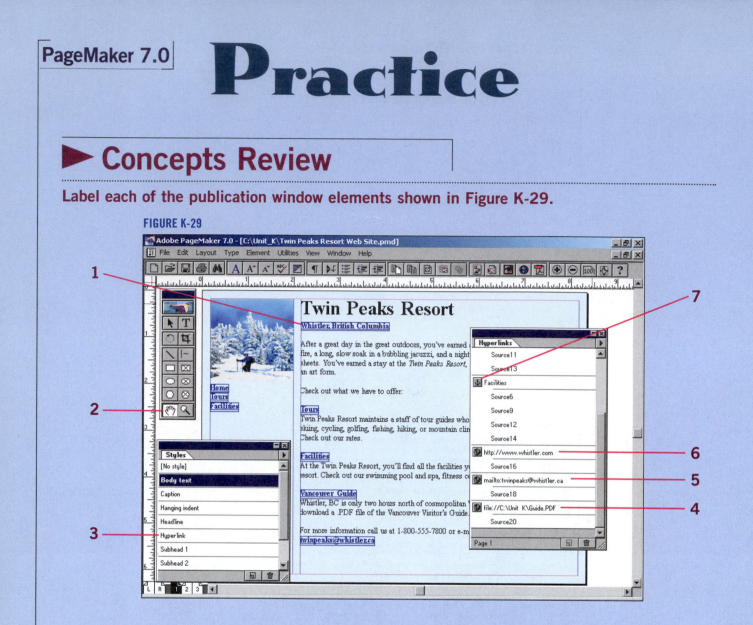

Match each of the terms with the statement that describes its function.

8. **HTML**
9. **World Wide Web**
10. **PDF**
11. **Thumbnails**
12. **Web browser**

a. A file format that can be viewed and printed from a Windows, Macintosh, or Unix platform

b. A network setup that allows use of a graphical interface on the Internet

c. Language used to create files for viewing on the World Wide Web

d. A program for finding and viewing Web pages

e. Page preview icons

13. **HTML is an acronym that stands for:**
   a. Hyper Text Marking and Linking.
   b. Hypertext Markup Language.
   c. Higher Text Marking Language.
   d. None of the above.

14. **PDF is an acronym that stands for:**
   a. Portable Document File.
   b. Portable Distribution Format.
   c. Passive Document Flexibility.
   d. None of the above.

15. **Which of the following tasks should be completed first when designing a Web site?**
    a. Export a publication as HTML pages.
    b. Develop a clear and easy-to-use navigation scheme.
    c. Insert attractive graphics.
    d. Create hyperlinks between the various pages in the Web site.

16. **Hypertext links can be used to connect to:**
    a. Text or graphics within the Web site.
    b. An e-mail address.
    c. Another page on the World Wide Web.
    d. All of the above.

17. **Which palette do you use to create hypertext links in PageMaker?**
    a. Hypertext palette
    b. Links palette
    c. Hyperlinks palette
    d. Web links palette

18. **What is the term used to designate the location that a hyperlink jumps to in a Web site?**
    a. Source
    b. Destination
    c. Anchor
    d. Location

19. **Which tool in the PageMaker toolbox do you select to show hyperlinks in a publication?**
    a. Link tool
    b. Hyperlink tool
    c. Hand tool
    d. Show tool

20. **Which letters are used to preface a link to a URL?**
    a. file://
    b. mailto://
    c. ftp://
    d. http://

21. **A uniform resource locator (URL) is a(n):**
    a. Programming language for creating Web pages.
    b. PDF viewer.
    c. Address of a Web page on the World Wide Web.
    d. Prefix for an anchor to a local file.

22. **Which of the following statements is true regarding the export of PageMaker features to HTML?**
    a. Imported pictures are exported to HTML as .jpg or .gif files.
    b. Drawn objects are exported to HTML as .htm files.
    c. HTML preserves text leading, tracking, and tab positions.
    d. Publications formatted in columns are exported to HTML as a single column of continuous text.

23. **Which of the following statements is true about a document converted to a PDF file?**
    a. The document's layout and graphics are retained.
    b. The user can add text to the file.
    c. The file extension is .html.
    d. The user must install Acrobat Viewer to read the document.

▶ Skills Review

1. **Set up a publication for a Web site.**
   a. Start PageMaker, open the file PM K-3.pmd from the drive and folder where your Project Files are located, then save the file as **Boston Web Site**.
   b. View the three pages in the publication to get an idea of its contents.
   c. Change the document setup to 600 × 450 Browser – Large.
   d. Change the layout for page 1 to 2 columns, then change the width of column 1 to 2".
   e. Change the layout for pages 2 and 3 to two columns, then adjust the width of column 1 on both pages to 2".
   f. Size and position the text block on each page so that it fits in column 2, then save the publication.

2. **Create a navigation scheme with hyperlinks.**
   a. Show the Hyperlinks palette, then create an anchor at the top of page 1 called Home.
   b. Create an anchor at the top of page 2 called Sightseeing, then create an anchor at the top of page 3 called Nightlife.
   c. In column 1 on page 1, type the following three entries for the navigation scheme: **Home**, **Sightseeing**, and **Nightlife**.
   d. Select Home in the list of entries for the navigation scheme, then associate it with the Home anchor.
   e. Associate the Sightseeing and Nightlife entries with their respective anchors, then save the publication.

3. **Format hyperlinks.**
   a. Click the Hand tool to show the hyperlinks, click the Sightseeing hyperlink, return to page 1, click the Nightlife hyperlink, then return to page 1.
   b. Create a new style called Hyperlink that includes the following character attributes: bold, underline, and blue text.
   c. Apply the Hyperlink style to the three entries in the navigation scheme on page 1.
   d. Copy the navigation scheme to column 1 on pages 2 and 3 of the publication.
   e. On page 1, associate Sightseeing and Nightlife in the text in column 2 with their respective anchors, then format both links with the Hyperlink style.
   f. Click the Hand tool, test the links on each page of the publication, then save the publication.

4. **Create hyperlinks to URLs and E-mail addresses.**
   a. Click the right arrow on the Hyperlinks palette, then click New URL.
   b. Type **http://www.boston.com**, then click OK.
   c. Select www.boston.com toward the top of page 1, click the URL button next to http://www.boston.com in the Hyperlinks palette, click OK, then apply the Hyperlink style to the selected text.
   d. Click the Hand tool, check the link, then close the browser window.
   e. Move to the end of the last paragraph on page 1, press [Enter] twice, type **For more information call us at 1-800-555-1200 or e-mail us at:**, press [Enter], then type **bostonvisitor@bguide.com**.
   f. Click the right arrow on the Hyperlinks palette, click New URL, type **mailto:bostonvisitor@bguide.com**, then click OK.
   g. Select the e-mail address in the publication, associate it with the mailto: URL, apply the Hyperlink style to the e-mail address, then save the publication.

5. **Export a PageMaker publication to an HTML file.**
   a. Click File on the menu bar, point to Export, click HTML, then click Untitled1.
   b. Click Edit, type **Boston Visitors Guide** in the Document Title text box, then click Done.
   c. Click Document in the Export Files to Location section, navigate to the location where you save files for this book, type **boston** in the File Name For HTML Document text box, then click OK.
   d. Click Graphics, then select the same location you selected for the boston.htm file.
   e. Click Export HTML.
   f. Open the Web browser you normally use, click File on the menu bar, click Open, click Browse, navigate to the location where you saved the boston.htm file, click boston.htm, click Open, then click OK.

g. Test the navigation scheme in the Web browser, test the link to boston.com, return to the Web site, test the e-mail link, close the new e-mail messaging window, then return to the PageMaker publication.

h. Save the publication.

6. Modify an HTML file in PageMaker.

a. Select the text Visit Boston! at the top of page 1, apply the Headline style, then deselect the text.

b. Show the Colors palette, then change the color of the paper to Blue: 185. The resulting color is a light yellow.

c. Move the list of hyperlinks in column 1 down to 1.25 on the vertical ruler bar.

d. Make sure a copy of the file bus_logo.GIF from your Project Files is saved in the same location as the boston.htm file, click File on the menu bar, click Place, navigate to the location of the bus_logo.GIF file, click it, then place it at the top left corner of column 1 on page 1.

e. Resize the graphic so it fits above the navigation scheme in column 1, save the publication, then export it again.

f. Refresh the revised Web site in your browser.

7. Create a PDF File.

a. In PageMaker, open the file PM K-4.pmd from the drive and folder where your Project Files are located, then save the file as **Boston Visitors Guide** to the same location you saved other files for this unit.

b. Click File on the menu bar, point to Export, click Adobe PDF, then click Export.

c. Type **Boston**, then click Save.

d. Click the Zoom list arrow on the Acrobat Reader toolbar, then click Fit in Window.

8. Use Acrobat Reader to View a PDF File.

a. Show the navigation pane, if necessary, then view large thumbnails.

b. View page 3, then click Culture in the Contents list to move to the Culture page.

c. View the Bookmarks, expand the Contents, if necessary, then click Transportation.

d. Close the Acrobat Reader file, then in PageMaker, close the Boston Visitors Guide publication.

9. Add a PDF file to a Web site.

a. In Windows Explorer, navigate to the location of the Boston.pdf file, then write down the complete folder path.

b. Click the right arrow on the Hyperlinks palette, then click New URL.

c. Type **file://**, type the path of the Boston.pdf file, then click OK.

d. Click the text Boston Visitors Guide on page 1 of the publication, then associate the selected text with the file:// URL you created in step c.

e. Apply the Hyperlink style to the selected text.

f. Save the publication, export it to HTML, then test the link to the PDF file.

g. Print the Web page from the browser, close the browser, close the publication in PageMaker, then exit PageMaker.

▶ Independent Challenge 1

You work for a new and prosperous company known as WorldLink, which specializes in helping businesses establish Web sites. A local music store named Rocket Music Connection wants you to create a Web site for their stores. The Rocket Music Connection wants a site that gives their viewers a brief overview of the more complicated Web site they're working on. Viewers would then be able to use hyperlinks to connect with Web pages focusing on their music preferences. These Web pages would have information about the latest releases as well as weekly updates on specials at the Rocket Music Connection.

a. Plan and sketch a three-page Web site that includes a home page and two additional pages. You determine the contents of these two additional pages. For example, one page could provide information about rock music releases and the other page could provide information about classical music releases.

b. Open a new publication, choose the large browser page size, then set up each page of the publication with two columns. Column 1 should be approximately 2" wide to accommodate the navigation scheme.

c. Write text for each of the three pages in the publication. Page 1 should contain the name of the music store and a general description of it. Make sure you format text with PageMaker's built-in styles rather than with specific commands.

PageMaker 7.0

d. Save the publication as **Web Site for Rocket Music Connection**.

e. Include one or two pictures if you wish. You can find pictures on the PageMaker CD. Show the Picture Palette, search for an appropriate category, then insert the picture. Note that pictures are converted to .gif files when the publication is exported to HTML. Make sure you insert the pictures above or below text to ensure they appear correctly after exporting to HTML.

f. Create a navigation scheme on page 1 that includes hyperlinks to each of the three pages in the publication. Remember that you need to create an anchor at the top of each of the three pages and then associate the anchors with the appropriate source text.

g. Create a new hyperlink style, format each hyperlink, then copy the navigation scheme to pages 2 and 3.

h. Open the Export HTML dialog box, create a title for the HTML document, then identify a filename and location. Use the filename **rocket.htm**. Identify the same location for graphic files.

i. Export the publication to HTML, then view it in the browser.

j. In PageMaker, modify the publication by adding a hyperlink to the Web site of your choice and a hyperlink to an e-mail address to contact for more information.

k. Change the background (paper) color of the publication, save and export the publication to HTML again, then refresh the view in the browser.

l. Print a copy of the Web page from the browser.

► Independent Challenge 2

As you have already learned, creating a PDF file is an alternative to traditional publication creation and distribution. Use one of your favorite PageMaker publications that you have already completed to create a PDF file using PageMaker and Adobe Acrobat.

a. Open a publication containing at least four pages in PageMaker.

b. Add a table of contents to the publication. Remember that you need to format each of the headings for the table of contents with a style and specify that the style should be included in a table of contents.

c. Export the publication to Adobe PDF.

d. View the publication in Acrobat Reader, then use the buttons on the toolbar to change the view of the publication and to scroll from page to page in the publication. Spend some time exploring the various ways in which you can view a publication in Acrobat Reader.

e. Print a copy of the publication from Acrobat Reader, then close Acrobat Reader.

► Independent Challenge 3

Seaside Cycles has created a four-page business proposal for expanding their presence on the World Wide Web. They would like to make this proposal available to all their investors from a link on the Seaside Cycles Web site. The author of the proposal has asked you to create a PDF file for the proposal that includes bookmarks.

a. Open the file PM K-5.pmd from the drive and folder where your Project Files are located, then save the file as **Seaside Cycles Proposal**.

b. Modify the Headline style so that it will be included in the table of contents.

c. Use the Create TOC command to create a table of contents for the publication. Use the default title for the table of contents.

d. Place the table of contents even with 7 on the vertical ruler bar and the left margin on page 1.

e. Use the Text tool to select all the entries in the table of contents.

f. Click Type on the menu bar, click Indents/Tabs, click at 6 on the ruler bar, click Leader, select the leader style you prefer, then click OK.

g. Position the table of contents on page 1 as shown in Figure K-30.

h. Save the publication, then export the publication to Adobe PDF as a file called **Seaside.pdf**.

i. In Acrobat Reader, show the thumbnails, show the bookmarks, then test the links on the table of contents.

j. Print a copy of the proposal from Acrobat Reader, then close Acrobat Reader.

k. Save and close the publication in PageMaker.

FIGURE K-30

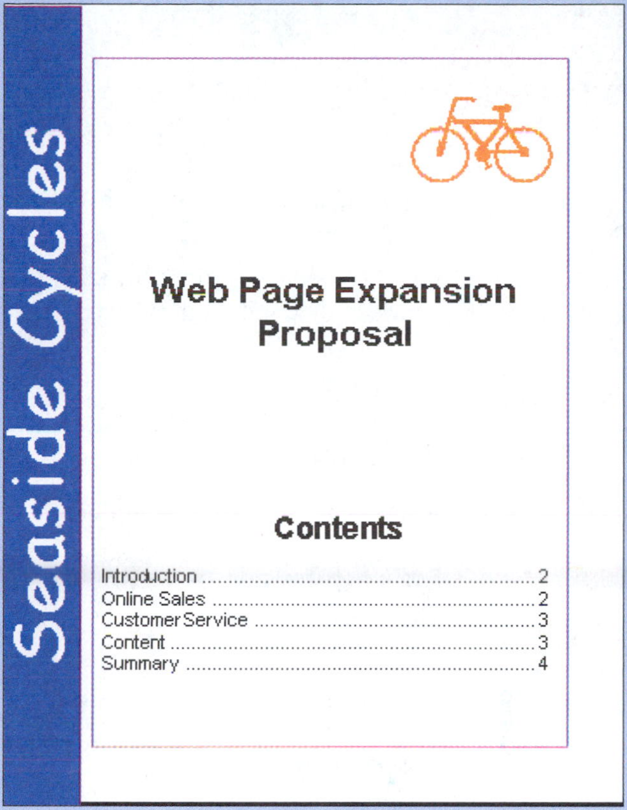

Seaside Cycles

Web Page Expansion Proposal

Contents

e Independent Challenge 4

Because so many people today are "surfing the Net," any company interested in doing business on the Internet should have a Web site that provides viewers with useful information and captures their attention before they jump to another Web site. You have been asked by your employer to critique some of the Web sites launched by your competitors to determine whether or not your company's Web site needs to be redesigned in order to be more attractive and informative to your customers.

a. Search the World Wide Web for at least two Web sites belonging to companies in the industry of your choice. Bookmark these pages so that you can easily jump from page to page. Explore some of the links that you find on each of the company's Web sites.

b. Critique each Web site using the following guidelines:
   • Are graphic images used attractively?
   • Is the download time for the site about right, or is it too long?
   • Is the navigation scheme easy to find and use?
   • Does the site include downloadable files for graphical images or long publications?
   • Does the site include a link to an e-mail address?
   • How would you improve the home page on each Web site?

c. Sketch the home page for your company that includes the best qualities from each of the home pages that you have explored. Include a navigation scheme for a Web site that would eventually include five pages.

PageMaker 7.0

▶ Visual Workshop

As the marketing director for a local retail center called The Galleria, you've been asked to create a Web site for the center. Set up a two-page publication called **Galleria Web Site** in PageMaker that appears as shown in Figure K-31 and Figure K-32 when exported to HTML and viewed in a Web browser. You need to select the 640 × 480 document size, format the publication in two columns, insert the image called Retail.gif from the drive and folder where your Project Files are stored, and change the paper color to Blue: 200. Include a hyperlink to the Web site of your choice from the text "Store of the Month." Export the publication to HTML as a file called **galleria.htm**. View the HTML document in the Web browser, then print a copy.

FIGURE K-31

FIGURE K-32

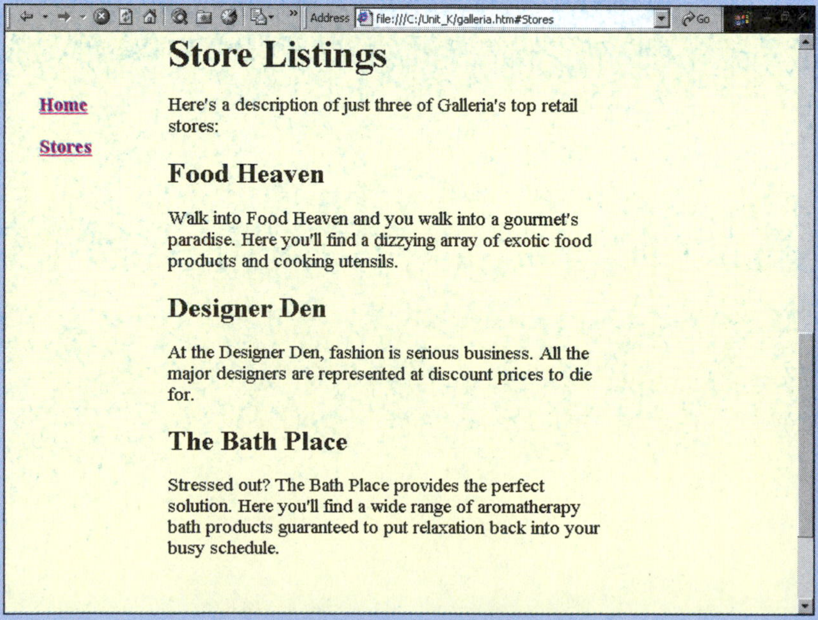

PageMaker 7.0

Unit L

Additional
Projects

Objectives

- ▶ **Create a letterhead**
- ▶ **Create a calendar**
- ▶ **Create an advertisement**
- ▶ **Create a poster template**
- ▶ **Create a brochure**
- ▶ **Create a newsletter**
- ▶ **Create a report and export it to PDF**

This unit provides seven additional projects for you to practice the skills you learned in this book. As you work through the steps, you'll refer to the completed publication shown in the figures. The process of creating each publication is similar to the process required to create a publication "from your head." Often, you work from a sketch or even just an idea of a finished publication, and then use your skills to bring that sketch or idea to the screen. In this unit, you create all the publications from scratch to replicate the challenges you face when creating your own publications. The seven projects in Sara's in-basket cover a wide range of publications—from a simple letterhead to a multiple-page report to a Web site.

Creating a Letterhead

Sara's first project is to create the letterhead for Red Rock Tours shown in Figure L-1. Red Rock Tours takes cyclists on day and overnight guided tours through the magnificent red rock canyons of Utah. The letterhead includes the company's business address and a logo that consists of geometric shapes that Sara creates right in PageMaker. In addition, the letterhead includes the company's slogan and, most importantly, the company's Web site address. Sara wants to create a letterhead using a clean design that effectively projects a positive image for the company.

Steps

1. Start PageMaker and open a new publication, then set up the document with the **Letter** page size and **.75"** margins on all four sides of the page

2. Save the publication as **Red Rock Tours Letterhead**

3. Create the text block containing **Red Rock Tours** as shown in Figure L-1

   The text is formatted in Century Gothic with bold and italics. The first letter of each word is 48-point, and the remaining letters are 24-point. You can use a different font if Century Gothic is not available.

   > **QuickTip**
   > Select the first two letters in a word, click Type, click Expert Tracking, then click Very Tight.

4. Adjust the tracking to reduce only the space between the first and second letters in each word so the completed text block appears as shown in Figure L-1

5. Create the text block containing the company address, phone number, and Web site information

   The text is formatted in 9-point Century Gothic. You can use a different font if Century Gothic is not available.

6. Add a text block with the slogan **Cycling Just Doesn't Get Any Better!** in 12-point, bold, and italics

   > **QuickTip**
   > Click Element, then click Polygon Settings to set the number of sides at three before drawing the triangles.

7. Draw a triangle with the settings shown in the Control Palette in Figure L-2

8. Copy the triangle, then fill the two triangles with the two shades of brown shown in the Color palette in Figure L-3

   You need to create two spot colors: PANTONE 1675 CVC for the front triangle and PANTONE 159 CVC for the back triangle.

9. Position the triangles as shown in the completed letterhead, print a copy, then save and close the publication

FIGURE L-1: Completed letterhead for Red Rock Tours

FIGURE L-2: Control Palette settings for triangle

Set the Width at 0.6 inches

Set the Skew at 25 degrees

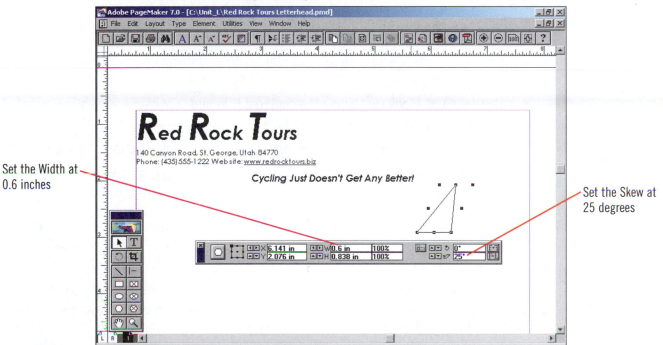

FIGURE L-3: Triangles filled with color

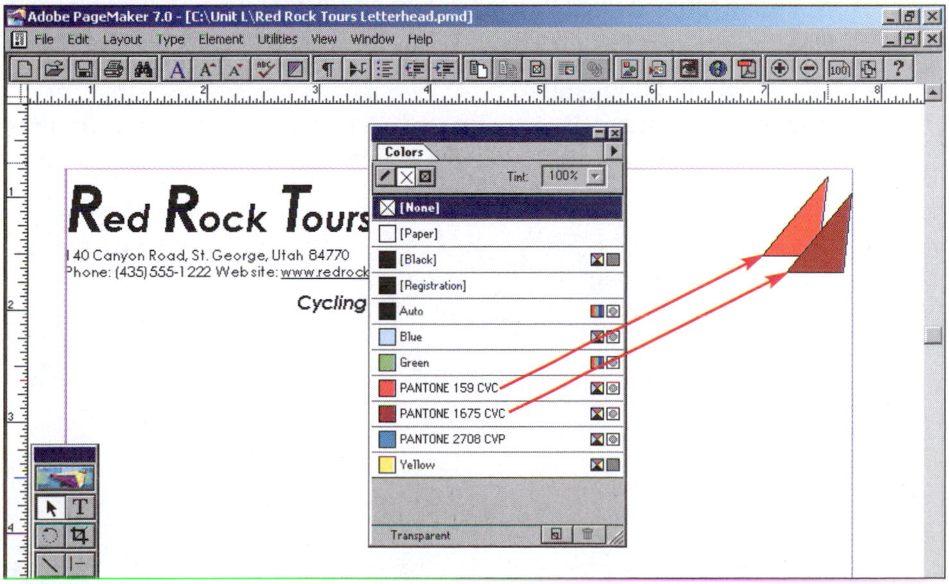

PageMaker 7.0

Creating a Calendar

The Rocky Mountain Music School in Banff, Alberta, runs a summer music program that attracts students from all over the world. The school has asked Sara to prepare a calendar advertising the concerts the students perform each week. The school plans to distribute the calendars throughout Banff and the neighboring communities. Sara suggests that they print the calendar with one spot color on standard-size paper. She uses Adobe Table to create and format the calendar. She prints the publication in landscape orientation, as shown in Figure L-4.

Steps

1. Open a new publication, then set up the document with the **Letter** page size, in **Wide** format and with **.5"** margins on all four sides of the page
   The publication is formatted in landscape orientation to best fit a full seven-day week.

2. Save the publication as **Rocky Mountain Music School Calendar**

3. Create the text block containing the name and address of the school at the top of the page, as shown in Figure L-4
   The company name is formatted in 24-point Arial Narrow with bold and italics. The address text is formatted in 12-point Arial. You can use a different font if Arial is not available.

4. Create the text block containing the centered title and subtitle as shown in Figure L-4
   The title is 36-point Arial, and the subtitle is 18-point Arial.

Trouble?

If Adobe Table 3.0 does not appear on the Insert menu, click Start on the taskbar, point to Programs, point to Adobe, point to PageMaker 7.0, and then click Adobe Table 3.0.

5. Click **Edit** on the menu bar, click **Insert Object**, click **Adobe Table 3.0**, then click **OK**

6. Enter **12** for the rows and **7** for the columns, make the table **5.5"** high and **10"** wide, then click **OK**

7. Click the upper-left corner of the table to select all the cells in the table, click **Window** on the menu bar, click **Show Text Palette** if necessary, then select the **Arial** font
   You can use a different font if Arial is not available.

8. Enter and enhance the text required for the schedule as shown in Figure L-4
   Use the Table Attributes and the Text Attributes palettes to format cells as you work. To merge all the cells in one row into one cell, click to the left of the row, click Cell, and then click Group. To enter the date numbers, enter the number, press [Enter], then change the horizontal alignment back to Center and type the concert title.

QuickTip

If you need to make changes to the table, double-click it to return to Adobe Table 3.0.

9. When the table is complete, click **File** on the menu bar, click **Exit**, and return to **Rocky Mountain Music School Calendar**, print a copy of the completed calendar, then save and close the publication
   If an Acrobat Distiller dialog box opens, go to the Acrobat Distiller printer properties, Adobe PDF Settings Page and turn OFF the option 'Do not send fonts to distiller.'

FIGURE L-4: Summer Concert Calendar for Rocky Mountain Music School

Rocky Mountain Music School

1601 Mountainview Road, Banff, Alberta T0L 0C3
www.rockymountainmusic.ca

Summer Concert Schedule

July 5 to August 31, 2004

July

Monday	Tuesday	Wednesday	Thursday	Friday	Saturday	Sunday
5 Strings Recital	6	7 Choral Recital	8	9	10 Band Concert	11
12	13	14	15 Piano Recital	16	17	18 Horn Recital
19 Jazz Piano	20	21 Harp Recital	22	23	24 Harpsichord	25
26	27 Singing Recital	28	29 Massed Choir	30	31	1

August

Monday	Tuesday	Wednesday	Thursday	Friday	Saturday	Sunday
2 Drum Recital	3	4	5 Solo Clarinet	6	7	8 Lute Recital
9	10 Piano Recital	11	12	13	14 Sax Trio	15
16 Horn Recital	17	18 Jazz Recital	19	20	21	22 Jazz Trio
23	24	25	26	27 Massed Band	28	29
30	31					

Creating an Advertisement

Perched atop Oregon's spectacular sand dunes, the Breakers Inn overlooks the endlessly breaking waves of the Pacific Ocean. The inn has recently started promoting winter weekend getaways. Guests can relax in luxurious warmth while watching the often violent winter storms rage outside the sturdy picture windows of the inn. The owner has asked Sara to design a half-page advertisement that will run in various local and national travel magazines. The advertisement includes a color photograph and provides details about the Breakers Inn and its winter packages. The completed advertisement appears in Figure L-5.

Steps

1. Open a new publication, then set up the document with a Custom page size that is **8.25"** in Width and **5.25"** in Height with **0"** margins on all four sides
The publication is sized to fit on one-half of a typical magazine page.

2. Save the publication as **Breakers Inn Winter Package Advertisement**

3. Place the **Oregon.jpg** photo from your Project Files into the publication

4. Position the photo as shown in Figure L-5

5. Draw the two rectangles, and fill them with **cyan**

6. Create the two rotated text blocks contained in the cyan rectangles
Use 30-point Arial Black or a similar font, and reverse the text. You need to rotate both text blocks.

7. Create the three text blocks containing the information for the advertisement as shown in Figure L-5
The text in the sky is 14-point Arial in bold and italics. The information about the weekend packages is 12-point Arial and the company name and address are 10-point Arial, with the company name in bold and italics. In addition, you need to bold and italicize "winter weekend getaway package," and enhance "$225" and the phone number with bold.

8. Print a copy of the completed advertisement so that it fits on one page

9. Save and close the publication

FIGURE L-5: Completed advertisement for the Breakers Inn

The Breakers Inn

Experience the power of the Pacific Ocean from the snug warmth of the luxurious Breakers Inn.

Our *winter weekend getaway package* includes two nights' accommodation, two breakfasts and two five-course gourmet dinners for only **$225 per person!**
Call **1-800-PACIFIC** to book your winter getaway.

The Breakers Inn, Route 99 South, Florence, OR 97439 Web site: www.oregonbreakers.biz

Winter Getaways

Creating a Poster Template

Every month Madison Books in Cleveland hosts a book signing event that features the author of a newly released book. The owner has asked Sara to create a poster template that can be adapted each month to feature a new author. The appearance of the poster will mostly stay the same from month to month. Only the name of the author and specific information about the book will change. The poster will be printed with one spot color on standard letter-size paper, and then distributed to libraries, recreation centers, and local stores. Figure L-6 shows the poster template and Figure L-7 shows a completed poster that includes information about Olga Hanson, the author who will be signing her new book on November 3, 2003.

Steps 1234

1. Open a new publication, then set up the document in Letter size with .5" margins on all four sides

2. Click **File** on the menu bar, click **Save As**, type **Madison Books Poster**, click the **Save as type list arrow**, click **Template**, then click **Save**
   You can base the poster for each event on the poster template.

3. Create a new spot color called **Teal** from **PANTONE 320 CVC** in the PANTONE® Coated library

4. Draw and position the **star shape**, then fill it with the **Teal** spot color
   The shape contains 12 sides with a 45% star inset.

5. Draw a rectangle with rounded corners, fill it with a **10% tint** of Teal, then change the Stroke color to **100% Teal** and the Stroke width to **6 pt**

6. Use the **Times New Roman font** to create all the text blocks shown in Figure L-6
   Make sure you enclose the text block containing the description text in a frame that is 5.5" wide and 3.5" high. The text in the star shape is 24-point in bold and reverse; "Book Signing Event" is 48-point and Teal; "Featured Author" is in 36-point, bold and italics; "[Name]" is 36-point, and "[Date]" and "[Time]" are 18-point. The text in the frame and the bookstore address information are both 12-point.

Trouble?

You may need to insert the PageMaker Content CD in order to access the pictures.

7. Insert the pictures from the Business & Finance Category in the Pictures palette (select Images), reduce their size, place them as shown in Figure L-6, save the poster template, print a copy, then close it

8. Open the template, save the new publication as **Madison Books Poster_Olga Hanson**, remove the text from the frame, place the text file **PM L-1.txt** in the frame, add a **2-line drop cap**, as shown in Figure L-7, then slightly reduce the height of the frame

9. Insert the author's name and the date and time of the event as shown in Figure L-7, print a copy, then save and close the publication

FIGURE L-6: Completed poster template

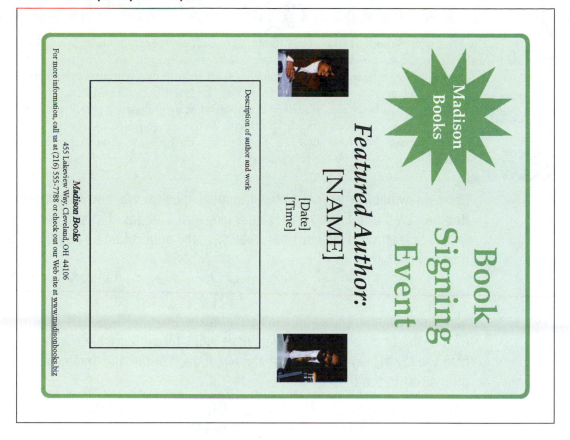

FIGURE L-7: Completed poster for Olga Hanson event

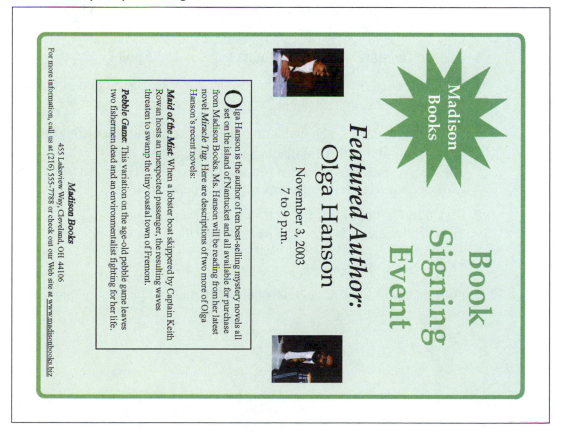

Creating a Brochure

The Footlights School of Drama in Atlanta, Georgia, provides students with a full-year program in the dramatic arts, including acting, theater history, stagecraft, and directing. The principal of the school has asked Sara to create a three-panel brochure that contains information about the school and its one-year dramatic arts program. The brochure will be printed on light-colored, letter-size paper in black and white for distribution at local high schools, employment centers, and theaters. The school has provided Sara with all the text required for the brochure in an RTF (Rich Text Format) file. Now she needs to transform the text into an attractive and easy-to-read brochure. Figure L-8 shows the two sides of the completed brochure.

1. Open a new publication, set up the document in **Letter** size and **Wide** orientation with **Double-sided** and **Facing pages** selected, with **2 pages** that start on **page 2**, and with **.5"** margins on all four sides, then save the publication as **Footlights School of Drama Brochure**

   You set up the publication so that you can see both pages of the brochures in the same window.

2. Add three column guides on each page, place the file **PM L-2.rtf** from your Project Disk in the first column on the left page, click the **windowshade handle**, press and hold the **[Shift]** key, then click at the top of each of the next three columns to place all the text in the file

3. Define a new style called **Theater1** that formats text in the **Arial font**, **16-point**, **bold**, **italic**, then define a second new style called **Theater2** that formats text in **Times New Roman**, **14-point**, **bold**

4. Apply the **Theater1** style and **Theater2** style to selected headings and subheadings as shown in Figure L-8

5. Edit the **Theater2** style to change the font size to **12-point**

6. Slightly reduce the height of column 2 by dragging the bottom sizing handle up so that the list of courses in Term 2 appears at the top of column 3

7. On panel 2 of page 2, add and format the two text blocks, then draw the rounded rectangle, and fill it with **10% black**, as shown in Figure L-8

   The contact sentence is formatted with the Theater1 style. The school name is 18-point bold Arial, and the school contact information is 14-point Arial.

8. Create the front cover of the brochure as shown in Figure L-8

   The school name is 36-point Arial and bold, and the slogan is 18-point Arial, bold and italic. The rectangle is filled with 30% black and enclosed in a Custom stroke that uses one of the Thick-Thin Stroke styles with a weight of 10-point.

9. Print a copy of the two-page brochure, then save and close the publication

FIGURE L-8: Completed brochure for Footlights Theater School

Program Objectives

The Footlights School of Drama in Atlanta, Georgia, offers students a wide range of courses in acting, directing, and stagecraft.

This one-year intensive program provides students with the training required to develop professional-level skills in all areas of theatrical production.

Upon successful completion of the Footlights School of Drama program, graduates receive a certificate recognized as equivalent to 18 credits at the university level. Students may then enter university in the sophomore year where they can fulfill the requirements for a Bachelor of Fine Arts in Drama.

Admission Procedures

Auditions for the Footlights School of Drama are held at the school in March and April of each year for admission to the school in September. Candidates may apply for an audition by calling the School Registrar at (404) 555-1220.

The following materials must be provided to the Audition Committee two months prior to the audition date:

- Resume detailing performance experience and drama-theater education
- Transcript from the last educational institution attended

- Reference letter from two or more instructors (one of which should be a drama instructor)
- Video of a recent performance (acting students only)
- Directing script of a recent production (directing students only)
- Costume, lighting, or set designs of a recent production (stagecraft students only)

The audition will consist of the following elements:

- Sight analysis of a selection from a contemporary play chosen by the audition committee
- Thirty-minute interview

In addition, acting students must present two prepared speeches and perform one sight reading of a role chosen by the audition committee.

Program Content

The Footlights School of Drama program is divided into two 4-month terms.

Term 1:

DRA 100	History of Theater 1
DRA 101	Dramatic Theory 1
DRA 102	Elective 1
DRA 103	Elective 2
DRA 104	Production

Term 2:

DRA 200	History of Theater 2
DRA 201	Dramatic Theory 2
DRA 202	Elective 3
DRA 203	Career Choices
DRA 204	Production

Course Descriptions

DRA 100: History of Theater 1
Evolution of theater from the Greeks to the English Restoration. Special emphasis on Shakespearean drama.

DRA 101: Dramatic Theory 1
The fundamentals of dramatic theory, including techniques for dramatic criticism.

DRA 102: Elective 1
Choice of Acting 1, Directing 1, or Stagecraft 1.

DRA 103: Elective 2
Choice of Improvisation 1, Production 1, or Graphic Design 1.

DRA 104: Year 1 Production
Participation in a full-length production of a play selected by the students.

DRA 200: History of Theater 2
Development of the theater from the 19th century in England and the United States with special emphasis on contemporary US playwrights.

DRA 201: Dramatic Theory 2
In-depth analysis of selected plays from a variety of genres and historical periods.

DRA 202: Elective 3
Choice of Acting 2, Directing 2, or Stagecraft 2.

DRA 203: Career Choices
Development of job search skills to obtain employment in theater or film.

DRA 204: Year 2 Production
Participation in a full-length production of a musical selected by the students.

Faculty

All the instructors at the Footlights School of Drama continue to work professionally in theaters throughout North America. In addition to our regular faculty, we are proud to welcome the following artists-in-residence for the 2004 program:

Merilee Montcalm: Acting
Ms. Montcalm has won acclaim for her performances on and off Broadway. Her most recent triumph was playing Lady Macbeth in the recent production by the New York Theater.

Mark Levine: Directing
In 2002, Mr. Levine won the coveted Players Trophy for his production of *A Streetcar Named Desire* at the Old Vic Theater in London, England.

Rachel Goldblum: Stagecraft
Ms. Goldblum has won numerous awards for her costume and set designs. Recently, she designed the costumes for the Oscar-winning film adaptation of *Wuthering Heights*.

Call to book an appointment for an admissions interview!

**Footlights
School of Drama**
180 Westside Road
Atlanta, GA 30314
Phone: (404) 555-1220
www.footlights.com
e-mail: info@footlights.com

Footlights
School
of
Drama

*Where All the World's
Your Stage...*

Creating a Newsletter

Twice a year, the Baird Street Gallery in San Francisco sends its customers a newsletter that provides information about upcoming shows, featured artists, and other information of interest to art lovers. The owner of the gallery has decided to have the newsletters produced professionally, so she has asked Sara to transform the current text files into a four-page newsletter that includes a table of contents and photographs of various art works. The completed newsletter will be printed on 17" x 11" glossy paper as a booklet, and then folded. The completed newsletter appears as shown in Figure L-9.

Steps 1 2 3 4

1. Open a new publication, set up the document in **Letter** size and **Tall** orientation, with **Facing pages** and **Double-sided** selected, with **4 pages** selected, and with **.5"** margins on all four sides, then save the publication as **Baird Street Gallery Newsletter**

2. Add two column guides on each page, then create the masthead for the newsletter, as shown in Figure L-9
   The gallery name is 36-point Arial Black in blue, and the date information is 12-point Arial. The line is 6-pt wide and blue. Use any font for this step if Arial Black is not available.

QuickTip

Click the L and R icon at the lower-left corner of the document window to show the master pages.

3. In the Master Pages, place and format the **footer text** required for the left and right pages
   The page numbers are 14-point Arial in bold, and the text is 10-point Arial. Use the [Ctrl][Alt][P] keystrokes to insert the page numbers.

4. Place the file **PM L-3.rtf** from your Project Files in the first column on the left page, click the **windowshade handle**, press and hold the **[Shift]** key, then click at the top of each of the next three columns to place all the text in the file

5. Create a new style called **Art Headings** that formats text in **Arial**, **24-point**, **bold**, and **blue** and is included in the table of contents, then format headings with the Art Headings style, as shown in Figure L-9

6. Place the pictures from your Project Files as follows: **Art1.jpg** on page 1, **Art2.jpg** on page 2, **Art3.jpg** on page 3, and **Art4.jpg** on page 4, then size and position the pictures as shown in Figure L-9, wrapping text as required

7. Create and then format the table of contents on page 1 as shown in Figure L-9
   You need to change the size of the TOC Art Heading style to 18-point, and increase the width of the text block to span the two columns and show the dot leaders.

8. Add lines and drop caps where required, create the pull quote on page 3, then adjust the positioning of the text and pictures so that the completed newsletter appears as shown in Figure L-9

9. Save the publication, use the Build Booklet plug-in palette to format the publication for printing in the 2-up consecutive layout with the default settings for creep and gutters, save the new copy as **Newsletter Booklet**, print a copy of the four-page newsletter, then save and close the publication

FIGURE L-9: Completed newsletter for the Baird Street Gallery

Baird Street Gallery

Winter/Spring 2004

Upcoming Exhibitions

We have a fabulous sched ule of exhibitions lined up for January–June, 2004. First up on January 2 is **Eduardo Lopez** with his *Tribal Memory* exhibition. This exciting and vibrant series of work reflects a synthesis of imagery derived from the artist's Mayan and Aztec ancestors with the art of the native cultures of the Pacific Northwest. Eduardo's exhibition runs to January 27.

On February 4, photographer **Jenny Smith** presents *Classic Mode*, an exhibition of black and white photo- graphs of subjects ranging from neo-classical

statuary, temples, and fountains in Rome, Flo- rence, Paris, and London to Roman ruins in

Contents

Italy and the south of France. Jenny's exhibi- tion runs to February 28.

Heinrich Strubel's exhibition called *Post Apocalypse* opens on March 3 and runs to March 31. These large paintings and charcoal drawings appear to depict the results of an archaeological dig. Through a variety of scraping and pouring techniques, Strubel creates a series of layerings to invoke the imbedded shapes and forms.

Kicking off the Spring season on April 8 is *Landscape Constructions*, an exhibition of mixed media assemblages by long-time artist **Ed Sloan**. The works in this exhibition com- bine natural materials such as wood, leaves, and found objects with acrylic paste and paint. All these elements are used to heighten densi-

ties and textures and to create an alternative approach to landscape painting. Ed Sloan's exhibition runs to April 28.

On May 5 the stunning abstracts of **Petra Watson** will give San Francisco audiences something to talk about! Her large canvases reverberate with subtle tones and sweeps of color, as dense as they are passionate. Petra's exhibition runs to May 31.

Hiromi Tanaka brings her series of delicate mixed media works to the Baird Street Gallery on June 3. Her works reflect an ongoing dialogue with the misty landscapes of her native Japan, combined with her interpretation of the west coast rainforests of her adopted land. Hiromi's show runs to June 30.

Film Rentals

The Baird Street Gallery is going Hollywood! In recent months, we have received several requests from film companies to rent artwork for film sets. Here's a list of some of the productions to watch out for:

- *First Chance* is using the work of Patricia Gardiner to decorate the hallways of a hospital.

- *The Fortune Seeker* is using the work of **Petra Watson** in a variety of office sets.

- **The Last Hurrah** is using the work of Eduardo Lopez on the set of a mansion.

Baird Street Gallery Online

We're online at www.bairdgallery.com. All of our artists are represented, along with images of their work. In a few more months,

You'll even be able to purchase art online

you'll even be able to purchase art online! We're working with a Web site developer right now to enable our site for e-commerce.

Video Openings

If you miss one of our openings, you can log on to our Web site and watch a video of the opening! We've installed a Web cam in the gallery so if the wind is blowing hard outside or your car has a flat tire, relax! Fire up your computer and come to a virtual opening. Here's the schedule of openings for the next six months:

January 2:	Eduardo Lopez	7 p.m. to 10 p.m.
February 4:	Jenny Smith	7 p.m. to 10 p.m.
March 3:	Heinrich Strubel	2 p.m. to 5 p.m.
April 8:	Ed Sloan	7 p.m. to 10 p.m.
May 5:	Petra Watson	2 p.m. to 5 p.m.
June 3:	Hiromi Tanaka	7 p.m. to 10 p.m.

Featured Work

The theme of the 2003 Christmas show was *The Abstract Eye*. Each gallery artist exhibited three paintings that represented their most abstract visions, even if normally they do not create work in the abstract style. Shown at the right is the image that was used as the cover photo for the 2003 Christmas Show invitation. Entitled *Traces*, this luscious canvas is the work of Petra Watson.

New Volunteers

We are always ready to welcome new volunteers! If you are interested in the arts and enjoy meeting artists, helping to run exhibitions, and lending a hand at openings, then please give us a call. We need your skills and your enthusiasm. For more information about the rewards of being a volunteer, read about Beth Rowan, our featured Volunteer of the Season!

Volunteer of the Season

Marge Rowan is our Volunteer of the Season – the Summer/Fall Season in this case! On more than one occasion, Marge has gone above and beyond the call of duty in her tireless efforts to ensure that the Baird Street Gallery remains one of San Francisco's best. We honor her this season specifically because of the support and help she provided for one of our artists who has been undergoing a difficult time in his personal life. Marge was there for him with the result that he was able to organize and mount his exhibition—and feel better about his life. Marge continues to inspire all of us with her caring attitude and her enthusiasm for art.

PageMaker 7.0

Creating a Report and Exporting to PDF

Clarity Communications runs seminars in oral and written communications for companies throughout North America. Recently, the company has decided to partner with Tech Trend Training to offer seminars in various software programs. The company would like to distribute the report from its Web site as a PDF file that companies can download and then print. The text for the report is contained in an RTF (Rich Text Format) file. Sara needs to format the report attractively over four pages, add a simple index, and then convert the publication to a PDF file and view it in Acrobat Reader. The four pages of the completed report are shown in Figure L-10.

Steps

1. Open a new publication, set up the document in **Letter** size and **Tall** orientation, deselect **Double-sided**, select **4 pages**, set the Left margin at **1.5"**, the Right margin at **.75"** and the Top and Bottom margins at **1"**, then save the publication as **Clarity Communications Report**

2. In the Master Page, type Page in the lower-right corner, followed by the page number code (**[Ctrl][Alt][P]**), draw the two triangles filled with **25% black**, then remove the Master from page 1
   To remove the Master from page 1, click View, then click Display Master Items.

3. Format the title page of the report as shown in Figure L-10
   The stroke width of the rectangle enclosing the page is 6-point, and the triangle is filled with 25% black. The titles are 30-point Arial, and the authoring information is 14-point Arial.

4. Place the file **PM L-4.rtf** from your Project Disk at the top of page 3, then flow it to page 4, adjusting the text boxes so they don't overlap the gray triangles
   The text does not fit on the two pages. You fix this problem next.

5. In Story Editor, remove the section titled **Partnership Need** and the second paragraph in the Conclusion, then modify the height of the text blocks on pages 3 and 4 so that the text appears as shown in Figure L-10

6. Open the Styles window, double-click **Heading 1**, click **Para**, click the **Include in table of contents check box**, change the Before Paragraph space to **.2"**, click **OK**, click **OK**, then include **Heading 2** in the table of contents
   You may need to adjust the height of the text boxes to make sure they don't overlap the gray triangles at the bottom of each page.
   In a file saved in Rich Text Format, heading styles may be included; however, you often need to adjust these styles in PageMaker.

7. Generate the table of contents on page 2 so that it appears as shown in Figure L-10

8. Save the publication, then export it as an Adobe PDF file called **Clarity Report**, accepting all defaults

9. View the completed report in Acrobat Reader, print a copy, close Acrobat Reader, then close the publication in PageMaker

FIGURE L-10: Completed report

PARTNERING AGREEMENT

Clarity Communications and Tech Trends Training

Prepared By:
[Your Name]
Vice President: Sales

[Current Date]

Contents

INTRODUCTION

Clarity Communications has an opportunity to partner with Tech Trends Training, a local company that provides software training to small and large companies in the Bay Area. This proposal describes the issues related to the partnership in terms of three factors: Partnership Requirements, Products and Services, and Financial Considerations. If Clarity Communications and Tech Trends Training agree to the proposed partnership, the terms of the partnership will become active on June 1, 2004 and extend to December 31, 2006, at which time a renewal of the agreement will be negotiated.

PARTNERSHIP REQUIREMENTS

This section provides background information about Tech Trends Training and discusses how the partnership could benefit both Clarity Communications and Tech Trends Training.

Background Information

Tech Trends Training is conveniently located in the heart of San Francisco's business district, where most of its clients are also located. Few other training services in the area offer on-site training in state-of-the-art computer labs. Tech Trends Training's agreements with several very high-profile computer software vendors has ensured a continuing supply of the most recent—and powerful—software applications in categories ranging from Office suites to Web Page design packages to Networking packages. All levels are catered to—from the office assistant eager to learn PowerPoint to the Web page designer who needs to develop SQL skills.

Benefits

Tech Trends Training needs the seminars provided by Clarity Communications in order to offer an overall business-training package that will appeal to its corporate customers. In particular, Tech Trends Training requires business writing seminars, online publishing seminars, and database design seminars. By providing Tech Trends Training with these seminars, Clarity Communications extends its market. Customers to Tech Trends Training can purchase Clarity Communications seminars and then contact Clarity Communications directly should they require additional seminars or consulting services. Revenues are also expected to rise.

PRODUCTS AND SERVICES

This section discusses the proposed partnership in terms of the products and services each party will provide.

Tech Trends Training Services

Tech Trends Training provides the following categories of software training:
- Introduction to Office applications
- Advanced Office applications
- Introduction to Web page design
- Advanced Web page programming
- Advanced Networking

The attached appendix lists the specific courses provided in each of the five principal categories.

Clarity Communications Products

Tech Trends Training is most interested in our business writing seminars and online publishing seminars, since these areas are most in demand by their current clients.

Package Opportunities

Tech Trends Training will offer Clarity Communications seminars as supplements to software training courses. In addition, Tech Trends Training and Clarity Communications can create custom training packages.

FINANCIAL CONSIDERATIONS

Tech Trends Training has provided information related to their course sales over the past three years. Based on this information, Clarity Communications could expect a minimum 20% increase in revenues on the sale of seminars used by Tech Trends Training to supplement its software training courses. In addition, Clarity Communications could work with Tech Trends Training to generate revenue from the sale of seminars to Tech Trends Training customers and the inclusion of customized seminars in Tech Trends Training packages.

Financing Required

Tech Trends Training has agreed to cover all costs associated with the packaging of Clarity Communications course materials for the first six months of the partnership agreement.

CONCLUSION

Clarity Communications has the opportunity to increase its market share by partnering with Tech Trends Training. Both companies are seriously committed to providing their clients with complete, personalized training packages and to develop training materials that conform to the highest standards of usability and effectiveness.

Project Files List

To complete the lessons and practice exercises in this book, you need to use the Project Files supplied by Course Technology. Below is a list of the files that are supplied, and the unit and exercise to which the files correspond. The name you save the file with is also provided, along with the names of files you create from scratch. For information on how to obtain the Project Files, please see the inside back cover of this book.

In the steps and practice exercises in this book, the Project Files are referenced with the phrase "the drive and folder where your Project Files are stored." You will save your files in the location designated by your instructor. This location is referenced in the book as "the location where your Project Files are stored." Please note that the files created by PageMaker are quite large, so you will need to store them on a Zip disk, hard drive, network drive, or another location as specified by your instructor.

Unit and Location	Project File Supplied	Student Saves File As	Student Creates File
Unit A			
Lessons	PM A-1.pmd		
Skills Review	PM A-2.pmd		
Independent Challenge 1			
Independent Challenge 2			
Independent Challenge 3			
Independent Challenge 4			
Unit B			
Lessons	Logo.tif		Twin Peaks Letterhead.pmd
Skills Review	Logo.tif		Memo.pmd
Independent Challenge 1	Hilltop Ski Shop Logo.jpg		Hilltop Letterhead.pmd Hilltop Memo.pmd Hilltop Business Card.pmd
Independent Challenge 2	School.tif		New Letterhead.pmd
Independent Challenge 3	Corner Bookstore.jpg		Manager Business Card.pmd Buyer Business Card.pmd
Independent Challenge 4	CD Logo.jpg		Music Letterhead.pmd
Visual Workshop	Island Paradise Logo.jpg		Island Paradise Letterhead.pmd
Unit C			
Lessons	PM C-1.pmd PM C-2.doc PM C-3.doc PM C-4.doc	Mouse Pad Fact Sheet.pmd	
Skills Review	PM C-5.pmd PM C-6.doc PM C-7.doc	My Fact Sheet.pmd	

Unit and Location	Project File Supplied	Student Saves File As	Student Creates File
Independent Challenge 1	PM C-8.doc Building.tif PM C-9.doc		Computer Science Fact Sheet.pmd
Independent Challenge 2	Placehld.jpg Texthld.doc		New Fact Sheet.pmd
Independent Challenge 3	Keyboard.jpg Texthld.doc		Grades Fact Sheet.pmd
Independent Challenge 4	Skis.jpg Hiker.jpg Texthld.doc		Sporting Fact Sheet.pmd
Visual Workshop	Plant1.jpg Plant2.jpg Placehld.jpg PM C-10.doc		Independence Landscape Brochure.pmd
Unit D			
Lessons	PM D-1.pmd	Seaside Cycle Web Proposal.pmd	
Skills Review	PM D-2.pmd	Sunrise Proposal.pmd	
Independent Challenge 1	Peterson Consultants.jpg Proptxt.doc		Peterson Consultants Proposal.pmd
Independent Challenge 2			
Independent Challenge 3	Springfield Text.doc SU Logo.jpg Springfield University.jpg		Computer Science Proposal.pmd
Independent Challenge 4	Volunteer Corp.jpg		Volunteer Trip Proposal.jpg
Visual Workshop	PM D-3.pmd	Hawthorne Report.pmd	
Unit E			
Lessons	PM E-1.pmd	Swan Report.pmd	
Skills Review	PM E-2.pmd	Health Notes.pmd	
Independent Challenge 1	PM E-3.doc PM E-4.doc PM E-5.doc PM E-6.doc		BioBuilder.pmd
Independent Challenge 2	Book.jpg Apple.bmp Texthold.doc		BookBuzz.pmd
Independent Challenge 3	Apple.bmp		My Cause.pmd
Visual Workshop	PM E-7.pmd PM E-8.doc PM E-9.doc PM E-10.doc PM E-11.doc Apple.bmp	Health Connection.pmd	

Unit and Location	Project File Supplied	Student Saves File As	Student Creates File
Unit F			
Lessons	PM F-1.pmd PM F-2.pmd Waves.jpg PM F-3.pmd	Art Exhibit Ad.pmd Photo Exhibit Ad.pmd Nature Photography Ad.pmd	
Skills Review	PM F-4.pmd PM F-5.pmd	Lobster Lounge 1.pmd Lobster Lounge 2.pmd	
Independent Challenge 1	Big Ben.tif PM F-6.doc		London Ad.pmd
Independent Challenge 2			
Independent Challenge 3			Product Ad.pmd
Independent Challenge 4			Cruise Ad.pmd
Visual Workshop	Paris.tif PM F-7.doc		Paris Ad.pmd
Unit G			
Lessons	PM G-1.pmd	Windward Cafe.pmd	
Skills Review	PM G-2.pmd	Bistro Menu.pmd	
Independent Challenge 1	PM G-3.doc PM G-4.doc PM G-5.doc		Pizza Place.pmd
Independent Challenge 2			Copied Menu.pmd
Independent Challenge 3	PM G-6.doc PM G-7.doc PM G-8.doc		My Restaurant Menu.pmd
Independent Challenge 4			London Menu.pmd
Visual Workshop	PM G-9.pmd	Neptune Lounge.pmd	
Unit H			
Lessons	PM H-1.pmd CapFerat.jpg Violin.jpg Violin2.jpg	Concert Poster.pmd CapFerat.jpg Violin2.jpg	
Skills Review	PM H-2.pmd Russia.tif Piano.jpg Music.jpg	Audition Poster.pmd Russia.tif Music.jpg	
Independent Challenge 1	Apple.bmp		Play Poster.pmd
Independent Challenge 2			Redesigned Poster.pmd
Independent Challenge 3			Event Poster.pmd
Independent Challenge 4			Tour Poster.pmd
Visual Workshop	PM H-3.doc Guitar.jpg		Guitar Lessons Poster.pmd

Unit and Location	Project File Supplied	Student Saves File As	Student Creates File
Unit I			
Lessons	PM I-1.pmd PM I-2.pmd PM I-3.csv	Arcadia Tours Brochure.pmd Arcadia Tours Envelope.pmd	
Skills Review	PM I-4.pmd PM I-5.pmd PM I-6.csv	Chicago Meeting.pmd AP Envelope.pmd	
Independent Challenge 1	Hawaii1.tif Hawaii2.tif HawaiiText.doc		Hawaii Brochure.pmd
Independent Challenge 2			GreenArt Envelopes.pmd GreenArt Data.txt
Independent Challenge 3			CD-ROM Brochure.pmd
Independent Challenge 4	Alaska1.tif Alaska2.tif Alaska3.tif		Alaska Brochure.pmd
Visual Workshop	Provence1.tif Provence2.tif Provence3.tif FranceText.doc		Provence Brochure.pmd
Unit J			
Lessons	PM J-1.pmd PM J-2.pmd	Vancouver Visitor Guide.pmd Vancouver Visitor Guide Complete.pmd Vancouver Visitor Guide Booklet.pmd	
Skills Review	PM J-3.pmd	New World Airlines Information.pmd New World Airlines Information Booklet.pmd	
Independent Challenge 1	PM J-4.pmd	Reno Investors Group Information.pmd Reno Investors Group Booklet.pmd	
Independent Challenge 2	PM J-5.pmd	Partnership Proposal.pmd	
Independent Challenge 3	PM J-6.pmd	Art Festival Report.pmd	
Independent Challenge 4			Chicago Guide.pmd Chicago Booklet.pmd
Visual Workshop	PM J-7.pmd	Fitness First News.pmd	
Unit K			
Lessons	PM K-1.pmd Skiing.jpg	Twin Peaks Resort Web Site.pmd index.htm skiing.jpg	
	PM K-2.pmd	Vancouver Visitors Guide.pmd Guide.pdf	

Unit and Location	Project File Supplied	Student Saves File As	Student Creates File
Skills Review	PM K-3.pmd bos_logo.gif	Boston Web site.pmd boston.htm bos_logo.gif Boston1.jpg Boston2.jpg	
	PM K-4.pmd	Boston Visitors Guide.pmd Boston.pdf	
Independent Challenge 1			Web Site for Rocket Music Connection.pmd rocket.htm
Independent Challenge 2			
Independent Challenge 3	PM K-5.pmd	Seaside Cycles Proposal.pmd Seaside.pdf	
Independent Challenge 4			
Visual Workshop	Retail.gif		Galleria Web Site.pmd galleria.htm Retail.gif
Unit L			
Creating a Letterhead			Red Rock Tours Letterhead.pmd
Creating a Calendar			Rocky Mountain School Calendar.pmd
Creating an Advertisement	Oregon.jpg		Breakers Inn Winter Package Advertisement.pmd
Creating a Poster Template	PM L-1.txt		Madison Books Poster.pmt Madison Books Poster_Olga Hanson.pmd
Creating a Brochure	PM L-2.rtf		Footlights School of Drama Brochure.pmd
Creating a Newsletter	PM L-3.rtf Art1.jpg Art2.jpg Art3.jpg Art4.jpg		Baird Street Gallery Newsletter.pmd Newsletter Booklet.pmd
Creating a Report and Exporting to PDF	PM L-4.rtf		Clarity Communications Report.pmd Clarity Report.pdf

Adobe Certified Expert (ACE) Requirements for Adobe PageMaker 7.0 Product Proficiency Exam

Below is a list of the Adobe Certified Expert (ACE) Product Proficiency Exam requirements for Adobe PageMaker 7.0 and where in the book the skill is covered. For more information, please visit www.adobe.com and follow the links for Training.

Skill title	Unit(s) where skill is covered
1. General Knowledge	
Describe common terms in areas of print and electronic publishing, typography, and color theory (e.g., half-tone, trapping, knock-outs, leading, kerning, etc.)	Units A, G, I
Discuss issues related to cross-platform file sharing in PageMaker (e.g., font and graphic file formats)	Units B, D
Describe appropriate workflows related to PageMaker (e.g., import by using filters, templates, converting files, etc.)	Units C, E, I, K, L
2. Page Layout	
Use commands to set up a publication (e.g., Document Setup Command, View Commands, changing preferences)	Units A, B
Manage the layout by using tools and resources (e.g., column guides, ruler guides, master pages, etc.)	Units A, B, C, E
Place and arrange elements on page by using tools (e.g., placing text and graphics, using the Control Palette, grouping, locking, etc.)	Units B, C, F, G, H
Create and manage layers	Unit H
Use the Adjust Layout Command	
3. Working with Text	
Format text using Type menu, Control Palette, explain difference between text frames and text blocks, edit text in story editor and layout view	Units B, C, D, E
Create and manage styles by using the Styles Palette (including defining, modifying, removing and importing styles to the list, etc.)	Unit E
Explain different Font use	Units B, G
4. Working with Graphics	
Create basic objects in PageMaker	Units B, F, H
Modify graphics by using commands from the Elements menus	Unit H
Crop graphics by using various tools including resizing a frame, Cropping tool, Frame options, etc.	Units F, H
Colorize and tint imported graphics	Unit I
Given a scenario, determine the appropriate graphic file format to use	

Skill title	Unit(s) where skill is covered
5. Working with Color	
Explain spot and process colors and appropriate uses	Unit I
Working with the Color Palette	Unit I
Import colors from another PageMaker file	Unit I
Color management features	Unit I
6. Importing and Exporting Files	
Import text/graphics from outside publication	Units B, C, D, F
Export text/graphics from PageMaker publication	Units D, F
Manage links between PageMaker and imported text and graphic files	Unit H
Options for cutting and pasting objects into and between PageMaker publications	Unit D
7. Working with Utilities	
Using Plug-Ins	Units E, I, J
Working with long documents	Unit J
Create and modify tables by using Adobe Table	Unit D
Export Adobe Table files	Unit D
Use the Library and Scripts Palette	Unit I
Describe and use the Data Merge palette	Unit I
Use the Build Booklet plug-in	Unit J
8. Printing and Prepress	
PostScript and non-PostScript printing	Unit B
Prepare a file for printing color separations and composites	Unit I
Create a package by using the Save For Service Provider Plug-In	Unit I
9. Electronic Publishing	
Create an Adobe PDF file from a PageMaker publication	Unit K
Create an HTML file containing text, graphics, hyperlinks and anchors	Unit K
Create a marked PDF file by using option in the Export Adobe PDF dialog box	Unit K
Exporting PDF files	Unit K

Glossary

Abstract   A summary at the beginning of a report.

Adobe Acrobat Distiller   An application that converts an exported PostScript file into a portable document format (PDF) file.

Adobe Acrobat Reader   An application that allows you to view and print portable document format (PDF) files.

Alignment   The position of text within a page or column; left, right, centered, or justified.

Anchor   In a navigation scheme, the location that appears when a hyperlink is clicked.

Attach   To join content with a frame to create a single object that can be moved, edited, or resized as a unit.

Autoflow   A feature that places text automatically so that it flows from one column to the next, filling up as many columns and pages as necessary.

Balance columns   To align the tops or bottoms of text blocks that are threaded in a story on a single page or on facing pages.

Baseline   An imaginary line on which text rests.

Baseline leading   A leading setting that measures the leading from the baseline of a line of text.

Black   One of the four process colors. *See also* CMYK.

Bookmark   A hypertext link in a PDF publication.

Bullet   A small picture, usually a round or square dot, used to identify an item in a list.

Camera-ready copy   A publication printed on paper that can be sent directly to a printing company to be photographed for reproduction.

Character view   The view on the Control palette used to change character-related formats such as font, type style, leading, baseline shift, and other settings.

Clip art   Graphic images that are stored as electronic files.

Clipboard   A temporary storage area for cut or copied text or graphics.

CMYK   An abbreviation used to describe the use of the four process colors: cyan (C), magenta (M), yellow (Y), and black (K).

Color library   An industry standard color matching system used to identify specific colors.

Column guides   Blue, vertical, nonprinting lines that mark the right and left sides of columns on a publication page.

Comma-delimited text file   A data source file in which each data field is separated by a comma.

Crop   To modify a graphic image by eliminating portions.

Cross reference   An index entry that describes a related or additional topic.

Cursor   The blinking line in the publication window that indicates where text will appear when you type. *See also* Insertion point.

Cyan   A shade of blue; one of the four process colors. *See also* CMYK.

Data source file   In a data merge, the file that contains the information that varies from publication to publication.

Definition points   Diamond-shaped handles that appear on standoff lines and allow you to adjust the shape of text wrapping around a graphic.

Desktop publishing application   A software program that gives users the ability to integrate text, graphics, spreadsheets, charts, and other objects created in different programs into one document.

Document Master page   A non-printing page in a single-sided publication that contains text, graphics, and other objects that appear on every page in the publication.

Document Master page spread   Left and right non-printing pages in a double-sided publication that contain text, graphics, and other objects that appear on every page spread in the publication.

Dots per inch (dpi) A unit of measurement for the number of dots that together create an image; determines the resolution of an image. *See also* Resolution.

Drag-place method A method for placing text that allows you to define the size of a text block at the time you import the text.

Drop cap The first letter in a paragraph that is enlarged and lowered so the top of the letter is even with the first line of text in the paragraph, and the base of the letter drops next to the rest of the paragraph.

Edition A file that can be imported or subscribed to by other application programs.

Element An item, such as a text block or a graphic, that you can select and resize, move, or transform. *See also* Object.

Fact sheet A publication that describes a product or service.

Field A unit of variable information in a data source.

File extension The three or more letters after the period in a filename that identify the program in which the file was created.

Flag The area on the first page of a periodical that contains the publication title, date of issue, and other information; also known as a nameplate or masthead.

Floating palette A moveable window within the publication window.

Font The specific design of a complete set of characters.

Footer Text that appears at the bottom of every page in a publication.

Format To change the appearance of text.

Frame An object that can hold graphics or text and can act as a placeholder for content.

Full-color A term used to describe a publication that uses process colors.

Grabber hand A pointer that acts like a hand on a piece of paper and allows you to move the publication page in any direction in the publication window.

Graphic element An umbrella term that describes anything on a page other than the text.

Graphic A picture, chart, or drawing object.

Graphical interface A computer interface in which the user interacts with the computer by clicking pictures, icons, and words rather than typing commands.

Guides Non-printing lines in the publication window that to help you place and align objects.

Gutter The space between columns.

Header Text that appears at the top of every page in a publication.

Home page The first Web page viewers see when they open a Web site.

Horizontal ruler The bar located on the top edge of the publication window that helps users to size and align text and graphics.

HTML Author A PageMaker plug-in that converts a publication into an HTML file that can be viewed on the Internet.

HTML Hypertext Markup Language; a programming language used to create Web pages.

Hyperlink Specially formatted text or a graphic that when clicked opens another Web page or jumps to a different location on the same Web page. *See also* Hypertext link.

Hypertext link Specially formatted text or a graphic that when clicked opens another Web page or jumps to a different location on the same Web page. *See also* Hyperlink.

Hyphenate To insert hyphens between syllables in words in order to allow words to break across lines in a text block.

I-Beam The shape of the pointer when the Text tool is active.

Image control A PageMaker feature that allows you to adjust the lightness and contrast of black and white images.

Imposition In preparing a booklet for printing by a commercial printer, a multiple-page spread that prints on a single sheet and can be folded to create the completed publication.

PageMaker 7.0

Indent A set amount of space between the first or last word in a line of text and the right or left margin.

Index entry A word or group of words included in an index.

Index marker A nonprinting character that designates text to be included in an index and is visible only in story editor.

Informational brochure A publication that includes detailed information about a product or service.

Inline graphic A graphic that is placed within a text block and is part of a line of text.

Insertion point The blinking line in the publication window that indicates where text will appear when you type. *See also* Cursor.

Internet A network of millions of interconnected computers worldwide.

Jump line A short line of text that tells the reader a story is continued on or continued from another page.

Kerning The space between a pair of characters.

Key words The major topics in a publication's text that are pulled out to create an index.

Laminate To cover publications with a permanent plastic coating in order to preserve them.

Landscape A term used to refer to horizontal page orientation; the opposite of portrait, or vertical orientation.

Layering Placing text and other objects on top of each other to create reverse text, graphics, or other visual effects. *See also* Stacking.

Layers A layout feature of PageMaker, akin to stacked sheets of transparency film, that allows you to place objects on different layers rather than directly on the page.

Leaders Characters that repeat between tabbed items, such as dots or dashes.

Leading The vertical space between lines of text, specifically, the total height of a line from the top of the tallest character in the line to the top of the tallest character in the line below.

Line art A graphic that is drawn with lines and shapes.

Link A connection between a PageMaker file and another file, such as a graphic file; a linked graphic appears in a PageMaker publication but is not stored as part of the PageMaker file.

Loaded A term used to describe a text flow pointer which "contains" text to be placed.

Magenta A shade of red; one of the four process colors. *See also* CMYK.

Margin guides The magenta-colored lines on the publication page that indicate the page margins.

Master page(s) Nonprinting page(s) used for placing text and/or graphics that appear on every page in a publication.

Master page(s) icon An icon that appears in the lower-left corner of the publication window and provides access to the master page(s).

Masthead The area on the first page of a periodical that contains the publication title, date of issue, and other information; also known as a flag or nameplate.

Menu bar The horizontal bar below the title bar in the PageMaker program window that contains the names of the PageMaker menus.

Misregistration The gap between colors that occurs when one or more of the process colors is not printed in exact alignment with the other colors.

Nameplate The area on the first page of a periodical that contains the publication title, date of issue, and other information; also known as a flag or masthead.

Navigation scheme A plan for linking the Web pages of a Web site with hyperlinks.

Nudge buttons Arrows on the Control palette that allow you to make incremental changes to a format setting.

Object view The view on the Control palette used to size, position, and transform graphics.

Object An item, such as a text block or a graphic, that you can select and resize, move, or transform. *See also* Element.

Orientation The position of a rectangular page, either portrait (vertical) or landscape (horizontal).

Orphan A line of text that ends a paragraph at the top of a column or page.

Page icons Numbered rectangles at the bottom of the publication window that are used to navigate between the pages in a publication.

Page information On a separation, the filename, date, and separation name at the bottom of each separation page.

Page view The degree of magnification of the page in the publication window.

Paragraph view The view on the Control palette used to change paragraph-related formats such as indents, alignment, and styles.

Pasteboard The white area surrounding the publication page that is used as a work area for creating and storing text and graphics before they are placed in the publication.

PDF Portable Document File; a type of file created from a PageMaker file that retains the page design and layout of the original file, but which can be viewed and printed using Adobe Acrobat Reader.

Pica A unit of measurement equal to 12 points or 1/6"; used by many commercial printers.

Pixel Dots that comprise a graphic image.

Place To insert or position text or graphics in a PageMaker publication.

Plug-in A software utility that comes with PageMaker that automates repetitive or complex tasks.

Point of response In a fact sheet or other informational publication, the phone number, Web site, or address that the reader can use to respond to information in the publication.

Point A unit of measurement equal to ½ of an inch; used to measure font size, leading, and line weight.

Pointer guides Dotted lines on the horizontal and vertical rulers that indicate the position of the pointer on the publication page.

Portrait A term used to refer to vertical page orientation; the opposite of landscape, or horizontal orientation.

Power points Areas of a publication that are read first by readers.

Primary index topic A main index entry.

Printer marks The cropping and registration marks used by commercial printers to align separations on the printing press and then to trim the print job to the final size after it's printed.

Process color A type of color used in commercial printing where four basic colors (cyan, magenta, yellow, and black) are combined in percentages to create other colors. *See also* CMYK.

Program window A window that contains the running PageMaker program; includes the PageMaker menus, toolbars, palettes, and publication window.

Proof A smaller, less-costly version of a publication that is used for editing.

Proportional leading The default setting for leading that allows for proportional amounts of space above the tallest character and below the lowest character in a line.

Proxy A graphical representation of the selected object on the Control palette that shows the reference point. *See also* Reference point.

Publication page The boxed area in the publication window in which you build a publication.

Publication window The workspace in the PageMaker program window that displays the current publication.

Publication Any document produced using PageMaker.

Publishing application program The application program used to create a text or graphic file that is imported into a PageMaker publication using PageMaker's Publish and Subscribe feature.

Pull quote A small amount of text that is enlarged within a story to catch the reader's attention.

Record In a data source, all the fields required for one item, such as a recipient.

Reference point The edge, corner, or center of a selected object that remains fixed when you make adjustments to the object using the Control palette. *See also* Proxy.

PageMaker 7.0

Reflect To flip an object from top to bottom or from right to left.

Resolution The print quality of a graphic, measured in dots per inch.

Reverse text White or lightly-shaded text or lines on a black or dark background.

Rotate To change the angle at which an object appears.

Ruler guides Nonprinting lines that are used to help align text and graphics on a page.

Sans serif A term used to describe fonts that do not include small strokes at the ends of characters. *See also* Serif.

Save for Service Provider A PageMaker plug-in that copies the publication file, all the linked image files, the fonts used in the publication, and all other files required to print a publication; used to save a publication for a commercial printer.

Scale To change the dimensions of an object either proportionally or non-proportionally.

ScreenTip A small box that appears when you point to a button in the PageMaker program window and identifies the name of the button.

Scroll bar Bars located at the bottom and right edges of the publication window that are used to display the parts of the publication and pasteboard that are not currently visible in the publication window.

Secondary index topic An index entry that appears subordinate to the main or primary index entry.

Selection handles Small black squares at the corners and sides of the graphic that indicate the graphic is selected.

Select To highlight an item so that a subsequent action can be carried out on the item.

Separations Printouts of a publication on paper or film, one for each of the four process colors.

Serif A small stroke at the end of characters in a font.

Serif font A font that includes small strokes at the ends of its characters. *See also* Sans serif.

Shadow box A rectangle or square with a drop shadow on two sides.

Skew To stretch an object at an angle, giving it a distorted appearance.

Snap to guides A feature that causes objects to align with guides as you draw or place the objects.

Source file A file, such as a graphic file, that is linked to a PageMaker publication file.

Source In a navigation scheme, the text a user clicks in order to jump to an anchor.

Spot color A type of color used in commercial printing where a specific ink is used to create a color.

Spread Two facing pages in a publication that are designed to work together as a unit.

Stacking Placing objects on top of each other to create interesting visual effects. *See also* Layering.

Standoff The blank space between an object and wrapped text.

Standoff lines The dotted border that surrounds a graphic to illustrate the boundary for wrapped text.

Story editor A word processing program within PageMaker.

Stroke Another name for a line in PageMaker.

Style bar The area on the left side of the story editor window that displays the name of the style applied to each paragraph in the story.

Style A set of format settings that you name, save, and apply to paragraphs; also, the design of a line.

Tabs Nonprinting characters used to position text at specific locations within a text block.

Target publication In a data merge, the PageMaker publication that includes placeholders for the variable data and all text and graphics that remain the same in each merged publication.

Teaser brochure A publication designed to motivate the reader to request more information about a product or service.

Template A professionally-designed publication that contains placeholder text and graphics that you can replace with your own text and graphics.

Tertiary index topic   An index entry that appears subordinate to a secondary index topic entry.

Text block   An object that contains text.

Text only   A format for exporting text from PageMaker that saves the text without the associated formatting.

Threaded   A term used to describe text that is connected to another text block so that the text in the story flows from one text block to another, often across columns or pages.

Thumbnail   A miniature version of a publication page.

Tint   A color that is based on a percentage of a color you created or a default PageMaker color.

Title bar   The bar at the top of the PageMaker program window that displays the name of the program and the name of the publication.

Toggle button   A button that can be used to turn a feature both on and off.

Toolbar   The horizontal bar below the menu bar in the PageMaker program window that contains buttons for thirty of the most commonly used menu commands.

Toolbox   A floating palette that contains tools used to create and modify text and graphics.

Top of caps leading   A leading setting that measures the leading from the highest point on any character in a line.

Tracking   The space between two or more characters.

Transform   To change an object's appearance by rotating, skewing, or reflecting it.

Trapping   A technique used to compensate for gaps that can appear between colors when creating color separations.

URL   Uniform Resource Locator; the unique address assigned to each Web page on the World Wide Web.

Variable data   In a data merge, the information that varies in each version of a merged publication.

Vertical ruler   The bar located on the left edge of the publication window that helps users to size and align text and graphics.

Web browser   A computer program, such as Netscape or Internet Explorer, that is used to read Web pages on the Internet.

Web page   A file that can be viewed with a Web browser.

Web site   A group of related Web pages that are linked to each other by hyperlinks.

Web   A collection of Web pages available to computer users around the world through a graphical interface; also know as the World Wide Web or WWW. *See also* World Wide Web.

Weight   The thickness of a line, measured in points.

Widow   A line of text that begins a paragraph at the bottom of a column or page.

Windowshade handles   Icons at the top and bottom of a selected text block that mark its beginning and end.

Word wrap   A feature that forces text to flow automatically to the next line as you type.

World Wide Web   A collection of Web pages available to computer users around the world through a graphical interface; also know as the Web or WWW. *See also* Web.

Wrapping   A technique for formatting text so that it flows around an object rather than behind it or through it.

Yellow   One of the four process colors. *See also* CMYK.

Zero point   The point at which the zero marks on the horizontal and vertical rulers intersect.

Zero point marker   The box at the intersection of the horizontal and vertical rulers.

PageMaker 7.0

Index

Index

Index

working with, 12
  Ellipse tool, 12, 13
  Pointer tool, 12, 13, 34, 90
  Text tool, 12, 13, 34, 66
tracking
 text, 190
  examples, 191
trapping, colors, 256
.txt file extension, 56
typographer's quotes, 181

▶ U

Uniform Resource Locator (URL)
 creating hyperlink to, 320
 types of URLs, 321
URL. *See* Uniform Resource Locator

▶ V

View menu, 14. *See also* page views
 changing page views, 14
 character view, 182

paragraph view, 182
publication page views, 15

▶ W

Web browser, 310
Web site, 310
 adding PDF file to, 330
 design, 332
 planning, 312
 setting up publication for, 314
white space, around inline
 graphics, 220
widow, 92
windowshade handles, 56
.wks file extension, 56
word processor. *See also* text
 exporting text to, 81
 story editor, 80
World Wide Web (WWW), HTML
 and, 310
.wpd file extension, 56

wrapping. *See also* text
 text, 158
  custom text wrap, 160
writing style, reports, 78
WWW. *See* World Wide Web

▶ Z

zero point, setting, 10
zero point marker, 8
Zoom tool, 13, 14